LATE CITY EDITION
U. S. Weather Bureau Report (Page 78) forecasts:
Sunny today; clear tonight.
Fair and milder tomorrow.
Temp. Range: 63—48; yesterday: 60—48.

, NOVEMBER 4, 1964.   TEN CENTS

PS GOLDWATER
BEATS KEATING;
N LEGISLATURE

TURNOUT IS HEAVY

60% Margin Expected for President, Victor in G.O.P. Bastions

By TOM WICKER

Lyndon Baines Johnson of Texas compiled one of the greatest landslide victories in American history yesterday to win a four-year term of his own as the 36th President of the United States.

Senator Hubert H. Humphrey of Minnesota, Mr. Johnson's running mate on the Democratic ticket, was carried into office as Vice President.

Mr. Johnson's triumph, giving him the "loud and clear" national mandate he had said he wanted, brought 44 states and the district of Columbia, with 486 electoral votes, into the Democratic column.

r Barry Goldwater, the n candidate, who o offer the people "a t an echo" with a onservative campaign, five states in the h and held a narrow s home state of Ari-arrying it would give him a total of 52 electoral vote-

LYNDON BAINES JOHNSON

The New York Times

HUBERT HORATIO HUMPHREY

SOUTH REVERSES VOTING PATTERNS

Goldwater Makes Inroads, but More Electoral Votes Co to the President

Democrats Are Assured Of Majorit

House Gain for Democra

By JOHN D. MORE

The Democr easily r
tained   se of tained

The Road to the White House

McGraw-Hill Book Company
New York   Toronto   London

The Story of the 1964 Election
by the Staff of The New York Times

The Road to the White House

Edited by Harold Faber

THE ROAD TO THE WHITE HOUSE
Edited by Harold Faber

written and edited by

Paul Greenfeder	Robert H. Phelps	Robert Slosser
Lee Kanner	Alvin Shuster	Warren Weaver, Jr.

with contributions by

Russell Baker	E. W. Kenworthy	James Reston
Lawrence E. Davies	Arthur Krock	Nan Robertson
John Fenton	Anthony Lewis	M. J. Rossant
Max Frankel	Joseph Loftus	Murray Schumach
Ben A. Franklin	Earl Mazo	Eileen Shanahan
Jack Gould	Charles Mohr	Claude Sitton
John Herbers	Cabell Phillips	Wallace Turner
Gladwin Hill	John D. Pomfret	Tom Wicker
Donald Janson	John D. Morris	Fendall W. Yerxa
	Jack Raymond	

*This book is a team effort of members of the staff of
The New York Times, many of whose names are familiar to readers
of The Times, but many more who are known only to their
colleagues. Without the work of these anonymous men and women—
reporters, copy readers, editors and many more—neither The
New York Times nor this book would be possible.*

Library of Congress
Catalog Card Number: 65-20111

FIRST EDITION

46370

Contents

Introduction   *vii*

1. An End and a Beginning   *1*
2. The Republicans: "An Engagement of Principles"   *11*
3. New Hampshire: "I Goofed Up Somewhere"   *19*
4. California: "A Pillow Fight Under Water"   *32*
5. "President of All the People"   *45*
6. San Francisco: "Eau de Convention"   *55*
7. "Just Poopin' Along": How Goldwater Did It   *72*
8. The Senator and the "Arizona Mafia"   *82*
9. William Edward Miller: "He Drives Johnson Nuts"   *92*
10. Atlantic City: "Not a Convention, but an Appreciation"   *104*
11. H. H. H.: "If You and I Just Apply Ourselves"   *112*
12. L. B. J.   *125*
13. The New Mathematics: The Republican Strategy   *141*
14. The Middle Ground: The Democratic Strategy   *151*
15. "I Possibly Do Shoot from the Hip"   *161*
16. "This Is What America Is Really All About"   *175*
17. The "Niagaran" and "The Happy Warrior"   *185*
18. A Choice not an Echo   *194*
19. Some Non-Political Speeches   *208*
20. The Other 495   *221*
21. "Tell Mum I'll Be Home after the Election"   *230*
22. "Come On, Now, Let's All Go to the Speakin' "   *242*
23. "I Have Spent My Life Getting Ready for This Moment"   *250*
24. Election Day   *264*
25. "Poor Strategy, Poor Content, Poor Delivery"   *273*
26. "The Republican Party Has Been Hurt . . ."   *281*
27. Another Ending, Another Beginning   *287*

    Tables (Popular Vote): President, Senator, Governor   *295*

    Index   *299*

Introduction

By Tom Wicker

Each Presidential election tends to take on a character of its own. Some precipitate great events; some produce political giants. The elections of 1860 and 1932 did both. It is too early to say that the election of 1964 did either; yet, it was an election that is likely to be long remembered and studied—perhaps even if its participants and its issues find some relatively minor place in American history.

The campaign between Lyndon B. Johnson and Barry M. Goldwater and Johnson's victory by the largest popular majority in history was an important event because never before had a Presidential election so dramatically and so fully disclosed the nature of American politics. Never before had the rules of the game or even its clichés been so sharply challenged, and probably never again will a candidate be more thoroughly rebuked and penalized for such transgressions.

Of course, the 1964 election had its more concrete results and many of these may prove historically important. If Lyndon Johnson can mobilize consensus politics to move the nation measurably toward a "great society"—if, indeed, he achieves nothing more than the education program already before Congress, his four years in office might prove to have been crucial. Already, as a result of his budget and economic messages, it may be possible to say that his election was a significant endorsement of the shift begun by John F. Kennedy toward a modern economics—the deliberate use of Federal budgetary policy for the shaping of the national economy.

Politically, the 1964 election gave ignominious burial to a divisive idea that had polluted the political atmosphere for a quarter-century and more—the notion that if only a "real conservative" could be nominated for President, millions upon millions of Americans, who had refused in disgust, election after election, to choose between two moderate-to-liberal candidates, would come out of hiding with whoops of patriotic joy and send the "real conservative" into office to save the Constitution and repeal the income tax.

In 1964, not only was a "real conservative"—in the cant meaning that the term has come to have in American politics—nominated; Goldwater also was a vigorous and attractive candidate with what was probably the largest personal following of any politician in the nation (after the death of Kennedy).

Yet, in every primary contest in which he was entered and in the election itself, Goldwater failed miserably to draw the "hidden" conservatives out. In New Hampshire, he lost to a moderate who was not in the race, Henry Cabot Lodge; in Nebraska, another moderate non-candidate, Richard M. Nixon, cut heavily into what should have been a huge Goldwater majority; in Illinois, Senator Margaret Chase Smith repeated the Nixon feat; in Oregon, Goldwater dropped out of the race and finished behind Lodge and the dogged Governor Nelson Rockefeller of New York; in California, the conservative hero managed a bare 51 per cent of the Republican vote; and on November 3, he was crushed everywhere but in his home state and in the Deep South.

The conclusion is inescapable: There is no hidden conservative vote. Early in 1965, a national poll reported that of the 27,000,000 votes cast for Senator Goldwater, only about 6,000,000 were right-wing conservatives. How many of the remaining 21,000,000 were simply regular Republicans, voting by reflex for their party's candidate, never will be established. And how many of them may have met the description of hidden conservatives is equally a mystery. What is certain is that even the full total of 27,000,000 will never again be enough to elect a President of the United States in a two-party election.

As a result of the failure of the hidden conservative theory, the Democrats were enabled to make a huge expansion of their party—historically, the signal for a long period of one-party dominance in our politics. Northeastern and Western states with a long record of Republican leanings went solidly Democratic—in Maine, for instance, by more than two to one, and in Indiana by more than a quarter-million votes. Farmers swung in great numbers from the Republican ranks to the Democratic. Negroes voted, almost to a man, for the Southerner in the White House. For the first time in memory, a preponderance of businessmen and newspaper editorial pages shifted to the Democrats. From the Republican near-landslide of 1956, when 57 per cent of the voters supported Dwight D. Eisenhower, to the Democratic landslide of 1964, when 61 per cent backed Lyndon Johnson, roughly one-fifth of the American electorate changed their party preference from the Republicans to the Democrats.

In terms of party power, such gains have to be cultivated and maintained if they are to be repeated in future elections. If one adds up all the votes cast for all Democratic Presidential candidates since Harry Truman won his narrow victory in 1948, the total comes out roughly equal to all the votes cast for all Republican Presidential candidates in the same period. And if it is true that 64 per cent of voters in the twenty-one-to-twenty-nine age group voted for Johnson last year (as against only 54 per cent for John F. Kennedy in 1960), that is not necessarily as hopeful a sign of future support as it may appear; in 1956, 57 per cent of the voters then in that age group liked

Ike. As the generations change, so do political personalities and political preferences.

Nevertheless, the huge Democratic majority of 1964, whether or not it can be held together and whether or not it ushered in another long period of Democratic hegemony, held one clear meaning. The mightiest popular endorsement in history was given to a candidate and a party who were in the most direct sense heirs of F.D.R. and the New Deal tradition of a strong central government with a direct interest in the people's economy and welfare, and who promised not only to maintain but to expand their work. What candidate and what party in the foreseeable future can attempt seriously to maintain that the New Deal revolution was a perversion of the will of the people—much less a subversive plot?

In this light, it is now crystal clear that the elections of Dwight Eisenhower were uniquely personal triumphs; and that the virtual split decision by which Kennedy narrowly won the Presidency from Nixon in 1960 was a result of Kennedy's Roman Catholicism, his slight national stature, and Nixon's head start as a well-known national and party leader. Even granting that a stronger politician than Eisenhower might have consolidated a powerful Republican party around his personal standing, the election of 1964 suggests that such a party would have had to be moderately progressive —as indeed Eisenhower was most of his time in office. Further granting that a stronger Republican ticket or a better effort by Nixon (another moderate progressive) might have defeated Kennedy in 1960, the real political meaning of 1964 may be that the long line of American politics since 1932 runs virtually unbroken from the New Deal to the Great Society. The truth is not merely that except in 1964 the Republicans have been a "me-too" party; the larger truth is that they cannot win in this era of American history as anything else. Their problem is to find a candidate who can win like Eisenhower and who unlike Eisenhower can build and inspire a stronger party than the Democrats.

The election of 1964 also provided clues to the succession four or eight years hence. Barring disaster not now conceivable, Johnson seems sure of another term if he wants it; but his departure will be forced by the two-term amendment in 1972 and it now is hard to picture a Democratic ticket in that year (or in 1968, if the President should retire to the Pedernales), that would not include either Vice President Hubert H. Humphrey or one of the Kennedy brothers; a Humphrey-Kennedy ticket is another possibility. For if Robert Kennedy's victory in the New York Senatorial race was something less than overwhelming, it was a victory nonetheless and—coming in such an important state—it made him overnight a power in American politics to an extent that even his name could not otherwise have done. In alliance with Edward Kennedy, the most underrated member of a remarkable family, and cultivating the memory and mythology of his murdered brother, Robert Kennedy obviously must be reckoned with at Democratic National Conventions for years to come.

On the Republican side, only Governor George Romney of Michigan and Representative John V. Lindsay of New York, among major state candidates, emerged with much credit; and both suffered in the eyes of brass-collar Republicans by achieving their victories at the expense of repudiating Goldwater and the national ticket. Lindsay, moreover, has no immediate hope of breaking into the Senate or the New York governorship. Governor William W. Scranton of Pennsylvania reversed the process; he gained in party stature by going down the line for the ticket but his last-minute, inept effort to stop Goldwater's nomination cost him dearly in public esteem. Nixon characteristically had somewhat the best of both worlds; he stuck by Goldwater and built up his bank balance in the party, and after the debacle he re-emerged into public prominence as peacemaker, conciliator and spokesman. From this quartet, in all probability, a 1968 candidate must be found although the present trend of Republican reconstruction suggests that if any one of them should be nominated for President, a Vice President of a far more conservative hue might have to be drafted as a silencer for the still vociferous right-wing and for the growing Republican parties of the South.

Ironically enough, the one Republican gain from what was otherwise sheer disaster was that in a year when it lost in almost every state of the Union, the Grand Old Party finally became what it had never been in its 110-year history—a truly national party with solid showings in the Southern states. Not only did Goldwater carry five Southern states (one of which, Georgia, in all its long history, had never voted Republican, not even for Dwight Eisenhower or against Al Smith), but the party elected sixteen members of the House (it already had Senator John G. Tower of Texas) and mounted strong challenges in the Presidential election in every Southern state; overall, Goldwater got just under 50 per cent of the popular vote cast in the Old Confederacy.

It is certainly true that Goldwater's strong showing in the South resulted primarily from his vote against the Civil Rights Act of 1964 and a tone in his campaign that suggested a willingness to let the South handle its own racial affairs. In the prevailing atmosphere of the Negro drive for civil rights, for instance, Alabama did not even let Johnson on the ballot, with the result that he got no votes in that once rigidly Democratic state and Goldwater polled just under a half-million. In Mississippi, where Johnson did get on the ballot, he was beaten seven to one. Without these decisive margins (totalling just under 800,000 votes), Goldwater's overall percentage in the South would have been sharply reduced.

The Goldwater candidacy was pitched, however, not only to a sort of unspoken segregationism but to the kind of conservatism that appealed strongly to the expanding managerial and high-income classes of the prospering Southern states, and to the States' Rights sentiment of the region.

For the past decade, a strong conservative sentiment has flowered in the South—spurred by the resistance to Federally enforced desegregation, which has tended to discredit both the Federal Government and all its works as well as the Democratic party that has been responsible for so many of these; and spurred at the same time by increasing prosperity, by the invasion of huge national corporations and their non-Southern employes and managers (many) of them Republican), by the obvious and increasing power in Federal elections of the big urban states and their minority groups, by the age and reactionary nature of the Southern political leadership produced and frozen in office through the one-party system, and even by such specifics as international competition for textile and plywood industries, competition that caused the South to abandon its historic free-trade views and move to a more conservative position on tariffs and import quotas.

All these forces produced a huge potential to be exploited by such a candidate as Barry Goldwater. Scattered victories by Eisenhower and Nixon and by Congressional candidates had demolished the old Southern social taboo on voting Republican; and in some states, North Carolina for instance, active and ambitious Republican organizations had replaced the squalid and slothful Republican parties that ever since the Civil War had existed in the South for virtually no purpose but to be bought—with patronage, preference and cold cash—by Presidential candidates desiring their votes at Republican National Conventions.

Goldwater's campaign greatly accelerated the trend toward live-wire Republican organization in the South. Georgia Democrats, totally unused to general election opposition and geared only to Democratic primary politics, were startled to find Republican campaign headquarters and other activities in backwoods towns where no Democratic effort had been necessary in this century or the last. Hard-working, hot-eyed young conservatives like John Grenier in Alabama had set up efficient statewide organizations manned by the eager volunteers the right-wing produces in profusion. Goldwater lent his presence to these campaign efforts, money was plentiful, the vital ingredient of enthusiasm was in over-supply, and the result was a significant Republican expansion—the only one of the election. And it was one that cannot be totally dismissed as due only to diehard segregationist sentiment, and thus as a national handicap to Republican recovery. Not all Republican candidates in the South were, like Goldwater, to the right of their opponents, and not all were more segregationist. And the excellent Republican showings throughout the South were due at least as much to general conservative sentiment and to hard, efficient Republican work as they were to Goldwater's civil rights stand; that stand, in fact, cost the party in the South what had been a sizeable share of the Southern Negro vote.

Thus, at least two things can be said for Goldwater's candidacy, as it developed in the South. He helped give his party for the first time in its history a solid base in the South, and there is no fundamental reason why a Republican candidate with civil rights posture more acceptable to the whole country cannot build upon this Southern base in the future—just as recent Democratic Presidential candidates usually have managed to win large areas of the South without endorsing segregation.

What this means was expressed succinctly by a professional political analyst who studied the 1964 returns closely. Despite that landslide, in his view it was possible to look ahead to 1966 and 1968 and say for the first time since Reconstruction that there was no state where the Republicans didn't have a chance to win statewide elections.

Moreover, it is altogether likely that had not Goldwater voted against the Civil Rights Act, then won the Republican nomination, the fanatical Governor George Wallace of Alabama would have run on a sleazy third-party ticket of white supremacy and Ku Kluxism. If Wallace had carried the five Southern states that ultimately went to the Goldwater-Miller ticket, he would have run second in the Electoral College, the Republican party would have been shut out even in the South, and a new and poisonous se-cession—from the two-party system—would have taken place, resulting in untold bitterness and alienation. Even if Wallace had only split the conserva-tive-segregationist vote and allowed Johnson to carry all but Alabama and Mississippi, the sole Republican gain of the campaign still would have been thwarted, Johnson would have been strengthened not a whit except for an even more swollen electoral total, and the Southern state campaigns would have inflamed racial feelings far more than was the actual case.

So let us give thanks to Barry Goldwater for this achievement, at least. He kept George Wallace out of the race and the South in the two-party system. Not a few Presidential candidates have contributed less.

But the real significance of the 1964 election was larger than any of these concrete results. This was the election that illuminated, as few others have, the fundamentals of our politics; and this was the election that of all—at least in the twentieth century—told us more about ourselves and our necessities.

Surely it was the strangest of American elections—and in its very strange-ness, we can find its truth.

We have seen that Democratic Georgia went Republican for the first time and that a Republican base was established in the South. It is a part of the same picture that Republican Vermont, never carried even by F.D.R., went Democratic—and for a Southern politician who might never have been nominated for the Presidency had not fate first thrown him into the White House. All over the East and West, Republican strongholds fell to the Demo-crats. In New York, the legislature went Democratic in both Houses for the first time since 1935; the same thing happened in Indiana. In Colorado, where in 1960 and 1962 a hard-working Republican organization had swept the boards in statewide elections, the Democrats recaptured the legislature and went for Johnson by nearly 200,000 votes.

Despite Goldwater's massive defeat, Republican strength popped up al-most everywhere. In Rhode Island, the President took an amazing 80 per cent of the vote; but Republican Governor John Chaffee, a moderate, was re-elected by an even more amazing 60 per cent. In California, Johnson won by more than a million votes in a state Nixon had carried in 1960; yet the same state chose Shirley Temple's former leading man as a Republican Senator over Pierre Salinger, who ran as a Kennedy man. In New York, not even a 2,700,000 vote victory for the President could give even Robert Kennedy a landslide over another moderate Republican, Kenneth B. Keating. But in Ohio, Robert Taft Jr., a candidate bearing another of the great names of American politics, running in one of the great Republican strongholds— also carried by Nixon in 1960—fell before the Democratic landslide.

Thus, it was at the Presidential level that the enormous Democratic expansion was generated; at other levels, plenty of Republican strength could be found and the sum of other Democratic gains was not necessarily permanent. There can be no doubt that the Republican disaster traces straight to the nomination of Barry Goldwater for President on July 15 in the Cow Palace at San Francisco.

Our political history has amply demonstrated—and 1964 confirmed beyond doubt—that an American political party, in order to win, must be an amorphous national coalition loosely held together by its allegiance to a man or (rarely) to an issue or (even more rarely) to both. That is so because of the vast diversity of sections, interests, groups, nationalities, views and states, the votes of which must be won if a party and its Presidential candidate are to win a national election—and the support of which must be held if that party and that candidate, once in office, are to be able to govern. It may be theoretically possible to put together, on the one hand, a group of less populated Southern and Western states that will make up an electoral majority; it may be mathematically correct, on the other, as some liberals argue, that a liberal candidate could win with nothing more than the votes of the major urban states. But the fate of Goldwater in 1964 and the hairbreadth victory of Kennedy in 1960 illustrate the pitfalls of these theories. One was smashed; the other had too little mandate and too little power to govern as he wished.

What is needed for real victory and real government in a nation that is itself no more than a coalition is a sprawling national grouping of interests, sections, views—all united, if no more often than every four years, upon a single object, the election of a President and the legal seizure of national power. The object of an American political party, first and foremost, must be to win; only if it wins substantially can it govern; and only if it intrudes into every section and interest and point of view and commands some loyalty in each can it do either.

Thus, by simple definition, a winning political party cannot be ideological or tightly disciplined to a narrow aim. Its machinery cannot be captured by a faction, however demanding or deserving. It cannot be actively hostile to any respectable group, section or interest. It must be hospitable to the most widely differing views and interests and it is the unavoidable and high duty of political leadership to find the man or the issue or the common ground of ambition upon which the most opposed men can stand —for at least a few months, every four years.

All these imperatives were cast aside by the Republican party in 1964, first by Goldwater and the right-wing conservatives and then by the moderates and liberals who opposed him so ineffectively. Goldwater's nomination was not the product of necessary and healing compromise and accommodation; it was a coup d'état and in some ways a coup de main. Whatever it was, it was not politics.

Goldwater was bound to be a weak and divisive national candidate and party leader, despite his attractiveness and personal following, because he had taken for twelve years in national politics a rigidly "conservative" position that amounted to a radical rejection of the norms of post-New Deal politics. He repudiated that politics from stem-to-stern, then repudiated two post-war developments that also had broad national support: The nuclear test-ban treaty and the Federal Government's support for the civil rights movement. In doing so, he alienated all those who believed in these things and he left little or no room for compromise or accommodation with them.

Moreover, by July 15, he had shown conclusively that he could not command a broad national following; every primary he entered made that point more obvious. Readers of this book will see that he won the nomination at San Francisco for only two reasons:

—The moderate to liberal opposition was divided, confused, leaderless, vacillating and relying on the Goldwater movement to collapse of its own weakness; the primaries only confirmed their hopes.

—The Goldwater faction, ably led by underrated professionals, swept state and local conventions and put together a disciplined delegate force not responsive to public opinion; the razor-thin California primary victory gave this skillful campaign the impetus it needed to capture the convention.

By July 15, neverthelesss, it was clear that Goldwater could not conceivably put together a national majority, and probably could not even hold his own party together. If ambition and pride blinded him to that fact, his allies in the conservative cause should have had no such human failings. If they believed in the conservative cause, on the eve of San Francisco that cause called for a compromise on a candidate who might win but who could be nominated only by alliance with and concessions to the conservatives—say, Nixon.

Probably it was too late for such a compromise, even if the need for it had been realized. As one Goldwater leader put it: "We didn't come here to nominate a conservative. We came here to nominate Goldwater." The enthusiastic Goldwater delegates were in no mood for compromise; they scented blood.

When Goldwater had had his moment of triumph, he compounded the problem with a militant acceptance speech extolling extremism and rejecting in advance the votes of those who disagreed with him. He also installed rigidly conservative leadership in the national committee and chose a conservative party functionary, William E. Miller, as his running mate.

This book documents what followed, with almost tragic inevitability. Republicans who could not accept Goldwater's views, and who saw little effort on his part to modify them or accommodate their own, defected in droves. Republican candidates who could not hope to win on a Goldwater-Miller ticket (in urban industrial states and areas) openly repudiated him.

Thus, the party cracked like a pane of glass. Worse, by hewing to his narrow, ideological course, Goldwater opened up the entire middle of the American political spectrum as represented in both parties, to his Democratic opponents. Johnson, opposed by an appealing moderate, might have been forced to a fairly liberal position; conceivably, he might even have moved to the right, exploiting his own Southern background and his occasionally conservative record. Instead, the Goldwater candidacy gave him the golden political opportunity of this century. He spread his arms all across the middle and to the moderate left; he avoided specific issues, ran as "President of all the people" and—far more important—as the safe candidate, the known quantity, the man of responsibility, the link between past and future.

For the first time since the New Deal, a Democratic candidate on a Democratic platform became the candidate of continuity and stability— which is to say the respectable candidate. In that position, Johnson could and did appeal in all sections, to all interests and groups, across party lines. It is symbolically satisfying that this opportunity came to a Southerner leading the party of urban liberalism—a true accommodation to political realities.

Its factions still at war, its interests unreconciled, its candidate repelling support rather than seeking it, the Republican party was as helpless as a whale washed ashore. The nature of the Goldwater nomination and candidacy made the result predictable. It remained only for the brilliant campaign of Johnson and an increasingly inept performance by Goldwater to turn inevitable defeat into shattering disaster. The rules and truths of American politics, after all, were not drawn up by some council of elders constructing a system; they emerged, instead, pragmatically and out of human necessity from the nature of the United States of America—from its geographical hugeness, its economic rivalries and conflicts, its ethnic patchwork, its historical traditions, its federal and electoral systems, its religious freedom and prejudices, its racial cruelties and class feudings, its simultaneous belief in the common man and its glorification of the uncommon "rugged individual."

That is something we need to understand more clearly. Great political leadership in this marvelous cacophony we call our country requires, at its roots, an ability to put together or to inspire from all these volatile elements a national coalition that can win and govern. Yet, we call it shameless demagoguery if a candidate makes an open appeal to the Jewish voter and a noble stand for principle if a liberal or a conservative denounces the other as immoral, selfish or subversive.

The two-party system—two such great national coalitions, by definition somewhat similar to each other, since they must be constructed from essentially the same elements—with all its flaws, ambiguities and irrationalities, is something that meets our national needs. In their contests for power, the two great coalitions provide and protect the vital necessity of the American system—a politics of the center, in which no faction and no section and no group gains unchallenged supremacy over all others. The politics of the center, in turn, guarantees the necessary minimum of national unity, the protection of variegated interests, the existence of diverse views, the concentration of effort on the greatest good for the greatest number. In a multi-faceted society, the two-party system and the politics of the center mean stability, continuity, and the nearest equivalent to justice for all.

They do not always guarantee swift progress, and it is true that, as in any system, some groups and elements are more equal than others; power always expresses itself. But when theorists suggest that the country might be more efficiently run by a narrower, disciplined faction—say, a liberal party, or a conservative party—they would do well to study the debacle of Barry Goldwater in 1964. A better system of winning political power in America cannot be devised so easily; it can only emerge as our necessities change and make their inevitable demands.

An End and a Beginning

"I do solemnly swear that I will faithfully execute the office of President of the United States and will to the best of my ability preserve, protect and defend the Constitution of the United States."

It was 2:40 P.M., Central standard time, on November 22, 1963, in the rear compartment of the huge Presidential jet, *Air Force 1*. Less than two hours earlier, Lyndon B. Johnson had been about a dozen car lengths behind President Kennedy's car in the motorcade through the streets of Dallas. President Johnson recorded his memories before the Warren Commission on the Assassination of President Kennedy:

> . . . I was startled by the sharp report or explosion, but I had no time to specu-
> late as to its origin because Agent Youngblood turned in a flash, immediately after
> the first explosion, hitting me on the shoulder, and shouted to all of us in the
> back seat to get down. I was pushed down by Agent Youngblood. Almost in the
> same moment in which he hit or pushed me, he vaulted over the back seat and
> sat on me . . .
> When we arrived at the hospital, Agent Youngblood told me to get out of the
> car, go into the building, not to stop, and to stay close to him and the other
> agents . . .
> It was Ken O'Donnell who, at about 1:20 P.M., told us that the President had
> died. I think his precise words were, "He's gone." O'Donnell said that we should
> return to Washington and that we should take the President's plane for this
> purpose.
> I found it hard to believe that this had happened. The whole thing seemed
> unreal—unbelievable. A few hours earlier I had breakfast with John Kennedy; he
> was alive, strong, vigorous. I could not believe now that he was dead. I was
> shocked and sickened.

An unmarked police car, its siren stilled, brought Johnson from Park-land Hospital to Love Field. Throughout the trip the Vice President, at the insistence of the Secret Service, crouched below the window level of the automobile.

> When O'Donnell told us to get on the plane and go back to Washington . . . I
> did not want to go and leave Mrs. Kennedy in this situation . . . but I agreed
> that we would board the airplane and wait until Mrs. Kennedy and the President's
> body were brought aboard the plane . . .

We were ushered into the private quarters of the President's plane. It didn't seem right for John Kennedy not to be there. I told someone that we preferred for Mrs. Kennedy to use these quarters.

Shortly after we boarded the plane, I called Robert Kennedy, the President's brother and the Attorney General. I knew how grief-stricken he was, and I wanted to say something that would comfort him. Despite his shock, he discussed the practical problems at hand—problems of special urgency because we did not at that time have any information as to the motivation of the assassination or its possible implications . . . He said that the oath of office should be administered to me immediately, before taking off for Washington . . .

I thought of Sarah Hughes, an old friend who is judge of the U.S. district court in Dallas . . . A few minutes later Mrs. Kennedy and the President's coffin arrived. Mrs. Johnson and I spoke to her. We tried to comfort her, but our words seemed inadequate. She went into the private quarters of the plane . . .

About a half hour later, I asked someone to find out if Mrs. Kennedy would stand with us during the administration of the oath. Mrs. Johnson went back to be with her . . .

I'm told that the oath was administered at 2:40 P.M. Mrs. Johnson and Mrs. Kennedy were at my side as Judge Hughes administered the oath of office.

With his left hand on a black leather-bound Bible, and his right hand raised, Lyndon Baines Johnson repeated the oath and became the thirty-sixth President of the United States. The new President embraced his wife and Mrs. Kennedy. Then he said, "Okay, let's get this plane back to Washington."

The jet landed at Andrews Air Force Base near Washington at 6:05 P.M. After the body of the assassinated President, accompanied by Mrs. Kennedy, was removed in a Navy ambulance, the President and Mrs. Johnson slowly walked to a battery of microphones and cameras. Struggling for composure, Johnson made his first public speech as President.

"This is a sad time for all people," he said. "We have suffered a loss that cannot be weighed. For me it is a deep personal tragedy. I know the world shares the sorrow that Mrs. Kennedy and her family bear. I will do my best. That is all I can do. I ask for your help—and God's."

In the capital on the Potomac, where government and politics are inseparably linked, the governmental machinery continued to function and the attention of office holders and politicians turned inevitably to the new President, his policies and his politics. In Washington they were already asking the inevitable questions: "What will happen now?" "What will happen next November?" Despite the shock and grief, they knew that the campaign for the Presidency in 1964 now had a new beginning. The assassination of President Kennedy removed the man who would have been renominated for a second term by acclamation nine months later, and elevated into the Presidency and the leadership of the Democratic party an older, more conservative man still emerging from his Southern heritage. For the moment, it seemed to the leaders of the Republican party that their prospects of electing a President the following November had increased.

Warren Weaver Jr. of The Times reported from Washington that day that the shock of the President's death had stilled the official voices of politics in the capital, but that the potential effect on the government and leadership was so profound that private consideration could not be silenced. Before the assassination there had been facts and strong probabilities on the national political scene: Kennedy would run again; he would be stronger in some states, weaker in the South; he would run with Lyndon B. Johnson again; he would debate his opponent; and he would be favored to win. Now, Weaver said, there were sudden questions with no answers: Would President Johnson be able to insure his own nomination next August, on the basis of an inherited nine months in the White House? Would liberal elements in the Democratic party make any attempt to dislodge Johnson in favor of a candidate more to their liking? Could Johnson win support in the South despite his espousal of the civil rights cause?

Kennedy, dead at forty-six, left a void that many believed Johnson would never be able to fill. Kennedy had become a symbol of hope for millions who yearned for a peaceful and better world. Intellectual, witty, sophisticated, he had occupied the White House with a style long sadly absent. Assisted—and sometimes led—by Mrs. Kennedy, he had established an atmosphere of artistic patronage; not since Thomas Jefferson had there been so keen an interest in culture in the White House. He exuded vigor and strength and confidence; he made Khrushchev back down in the Cuban missile crisis; he pushed the strongest civil rights bill in history; he signed a nuclear test ban treaty with the Soviet Union. If, as James Reston wrote on the day of the assassination, "America wept tonight, not alone for its dead young President, but for itself," it was with justification. The grief that overtook the nation was far more than shock over Kennedy's death, over what he might have accomplished had he lived—it was a wave of fear of what the future held, of uncertainty over the capabilities of the new President so suddenly thrust into the White House.

Saturday, November 23, was Johnson's first full day in office. The morning was bleak, with rain falling slowly out of gray skies. At 8:40, Johnson left his suburban Washington home, his limousine flanked by motorcycle out-riders and followed by a Secret Service car, and sped to the White House. He conferred with officials on foreign and defense policies; he received intelligence briefings; he met with former Presidents Dwight D. Eisenhower and Harry S. Truman; he spoke at length with legislative leaders of both parties; he visited Kennedy's widow; he held his first Cabinet meeting, opening it with a minute of silent prayer for the late President, and then asking all members of the Cabinet to serve as before; with Mrs. Johnson, he attended a special prayer service in St. John's Episcopal Church across Lafayette Square from the White House; and he designated Monday, November 25, as a day of national mourning, calling on all Americans to go to their churches and pay "the homage of love and reverence" to the memory of his slain predecessor.

In the new President's first day in office, some of the old Johnsonian habits —an affable carelessness about time, for instance—vanished. He kept to his schedule with precision. One official close to the new President said he was moving with the "natural grace of the gentleman he is, but also with a sense of responsibility." When he was seen publicly at the White House or in the corridors of the Executive Office Building, his demeanor was a mixture of sorrow and constraint.

Throughout the long day, Americans read reassuring articles in their newspapers and heard discussions on television attesting to Johnson's intensive preparation for his new responsibilities. As Vice President he had attended all Cabinet meetings; he had served as chairman of the important National Aeronautics and Space Council; he had been responsible for setting up the President's Committee on Equal Employment Opportunity; he had been President Kennedy's special emissary abroad; he had been a member of the National Security Council, the group most closely concerned with the nation's military and diplomatic secrets.

Politically, this experience and its instant application began to have effects. Barely twenty-four hours after Kennedy's death, party leaders reached one major conclusion: The new President seemed almost certain of nomination at the Democratic convention in Atlantic City. Although Johnson was silent on politics, no one among his associates questioned that the former Vice President would expect the nomination and fight for it, if necessary, as hard as he had fought against Kennedy for the same prize in 1960.

A day after Kennedy's death, Warren Weaver Jr. reported from Washington:

One of the major advantages that President Johnson will enjoy is that his potential opposition is almost hopelessly divided.

When the political harmony of Washington's present crisis mood has faded, the President can expect to face two major groups of detractors within his own party: those liberals who find him too conservative and those Southerners who feel he has deserted their cause.

Both of these groups may feel next August that they might prefer one of their own as a nominee. But the possibility of their agreeing on a candidate seems dim.

Time is also on Mr. Johnson's side. The tragedy that projected him to national leadership seems certain to produce Democratic—even partisan—unity for some time to come. The President and the people still expect it.

When that feeling dissolves, there will be little time before the convention for an organized effort against Mr. Johnson.

History would seem to favor the new President. Three twentieth-century Vice Presidents before him have moved into the White House: Theodore Roosevelt, Calvin Coolidge and Harry S. Truman.

All were nominated at the next convention—and elected. Even Mr. Truman, who was very unpopular in some Democratic quarters in 1948, was not denied the nomination.

The emerging conviction that President Johnson will head the ticket immediately focused Democratic interest on his choice of a running mate.

The name mentioned most frequently was that of Senator Hubert H. Humphrey of Minnesota.

The feeling among party leaders is that Mr. Johnson, as a conservative—or at least moderate Democrat—will need some strong liberal sponsorship if he is to make a good showing in the urban, industrial states.

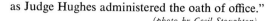

"I'm told that the oath was administered at 2:40 P.M.
Mrs. Johnson and Mrs. Kennedy were at my side
as Judge Hughes administered the oath of office."

(photo by Cecil Stoughton)

Opposite right:
November 22, 1963: "I will do my best.
That is all I can do. I ask for your help and God's."
(Associated Press photo)

Opposite left:
November 23, 1963. The President, Bill D. Moyers,
McGeorge Bundy, aides and Secret Service men leave
the Executive Office Building for the White House.
(photo by George Tames, The New York Times)

"I will offer a choice, not an echo.
This will not be an engagement of personalities.
It will be an engagement of principles."

Mr. Humphrey, it is suggested, would supply that precious commodity.

Another possibility is Senator Eugene J. McCarthy of Minnesota, who is not as well known as his colleague but who would put a Roman Catholic on the Democratic ticket.

Whatever doubt existed about Johnson's political outlook, he dispelled it with his address to the joint session of Congress on November 27, a speech aimed as much at the voters as at Congress. Within the chamber of the House of Representatives, many were moved to tears as Johnson, in a slow, deep voice, said solemnly, "All that I have, I would have given gladly not to be here today." He called for the translation of Kennedy's ideas and ideals into effective action, requesting quick action on tax reduction and on virtually every other point of the Kennedy legislative program. He rededicated his Administration to the support of the United Nations, to its commitments to its allies, to the maintenance of a military strength "second to none," to the stability of the dollar and to continued foreign aid. He left no doubt that he wanted Congress to move ahead at once rather than in January with civil rights, tax reduction and other phases of the legislative program. "Our most immediate tasks are here on this hill," he said. "This is no time for delay. It is a time for action."

On an occasion that had many moments of drama, one of the highest came near the end of the twenty-seven-minute speech, when Johnson said firmly and with deep feeling, "The time has come for Americans of all races and creeds and political beliefs to understand and to respect one another. So, let us put an end to the teaching and the preaching of hate and evil"—here Johnson's voice rose sharply—"and violence." That brought a burst of sustained applause, the most prolonged that he received.

Almost as great was the ovation for Johnson's statement on civil rights— the climax of an address that surprised even his admirers with its force, its eloquence and its mood of quiet confidence. He first mentioned the issue in an early passage on American dreams that he said had been given vitality by Kennedy's "drive and dedication." Among these dreams, he said, was "the dream of equal rights for all Americans, whatever their race or color." The stress on American dreams was an obvious allusion to an address by the Rev. Dr. Martin Luther King Jr. to the massive civil rights demonstration in Washington on August 28, 1963. Speaking to more than 200,000 persons at the Lincoln Memorial, Dr. King, amid cheers, had told his audience, "I have a dream that my four little children will one day live in a nation where they will be judged not by the color of their skin but by the content of their character."

The President also urged action on education bills, youth employment opportunities, foreign aid, the remaining appropriations bills and "the dream of care for our elderly." Tax reduction, he said, "if passed without delay, means more security for those now working and more jobs for those now without them and more incentive for the economy." He also prudently mentioned the importance of fiscal responsibility.

In his address Johnson used "continue"—he pronounced it "continyuh"—five times, and "act" or "action" seventeen times. These words were the keynote of his first week in office, as seen by James Reston:

President Johnson is probably going to have the shortest political honeymoon in the history of the White House, but he's enjoying it while it lasts.

The man is all over the place. He's on the phone night and day. Visitors go in and out of his new office as if he were still on Capitol Hill, and after only a week in office he already has the Republicans worried.

George Meany, president of the A.F.L.-C.I.O., was at his house this morning before breakfast. After that, the Rev. Martin Luther King Jr., the Negro leader, conferred with him for almost an hour, and at breakfast the Democratic leaders got the word—full speed ahead on civil rights and a tax cut.

"This is Lyndon," he says on the phone to reporters, Congressmen, and anybody else on the list, not having time to remember he is President. It isn't that he thinks about politics; it's just that it wouldn't be natural for him to think any other way.

Lyndon the friend of the Negro, Lyndon the friend of the unemployed, and Lyndon the tax-cutter are all at work building his strength in the urban North. Meanwhile Lyndon the economizer is reassuring his friends in the South that he's for watching Government costs and keeping next year's budget below the $100 billion mark.

In a single week he has seen all the leaders of the Western world, put Chief Justice Warren and Senator Richard Russell, of all people, on the same commission to look into the assassination of President Kennedy, talked to the Congress, addressed the nation, met with two other Negro leaders besides Dr. King, written to all defense contractors to hold down costs, and talked Kennedy's White House staff into staying on the job.

To one member of the Kennedy staff, he used the direct Johnson approach. "Give me three months to prove to you I'm worthy of your loyalty," he said. What can a man reply at a time like this to such a proposal from the President of the United States?

At this rate he shouldn't have much trouble taking off those extra ten pounds he's worried about. He's in a hurry. There are only a few days left to get his budget ready for the Congress and to get the Congress ready for the civil rights bill, and only a little over a hundred days to the first Presidential primary election.

This puts the Republicans on the spot. They are confronted by a wholly new political situation. The new President is dominating the headlines and emerging as a commanding figure, but his opponents do not feel that they can answer back without seeming to be too hasty in criticizing the former President or the new.

Even after the President completed his first month in office, the political "honeymoon" was still on—and Times writers were prophesying that it could not last much longer. On December 22, Tom Wicker reported that Johnson's first thirty days had been full of furious action, copious statements, ringing telephones, flying memos and speeding limousines. He summed up Johnson's major achievements in office this way:

(1) With considerable force and skill, he has established the continuity of the Government in the face of a disaster of which no one had conceived. And he has conveyed to the country the strong impression of a man who is up to his job if not yet altogether on top of it.

(2) The world's leaders, too, seem cautiously confident that they will have in Mr. Johnson's likely policies no radically different departures to deal with. Still an unknown quantity as far as his personal impact on world affairs is concerned, he has made it clear that the broad outlines of American policy are unchanged.

(3) Politically, he has managed so far—in the words of a dismayed Republican —to "carry water on four shoulders." Solidly committing himself to the Kennedy civil rights policies, he also has avoided an open break with the South. This could prove an ephemeral accomplishment when the civil rights battle gets under way in Congress.

(4) Administratively, he has managed to keep on the job virtually the entire Kennedy staff and all the department heads. This has been of untold value in running the Government, in building public confidence in a new President's capabilities and intentions, and in the political connections that are vital to his re-election campaign next year.

(5) Legislatively, Mr. Johnson has produced no rabbits from his Stetson and has fallen on his face as hard as had Mr. Kennedy and President Eisenhower in attempting to nullify Representative Otto Passman, the scourge of foreign aid. He had an important personal hand, however, in foraging for the votes necessary to pass the far-reaching college aid bill, and his insistence stirred Senator Harry Byrd and Representative Howard Smith, the Virginia stalwarts, into creeping concessions on the tax and civil rights bills.

All in all, Wicker concluded, Johnson had performed the one indispensable task—he kept the Government going, kept its gears turning, and had given the country a President. No man, cast into such an office by fate, could be asked for much more than that in his first month in office.

Johnson himself, however, proposed much more. It was clear that he would not be satisfied merely to carry on in Kennedy's tradition. With the New Year, on January 8, the President went before Congress once more, this time to deliver his first State of the Union message, a combination of legislative program and political document designed to capture for himself the middle ground of the American political scene at the very beginning of the Presidential campaign. The Republicans complained at once that Johnson was offering more for less, both security and solvency and a bargain-basement Utopia. The President de-emphasized foreign affairs while he called for a new war against poverty and ignorance. He pleaded for his $11,000,000,000 tax cut by February 1. He cut back enriched uranium production for nuclear weapons by 25 per cent and challenged "our adversaries" to do likewise. He pared the budget to $97,900,000,000, $500,000,000 below Kennedy's last budget; and he committed himself to reduce the Federal payroll substantially —a clear appeal to conservatives and Republicans.

There was scarcely a sentence in the speech that was not applauded, but most of the eighty rounds of applause from the floor of the House came from the Democratic side. It was inevitable that, despite his moves toward economy in government, there would be strong opposition on the Republican side, precisely because his poverty program was so reminiscent of the New Deal programs the G.O.P. fought for many years.

What the speech did more clearly than anything else was to indicate the President's approach to his new responsibilities. He seemed to feel that there was enough of a détente to enable him to give a new emphasis to home affairs. He explained, for example, to President de Gaulle that he could not agree to meet him in Martinique because he had an important legislative program before him in an election year.

Also, it was clear that the President had rejected the advice of those who would have him take a tougher line toward the Communists and avoid new explorations looking toward a wider accommodation with Moscow. He emphasized a dual program: To be strong enough to deter aggression and flexible enough to seek every possible chance to reduce international tensions. Thus, he accepted the political challenge of Senator Barry Goldwater, who had been arguing against the test ban treaty, the sale of wheat to Communist nations, and a policy of patience on Cuba.

The home front part of the speech illustrated a great deal about Johnson's ties to Franklin D. Roosevelt. It was not only an outline of a program but also a platform for the Presidential campaign. He left the Republicans very little. He blunted the economy issue, and he came forward with proposals that helped the major urban centers, which were vital to victory in November.

Washington observers, noting that Johnson was cultivating former President Eisenhower, courting business, proclaiming national unity and wrapping government economy in the flag, agreed that the issue of the 1964 campaign would be Lyndon Johnson himself—an early indication that personalities, not policies, might dominate the election campaign. Tom Wicker wrote from the capital on January 19 that when a President sought re-election as Johnson strongly hinted he would do, the only real question was whether the people wanted him around for the ensuing four years.

But it was not to be all clear sailing for Johnson. In the first few months of the new Administration a problem arose that was to haunt the President throughout the campaign. In the complex affairs of Bobby Baker, the Senate page from South Carolina who rose to become "Lyndon's boy" and secretary of the Senate, and who engaged in all sorts of peculiar financial dealings before he resigned under pressure, the Republicans tried to find a basis for their charges that Johnson himself was somehow involved. Republicans and others also made an issue of the fact that the lone television station in Austin, Texas, was owned by Mrs. Johnson. There were charges, promptly denied, that Walter W. Jenkins, the President's close friend and aide, had exerted pressure for advertisements for that station.

On Capitol Hill, however, Johnson was having considerably more success. For years he had been a member of Congress's "inner circle" and he knew how to woo and persuade its leaders. At Kennedy's death, the record of the Eighty-eighth Congress was by no means so weak as some contended. The Senate had ratified the test ban treaty; the House had passed the tax bill and Congress had approved a precedent-setting measure that helped head off a national railroad strike (ordinarily, the average Congressman would rather break a metatarsal than a precedent). Moreover, two major education bills were on the verge of passage. When Johnson took over, his most important objectives on the Hill were to move the civil rights bill through the House Rules Committee and the House itself and to get the tax reduction bill through the Senate Finance Committee and the Senate itself. In these two instances, Johnson intervention, both publicly and, probably more important, behind the scenes, helped push the measures through what had previously been a reluctant Congress.

On March 2, 1964, Johnson completed his first hundred days in office. Fourteen months earlier, when Kennedy had completed half of his first term as Chief Executive, he had been interviewed by reporters of the three national television networks. Seated in his famous chair, gently rocking back and forth, jabbing the air with his finger as he made his points, Kennedy had spoken with wit and eloquence about the responsibilities of the office. Now, on the same sort of program, it was Lyndon Johnson who was being interviewed. The President displayed patience and confidence and tact, particularly in reference to questions about the pressure being exerted to select Robert Kennedy as his running mate in the fall. James Reston discussed the television appearance:

There have always been two Lyndon Johnsons since he came to Washington more than thirty years ago: the political tactician, whose genius for backstairs manipulation was well publicized; and this other Johnson who appeared on the TV sets tonight: the quiet, philosophic, almost fatherly Johnson who never has a bad word for anybody.

This latter Johnson has never had an effective Boswell. The other one, the wheeler-dealer Johnson, has been well reported. Maybe in the TV conversation he has found the medium for making the whole of this remarkable and almost contradictory personality vivid to the American people.

The reporters confronted him with all the current political hobgoblins supposed to trigger the famous Johnson temper—Bobby Baker, President de Gaulle of France, Bobby Kennedy and even Barry Goldwater. He never even blinked.

He talked about de Gaulle as if the general were a temporarily misguided friend: a little difficult, maybe, but doing what he had every right to do. He talked about his relations with Bobby Kennedy as if the two of them were merely the victims of a vicious press, and went out of his way to commend the Attorney General for his part in the civil rights program.

As for Bobby Baker, the President threw him to the Senate of the United States, and referred to him as if he were sort of a remote official acquaintance who just happened to be in office as a result of the votes of all Senators and certainly not as a result of any friendship with Lyndon Johnson.

None of this set any records for candor in Washington and it was certainly not the whole truth, but it demonstrated the art of the political Johnson, and who could complain? After all, there is nothing in the Constitution that obliges a man to dramatize every single personal difference on nationwide television.

Beyond that, Mr. Johnson's performance was almost an official refutation of all the charges his opponents make against him. He is charged with vanity; he was, in contrast, the very soul of modesty.

No doubt, he said, he had made "many mistakes" in the first one hundred days. He may not be a "great President" but he wanted to do the best he could. Vanity? He was positively self-effacing.

He is supposed to be political and partisan in every waking and sleeping act. Tonight he was as nonpartisan as the Ten Commandments: a disciple of unity, confident in the fairness and wisdom of the Congress, a man who was served by a great staff, a man who merely wanted to be "a people's President" and who sounded as if he dreaded the very day when the Presidential campaign would force him to utter a partisan word.

His enemies say he is tough and impatient. Tonight he was sensitive about everybody, particularly Mrs. John F. Kennedy and the Kennedy staff. As for the rest, he was in turn patient, nostalgic and quietly confident.

"Compassionate" was the word he used to describe the kind of Administration he wanted. "A better deal" for the poor was his slogan to carry out this ideal. He defined his political position as "a progressive who is prudent."

If the commanding ground of American politics is the center, President Johnson captured it this evening. Economically, he defended the free enterprise system with more eloquence than has been heard from the United States Chamber of Commerce since the early days of Eric Johnston. Militarily, he made Barry Goldwater's suggestion about landing the Marines in Cuba sound like the proposal of an impulsive boy.

The President was even detached, almost indifferent, about himself. He discussed his health objectively, as if he were giving a clinical report on the incidence of rickets among the Eskimos. He talked about his 18-hour or 19-hour work-day as if this were the least he could do to show his "gratitude" for having a good job.

Thus he has come to the end of the experimental period in the public relations of the President, and he has covered a wider range than any President of our time.

He has had news conferences off-the-cuff, on television tape and live. He has had fireside chats on Thanksgiving, and Congressional appearances, and reports on the tax bill, half on TelePrompter and half extemporaneous.

Beyond that, aside from having telephoned most of the characters in Who's Who, he has had every member of both Houses of Congress to a sort of combination cocktail party, dinner, official briefing and dance at the White House while the legislators' ladies were touring the upstairs bedrooms. And if you think this isn't effective politically, ask the chairman of the Republican National Committee.

2

The Republicans: "An Engagement of Principles"

While Johnson took full command of the Democratic party immediately after the assassination, the Republican party was divided and in disarray; even its leaders could not assess the extent of the disarray because all politics of a public nature had come to an automatic halt. On the day of President Kennedy's funeral, the opposition party announced a moratorium on political campaigning during the period of national mourning. Governor Nelson Rockefeller of New York, then the only announced candidate for the Republican Presidential nomination, had two days earlier canceled a campaign tour of New Hampshire, where, on the next March 10, the nation's first Presidential primary election would be held. Senator Barry Goldwater, the other principal G.O.P. contender at the time, had been in Muncie, Indiana, for his mother-in-law's funeral on the day of the assassination; he called for political unity and support:

I have confidence in Lyndon Johnson. And I think now is a time that will test Americans of all faiths and both parties. We must give this man our full cooperation and our prayers and work with him; and let's see the kind of President that he will be. President Johnson certainly has the training; he has the instincts; he has the ability. I think we must now, as a nation, unite behind him and help him all we can; and go the usual course of helping a President—of being critical when it's needed and helpful when that's needed.

The Republican national chairman, Representative William E. Miller of New York, postponed a national committee meeting scheduled for mid-December in Minneapolis, which was to have issued a formal call for the Republican National Convention in July in San Francisco. He reported absolute unanimity among Republicans that the nation should have a respite from partisan activity and that he wanted no campaigning for the rest of the year. "I pledge that our party will stand with the new Administration in this tragically unexpected process of transition," he said.

But within the two parties, the leadership level—persistently questioned as always by the political columnists and reporters—continued to debate the Republican problem: Who would be the Republican candidate? Politicians in general agreed that the imminent prospect of a Johnson nomination appeared likely to produce a liberal Republican opponent. The reasoning: The new President was a Southerner with little apparent appeal for liberal and independent voters in other sections of the country. To capitalize on such shortcomings, the theory ran, the Republicans would nominate a man who did appeal to these liberals and independents—someone like Rockefeller or Governor William W. Scranton of Pennsylvania or, perhaps, as a compromise, former Vice President Richard M. Nixon, who lost to Kennedy by only 118,500 votes in 1960. Under this rationale, it seemed less likely than ever that a conservative like Goldwater could succeed in winning the nomination.

Of the Republican contenders, Rockefeller had the strongest national reputation as a liberal. But his political career had been clouded on the personal level by his divorce and early remarriage and by party dissension and governmental corruption in New York on the public level. Nixon was regarded as too conservative by some Republican liberals and too liberal by many conservatives. His loss in the California gubernatorial election of 1962 to Edmund G. Brown, his embittered farewell press conference after that loss, his unexpected shift of residence to New York, leaving him without a power base, the residue of criticism that still existed regarding his 1960 campaign (he should have wooed the South, he should have written off the South, etc.), all were regarded as serious drawbacks to his chances. Still, he inescapably occupied a comfortable middle ground between Rockefeller and Goldwater and he saw himself as a likely compromise candidate if the convention could not accept either of the two.

The Republican increasingly mentioned for the Presidential nomination, however, was Scranton. Although he was not even privately a candidate, the young Pennsylvania Governor seemed to have gained the most, in a political sense, from the removal of Kennedy from the national scene and his replacement by Johnson. For in some ways, Scranton appeared to be a Republican version of John Kennedy. A young, handsome, Ivy League type, he seemed the kind of candidate who might run well against an older, somewhat conservative professional politician from the South. The big question: Was he prepared to assume an active national role that he had thus far shunned? The answer was to perplex Republican liberals for many months.

While Goldwater's qualifications for running successfully against Johnson were suspect, few observers discounted his chances. He was simply too popular with too many Republican leaders and party workers across the country to write off his candidacy eight months before the convention. For years Goldwater had been crisscrossing the country, speaking at innumerable party affairs, raising money, expounding his own particular philosophy of conservatism. There were many right-wingers, rank and file Republicans, party leaders, businessmen and others who shared his belief that true conservatism had never really received a fair test at the polls in the modern political era. To them, the Eastern liberal establishment that had captured the Republican party twenty years before was again trying to lead it to defeat.

Goldwater, whatever his own private doubts about running, had to be reckoned, on a basis of strict mathematics, the leading Republican candidate as 1964 opened. Since not a single delegate had as yet been chosen, either by primary or state convention, no contender had any demonstrable convention voting strength. But the Goldwater backers claimed they had several hundred of the 655 votes needed for nomination already secured, and even their opponents conceded him 300 or more at this early date. However, the anti-Goldwater forces were convinced he could not win the nomination; it was an article of political faith in both parties that a candidate, to be successful, must necessarily move toward the center, toward the broadest available consensus that can unite all factions of a party. Goldwater showed no signs of moving in that direction. Rockefeller early demonstrated his willingness to move there, but his personal handicaps were judged insurmountable. The collective theory of the anti-Goldwater Republicans—and a good many Democrats—remained that Goldwater and Rockefeller would eliminate each other over the preconvention route, leaving the nomination for Scranton, Nixon or perhaps Governor George Romney of Michigan.

Rockefeller had announced his candidacy on November 7 in his own capital, Albany, and in Nashua, New Hampshire. James Reston reacted to the long-expected entry in this way in The Times:

An honorable man takes responsibility for his own acts, and this is what Governor Rockefeller is doing by entering the race for the Presidency.

He could not, in good conscience, do otherwise. Political courtesy forbids him to say so, but he is unalterably opposed to the candidacy of Barry Goldwater. Yet the Governor, by his divorce and remarriage, has opened the door to Goldwater, and he now feels obliged to try to close it . . .

So the Governor has now started out on the long, agonizing, exhausting trail of endless speeches and hand shakings and midnight plane rides, not because he really thinks he can win the nomination and save himself (he may merely have thrown Nixon's hat into the ring), but because he thinks it is his duty to try to save his party from the policies of Goldwater.

For the moment this may seem a hopeless and to many even a presumptuous adventure, but Rockefeller at least has the power to make Goldwater speak up, and when Barry speaks up, anything can happen . . .

This is the main significance of Rockefeller's campaign. He can dramatize the issues and force his party to consider whether it wants to be identified with Goldwater's policies . . .

With Rockefeller in the race, attention immediately centered on his ideological opponent, Goldwater. It had seemed clear for many months that the Arizona conservative would, at a time of his own choosing, declare himself and fight for the nomination; a well-financed Draft Goldwater organization had been operating efficiently for many months, apparently with the Senator's tacit blessing. But those closer to Goldwater knew that late in 1963 his active

Presidential candidacy was in real doubt. Characteristically, the Senator postponed taking either himself or the possibility of a national campaign very seriously.

In the early stages of the draft movement, he had "sort of laughed" at the prospect, saying, "It's not going any place; at least they'll work off some steam." But in the fall of 1963, Goldwater began to convince himself that he should make the race. He had been talking for years about conservatism, the responsibility of the individual to work for a truly American system of government and against a drift toward liberalism, statism, socialism and worse. His view, expressed privately to his friends, was, "I do not particularly want the Presidency, but I cannot let the conservative movement down."

Then the assassination of Kennedy affected Goldwater not only politically but also personally. They had been friendly colleagues in the Senate for years and Goldwater had some warm memories of Kennedy. He recalled, later, that at the time of the Bay of Pigs crisis, he had been summoned to the White House by Kennedy. He went into the President's empty office and sat down in his rocker. Goldwater had been consulting Dr. Janet Travell, Kennedy's doctor, about his own back trouble, and he gave the rocking chair a stiff workout as he waited for the President. Finally Kennedy came in, smoking a cigar, looked at Goldwater and said, "Do you want this job?" Goldwater replied, "No, not in my right mind." They both laughed. Kennedy said, "Well, I thought I had a good thing going until this morning." That was the day the invasion turned into a fiasco.

After the assassination, Goldwater at first lost all interest in the Presidency. He told his wife, "To heck with the Presidential thing." Adding to his personal doubts, public opinion polls indicated that his chances had been impaired by Kennedy's death and the elevation of Johnson to the Presidency. For Goldwater would have to depend heavily on carrying the Southern states, and it was precisely there that Johnson, the Texan, enjoyed his most natural strength.

Goldwater had liked Johnson personally in their Senate dealings, but he had come to doubt his dedication to political principle. The Arizonan had respected Kennedy—even though privately he had called him "a public liberal," and jokingly said he would complain to Kennedy's father—but he was disturbed by what he viewed as Johnson's shifting progress from conservatism to liberalism. Curiously, at the opposite end of the political spectrum, this same progress was being viewed with suspicion by Northern liberal Democrats; Goldwater was afraid it had really happened, they were afraid it hadn't.

The days following the assassination were long and agonizing for Goldwater. He wavered . . . should he run? . . . should he not run? . . . until, sitting at his desk in the den of his Arizona ranch home, he reached a second —and final—decision. Later, he said: "I'd finally just said to myself, you've got to do it. I realized that I had a responsibility to conservatism and to the young people who had become interested in it. I felt, too, that if I didn't do it that those young people who were voting, many of them for the first time, might drift away. I had a question in my mind all the time—all through the year—whether or not this was the right time for a conservative candidate to offer himself. Because I felt if he—if he were clobbered at the convention— that would be the end of conservatism in the party. Or if he were clobbered in the general election, should he be the nominee, that would write off conservatism in this country. And I wasn't convinced, frankly, at the time I made the decision, that this was the year."

His mind at last made up, Goldwater waited for the expiration of the political moratorium, then called a news conference for Friday, January 3, at his home in Paradise City, a suburb of Phoenix. He said only that he would announce his political plans, but the nation was certain this meant he was off and running.

On Friday morning, Goldwater sat at his desk, in blue jeans and a bedroom slipper, his right foot in a cast because of a bone spur operation on his heel. He talked to some other hams over his short wave radio, more or less oblivious to the mounting confusion around him. After a while he put on a suit and a tie and went into the living room where all of Arizona's top Republican figures had gathered and told them he was going to announce for the Presidency. This was just what the politicians had expected and wanted, and they applauded loudly.

Using crutches, Goldwater hobbled out to the sunny patio of his ranch house near Camelback Mountain. Around him were clusters of yellow roses, marigolds and bougainvillaea. In front of him were scores of reporters and television cameramen. The American flag was back atop the automatic flagpole, after having been at half-staff for the period of mourning for President Kennedy. It was in this unusual but typically Goldwater setting, under open Western skies, that the Senator read a statement and then answered questions.

The day of the Goldwater announcement was a day of paradoxes. Suburban Paradise City, looking as new as if it had somehow magically sprung up overnight, seemed to symbolize the New America—the new life and the need for new political devices to deal with it; and yet, there was Goldwater, looking down on a city with one of the fastest growing populations—and crime rates—in the nation, arguing the case for the Old America. And why did he start running for President on crutches? The health, the stamina, of the President had become a matter of legitimate national concern; surely a new candidate should look as vigorous and confident as possible at his debut. Goldwater's advisers pleaded with him to wait a few days until his foot had healed, but he was adamant and hobbled out to meet the nation on television with his foot in a cast. And why on Friday? The big story would then appear in the Saturday papers, traditionally the least read of any in the week. Why not Saturday, for a story in the widely circulated Sunday papers, or Sunday, for even more prominence in the uncrowded pages of the traditionally dull Monday papers? The Senator listened to the public relations experts—and chose Friday.

Then he insisted on staging the perfectly predictable mob scene that followed not at a downtown Phoenix motel where the crowd could be contained but in the patio of his home. This decision, literally, brought the campaign into the Goldwater family's front yard. For it meant that Peggy Goldwater, the Senator's shy wife, had to have all the Arizona county chairmen in her living room for the pre-announcement meeting, get the Maricopa County sheriffs in their tight dark brown pants and their dark brown ten-gallon hats to fend off the neighbors, arrange for tuna fish and cream cheese sandwiches and coffee for the throngs, turn the carport over to the telephone company and Western Union for communications and let the television experts take over and trample the garden. Peggy Goldwater didn't look wildly enthusiastic, and it was no wonder. She had to marry off a daughter in June, see a husband nominated for the Presidency in July and suffer through months of politics, and then try to bring him home alive in November. So the day understandably seemed a bit too much for her.

But the weather was perfect, and the house looked like a color picture out of the magazine *Arizona Highways*. It was nonetheless modest by contrast with the LBJ Ranch in Texas, and the atmosphere was precisely as informal and individual as the candidate himself. The Senator welcomed one and all to "Be-Nun-I-Kin"—his spelling—meaning "The House on Top of the Hill" —in his interpretation of the Navajo language. After the crowd took in the placid surroundings, many wondered why, with a home like that, he wanted to run again for the Senate, let alone for the Presidency. It clearly would be a long time before he could relax again with his ham radio, its shiny antenna bristling up from the house with an electric Christmas star on top.

In his statement to the news conference, Goldwater said:

I won't change my beliefs to win votes. I will offer a choice, not an echo. This will not be an engagement of personalities. It will be an engagement of principles.

I've always stood for government that is limited and balanced and against ever-increasing concentrations of authority in Washington.

I've always stood for individual responsibility and against regimentation. I believe we must now make a choice in this land and not continue drifting endlessly down toward a time when all of us, our lives, our property, our hopes and even our prayers will become just cogs in a vast Government machine.

I believe that we can win victory for freedom both at home and abroad. And I believe that we can be strong enough and determined enough to win those victories without war.

And I believe that appeasement and weakness can only bring war. I have asked and I will continue to ask across this country: Why not victory—why not victory for sound Constitutional principles in government? Why not victory over the evils of communism?

I am convinced that in this year of 1964 we must face up to our conscience and make a definite choice. We must decide what sort of people we are and what sort of a world we want—now and for our children.

My candidacy is pledged to a victory for principle and to presenting an opportunity for the American people to choose.

In the question period that followed, Goldwater was asked about the impact of his candidacy on the conservative movement:

QUESTION. Senator, was it basic in your decision to run that you could poll at least 45 per cent of the popular vote so that your conservative movement would not be . . . ?

ANSWER. Yes. I would—That was one of the factors that—I felt that if I—if I were beaten and didn't lose by more than the magic five—55, 45 or in which direction you approach it—that this would not harm the conservative movement. It would actually help it and the closer we could get to even-Stephen the better it would be. And I feel that that will happen.

Thus, against the advice of some of his friends and advisers, Goldwater started his campaign in his own special way. "This will not be an engagement of personalities," he said. "It will be an engagement of principles." Yet, from that day forward, confident Democrats and confused Republicans were rarely able to disentangle the principles that Goldwater insisted he was stressing from the warm, complicated, shifting force of his personality.

On the same day in Boston, John Fenton reported two developments:

BOSTON, Jan. 3—Rival Republicans opened Presidential campaigns today in support of Ambassador Henry Cabot Lodge and Senator Barry Goldwater of Arizona.

Despite indications that the Ambassador is not a candidate, a national draft-Lodge campaign opened in a former yarn shop on State Street in Boston's financial district.

Two blocks away, on Federal Street, Lloyd K. Waring, chairman of a loose confederation of Goldwater supporters, said the Senator's announcement today that he would run "puts us in business."

At the time, the Lodge movement did not appear to pose any serious threat to Rockefeller, Goldwater and the others. A less than vigorous campaigner in 1960 when he had run for Vice President with Nixon, the one-time Massachusetts Senator apparently lacked any broad-based support. His protests of disinterest, however, were taken about as seriously as the draft movement; it was clear that he could resign his diplomatic post and return to campaign if his candidacy gained any real headway.

Before January ended, there was another Republican candidate in the field, Senator Margaret Chase Smith of Maine. On January 27 in Washington, the sixty-six-year-old Senator announced her intention of entering the New Hampshire primary. Mrs. Smith conceded that the odds against her would be heavy. No woman had ever been named either Presidential or Vice Presidential nominee by a major political party. Mrs. Smith would not admit it, but she wasn't really running for President and would be quite happy to be considered for the Vice Presidential nomination. But it is a shibboleth of American politics that nobody runs for the second spot; by custom, you only run for the Presidency and then accept the Vice Presidential nomination graciously as a duty to party and country.

Thus, by the end of January, the full cast of characters had made its initial appearance in the big drama of the year, some already trying to elbow their way into the spotlight, others protesting that they had no intention of seeking a larger role. For the Democrats, the script was pretty much written: Lyndon Johnson was playing the lead, he would choose the chief supporting players and the scenario was the record of the Kennedy-Johnson Administration as it continued to unroll.

The Republican problem was altogether different. The script could not be written until the tryouts were held, and these threatened to be unruly indeed. Goldwater and Rockefeller were each insisting on star roles in their kind of show, or none at all. There appeared to be a number of other promising actors—Scranton, Romney, Nixon, even Lodge—but each seemed more reluctant than the other to play a major role in the early scenes of the Republican drama or to offer script suggestions. Some columnists even intimated that fears that the G.O.P. production would turn out to be the flop of the year motivated them.

Against this makeshift backdrop, the first of the agonizing Republican tryouts was to ring up the curtain on political 1964—out of town, of course, in the spare, old communities and snowy windswept hills of New Hampshire.

3

New Hampshire:
"I Goofed Up Somewhere"

To me the high point of the whole primary campaign remains the frosty night in New Hampshire when we were informed that Goldwater would participate in a torchlight parade. And here he came, sitting with an embarrassed and foolish grin in a pony cart pulled by a grotesquely small horse. Ahead of him was a high school drum and bugle corps dressed in Indian feather bonnets, playing "Blue Moon." And ahead of them was a pudgy high school girl, with blue and frozen knees, carrying, of all things, a United Nations flag.

Thus wrote Charles Mohr to his colleagues on The Times, in a piece printed in Times Talk, the magazine for staff members, about the campaign in New Hampshire—where fewer than 100,000 voters gave the nation on March 10 the first concrete evidence of the impact of the candidates.

Another picture that reporters and residents carried away from the state primary fight was that of Nelson Rockefeller and his obviously pregnant wife of a year, crunching through the snow together, often holding hands on the streets, their affection obvious, trying desperately to dispel the image of home-breakers so that the Governor could campaign on the issues as he saw them. There was a lot of curiosity about the new Mrs. Rockefeller, and her fresh, wholesome appearance sharply contrasted with the femme fatale impression that many persons had formed as a result of the Governor's divorce and re-marriage. But if she and her husband were well received everywhere, there still were doubts expressed privately about his moral fitness for high office.

New Hampshire residents, who had just legalized the country's first modern state-operated lottery, are a breed apart from their New England neighbors. To reporters covering the primary, the citizens of New Hampshire seemed to be among the most intelligent and best-informed group of voters they saw all year. They had a very clear idea of Goldwater's public record, as well as of Rockefeller's private affairs; they asked penetrating questions; they showed a healthy skepticism. It was simply not true, as some said, that they were uninterested in such issues as the United Nations or the North Atlantic Treaty Organization except in terms of reduced government spending. The United Nations was a major issue (which it certainly was not in most states), and New Hampshire seemed to have a special feeling about it—some high schools consistently carried the United Nations flag in parades and displayed it at various times at school. New Hampshire was one of the toughest political audiences that any candidate had to play to.

A small industrialized state, with an area of 9,304 square miles (forty-fourth in the nation), wedged in between Vermont and Maine, New Hampshire and its primary over the years have assumed significance far beyond its size because it is the first primary of the year. The prize for months of arduous and intense campaigning through the rugged mountains of the state is only fourteen delegates, a handful of the 655 required for nomination, but the psychological impact is considerable.

It had long been obvious that Rockefeller and Goldwater would enter the New Hampshire primary. Rockefeller, who had been seeking the Presidency since the second Eisenhower Administration, had suspended his first attempt for the nomination late in 1959 when it became clear that he could not overtake Nixon. Primary victories in 1964 were a must for him because he had to prove to party professionals, doubtful of his appeal, that he was the choice of the Republican rank and file. Goldwater was not so dependent on the primaries, since he was busily rounding up delegates at local and state conventions.

However, Goldwater and his advisors began with a firm confidence that he could carry the two most important primaries, New Hampshire and California. They were led to this belief by polls that showed him the heavy favorite of Republican officials such as county chairmen; local politicians like Senator Norris Cotton in New Hampshire encouraged them. Goldwater was personally certain that Rockefeller could not make a close race of a primary and it was, therefore, with surprise and dismay that the Goldwater camp found—within a week of the opening of the New Hampshire campaign—that he was on the defensive, a position from which Goldwater never extricated himself all year.

Since the first primaries had been legalized in the early 1900's, with the intent of taking the choice of the nominees out of the hands of the professional politicians, the only certain pattern to emerge had been uncertainty. Overwhelming primary winners in the past had failed dismally of nomination (Republican Hiram Johnson in 1920 and Democrat Estes Kefauver in 1952); candidates who shunned all primary contests like a plague walked off with the nomination (Republicans Alfred M. Landon in 1936 and Wendell L. Willkie in 1940 and Democrat Adlai E. Stevenson in 1952.)

A primary victory might be no guarantee of nomination, but defeat in a key state often had effectively disposed of a strong contender—for example, Thomas E. Dewey's triumphs over Willkie in Wisconsin in 1944 and Harold E. Stassen in Oregon in 1948, and Kennedy's defeat of Hubert Humphrey in West Virginia in 1960. Still, it is comparatively simple to becloud that pattern by citing the New Hampshire primary of 1964, when the two major Republican hopefuls were soundly trounced by a non-candidate sitting it out on the other side of the world.

If Presidential primaries prove little, if they are widely regarded as a confusing bore, they are there, and they cannot be avoided. Voters, like politicians and analysts, look to the primaries for guidance on the strength of Presidential candidates; paradoxically, many voters resent the fact that often the decision is being made by a small number of voters in states far removed from them. A great deal of that resentment stems from a lack of understanding of how the primaries operate.

The ground rules are complex and vary from state to state. James MacGregor Burns wrote in The Times Magazine:

> The seeming disarray of the Presidential primary system reflects a great virtue
> —its openness. Presidential aspirants who otherwise might be closed out by party
> leaders can use the primaries as a way to demonstrate their popular appeal. In
> 1960 John Kennedy was cut off from two centers of Democratic party power:
> The old Presidential Democratic party leadership headed by Mr. Truman, and
> the Senate Democratic leadership under Lyndon B. Johnson. Kennedy outflanked
> these power centers by invading the primaries.

Today's primaries use one or both of two systems for allowing the voter a preliminary voice in the choice of party Presidential candidates. They are:

1. The preference poll, in which the enrolled members of a party can vote for the one candidate, among a number, they would like to see nominated. The winner of a state's preference poll may acquire its delegates' convention votes or part of them or nothing but good publicity, depending on state laws and, sometimes, party rules and regulations.

2. Election of delegates to the national convention. In some primaries voters can elect delegates pledged to an identified Presidential candidate. In others, they elect delegates "favorable" to a candidate. In still others, they elect delegates officially unpledged but known informally to be supporting one candidate or another.

In 1964, sixteen states and the District of Columbia conducted primaries, many of them of no national significance. At the outset, only two seemed of major importance—New Hampshire and California—and five of secondary importance—Oregon, Illinois, Indiana, Nebraska and West Virginia. Later, because of special circumstances, Oregon's importance mounted. In addition to the primaries, candidates vied for delegates at many state conventions, where delegates, not the voters themselves, decided on whom they would support for the nomination. In the primaries, the struggle was in plain view of the press and the public; in the state conventions the fighting was often as bitter and even noisier, but for much of the year the abrasive struggles were seldom covered by the national press. And no matter how much shouting took place on the floor of state conventions, the major decisions were made beforehand behind closed doors.

Th 1964 primary campaign actually got under way during the first two weeks of August, 1963, when George L. Hinman, the soft-spoken, efficient Republican national committeeman from New York, who was Rockfeller's political chief of staff, assured key Republicans in Congress that the Governor was prepared to fight for the nomination in at least two major primary contests—New Hampshire and California. Hinman also promised them in private meetings that Rockefeller would not pull out of the race abruptly, as he had in late 1959, when he became convinced of the futility of bucking Nixon's steamroller.

In September, 1963, Goldwater's intentions of entering the primary in New Hampshire had all but become official when Senator Cotton agreed to direct the Arizonan's drive, the first of many blows to Rockefeller's chances. Rockefeller had hoped that Cotton would either support him or remain uncommitted a few months longer, thus keeping the situation in New Hampshire fluid and encouraging other state party leaders to stay out of the struggle.

Still not in the race officially, Rockefeller toured New Hampshire for two days in mid-October. In a sharp attack, he charged that Senator Goldwater's opinions on international cooperation spelled "disaster for the future of freedom." He asserted that Goldwater wanted the United States to withdraw from the United Nations, opposed the activities of the World Bank and favored ending economic assistance to all foreign nations. "I disagree with Senator Goldwater's position on each of these three issues," the New Yorker went on, "because I feel that they are not in the best interests of the American people."

When Rockefeller formally announced his candidacy in early November, he was forced to hold two news conferences at Nashua because the weather delayed for more than two hours the arrival of a chartered plane carrying out-of-state newspapermen. The incident gave some indication of the difficult road ahead of him. He entered New Hampshire a definite underdog, yet as late as 1963 he had been the front-runner for the nomination, and as early as 1960, after Nixon's close defeat at the hands of Kennedy, he appeared to to be a leading contender for 1964 nomination. What caused the drastic decline in his prospects?

The long and well-organized drive for Goldwater cut into his lead, but there was little question that Rockfeller's own divorce and remarriage was a major cause. In March, 1962, the Governor had been divorced by Mary Todhunter Clark Rockefeller, his wife of thirty-one years and the mother of his five grown children. Although this shocked public opinion at the time, he had seemed to weather the storm, until his remarriage, on May 4, 1963, to Mrs. Margaretta Fitler Murphy, a divorcée of five weeks and the mother of four young children. The Governor was fifty-four and his bride thirty-six at the time of their marriage, and this disparity of ages, along with the fact that the lives of the Murphy children were so disrupted, turned many voters, particularly women, against Rockefeller.

When the divorce issue came up, as it often did in the early days of the campaign, Rockefeller was prepared. Readily, and with no trace of irritation, he conceded that his remarriage was an issue, one that each voter would have to weigh in his own conscience. Despite attacks by *The Manchester Union-Leader,* the state's largest paper, which called him a "wife-swapper," the Governor lost his temper only once when asked about his remarriage. The Times reported the incident, which occurred in the closing hours of the campaign, when Rockefeller was fatigued:

At the taping of an American Broadcasting Company radio interview, the Governor was asked about statements by William Loeb, publisher of The Manchester Union Leader. Bill Downs, the A.B.C. interviewer, said of Mr. Loeb:
"He brings up the wife-stealing issue—or tried to make it an issue—and has charged you with that. Do you think this has helped you in the long run?"
Mr. Rockefeller snapped: "I don't think it helps when you bring it up either, that way."
Mr. Downs apologized. "I don't mean it that way, sir," he said.

Goldwater's entrance into the race offered the New Hampshire electorate the country's first chance to make the "clear choice" he had suggested between the right wing and moderate-liberal elements of the G.O.P. For three years the Senator had been quietly building his strength with the party professionals, making hundreds of speeches from coast to coast, raising thousands of dollars at $25 to $1,000 a plate party banquets. Now he would test his appeal at the polls.

The Times was not so certain about Goldwater's "clear choice" and in an editorial on January 4 said: "If by that he means no one else is so explicitly *against* every aspect of the New Deal, Fair Deal and the New Frontier, he is quite right. If he means that every voter knows what Mr. Goldwater is *for*, the choice is not nearly so clear-cut."

The question of what Goldwater was for assumed more and more importance as the New Hampshire campaign progressed. The Senator, who made a fetish of frankness, would at one point tell a questioner he favored United States withdrawal from the United Nations if Red China were admitted, or that some poor people really did not want to work, or that the civil rights bill went too far, or that the nation must take new military moves against Cuba. Then, sometimes within minutes, he would modify his position for still another questioner. His views on the United Nations were a case in point. A questioner asked him at Lancaster if it were true that he was not "too strongly for the U.N." Goldwater said, "No, that's not true." Earlier, at Littleton, however, he said that the United Nations could and "probably would" become dominated by enemies of the United States. In that case, he said, "I see no advantages of staying in it."

Charles Mohr, in a Times article, documented the Senator's ambivalence on the United Nations:

There have been occasions on the campaign trail when Mr. Goldwater appeared to be in favor of either or both kinds of [United Nations charter] reform.
By that time, however, some voters appear to have lost the thread of his argument. Neither those who admire the United Nations nor those who despise it find much to jeer or cheer, and he is seldom applauded when speaking on this subject. . . .
In Laconia, N.H., last Friday Mr. Goldwater was asked whether, if he were the Republican nominee next fall and Communist China were admitted to the

United Nations, he would promise to take the country out of the United Nations.
"I would be inclined to do so," he answered.

Press association reporters were telephoning in this story when the Senator arrived a few minutes later on a street corner in nearby Meredith.

A resident said, "My wife wants to know what you would do about the United Nations."

The Senator said:

"We must stay in the United Nations, but we must improve it."

Asked if it were true, then, that he had never opposed the United Nations, Mr. Goldwater said, "No."

Soon afterward, at the Meredith High School, however, Mr. Goldwater told students that if Communist China were admitted "I think it blows the whole thing to pieces."

The day before, in a speech at Colby Junior College for Girls at New London, Mr. Goldwater said, "I've never said let's get out of the U.N. I don't know how the rumor ever got started."

It was on January 7 at Concord, during his very first day in the state, that Goldwater opened himself to an attack that was to dog him until the general election itself on November 3. At a press conference, Goldwater said he would suggest "one" change in Social Security, "that it be made voluntary." His own staff distributed the transcript of the press conference confirming this remark. Goldwater had made similar remarks in interviews the previous year, but this was different—he was now a candidate for the Presidential nomination. Rockefeller began to charge that Goldwater's views would destroy Social Security. Although he had a reputation for blunt political honesty, Goldwater did everything he could to blur this incident—at times he even denied he had made such a remark. He tortuously modified his opinion on Social Security to an argument that, while it should not be made voluntary, the withholding tax should not be allowed to rise to such high levels that it would preclude the purchase of private, "voluntary" pension plans.

Goldwater left even his own followers bewildered and uncertain about some details of his opinions on major questions. He was not trying to be evasive; his aggressiveness, his willingness to state his views and stand or fall on them actually were a big factor in the confusion. Also, his throwaway delivery of his lines on New Hampshire street corners did not soften his message when they were transformed into newspaper headlines. The Senator, his manner so unemotional and relaxed that it disarmed many of his severest critics, promised voters very little. After one speech, a man in the audience was overheard to say: "Well, that's one guy who can say four years from now, 'What are you complaining about? I never promised you anything.'"

In New Hampshire, the problem of extremism and the ultraconservative John Birch Society cropped up. Goldwater said he did not refuse the help of anyone as long as they did not advocate the overthrow of the government. He declared that attempts to stifle the conservative dissent had led to "fascism of the left."

The Arizonan spoke out on other issues—and his opinions were just as controversial. He suggested a resumption of U-2 reconnaisance flights over the Soviet Union. He said the United States should "interdict" supply lines not only from North Vietnam into South Vietnam but also from Communist China into North Vietnam. He said "brinkmanship is a great word."

"Have the people of New England or the people of the United States changed in the last two hundred years?" Goldwater asked his audience one night. He followed that up with perhaps the unhappiest political question of the year by asking, "Have we become a nation of cowards?"

He opposed Federal aid to elementary education and the medicare bill because they would weaken parents' sense of responsibility for educating their children and young people's sense of responsibility for taking care of parents. He asserted that the nuclear test ban treaty, which he had opposed, made it impossible to test the reliability of United States guided missiles. He suggested an investigation to see "why Johnny won't work," instead of the Johnson war on poverty. He proposed that the Marines turn the water on at the Guantanamo naval base, when Castro turned it off. He insisted that trends toward "handouts and circuses" were threatening the United States with a fate comparable to that of Rome or ancient Egypt.

Goldwater's utterances were merely affirmation of the conservative philosophies he had been advocating for years, but this time he was receiving national attention each time he spoke. Concern mounted, particularly in the East. The Times, in an editorial, said:

Senator Goldwater has told the voters of New Hampshire that eventually the United States will have to unleash another armed attack on Cuba. Whether this statement went over with a bang on the peaceful street corners of Concord, we know not. But his remark raises an interesting point. Can the Republican party afford to continue to unleash Barry Goldwater?

To those familiar only with the massively organized hoopla of a general campaign or a big primary such as California, the New Hampshire primary campaign would have been a revelation. Goldwater spoke to audiences as small as ten or twenty or thirty persons—in little town halls that would not have held many more people. Sometimes he dispensed with a speech entirely and merely answered questions, which were often tough. Seldom has a political candidate so frankly answered so many questions—and learned to regret it so much later. Although his remarks astounded many politicians and political observers when they read them in cold print the next day, they were delivered so casually and so unemotionally that the Senator seemed, on the scene, almost to be engaging in a private conversation with a group of friends.

When Goldwater formally entered the race, Rockefeller eagerly challenged him to a debate on the issues. The Arizonan steadfastly declined to accept, and the New Yorker made a strong point of this refusal in the early stretches of the campaign. The Senator's conservatism provided the Governor with ample ammunition for his appeal to New Hampshire voters to support a candidate in the "mainstream of American thought," a theme that would recur again and again throughout the primaries.

Rockefeller's moderation contrasted starkly with his opponent's position. He supported, without reservations, the United Nations and Social Security;

he decried the recklessness of Goldwater's remarks; he reaffirmed his belief in civil rights; he pledged a program of aid for small business. The Governor pounced on Goldwater's stand on helping the indigent and accused him of having a "restricted" understanding of the human problems of unfortunate people.

From the start of the primary race, Goldwater had attempted to depict his rival as a "me-too" or "echo" candidate. Rockefeller did not neglect this charge. He emphasized his differences with the Democrats, in their approach to social problems, and said: "I don't think that 'me too' label has any application, either to the Democratic party here or on the national level. There are fundamental differences between my views and their views. I think it was just a political statement on his [Goldwater's] part." The Governor found time, too, to assail "extremist" backers of Goldwater for "lies, deceit and tricks" in the campaign.

Only in their campaign style did the candidates manage to bridge the wide chasm separating them. The two men and their wives both braved cold weather and heavy snow to trek through the streets of New Hampshire's towns and hamlets, pumping numbed hands and making small talk, darting into supermarkets, variety stores or barbershops in their incessant search for voters. The Governor, however, was more at ease in this "supermarket" tactic than his opponent. He could pat babies' cheeks, buy dozens of ice cream cones for children, and appear as if he were enjoying himself. Goldwater suffered through it.

Both candidates resorted to jokes, Goldwater's being irreverent, Rockefeller's rarely witty.

A Goldwater sample: In a parish house he said he had once been asked if he were a high or low Episcopalian. Ask me on a Saturday night, he replied. This reference to weekend drinking left most of his Yankee audience as cold as the weather.

A Rockefeller sample: One time his grandfather, John D. Rockefeller, was discovered by an assistant crawling about the floor of his office. "What are you doing, on your hands and knees behind your desk?" the assistant gasped. "I'm looking for a dime I lost," Mr. Rockefeller replied. "Well," the assistant said, "you don't have to worry about a dime." Grandfather Rockefeller got up indignantly. "Young man," he said, "do you realize that dime represents 5 per cent interest . . . " the Governor hesitated for a moment, then finished, ". . . on two dollars for a year."

With the primary voting day four weeks away, John Fenton of The Times toured the state and summed up several impressions:

A Republican sipping coffee at a lunch counter in Laconia said that Senator Goldwater had been doing well in that area until he appeared in person and then was followed by Governor Rockefeller. "Goldwater," the man said, "told a couple of questioners in his audience, 'I don't want to answer that question now. Why don't you write me a letter and I'll answer it.' That went over like a lead balloon, and he looked worse after Rocky showed up, because he answered everything, and shook hands all over the place."

While Rockefeller and Goldwater were pouring hundreds of thousands of dollars into their campaigns (Goldwater less than Rockefeller), two men from Boston were working in a dingy vacant store in Concord on a project that was to undermine both the Governor and the Senator in the primary. David Goldberg, a lawyer, and Paul Grindle, an advertising man, had opened Draft-Lodge headquarters with little more than hope. They had virtually no money. Their candidate refused to give them public support because as an Ambassador he was prohibited by Foreign Service regulations from taking part in politics. And they had few of the local political leaders with them—almost all had lined up long before for Goldwater or Rockefeller. But they did have a plan based on Grindle's experience in direct-mail advertising. They sent pledge cards to every listed Republican voter in the state, going over the heads of the political leaders, appealing to the voters to enlist themselves on the side of the handsome moderate from neighboring Massachusetts, the man who had stood up to the Russians at the United Nations. All over the state they showed a movie of Lodge in action at the United Nations, with a message from Eisenhower calling him the kind of man the country needed (actually Eisenhower's statement was made in 1960, when Lodge was the Vice Presidential candidate).

The Draft-Lodge movement was a lifesaver for the Goldwater drive. The Arizonan's campaign had been going badly. Starting out with an admittedly long lead, he had seen Rockefeller steadily whittling it away. Lodge would draw votes from Rockefeller; so would Senator Margaret Chase Smith of Maine and even Harold E. Stassen, the perennial candidate who was trying once again. A new write-in campaign for Nixon, on the other hand, would probably hurt Goldwater more. In any event, though Goldwater might not win New Hampshire, neither would Rockefeller. In fact, the vote would be so split up it would mean nothing.

That is precisely what Rockefeller feared. As an adopted son of New Hampshire (Dartmouth, '30), he had high hopes of carrying the state. The people responded warmly to his folksy way of campaigning—the double wink, the firm handclasp, the arm around the shoulder, the "hiyah fella!" He was saying the right things because in-depth studies of voter sentiment had told him to speak up for the United Nations, to warn of the peril in Goldwater's Social Security views, to hammer away at Castro. Now Lodge backers were endangering all his careful plans. Something had to be done. The question was, what?

On February 18, Goldwater opened up on Lodge, accusing him of getting things "kind of balled up" in South Vietnam. The Lodge staff expected an immediate Rockefeller defense of their man. "We held our breath for days," Grindle said. "We thought sure Rockefeller would issue a statement backing up Lodge. We felt it would absolutely ruin us." If such a statement had come, Grindle said "we would have been frozen out of the picture." The Draft-Lodge strategists were ready to close their headquarters and go back to Boston. For two days all was silence. Then, on February 20, in Goffstown, Rocke-

feller refused to exonerate Lodge from responsibility for the "mess" in South
Vietnam. The next day Rockefeller, his worries about Lodge's impact in the
primary growing, telephoned the Ambassador in Saigon and asked him either
to come home and run or to pull out of the race. Lodge refused to commit
himself either way and Rockefeller's attitude hardened. Soon he expressed a
reservation about Lodge's qualifications to be President because of the Ambassador's limited administrative experience.

With each of these moves Lodge sentiment gained. Grindle and Goldberg
redoubled their efforts. Eventually Nixon issued the kind of a statement that
Grindle had feared Rockefeller would. Nixon said that there was evidence
that Lodge was getting a "bum rap" for the Vietnam situation. There were
those in the Rockefeller organization who had advised him to issue a statement supporting Lodge's performance in Saigon. One was even drafted, but
never issued.

By March it became more and more apparent that the support for Lodge
was unexpectedly widespread and contagious. Grindle was talking about
20,000 to 30,000 votes for his man. To make matters worse for the Goldwater and Rockefeller camps, a similar write-in drive for Nixon, mounted
by former Governor Wesley Powell, who had withdrawn from the race in
favor of Nixon, was daily growing more effective.

As March 10 approached, James Reston wrote:

The interesting thing about the New Hampshire election is that the reporters
spent their days following Goldwater and Rockefeller through dirty snowbanks,
and then retire to various bars and talk about the candidates who aren't in New
Hampshire at all: Lodge, Nixon and Scranton.

The vote will probably be fairly large, if it doesn't snow on Tuesday, not
because the people are excited about the national implications of the election, but
because they are excited about whether state lottery tickets are to be sold in their
local state liquor stores.

Meanwhile, what is clear is that the New Hampshire campaign has come to an
end without any candidate making much of an impression on the voters. About
all it has proved is that both Goldwater and Rockefeller are critical of the
President's conduct of foreign policy, but when the voters listen to the alternatives
offered by Goldwater—blockading Cuba, attacking North Vietnam, and maybe
even China, they look decidedly unenthusiastic.

There was snow and sleet in New Hampshire on primary day, but it did
not keep the voters from the polls. In cities and hamlets alike they slogged
through the streets to write in the name of Lodge as their preference for the
Republican nomination for President. Leading almost from the start, he
slowly pulled away from his two principal contenders, Goldwater and Rockefeller. The complete official returns were as follows:

Lodge	33,007
Goldwater	20,692
Rockefeller	19,504
Nixon	15,587

Lodge won more than a preferential "beauty contest" poll. He also won all the delegates. It was a spectacular and smashing victory for him. The reaction was immediate and, as it turned out, erroneous. James Reston said:

The political pros are now betting on Gov. William W. Scranton of Pennsylvania, former Vice President Richard M. Nixon or Ambassador Henry Cabot Lodge of Massachusetts for the 1964 Republican Presidential nomination.

They seem to agree that Ambassador Lodge's spectacular write-in victory in New Hampshire's primary election virtually eliminated both Senator Barry Goldwater of Arizona and Governor Rockefeller of New York.

At the same time, they expect Senator Goldwater to retain sufficient strength in a deadlocked convention to transfer about 250 delegate votes, most of them from the South, to the man of his choice—probably in favor not of Ambassador Lodge but of Mr. Nixon or Governor Scranton.

Lodge, in Saigon, voiced gratification at the result, but maintained his non-candidacy posture. "I do not plan to go to the United States," he said, "I do not plan to leave Saigon. I do not intend to resign."

Still, his victory posed a problem: Had he compromised his position as Ambassador by his sudden emergence into the political forefront? It was privately admitted by Lodge leaders that the Ambassador had called all the shots in his campaigning, passing instructions on through his son, George Cabot Lodge. It was a moot point, but only one opinion really mattered—that of President Johnson. He apparently did not think Lodge had violated regulations; the Ambassador remained at his post, and his followers began immediately to talk of seeking $1,000,000 to press his cause in other states, with the cry of "on to Oregon."

Rockefeller's staff was clouded in gloom. It had expected more from New Hampshire. But the Governor emphatically denied that New Hampshire had rejected him, and said that Lodge's triumph had been a "victory for a favorite [New England] son" and for opponents of "extremism in the party." Nothing daunted, he flew to another Concord, in California, the next day to renew his campaign on the Coast, but not before repeating that he was "happy" about the outcome, that he had been a five-to-one underdog when the New Hampshire primary began, and that "I feel [the] results are clear evidence of the strength I can develop by campaigning." Privately, however, there was no question about his disappointment.

Scranton's men saw in the Lodge victory hope for a "third force," but Scranton would have none of this. He called the results amazing and a tremendous compliment to Lodge. He also stressed that his own position was unchanged, that he was not a candidate and that he would respond only to a genuine draft.

It remained for Goldwater to offer the simplest explanation of all. He said he had "goofed up somewhere" in the race, but he reassured his followers that in politics it is possible to lose some battles and still win the war. Where had the Senator, the heavy favorite in New Hampshire, "goofed"? He had made more than 200 appearances in twenty-three days in New Hampshire, sometimes answering more than fifty questions a day from voters, exposing himself in staggering detail on every possible issue of the day. His over-prominence in the press, the Senator was to say later, seemed to distort his conservative views into "extremism" in the minds of the voters. To Rocke-feller, it was simply that Goldwater had been forced to expound his views in public and defend them and that the voters had rejected them and Goldwater, too.

Charles Mohr, in a Times article, described Goldwater's disorganized pre-sentation:

He speaks with great imprecision and often obviously has not done his home-work. The best example is when he discusses Social Security, on which he offers two opinions. One, that it would be difficult and inadvisable, on the basis of both politics and accounting, to abolish the system. But, two, that it violates his funda-mental principles and is a poor bargain for its costs to the beneficiaries.

This innate honesty seems to require him to say that many Federal programs ought to be abolished as wrong, illegal and destructive of social values, but then to add that it is politically impossible to abolish them leaves his hearers nowhere.

The New Hampshire debacle, in which he failed to capture a single delegate, made Goldwater change his tactics and campaign style drastically. On the friendly banquet circuit he could be as far-out in his observations as he pleased, because there was no one to dispute him among his captive audiences. On the tough primary trail, with the national press and television and rival candidates watching and listening, he could no longer escape the consequences of his remarks.

He was forced to think, to seek help and plan what he was going to say. He became more cautious in his utterances, if not in his viewpoints, resorted less to extemporaneous speeches and more to prepared texts; he modified his position on some politically potent questions (Social Security, for one) as he studied them more deeply; he cut down on his public appearances. It was a frustrating but essential shift for the Arizonan, who prided himself on his candor.

"My biggest strength is also my biggest weakness," he said. "I'm frank and I say what I think. Some people like it, but it bothers some people, even conservatives."

Denison Kitchel, his national campaign director and an old friend, defined the new aim this way, "We want to re-establish the identity of Barry Gold-water." The keys to that new identity were caution and less exposure. Whether they would unlock the door to the Republican nomination remained to be seen. But as days went by, and the first shock of New Hampshire receded, it became increasingly evident it had not been so great a disaster to Goldwater and Rockefeller as believed earlier. The Times, in an editorial, analyzed it this way:

In a real sense, the national contest for that [Republican Presidential] nomina-tion is almost as wide open now as it was before the astounding flood of write-in ballots that put Ambassador Lodge first with New Hampshire Republicans.

All the votes cast for Mr. Lodge came to less than one-twentieth of 1 per cent of the probable national total next November. Moreover, there is reason to suspect that the write-ins were votes against the two front-runners, Senator Goldwater and Governor Rockefeller, as much as expressions of positive support for our Ambassador to South Vietnam.

As for Senator Goldwater and Governor Rockfeller, both have been hurt by their rebuff in New Hampshire—but not fatally. California's primary in June will be a much more crucial test for both men.

Even this appraisal, events later proved, did not properly evaluate Goldwater's strength in the non-primary states where national convention delegates would be selected in state conventions. His chances could have been destroyed if his supporters in such states had reacted strongly to the New Hampshire defeat. At the Goldwater headquarters at Connecticut and L Streets in Washington, there were days of apprehensive waiting after March 10. But then it began to dawn upon his key supporters—as it did not to many sophisticated political experts until much later—that Goldwater still had his base of support and that it was more than enough to nominate him—if he could just get through the California primary alive.

4

California:
"A Pillow Fight
Under Water"

Crucial California was still months in the future, but there was no question about its overriding importance or its unpredictability. California, as Eugene Burdick wrote in The Times Magazine, is a "maddening state to evaluate." It has a high divorce rate, a high alcoholic rate, a high accident rate; its inhabitants, many immigrants from other states, are highly mobile; most of all, it is a haven for fringe groups with passionate convictions and for political mavericks—and the site of many political upsets.

The California primary would not be held until June 2, but the preliminaries had started as early as September of 1963. In that month, an advisory committee headed by former Senator William F. Knowland was formed to appraise the Arizonan's chances in the state and Goldwater made a number of visits to the Coast. His followers had taken over the Young Republican organization in California and had recruited 20,000 volunteers. Rockefeller was not idle either. In November, he hired a professional political management organization, Spencer-Roberts & Associates, boasting an imposing record of victories. Then early in 1964 George Hinman moved to the Coast to devote full time there, and Senator Thomas H. Kuchel, the state's most potent vote-getter, agreed to serve as the Rockefeller campaign manager.

For both Goldwater and Rockefeller, California was the big one. True, Goldwater was steadily increasing his delegate total by lining up votes at state and local conventions, but he needed a big primary victory to show that his appeal extended beyond party functionaries to the voters at large. Blocked in state and county conventions by Goldwater's meticulous advance work, Rockefeller had to win this vital primary to prove to the professionals that his national reputation could be transformed into votes. If he could defeat Goldwater in Oregon and in California, he still might have a chance. In any event, he might stop Goldwater.

Here is what happened in the earlier primaries:

Wisconsin, on April 7, picked thirty convention delegates ostensibly favoring the state's own Representative John W. Byrnes for the nomination, but actually leaning toward Goldwater. By the rules of the game, no national contender openly campaigned, in deference to Wisconsin's favorite son.

Illinois, on April 14, did not give Goldwater the 80 per cent vote his backers had confidently predicted; it gave him only 63 per cent of the total Republican vote. Although he gathered another forty delegates, he failed by about 150,000 to reach the rock-bottom estimate of what traditionally conservative Illinois was supposed to give him. Mrs. Smith, the only other candidate on a ballot permitting, but heavily discouraging, write-ins, did not even pretend to campaign in the state, still got 209,521 votes, compared with 512,840 for Goldwater, 68,122 for Lodge, 30,313 for Nixon, 2,048 for Rockefeller and 1,842 for Scranton.

Pennsylvania, on April 28, gave its Governor Scranton 58 per cent of the total vote after a spirited write-in drive by his supporters. Lodge got a surprising 21 per cent, but no candidates, major or minor, had entered this non-binding popularity contest, and all it proved was that in his own state Scranton evoked somewhat less enthusiasm than his friends had hoped.

Massachusetts, Lodge's home state, where nobody campaigned, on the same day gave the absent Ambassador 80 per cent of the write-ins registered. Nevertheless the state's thirty-four convention delegates were pledged to Senator Leverett Saltonstall, another favorite son, but loyal to Lodge.

Texas, on May 2, in a poll that didn't really count at all because its fifty-six convention delegates were to be chosen at a state party convention two weeks later, still stirred some interest. Instead of giving Goldwater a resounding vote of confidence, as had been expected, the state's Republicans gave him only a comfortable margin, despite active campaigning by Goldwater committees, and picked Lodge, who had done no campaigning at all, for second place.

Indiana, another conservative stronghold, on May 5 had only two choices on its ballot, Goldwater and Stassen, and write-ins were forbidden. Goldwater, as expected, won the state's thirty-two convention delegates. Yet Stassen startled everybody by collecting 25 per cent of the Republican total, an obvious protest vote by the G.O.P. rank and file.

Ohio, on the same day, had no Presidential candidates on its Republican primary ballot, but in a race for the party's Senatorial nomination, Representative Robert A. Taft Jr., son of the late Senator and a middle-of-the-roader himself, overwhelmingly defeated Ted W. Brown, an ardent Goldwater man.

West Virginia, one week later, added at least a psychological blow when Rockefeller, running unopposed there, after a short, jaunty and confident campaign, won the approval of two-thirds of the voters casting ballots. Although this verdict was not binding on the state's fourteen convention delegates, it all but assured the New York Governor of their support—the first tangible result he had to show for months of hard work.

And *Nebraska*, on the same May 12, dealt less kindly with Goldwater, the sole candidate listed on its primary ballot. Nebraska Republicans took the trouble to write in Nixon (31 per cent), Lodge (16 per cent) and assorted other names, leaving the Arizona Senator with slightly less than 50 per cent, another tarnished victory.

Still despite such minor setbacks as these, Goldwater's own confidence was rising steadily—and with reason. In behind-the-scenes politicking at state party conventions, he had already "locked up" about 280 delegates. He was not yet within sight of the magic 655 needed for the nomination, but even so the race appeared to hinge on one question: Could Goldwater be stopped? In retrospect, it is clear that he actually did have an unshakable hold on prospective delegates—that, in fact, he possibly could have been nominated even had he lost the California primary. But it did not appear that way at the time, especially to Goldwater himself. He often remarked that his nomination would be almost impossible if he lost California.

Oregon, on May 15, was not viewed as so vital. There was open murmuring in the Goldwater camp that it was assuming the appearance of another New Hampshire, a race in which there were too many candidates entered to give conservatism a decent chance. Goldwater had originally been optimistic about Oregon because it was a Western state, but as polls by his own organization came into his hands, he was suddenly faced with evidence that his cause was virtually hopeless there.

Oregon's Presidential primary law was unique. It required those "generally advocated throughout the United States" as potential candidates to be placed on the ballot. Under this mandate, the Oregon Secretary of State nominated Goldwater, Lodge, Rockefeller, Nixon, Scranton and Romney. The Michigan Governor withdrew before the March 9 deadline, but Mrs. Smith's name was added through a petition signed by more than 1,000. Oregon law states that a candidate may have his name removed if he signs an affidavit stating he "is not now and does not intend to become a candidate for President or Vice President in the forthcoming election." On March 6, three days before the deadline, Scranton, who consistently maintained he was available only for a draft, requested that he be eliminated because he was not an active candidate; then he added, "I cannot in conscience sign the affidavit." His name remained on the ballot. Lodge, on March 11, a day after his New Hampshire victory, had cabled the Oregon Secretary of State that he could not be a candidate in the primary because "I am precluded by Foreign Service regulations from engaging in any political activity." Since this was a day after the deadline for withdrawals, his disclaimer accomplished nothing except to strengthen the belief that he was a candidate.

About the time of Lodge's cable, an Associated Press poll of Republican county leaders in Oregon surprisingly disclosed Goldwater far ahead of the other contenders. Rockefeller and Nixon were virtually deadlocked for second; Lodge, Scranton, Mrs. Smith and Romney followed in that order. Even before March 10, both Rockefeller and Goldwater had made wearisome transcontinental flights to campaign in Oregon. The views they expressed, the strategy they followed were the same as they were in New Hampshire. Goldwater's margin appeared insurmountable; Rockefeller's campaign futile.

By mid-April the picture had changed radically; the undeclared candidacy of Lodge, still riding the tide of his upset victory in New Hampshire, swelled into Oregon. A poll taken by Louis Harris showed Lodge favored by 46 per cent of the Republican electorate in the state. Nixon, who had beaten Kennedy in the state four years earlier, was second with 17 per cent. Goldwater was third with 14 per cent, Rockefeller fourth with 13 per cent. Two other findings of the Harris poll were revealing: Four out of ten Republicans denounced Goldwater as being too far to the right and 34 per cent said they could not vote for him if he were chosen by the convention. Five out of ten voters criticized Rockefeller for his divorce and 27 per cent said they could not vote for him if he were nominated.

Lodge's followers, who had opened their campaign headquarters in a vacant store in Portland only two weeks before the poll, were skeptical of their findings. David Goldberg, the young Boston lawyer who had helped direct the Ambassador's New Hampshire drive, said: "It scares us. It's hard for me to believe before we have done much hard work in the state. We're not paying any attention to the polls. We're getting ready for an uphill kind of doorbell ringing type campaign, with no built-in organization or political leaders." William E. Walsh, Rockefeller's state chairman, asserted he could find no basis for the poll results.

"We've come up between the last two polls and Goldwater has gone down," he said. "We're still as well organized in Oregon as anybody else and, as of today, we're stronger than Goldwater. Nobody can gauge the Lodge deal. It could blow up and get big or be volatile and disappear."

The Goldwater strategist in Oregon, Stephen Shadegg, who once had been closest of all Goldwater's associates, said the latest polls did not agree with those taken for him. "The Senator is substantially ahead of the position given him in these other polls," he declared. "Harris pollsters went around and asked, 'Do you agree with Senator Goldwater that we ought to pull out of the United Nations?' But the Senator has not said so. You let me plan these questions and I'll give you any kind of answers you want." Shadegg's optimism for publication contrasted sharply with private pessimistic reports to the Goldwater leadership. The results of his own and other polls were the chief reason the Senator decided to bypass Oregon and concentrate on California. Although he could not withdraw his name from the ballot, Goldwater canceled all his remaining Oregon appearances and his organization there was left to its own devices.

But supporters of Nixon were heartened by the same polls and mounted a serious and determined drive for him. Wendell Wyatt, a former Republican state chairman who directed Nixon's Oregon race in 1960, offered this explanation: "We have been upset to see a vacuum developing here in Oregon and Nixon supporters drifting to Henry Cabot Lodge. These are people who would be glad to get out and work for Mr. Nixon if they had the incentive. We will do what we can to raise the necessary money locally and I will try to obtain outside funds wherever I can. We will undertake some television, radio and newspaper solicitation of votes."

In the closing weeks of the campaign, Rockefeller, clinging to the belief that the Lodge ratings were a flash in the pan, increased his efforts. He had the state to himself; there was no other active candidate. In rural areas and urban areas, in shopping centers and small stores, in large auditoriums and small clubhouses, the Governor flashed his smile, shook thousands of hands and tirelessly enunciated his philosophy of Republican moderation.

His backers boasted, "He cared enough to come to Oregon," and a typical day's schedule—a week before the election—showed how much he cared. Rockefeller campaigned in five communities in western Oregon; he began with a breakfast at 7:30 A.M. in Astoria, spoke in Tillamook, Salem and Dallas, and ended with an address at the University of Oregon in Eugene that night. The crowds ranged from a few hundred to a few thousand, usually warm and polite but seldom carried away with enthusiasm. Rockefeller gave an essentially standard speech in rather low key—a speech not designed to evoke an emotional response. His determination, his uphill struggle captured the imagination of the Oregon voters—and of the nation.

As primary day dawned, with fair weather in most areas, one big question still remained to be answered: Had the voters of Oregon, a state plagued by a high divorce rate, become reconciled enough to Rockefeller's divorce and remarriage to concentrate on the real philosophical differences between him and Goldwater?

Lawrence E. Davies of The Times reported their answer this way:

PORTLAND, Ore., May 15—Governor Rockefeller won a dramatic upset victory tonight in Oregon's Republican Presidential preferential primary election.

His "Lone Ranger" campaign to capture the state's 18-vote delegation to the Republican National Convention carried him into first place over Henry Cabot Lodge, who was favored, and four other rivals in the incomplete ballot count.

The final results showed Rockefeller the winner with 94,190 votes; Lodge, 79,169; Goldwater, 50,105; Nixon, 48,274; Smith, 8,087; Scranton, 4,509. The victory put Oregon's delegates firmly in Rockefeller's grasp for at least two convention ballots. The Governor viewed the victory as a trend in his favor that might carry over into California. He confidently declared that the brand of progressive Republicanism he represented would turn back the threat of extremists to take over the party. He contended that his forward-looking position on such basic issues as Social Security and the United Nations, compared with Goldwater's conservative outlook, was a major reason for the triumph. Goldwater's views, he asserted, "do not reflect the thinking of the great majority of Republican voters."

Numerically, Oregon's eighteen delegates were not vital to Goldwater's chances. He had almost matched them with twelve in Wyoming picked up

Top:
A mighty storm of cheering broke
through the Cow Palace.
(The New York Times photo)

Bottom:
William Scranton, sixteen,
and Susan Scranton, eighteen.
(Associated Press photo)

"I would remind you that extremism in the defense of liberty is no vice. And let me remind you also that moderation in the pursuit of justice is no virtue."

(photo by George Tames, The New York Times)

Left:
He turned his hobby into a wartime occupation,
ferrying bombers and fighters to India.
(Associated Press photo)

Right:
"The handle here is Barry
— Baker, Adam, Roger, Roger, Yankee
it sure is a pleasure to work you."
(Associated Press photo)

at about the same time. "I still have 325 delegates," he said. "I am glad he has some—it makes a better race of it."

Psychologically, the victory was like a tonic to the Rockefeller camp. It revitalized and rejuvenated the New Yorker and his followers, confirming again that Goldwater had still to prove himself in any tough popular competition. It forced the party leaders to take another hard look at the Rockefeller candidacy, to ask themselves if the issue of his divorce had not run its course. It abruptly braked the headlong candidacy of Lodge. And, most of all, it reaffirmed—if any reaffirmation had been needed—the importance of the California vote on June 2, a race in which only Goldwater and Rockefeller were contenders and in which write-ins were illegal.

James Reston wrote in The Times:

So long as he [Goldwater] was merely a symbol of conservatism in the Senate, talking primarily to partisan audiences, his views were not minutely studied, but in the primary campaigns they were. For the first time, his policies had to be considered seriously in Presidential terms, as the policies he would actually adopt if nominated and elected.

The response of the people who had a chance to vote for or against Goldwater in these terms has been clear enough. They have not responded as he said they would. Even within his own party he has not been able to transfer his personal popularity into a majority, and the progressive spirit of the party which chose Willkie, Dewey, Eisenhower and Nixon has again proved to be strong.

The professional Republican party workers, accordingly, are faced with an awkward and ironical situation. The more Goldwater has declined in popularity polls and in the contested primary returns, the more the pros have pushed him toward the nomination.

One hour after the polls closed in Oregon, Grindle, the national campaign director of the Draft-Lodge movement, in conceding victory to Rockefeller, said: "There is not the slightest question that Oregon voters have seen one of the greatest finishes in political history. They have seen an incredible fighter with lots of guts, who has gone on slugging since New Hampshire. I think the Oregon voters have gone along with us in expressing their admiration for Nelson A. Rockefeller."

Lodge's adherents, moderate Republicans like the Ambassador, were mired in a quandary of alternatives. Goldwater's extreme views were unpalatable to them. A California victory for the Senator would end all hopes for a convention deadlock—the only road open to their man. A Rockefeller triumph would undoubtedly check the Arizonan's onrush, and, more to the point, would pave the way to a compromise that would serve their cause of moderate Republicanism. Perhaps, too, it would lead to a convention deadlock and a choice of Lodge.

Rumors that the Lodge forces were going to throw their support in California to the New Yorker began to circulate almost as soon as the trend in Oregon became evident. Goldwater reacted sharply the day after the primary. Standing in the aisle of a chartered airplane, rocking on the balls of his feet, he told reporters, "If I dropped dead today, Rockefeller just can't get the nomination." He also asserted that Oregon had punctured the bubble for Lodge, and that if he [Goldwater] lost in California, it would be Nixon or Scranton who would benefit from it.

Rumor became fact on May 18. Joseph Loftus of The Times reported the next day:

LOS ANGELES, May 18—Henry Cabot Lodge's California friends decided today to work for the Rockefeller slate of delegates as a tactical move to save their own candidate.

The decision was meaningful for the Republican party nationally because it sharpened the conflict between conservatives and moderates to a point that could make or break Senator Barry Goldwater in the contest for the 1964 nomination for President.

If Senator Goldwater can beat the combined Rockefeller-Lodge forces, he will have compensated for his poor Oregon and New Hampshire showings and will have the nomination almost within his grasp.

Goldwater declared that liberal attempts to thwart his nomination could be "suicidal for the party" and that the alliance wouldn't work. However, he added: "It will have its effect. But we haven't yet been able to analyze what the effect will be. I haven't seen any visible support for Lodge in California— but I know there is some."

It was inevitable that the final weeks of this primary battle would be as bewildering as they were bitter. Gladwin Hill of The Times reported:

In metropolises and hamlets up and down the thousand-mile length of the state, impressive crowds daily coalesce, palpitate and titillate as a candidate's plane descends portentously from the sky, or as the luke-warm chicken, campaign literature and money receptacles are trotted out in banquet halls. On both sides there is all the panoply of a full-fledged Presidential showdown—the bands, the placards of "Modoc County" and "Buttonwillow," the fetchingly clad nymphets with plastic "Rocky" skimmers, the collegiate folk-singers twisting "Hello, Dolly" into "Hello, Barry."

Discerning the outlines of the primary scuffle is a little like watching an angry hippopotamus battle a swarm of bees.

The Goldwaterites, encompassing everything from the fanatical Birchite hard-core to many Republican moderates, present the unified image. Attacking from many directions, with Rockefeller as their queen bee, is an assortment of Republicans either militantly or wistfully enunciating disparate allegiances to everybody from Mr. Rockefeller to Harold Stassen.

The dogmatism on both sides precludes the usual campaign spectator-sport of following the sound and fury of suasion. A Goldwater crowd seems as unmotivated by specifics as a bunch of Beatle fans. Similarly, the Rockefeller-oriented are as dogmatic as a group of Catholic seminarians passing a Holy Roller meeting. Factional lines hardened months back—with roughly one third of the electorate crystallized one way, one third the other, and one third "undecided."

In sum, to a neutral observer on the scene, through a characteristically Californian confluence of typical circumstances, the primary has the dream-like aspect of a pillow-fight under water, with neither contender landing any telling blows, yet with either, or both, liable to sudden blackout—while galleries at the poolside shout encouragement only dimly linked with action below.

Goldwater supporters charged that liberal Republican enemies of the Senator were conducting the "most vicious and venomous campaign against a candidate the party had ever seen." Goldwater was more detached, but he, too, spoke out vigorously. He denied the reiterated accusations of extremism and recklessness, insisting he was not "out of the mainstream of Republican and American thought." He declared that his philosophies were not startingly at variance with those of many prominent Republicans and he charged that his positions on Social Security and the United Nations had been distorted by Rockefeller and his supporters.

On the other hand, Rockefeller forces charged a campaign of terror by the right-wing elements supporting Goldwater—threatening telephone calls, cars being forced off roads, social ostracism and even bomb scares. To Rockefeller himself, this was the most frightening aspect of the campaign, that there were extreme right-wing forces using tactics in an American election that were reminiscent of communism or fascism.

The Senator's supporters became irritated and bitingly sarcastic as the days passed. At one rally, Ronald Reagan, the actor, greeted his listeners with the words, "And good morning to all you irresponsible Republicans." He went on to say that there were two ways of introducing the Arizonan, one as the true voice of Republicanism, or, he asked rhetorically, "Should he be introduced as a Neanderthal man, a bigot, a warmonger, looking out at us from the nineteenth century?"

It was in Glendora one night that a wild-eyed Goldwater partisan rushed up to one of the Senator's aides, after watching newspaper reporters taking notes, and said: "You've got to warn the Senator right away. There are men out there taking down every word he says."

Rockefeller, pledging a last-ditch fight no matter the odds, told his listeners again and again that he represented a can-win Republican philosophy while Goldwater was outside the mainstream. He preached moderation at home and abroad. He supported the civil rights bill. He avoided any possible me-too labels by denouncing the Democratic Administration. At Anaheim, in the heart of the Goldwater country, 5,000 persons came out to hear Rockefeller, and the receptions became larger and more enthusiastic wherever he spoke. The Senator's lead began to dwindle, then, suddenly, it seemed as if his lead had vanished completely—and the polls were there to confirm it. Mervin D. Field, the reputable California poll taker, reported that there had been a massive switch in sentiment and that Rockefeller now was ahead in the struggle for the state's big bloc of eighty-six delegates.

The Governor, eager to retain the role of underdog that had helped him materially in Oregon, said he was not impressed and his Oregon experience had diminished his respect for polls. Goldwater himself acknowledged that he had slipped in the ratings, but he doubted his decline was as drastic as Field indicated. Nevertheless, uncertainty, if not gloom, settled over his organization—uncertainty over the probable result and over what went wrong and what could be done to correct it.

In the closing days of the California primary, Goldwater campaigned only in a perfunctory way. He spent hours in his hotel room watching westerns on TV. He spoke during the day only to precinct workers instead of searching for uncommitted voters. The atmosphere in his camp was one of resigned fatalism—that the decision of the voters could not be changed by oratory. Several times Goldwater surprised journalists by saying that it was up to the precinct workers to rebut and counter the charges that had hurt him most.

But while Goldwater's own campaign slipped into low gear, the precinct workers went to work feverishly. He had one of the best organizations of volunteer workers ever seen in a primary—and one vastly superior to Rockefeller's. Undyingly loyal and undismayed by polls, they looked for all possible pro-Goldwater voters and then made plans to get them to the polls. His organization concentrated its time and money in Southern California, where he was strong, to make sure of every possible vote.

Rockefeller supporters oozed confidence. A declaration by Eisenhower (under his byline on the front page of the stanchly Republican New York *Herald-Tribune*) added to their optimism. In it, Eisenhower belatedly drew up a statement of principles as a guide to the selection of a Republican nominee. All but shooting the elephant from under Goldwater, the statement said:

Many concerned people have urged me to indicate my preference among the possible Republican candidates or to try to dictate the Republican party's choice of a Presidential nominee. I do not intend to attempt this. It is not my proper role. I do fervently hope, however, that the person selected . . . will be a man who will uphold, earnestly, with dedication and conviction, the principles and traditions of our party. . . .

As the party of Lincoln, we Republicans have a particular obligation to be vigorous in the furtherance of civil rights. . . .

In the foreign field, the overriding concern of the Republican party—of either party—must be the maintenance of peace while protecting and extending freedom. This is not easily done in a dangerous, volatile and uncertain world.

It requires military strength second to none, backed by a vigorous and expanding economy . . . It requires loyal support for the United Nations in its peacekeeping efforts. It requires calm, painstaking study of all the infinitely complex situations that confront us . . . followed by firm decision and prompt but carefully conceived action. In today's nuclear-age diplomacy there is no time for indecision, but neither is there room for impulsiveness, not only to treat successfully with today's crises, but to probe into those areas where, step by step, the barriers between East and West can be lowered.

Goldwater at first refused to answer questions about the Eisenhower statement, but he showed his feelings in one of the memorable moments of the campaign. As he stepped before an audience the next day he slyly tucked an arrow (which he had picked up in a school gymnasium) under his armpit and turned sideways, making it appear that the arrow was imbedded in his back. Later, he charged that "a mysterious clique in the East" had prevailed on the General to publish his statement. Then he insisted that the former President had refused "to buy the extreme line he was probably asked to take," and added: "I don't think it points out any one person as Ike's favorite. If Eisenhower opposes me, all he has to do is pick up the phone and say, 'Barry, I don't think you're the man for the job,' and I might not agree with him, but it would have a great bearing on what I might do."

Goldwater was also asked if Eisenhower had intended a rebuff when he declared that impulsiveness was undesirable in the White House. His reply was: "No, my foreign policy position is precisely the Eisenhower-Dulles position, and I wouldn't call him impetuous when he went into the Formosa Straits and when he went into Lebanon, on very short notice, or on his attitude on Berlin. Nor do I think I'm in the least bit impetuous."

Goldwater did receive some encouragement when Nixon and Scranton both proclaimed their neutrality in the primary. Nixon, stressing the need for Republican unity, urged followers of all candidates to pledge immediate support for the party's nominee at the San Francisco convention. Scranton also emphasized his overriding interest in party unity and said, "I have refused to join 'stop Goldwater,' 'stop Rockefeller' or 'stop anybody' movements." Since both undeclared candidates were dependent on a convention deadlock to keep alive their chances for the nomination, their stand was no surprise.

Then Eisenhower, a day before the June 2 primary, gave Goldwater further comfort when he denied that his declaration of principles had been designed to drive the front-runner from the Republican party. Such an inference, he said blandly, was a complete misinterpretation of his newspaper article. Moderate Republicans had been waiting all year for the General to make his position clear. As a former President, one of the best vote-getters in history, Eisenhower might easily have tilted the scales in favor of his chosen candidate, but except for his declaration of principles, the General refused to intervene, insisting that it would be improper for him to dictate to the party and the convention, which must remain open for all contenders. As Tom Wicker later wrote, "General Eisenhower camped out for the winter in Palm Springs, marched up the hills against Senator Goldwater two weeks before the California primary, then marched down again the day before it."

A week before the primary, on May 27, Rockefeller suffered a serious blow when Loyola University of Los Angeles, a Jesuit institution, withdrew an invitation for him to speak as the result of pressure by a group of regents led by a John Birch Society member. The cancellation of the speech itself was of less importance than the impression it gave to some Roman Catholics of the area that the hierarchy opposed Rockefeller. In a speech in San Francisco two days later, Rockefeller was bitter about the methods used by Goldwater supporters in forcing the cancellation and charged that these were the kind of tactics that had resulted in "over 200 calls to our offices in the Los Angeles area saying that the offices were going to be bombed."

Just three days before California voted, another event happened on the other side of the continent that affected the vote; a child was born to Rockefeller and his new wife, a boy named Nelson Rockefeller Jr. The birth of the baby revived interest in the candidate's divorce and remarriage, a subject that he hoped had been closed. Most observers suspected that this would have some political impact and that Rockefeller would suffer because of it.

As primary day approached, Arthur Krock in The Times pointed out one effect of the polls:

> If Senator Goldwater should lose the Republican Presidential preference primary in California to Governor Rockefeller by even a fairly close margin, that would temper the impact of his defeat on his own prospects for the nomination. Also, it would preserve much of his power to influence the major decisions of the national party convention at San Francisco in the event of his failure to win the nomination.
>
> Goldwater would owe these important salvages to the pre-primary sample polls which forecast an emphatic victory for Rockefeller, and to the preponderance of opposition to his candidacy in the press.

The election was close, much closer than expected. Through a long night the outcome remained in doubt, although the Columbia Broadcasting System, using computer projections of early returns, said that Goldwater had won at 7:22 P.M., only twenty-two minutes after many, but not all, of the polling places had closed. The National Broadcasting Company said its computers indicated such a close vote that it would not name a winner. The American Broadcasting Company, at 8:12 P.M., designated Goldwater as the winner, but the two major newspaper wire services, The Associated Press and United Press International, shied away from projecting the victor.

The Times, in its final edition of Wednesday, said that Goldwater clung to a narrow and dwindling lead over Rockefeller. The official result was given in an article by Charles Mohr in the Thursday issue:

> WASHINGTON, June 3—Senator Barry Goldwater's victory in the California Republican Presidential primary yesterday has put him tantalizingly close to the nomination.
>
> The California race was a close one, with the outcome uncertain until late this morning. Senator Goldwater held a lead of about 59,000 votes out of more than 2 million.
>
> Complete returns from the state's 32,861 precincts gave:
>
> | | |
> |---|---|
> | Goldwater | 1,089,133 |
> | Rockefeller | 1,030,180 |
>
> With about 70 per cent of the state's registered Republicans voting, Mr. Goldwater received 51 per cent of the vote.
>
> The Senator may virtually wrap up the nomination at Republican state conventions this weekend in Alabama, Colorado, Hawaii and Washington.
>
> Mr. Goldwater's campaign headquarters maintained today that the eighty-six national convention delegates won in California brought to 454 the number of delegates "publicly committed" to the Arizona Senator.

In a group of precincts in which Roman Catholics predominated, Goldwater received a larger percentage of votes than had been expected, which suggested Rockefeller's divorce and remarriage were a contributing factor in his loss. Goldwater's role of underdog in the final weeks of the campaign did not hurt him. It was also noted that Goldwater received an unexpectedly heavy vote in metropolitan areas like Los Angeles, where his supporters had put on a massive drive.

Despite the close result, all in all, June 2 was a day that confirmed conservative optimism. Moderate party leaders in the state said the G.O.P. was in grave danger from the right wing, but former Senator Knowland, the top Goldwater leader in California, voiced a different opinion. "Ninety per cent of the members of our Goldwater delegate slate were supporters of President Eisenhower," he said. "They were not extremists when they did that and there's no basis for saying they are now."

Now there was little doubt that Goldwater was virtually sure of the nomination; there still was doubt, however, of the effects of his victory on the Republican party. James Reston wrote in The Times:

The 1964 Presidential primary campaign was remarkable in at least one respect. It lasted for three months without really coming to grips with a single major national issue or producing a single memorable speech.

Goldwater and Rockefeller in California ended merely by dramatizing the deep divisions within the Republican party about how to deal with the major problems of the day. They did not strengthen their party but weakened it for the campaign against the Democrats just ahead.

What dominated the debate through this long, strange campaign was a bedlam of obscurities about whether Goldwater was reckless about the Communists and heartless about the old and the poor; whether Eisenhower was for Goldwater or against him; whether Goldwater was "in the mainstream of the Republican party" —whatever that is—and whether Rockefeller and the "Eastern Liberal Establishment" were trying to "buy" or "kidnap" the Republican party.

Arthur Krock discussed a different aspect:

But because the Arizona Senator barely surmounted these high hurdles [in California], his party opponents will seek by every possible means to discount the effect on the delegates to the national convention at San Francisco. His accretion of a solid bloc of 86 delegates cannot be argued away. But in the six weeks remaining before the convention assembles there is time for another and finally desperate try at a stop-Goldwater movement.

. . . the remaining hope of a stop-Goldwater movement, if any, rests on the attitude toward it of Governor Scranton.

In the two weeks after the California primary the final state conventions were held. On June 6, as forecast, Goldwater picked up sixty-four more delegates; in Alabama (twenty), Colorado (fourteen), Hawaii (four), Virginia (four) and Washington (twenty-two). Two days later, Goldwater's forces obtained pledges from sixteen of Florida's thirty-two delegate votes. Utah, Missouri, Idaho, New Mexico, Connecticut and Virginia joined the Goldwater bandwagon in their conventions. The vote that put him over the once-elusive 655 came in Texas on June 16. There the Senator, in a confirmation of the earlier primary, won Texas's big bloc of fifty-six delegates. To Montana fourth in size with an area of 147,138 square miles but forty-first in population with 674,707, went the honor at its June 19 convention of giving him his final delegates—fourteen pledged to him for the first three ballots.

Goldwater had done it. He had rounded up most of his delegates at party conventions around the country. And, although the comparison was questionable, he could point to the fact that he had gathered more votes in primaries in 1964 than Kennedy had in 1960. Moreover, he could insist that he had proved in California that when the issue was not beclouded with a multitude of candidates, when there was the "clear choice" he had been calling for, the voters would choose a conservative over a liberal. The Republican moderates did not throw in the sponge until several weeks later at San Francisco, but few doubted that Goldwater's nomination was now a foregone conclusion.

5

"President of All the People"

While the Republican hopefuls had fanned out across the country for the primaries, President Johnson remained in Washington taking a seemingly aloof attitude toward the political sound and fury that reached the capital. On the surface, he tried to appear like a man simply doing his duty, giving no thought whatsoever to the fact that an election was coming up in November and that he would be heading his party's ticket. It was a "politics, what's that?" attitude. Apparently, Johnson had decided to run the country rather than run for election. The way he did it amounted to the same thing.

"The President believes," a White House aide said, "that the best politics is not to talk about politics." Another said, "Our job is to see to it that when the Republicans finally do settle on one man, the President is still months ahead and keeps that lead all the way." Like Johnson himself, the aides were keeping a sharp eye on the public opinion polls. They drew particular satisfaction from the Gallup Poll right after the New Hampshire primary in March that showed 73 per cent of the people approved of the way Johnson was handling his job.

The strategy of the-best-politics-is-no-politics appeared to be working. As The Times noted, Johnson seemed in the spring of 1964 to have decided on the greatest exhibition of running without really running since William McKinley's "front porch" campaign of 1896. But Johnson's frenetic energy precluded rocking on the White House balcony. Right up to the Democratic convention, he talked a good game of no politics. But he played a game of good politics. "I gave thought to what my course of conduct should be and concluded that I would not enter any primaries," he said, drawing, as The Times said, the American flag about his chest. "I would do the very best job I could as President for all the people up to convention time and then let the delegates at the convention make their choice freely. Then my conduct would be determined after they made their choice."

He was even cagey on whether he would run for election. He smiled at a news conference when he announced that he had asked Congress to appropriate $800,000 to provide staff help for an incoming President between his election and his inauguration. The Budget Director, he said, told him that "my re-election would save $800,000." Then he added, "And you all know how strongly I feel about economy." To some cheering Democrats in San Francisco, he came close, "I hope you love me in November as you did in May."

Meanwhile, all his "non-political" activities were making news—his trips to flood areas, his six-state tour to poverty pockets, his speeches calling on Americans in his evangelical way to join him in creating the Great Society. The advantages of a President seeking election soon became clear. Before he technically becomes the nominee, a President can command television time almost at will. He is surrounded by the majesty of his office and his moves and words are fully reported. He has the resources to gather all the information he wants or needs and he can use it all as he sees fit.

The President decided to take the high road and the center of the high road at that, though sometimes bearing a little right, sometimes a little left. He kept saying he was the "President of all the people" and did his best to broaden his political base. He wooed business with tax cuts, budget cuts and a rising economy. He appealed to the urban North and to the liberal left and the minority groups with strong words on civil rights and a highly dramatized campaign against poverty. He went South and admonished the Old Confederacy to accept the civil rights program and to bury the dead issues of the past. Labor found its place at the President's table. Consumers got a new champion in the Administration, Mrs. Esther Peterson, and the President talked of putting more women in high governmental jobs. Farmers received promises of higher income under a bill passed after the President's personal intervention in Congress. The elderly heard him express repeated hope for the medicare bill. For young people, the President established a program of Presidential scholarships for outstanding students.

Politics? Of course not. As James Reston noted in The Times in mid-March, Johnson sounds "as if he dreaded the very day when the Presidential campaign would force him to utter a partisan word." When Johnson completed his first six months in office, Tom Wicker took stock:

WASHINGTON, May 21—As President Johnson completed his sixth month in office today, he stood high in all the popularity polls, dominated the national political outlook, and was heavily favored to win the election next Nov. 3. He was firmly in command of the Administration.

Only half a year after the assassination of President Kennedy elevated Mr. Johnson from the Vice Presidency to the White House, he has a substantial record of achievement at home, and has not been heavily challenged or set back in affairs abroad.

Both at home and abroad, however, the President is still confronted with the two major problems that disturbed the last year of Mr. Kennedy's life.

In the United States, evidence is mounting that the civil rights crisis threatens not only social but political stability, and that its effects have reached into almost every state and section. Both Negro and white moderates—like Mr. Johnson— seem to have only a tenuous command of the situation, and in Congress there is no resolution of the bitter Senate debate on the Kennedy-Johnson civil rights bill.

In South Vietnam, most signs point to a deteriorating situation in the guerrilla warfare between the Vietcong, the Communist forces, and the Government troops with their United States advisors and support. . . .

These two problems—civil rights and South Vietnam—appear to many of Mr. Johnson's supporters and opponents to be the most likely—perhaps the only— areas in which he might suffer sizable setbacks between now and the Presidential election. Without such setbacks, few opponents and virtually no supporters believe that he can be defeated in November.

It was about this time of the spring, however, that Johnson stepped up the pace and pitch of the public relations of the Presidency. News conferences became more frequent. One Saturday a group of some one hundred tourists standing at the Southeast Gate were surprised to find the gate swinging open, the President at hand, and themselves led off on a tour of the South Lawn. "All of you ugly men get up front and all of you pretty girls come back here with me," he said. Any Congressman whose daughter got married could count on a surprise guest for the pew of honor; convention groups by the dozens got a stemwinding speech in the Rose Garden; every member of Congress was entertained at a reception, featuring policy briefings for the men, tours of the White House living quarters for the women. When the women guests weren't being shown the upstairs rooms at such receptions, the President was showing them his prowess on the dance floor. He took the poet Carl Sandburg into a bargaining session of the rail negotiators, and went swimming in the raw in the White House pool with staff members, television moguls and Administration officials.

On his visits to his LBJ Ranch near Johnson City, Johnson provided even more colorful news. He held a news conference on the bank of the Pedernales River using a bale of hay for a rostrum, and ended it by riding off on a Tennessee walking horse. He kept twenty-three family guests waiting dinner while Mrs. Johnson fumed, so that he could give two busloads of reporters a tour of his old stone-and-frame house. ("Don't pick up that white telephone, Cousin Oriole, Khrushchev might answer.") Later in the spring, giving some reporters a ranch tour in a Lincoln Continental, he was reported to have been speeding up to eighty miles per hour on Texas highways while drinking beer at the wheel. Once he took a Secret Service agent's pistol and blazed away at an armadillo; on another occasion, he went hunting deer and bagged a notable buck.

With reporters, Johnson became increasingly gregarious. He chafed under press criticism and tended to attribute it to his belief that he was under suspicion as a "Southern cornball." Yet, he held more news conferences, in more different places and manners, than any President in history. Many were informal and called in his own office on the spur of the moment, others were carefully planned and televised nationally; once he had four news con- ferences in the space of nine days. Sometimes, Johnson would read the routine White House press notices usually given out by his news secretary. Several times, he served coffee to the attending reporters. When the question- and-answer sessions ended, he frequently talked on informally to all who cared to listen. He talked often with individual news reporters, visited the executives of The New York Times, and had the officers of most major news media to lunch at the White House, lunches that often sprawled through most of an afternoon. In this manner, Johnson quickly became the most accessible and familiar President of the twentieth century. He was not particularly informative at his news conferences and his private interviews tended to be monologues, but so great was his exposure to the press that it is likely that no other President was ever made so intimately familiar to the people so rapidly.

Johnson was frequently criticized for his open sentimentality and unabashed exhortations. Yet, many observers believed that he touched fundamentally the aspirations and beliefs of large numbers of Americans, themselves sentimental, patriotic and optimistic. He went off on brief tours of poverty areas, talking of elevating the poor and dignifying the down-trodden. He sat down on the porch of a Kentucky shack with an unemployed miner and chatted in North Carolina with the family of a tobacco farmer. He proposed a Washington "Memorial to God." He got a lot of attention and criticism by pulling the ears of his beagles and making them yelp. He invited the wives and children of newsmen to a punch-and-cookies news conference on the White House lawn. This was a fatherly Johnson who never had a bad word for anyone.

As early as April, he told reporters that Goldwater "will be up there pretty high" when the Republican National Convention voted on a Presidential nominee in July. If in fact he believed then that his opponent would be the G.O.P. conservative, the middle was obviously the place for him, giving the impression of a moderate, responsible, safe candidate.

Nowhere did Johnson show his effectiveness better than in his relations with Congress. His intimate knowledge of its inner workings and pressure points enabled him quite often to make just the right move at the right time. Early in the session he fought a hot battle with House Republicans over an amendment that would have limited the President's freedom in such activities as the wheat sale to the Soviet Union. It took many phone calls—Johnson always found the telephone an effective political tool—and much pressure to ward off the Republican restriction. Then there was the tax reduction bill. The House had acted on it before Kennedy's death, but approval by the Senate Finance Committee and the Senate itself was in doubt. The President realized that the bill reducing Federal income taxes had little chance unless he moved to reduce Federal expenses. Undoubtedly this was the reasoning behind the President's early and continued talk of cutting the budget, of turning off the lights in the White House, of closing unnecessary military installations.

Johnson promised budget cuts though in fact he had accepted the Kennedy arguments that the expected deficit from the tax cut bill would be short-run and would help stimulate business so that tax revenues would rise to offset the reductions. It was reported that Senator Harry F. Byrd, Democrat of Virginia, agreed to allow a vote on the bill in his Senate Finance Committee only after a Johnson pledge to reduce government expenses wherever possible. "A dollar's worth from a dollar spent" became a favorite Johnsonism.

While most of the Johnson must list for Congress was made up of Kennedy bills, the President had one major addition—his war on poverty bill. Much of this program, too, consisted of items originally proposed by Kennedy, such as a youth corps to put unemployed young people to work. Johnson chose to send all to Congress under one umbrella, proposing a single administrator, on March 16. The program, he claimed, would help "one-fifth of our people who have not shared the abundance which has been granted to most of us, and on whom the gates of opportunity have been closed." Although some Republicans called it an election-year gimmick, Congress went on to pass it by a comfortable margin.

The President's major struggle with Congress during the spring and summer before the Democratic convention, however, was in the Senate over civil rights. Shortly after the first of the year, the House passed the Kennedy-Johnson civil rights bill. The President took little part in the strategy of the actual debate in the House, but he did all he could to maintain the bipartisan coalition that beat down the Southern opposition. Then the exhausting fight began in the Senate. Four months of the session were devoted to consideration of the rights bill, with the ordeal ending only after the first successful debate-closing closure vote against a civil rights filibuster in history. The President for the most part kept his efforts behind the scenes, avoiding any open attacks on the Southerners resisting the bill he wanted—and needed.

The key action came on June 10, when the Senate shut off the Southern talkathon by a vote of seventy-one to twenty-nine, four more than the two-thirds, or sixty-seven, votes needed for closure. Goldwater opposed closure, as expected, since he had to protect whatever bases of strength he had in the South. Similarly, he voted for the Russell amendment to delay for more than a year the effectiveness of the title banning discrimination in public accommodations on the ground that it involved Federal intervention in local affairs.

The South attempted a series of delaying actions. On June 14, Goldwater joined in a futile effort to kill the public accommodations section, regarded as vital by Negro leaders. The vote was sixty-three to twenty-three. On June 18, as the final showdown neared, Goldwater told the Senate that he would vote against the civil rights bill because the public accommodations and fair employment sections of the measure "fly in the face of the Constitution" and would lead to the "creation of a police state." He said, "If my vote is misconstrued, let it be, and let me suffer the consequences." The Senator went on to explain that his vote would be reluctantly cast and that he had hoped that the bill would have been altered enough by amendments to permit a vote for it. He said that he realized "fully that the Federal Government has a responsibility in the field of civil rights" and that he could have supported the bill without the two sections to which he objected.

On June 19, on the eighty-third day of the debate and nine days after closure had been invoked, the historic bill was passed, seventy-three to twenty-seven, with Goldwater voting against it, as he had said he would. On July 2, the President signed the bill, the most far-reaching civil rights legislation since

the Reconstruction era, covering voting rights, equal access to public accommodations, school desegregation, extension of the civil rights commission,
equal employment opportunities and the establishment of a community relations service.

Also illustrative of the Johnson technique with Congress was the way he
handled the foreign aid bill. The program had grown increasingly unpopular
over the years and a pattern had developed: The Executive would propose a
figure and the Congress immediately went to work hacking off what it thought
was just plain "fat." In 1963, for instance, the cut amounted to some 34 per
cent. In 1964, Johnson asked for $3,500,000,000, $1,000,000,000 less than
the year before, and convinced Congress the program was pre-shrunk. Very
little was cut. Before convention time in August, Johnson had won from
Congress not only the tax cut, civil rights and poverty bills, but also a food
stamp program, the wheat-cotton voluntary price supports bill, the interest
equalization tax on foreign securities, a pay raise bill for Federal workers,
and the 1964 wilderness preservation bill.

The President scored a major domestic triumph in the spring, too, with
the settlement of the long-standing rail labor dispute. James Reston commented in The Times:

Thursday he was back at it with the leaders of the railroad companies and the
unions. Some of his advisors told him it was the end of the road: There would be
a national strike at midnight; he would only lose face by intervening. He inter-
vened anyway.

He got them together in the Cabinet Room of the White House. He told them
labor and management had pledged him their support "on that tragic day in
November." He needed that support now, he said. He was the only President they
had, whether they liked it or not.

They told him they had been trying to settle this thing for four years and that
they had lost faith in each other. He turned to Roy E. Davidson, head of the
Brotherhood of Locomotive Engineers. "Have you lost faith in me?" he asked.
Davidson said, "No." The President asked J. E. (Doc) Wolfe, the chief negotiator
for the railroads, the same question and got the same answer, but still they
protested.

They said the White House had been involved in this dispute for years and it
had done no good. President Johnson said all he asked was the same chance they
had given President Kennedy. "Let me have 20 days," he requested.

Some aide told the President a key man in the dispute was Charles Luna,
president of the Brotherhood of Railroad Trainmen, who wasn't there. The White
House got him on the phone and the President sent a plane to Canada to bring
him in.

Then he called Walter Heller, chairman of the Council of Economic Advisers.
He wanted within an hour a memorandum on the effect of a national rail strike.
At 8 the negotiators were still deadlocked. He read them the Heller memorandum
and told them a story.

Once, he said, when he was a young Congressman he lost his temper in a
similar dispute in Texas and told everybody to go to hell. Later, a friend said to
him: "You can always tell people to go to hell but they don't have to go." The
President addressed himself again to Davidson and Wolfe. He asked them to
look at one another and say in his presence that they couldn't possibly agree and

wouldn't give him a chance. Were they going to tell the President of the United States to go to hell or weren't they? They didn't.

In the end, they gave him 15 days to try. "If the old atmosphere is poisoned, we'll create a new atmosphere," he said. Later that night, he telephoned Dr. George W. Taylor, a distinguished labor mediator at the University of Pennsylvania, whose wife was in a hospital. The President talked to him personally. "I'm not asking you," he said, "I'm telling you to be in my office at 9 in the morning." And so he was.

Maybe all this won't work, but this capital hasn't seen the like of the Johnson technique in many a year. It is an elemental force. It is directed in such a way that it cannot be ignored. It is highly personal and it is aimed directly at the personal honor of the men in dispute. It can be opposed only by equal force and only with great personal embarrassment, but it cannot be evaded.

This city is still muttering negatively about Johnson's style, but the complaints are really about appearance. If style in government is not merely the art of pleasing but the technique of getting things done and making stubborn men put the general interest above their special interests, then President Johnson has plenty of it. It is not the style of Tunney but the style of Dempsey; it is as obvious and as effective as a swift punch in the nose.

There is another point. This is not merely the brutal use of Presidential power. The emotional content of the Johnson appeal, the total absence of ideology, the passionate insistence on the general welfare, the willingness to talk endlessly through the night if necessary, the vivid earthy American language and optimistic faith that problems can be solved—all this is highly effective under Johnson.

He has that rare gift in a small room of antagonists, not only of telling men how he thinks they should feel, but of making them feel it, of forcing them to face the larger problems, as if they were sitting in his chair.

In a vast continental Federal Union, with inevitable conflicts between regions, parties, classes and institutions, this is a personal force of immense value to the nation.

To many observers Johnson in those weeks did not seem to be so adept at handling overseas affairs as he was at cutting the budget, wrestling with Congress, persuading rail negotiators, or keeping his secret on his choice of a Democratic running mate. He was heavily criticized for his handling of foreign affairs, but except in South Vietnam, there was little apparent deterioration of American strength and no major Communist advances. The Soviet Union did appear to be testing Johnson in March when they shot down an Air Force RB-66 that had strayed out of the Berlin air corridor into East Germany and captured the three-man crew. Johnson authorized strong representations and the fliers were soon released. Then came strong orders to American pilots to stay in the corridor. A month later came word from the White House that the United States would make a major reduction in the production of nuclear weapons materials and that the Russians were making similar reductions. Tensions between the two great powers eased even more— at least on the surface.

In Vietnam, Johnson made no changes in the policy against the Communist guerrillas. He engaged in some new psychological warfare by encouraging speculation that the war might be expanded to North Vietnam. At a news conference on June 3, he outlined the four basic themes that governed

United States policy in Southeast Asia. First, "America keeps her word." Second, "The issue is the future of Southeast Asia as a whole." Third, "Our purpose is peace." And fourth, "This is not just a jungle war, but a struggle for freedom on every front of human activity."

To help convey a flavor of bipartisanship, the President kept Ambassador Henry Cabot Lodge, a Republican Presidential hopeful, in Saigon throughout the spring. In June, when Lodge resigned to come home to try to stop the Goldwater drive for the Republican nomination, the President sent General Maxwell D. Taylor, chairman of the Joint Chiefs of Staff, to Saigon in a move designed to underscore United States determination to support the anti-Communist effort there.

There was a crisis for American policy makers in Panama when rioting erupted over what Panamanians regarded as an insult to their flag. Relations were broken. Panama demanded the renegotiation of the canal treaty. Johnson replied that the United States would discuss anything, when diplomatic relations were restored, but would not pledge renegotiations in advance. The President held firm and in the formula that was finally worked out he won his point.

Max Frankel, diplomatic correspondent of The Times, wrote:

The Johnson Administration is giving about equal weight to gestures of conciliation and defiance toward the Communist world as it braces to defend its policies in the election campaign.

Publicly, officials do not speak about the influence of politics on diplomacy. Even in private conversation they are unusually cautious and mindful of the President's prerogatives. . . .

The Democrats' basic theme, in the face of Mr. Goldwater's charge that they "cringe before the bully of Communism," will continue to be that different Communist countries must be treated differently.

The Administration's achievements were clear and the political strength of the President seemed formidable. But criticism was bound to come, for as Johnson himself told reporters, he had made "mistakes" in the first months of office. His style, particularly when compared to that of his predecessor, inspired many to refer to him as "Ol' Cornpone." Intellectuals, although recognizing the progress made in easing tensions with the South, Congress and the business community, felt uncomfortable and left out during the early months. Some members of Congress resented the constant intrusion of the White House, the frequent phone calls into the inner reaches of the Capitol for friendly chats that might just contain a little persuasiveness. Republicans complained that all the talk of economy and budget-cutting amounted to nothing more than politics and figure-juggling. Then there was Robert G. (Bobby) Baker.

Cabell Phillips, writing in The Times, gave this background to the case:

Baker came to Washington from a little town in South Carolina 20 years ago as a Senate page—one of those agile, blue-suited youngsters who run errands for the members. He was bright, ambitious and eager to please. He liked the Senate and the Senate liked him. His two-year term was extended a couple of times. Then he moved up to the Democratic Oak Room; then to the office of the majority secretary, and in 1955, with the solid support of the then majority leader, Lyndon B. Johnson, the Democrats elected him majority secretary.

In the meantime, Bobby Baker had finished high school, earned a law degree, gotten married, and taken to Senate politics the way a sponge takes to water. The only man more versed in this arcane art was his boss, Lyndon Johnson, who found in him a trusted first deputy in the intricate business of running the Senate. He was "Lyndon's boy," a title that carried weight not only in the Capitol but also in the market places downtown where no commodity is more sought after than influence.

How Mr. Baker got on the financial escalator is one of the unanswered questions of his career. When he got on is fairly clear. It was some time between 1954, when he declared a net worth of $11,025, and 1957 when he claimed it to $84,133. His Senate salary in those two years was $9,000 and $12,500, respectively. In February, 1963, his salary was $19,600 but his claimed net worth worth was $2,256,855. His financial statement was featured by an impressive portfolio of stock and real estate holdings, and by some equally impressive bank debts in cities as far away as Dallas and Oklahoma City.

The first intimation most of his friends had of his affluence came in the summer of 1962. He invited several bus loads of them down for the formal opening of a lavish resort motel at Ocean City, Md., of which he turned out to be a one-third owner.

But a full appreciation of his opulence did not occur until nearly a year later— September, 1963. In that month a $300,000 civil damage suit filed against him in a local court revealed him as a tycoon of the vending machine industry with contracts grossing approximately $3 million in the plants of a number of defense contractors. Inquisitive reporters began digging into his background and uncovered his connection in a wide variety of insurance, real estate and stock transactions. There were many unsupported intimations also of influence peddling and unsavory relationships.

When the Senate leadership called on him for a private explanation of his situation in October, Mr. Baker resigned. Two days later the Senate voted to have its Rules Committee investigate to determine if there had been conflicts of interest in his business affairs.

The most potentially damaging charge came next. Johnson was accused of having received a $500 stereophonic record player from Baker. Further, the Baker inquiry disclosed charges that Don B. Reynolds, a former business associate of Baker and an insurance salesman who sold Johnson a life insurance policy, had been forced by a Presidential aide, Walter W. Jenkins, into advertising on the Johnson family television station in Austin. Johnson and Jenkins denied the charges, but for the most part critics found the President's handling of the case evasive at best. A Times article noted that the President often referred to Baker as kind of a "remote official acquaintance who just happened to be in office as a result of votes of all Senators and not as a result of any friendship with Lyndon Johnson." When the Senate hearings on the Baker case concluded their first phase, the President was charged with having forced a halt to them. The only bright spot in the embarrassing situation was that the Baker case had started before Johnson became President. If the lawsuit had not been filed in September, Baker probably would have gone to the White House with other key aides and then Johnson could not have avoided a scandal touching the Presidency itself. For this fortuitous timing, Democratic politicians gave thanks. However, Cabell Phillips of The Times predicted that, whatever its ultimate resolution, the Baker case "will haunt the Democrats' table in 1964 like the ghost of Sherman 'Banquo' Adams."

Republican newsletters all through the summer bore down heavily on the Bobby Baker case. In that connection, they raised questions about the accumulation of the Johnson family fortune in general and the family television station, KTBC-TV, in particular. The stock of the station as well as other Johnson family interests were put in trusteeship when Johnson became President. Republicans, however, found it unusual that a city the size of Austin with a population of 200,000 had only one such station. They implied and vainly sought to prove that political influence might have been a reason.

The Republicans saved their biggest guns for Johnson's foreign policy. They saw the United States floundering and accused the Johnson Administration of losing friends abroad. On Panama, they felt the President handled the crisis badly and offended all of Latin America. On Cuba, they thought he overreacted in the Guantanamo crisis, when Castro cut the water supply to our naval base. On Vietnam, the Republicans complained about a "no-win" policy in which American soldiers were sent to "die, not fight."

If the Republicans saw their candidate standing before the television cameras around election time, pointing his finger at Johnson and raising all these questions, they were soon to be disappointed. A week before the Democratic convention, Senate Democrats (surely with the knowledge and probably with the urging of Johnson) voted to kill a bill suspending for the 1964 elections the "equal time" requirement of the Federal Communications Act. The action made it impossible for the networks to carry TV and radio debates between the Presidential nominees without also giving the same time to the multitude of minor party candidates, such as the Socialist-Laborite and the Prohibitionist. Such a bill had enabled the networks to carry the Kennedy-Nixon debates in 1960, which, everybody agreed, had resulted in a gain for Kennedy, the challenger. But the President obviously felt it was to his political advantage not to have to stand before the nation as President and candidate and debate a man whose name he might not even want to mention in his dignified, high-road campaign. Politically, he could only lose by appearing on the same platform as Goldwater and spreading the aura of the Presidency over him.

6

San Francisco:
"Eau de Convention"

From San Francisco, the scene of the twenty-eighth Republican National Convention, Russell Baker of The Times reported an esthetic clash between the baroque of the nineteenth century convention form, with its excesses of emotion, shouting, overstatement and farce, and the gossamer beauty of a city that exalted taste, beauty, serenity and restraint. He wrote:

As an art form, the political convention was designed to harmonize with slaughterhouses, as in Chicago; with railroad yards, as in Philadelphia, or with gasoline fumes, as in Los Angeles. To cast one in San Francisco is to set violets before hangmen.

Nevertheless, San Francisco is trying in its own way to make the accommodation. Delegates who venture out of the smoke to taste the Pacific air and shop for knickknacks can find a lovely assortment of imported alabaster elephants at prices ranging up to $250.

Away from the three major convention hotels, the manic mood is rarely visible. An occasional sound truck cruises up Market Street blaring, "We want Barry!" or "We want Bill!" It seems like a crude intrusion upon the throngs of well-wrought ladies in search of bone chinaware and tailored suits . . .

In the sweet Pacific air along these quiet streets, the convention seems as remote as Hong Kong, and much less provocative.

It reasserts itself on Nob Hill at the Mark Hopkins Hotel, where Senator Barry Goldwater and Gov. William W. Scranton are staying. Even at morning, the lobby air is sour, as though imported from Chicago to make the politicians feel at home.

This is a place where a thousand cigarettes have been smoking constantly for 24 hours, where rivers of bad coffee flow perpetually into failing stomachs. The television floodlights burn full-time, creating the impression that this is also a place of much hysteria.

The result is an essence so palpable that it can almost be bottled and labeled "Eau de Convention." It is an alien essence in San Francisco, which is more at home with the scent of cut roses at the corner flowerstands.

As the delegates gathered in San Francisco in early July, it became increasingly clear that the function of the convention was not so much to select a Presidential nominee as to ratify a selection already made by fervent Goldwater supporters at the precinct level and by the failure of the moderate wing of the party—of Eisenhower, Rockefeller, Lodge, Nixon, Scranton and Romney—to unite upon a candidate until it was far too late.

The month preceding the convention had been a time of frantic motion by the moderates, but no apparent progress. Two days after Goldwater's victory in California all but sealed his nomination, Rockefeller said he could no longer be responsible for leading the moderate campaign and that someone else must take the initiative. Unfortunately, there still was no leader to follow. Scranton, at first, refused to join in the move to stop Goldwater. Then, as Joseph A. Loftus recounted in The Times, he reconsidered:

On June 5, the nation's Governors started gathering in Cleveland for their annual conference. The agonizing of the Republican Governors shoved the bipartisan conference itself out of the news.

Some of the moderates had already resigned themselves to a Goldwater nomination. They were not stirred much when, last Saturday, the news broke that former President Eisenhower had talked with Governor Scranton. The General had set up the meeting and had urged the Governor to publicize the fact. The stated goal was to keep the convention open.

Governor Scranton went to Cleveland expecting to make himself "more available," as General Eisenhower had requested. Instead, he wallowed in the theme of party unity. The comedy and tragedy of errors mystified everybody until Monday when word leaked that General Eisenhower, having heard from George M. Humphrey, a close friend who is committed to Mr. Goldwater, called Governor Scranton. Whatever was said—and all versions are vague—it had been enough to dampen the Governor's enthusiasm for whatever he had planned to say, or do.

By last Wednesday, there was hardly a practicing politician in sight who would dare say anything but "the fight is over." It wasn't, though. A few politicians, notably Senator Hugh Scott of Pennsylvania, running for re-election, operated out of sight.

The telephones jangled day and night in Governor Scranton's office and home. The Governor himself put in calls for political friends from Oregon to Maine. By 8:05 Thursday night with Senator Scott and the Governor's own aides present, the Governor came to the decision that he was mad enough to fight. He seized the Maryland Republican party's offer of a forum and sounded the campaign cry Friday afternoon [June 12].

Scranton had thirty-one days before the convention to convince the Republicans that a Goldwater nomination would be a tragedy for the party. He made a valiant attempt, aggressively attacking Goldwater in his search for delegates. He got an important assist in late June when Lodge resigned as Ambassador to Vietnam to return home and "do everything I can to help Governor Scranton." Rockefeller and Romney joined in, as did Eisenhower's brother, Milton, and his son, John. But the General himself was conspicuous by his absence from the Scranton camp, as was Nixon, who apparently still had hopes that a convention deadlock might bring him the nomination. As the start of the G.O.P. convention neared, it was obvious that Scranton, despite a month of intensive campaigning, had failed dismally in his efforts to lure Goldwater delegates into his fold. Senator Dirksen, who had ignored one

Scranton overture, commented that the commitment of the delegates to Goldwater was "as tight as wallpaper."

Nevertheless, while there was little suspense in San Francisco, there were moments of excitement within the long tedious hours, and the fascinating spectacle of overwhelming victory and disastrous defeat. It was popular in San Francisco and elsewhere to say it was a dull convention, but actually it was one of the most significant in recent history. What made the convention dull for reporters and the television audience was precisely what made it dramatic for the historian. The convention marked a decisive change in political philosophy of one of the two major parties. The Republican party made a sharp swing to the right, challenging the whole trend of American foreign and domestic policy under both Democratic and Republican Administrations in the recent past.

Although the convention's first session did not take place until Monday, July 13, the platform committee had been holding hearings and drafting planks at the St. Francis Hotel for two weeks. It was during these hearings that the absolute control of the Goldwater group over the convention became fully apparent. Though Goldwater himself was rarely visible in San Francisco, remaining most of the time in his fifteenth-floor suite at the Mark Hopkins Hotel, his presence, as well as his organization, dominated the proceedings, evoking quiet desperation from the liberal Republicans and this comment from James Reston in The Times:

> The Republican liberals keep complaining that Barry Goldwater is an "impulsive" man, as if he were merely a careless blabbermouth, but the problem is much more serious than that.
>
> It is not what he says but what he deeply believes that is the issue in the Republican Convention. Nobody who has watched him carefully or read what he has written over the years can attribute his statements to a kind of offhand impulsiveness, or really think that he would not try to carry out his philosophy in the White House.
>
> It is time to be frank about this. This is a serious, strong-willed man with a fierce anti-Communist zeal, a fascination with military power, and the conviction that we must destroy or transform Communism, or be destroyed by it.
>
> The struggle in the world today, he asserts, "is a struggle between godless people and the people of God . . . between slavery and freedom." And it is precisely because he feels this so strongly and expresses it with such vigor that he is the one man in this convention who can make the galleries jump and scream. . . .
>
> The polls certainly don't indicate that Barry has convinced the country or even a majority of the Republican party on the rightness of his policies. But the delegates are going to nominate him anyway because they like him, because they admire his industry and his courage, because he beat Rockefeller in California and because—always underneath the surface—many of them vaguely feel that Goldwater's civil rights stand might just pick up enough votes in the North and South to win.
>
> It is a remarkable situation: for here is the party of "respectability," of "responsibility," of "equality," and of "peace" handing leadership in a cold war and a racial revolution to a militant man who wants to leave war to the soldiers, and the Negro to the states. They are giving us a choice in San Francisco all right, but what a choice!

It was the obvious imminence of this choice that drove the Scranton forces to what was variously described as a move of noisy desperation, a tactical miscalculation, even a piece of canny calculation that carried with it its own "backlash" (the political word of the year) and sealed Scranton's fate the night before the convention was even officially convened. The object of all this excitement was a letter sent over Scranton's signature to Goldwater challenging him to a debate before the convention on Wednesday "prior to the nominating speeches." Goldwater and Scranton had been (in Scranton's words) "warm personal friends" and had served together in the same Air Force Reserve unit for many years. To those unfamiliar with the machinations of American political life, it may seem peculiar that Scranton didn't walk down one flight from his suite on the sixteenth floor of the Mark Hopkins to propose the debate in person to his warm friend, or, as Arthur Krock remarked, "He'd better have used the telephone." If politics make strange bedfellows, they also end—sometimes only temporarily—warm personal friendships. Letters are usually considered a private form of communication, but this letter was not private; it was a public act.

The decision to send the letter was apparently taken when Scranton, Rockefeller and Lodge lunched together Sunday. Scranton gave his staff directions to follow through; a letter suggesting the debate was to be addressed either to Senator Thruston B. Morton of Kentucky, the permanent chairman of the convention, or directly to Goldwater. The staff was left to make the choice while Scranton went across the street to the Fairmont Hotel for his television appearance on "Meet the Press." Although the language of the letter sent later that day has been ascribed to one man, William Keisling, a twenty-eight-year-old assistant to the Governor, at least five other aides either participated in a draft or saw the letter before it was sent.

In any event, Scranton apparently did not write the letter, or sign it or even see it before it was taken downstairs to the Goldwater headquarters around 7 P.M. The letter, an extraordinary document, said:

As we move rapidly toward the climax of this convention, the Republican party faces continuing struggle on two counts.

The first involves, of course, selection of a candidate.

Here the issue is extremely clear. It simply is this: Will the convention choose the candidate overwhelmingly favored by the Republican voters, or will it choose you?

Your organization does not even argue the merits of the question. They admit that you are a minority candidate, but they feel they have bought, beaten and compromised enough delegate support to make the result a foregone conclusion.

With open contempt for the dignity, integrity and common sense of the convention, your managers say in effect that the delegates are little more than a flock of chickens whose necks will be wrung at will. . . .

All of us in San Francisco are so close to the hour-by-hour story unfolding here that there is a danger we may overlook the over-all impression being created in the minds of the American people.

Goldwaterism has come to stand for nuclear irresponsibility.

Goldwaterism has come to stand for keeping the name of Eisenhower out of our platform.

Goldwaterism has come to stand for being afraid to forthrightly condemn right-wing extremists.

Goldwaterism has come to stand for refusing to stand for law and order in maintaining racial peace.

In short, Goldwaterism has come to stand for a whole crazy-quilt collection of absurd and dangerous positions that would be soundly repudiated by the American people in November.

Meanwhile, we have tried as best we can in the rigged situation engineered by your organization to articulate another point of view.

These are not surface differences between you and the vast majority of Republicans. These are soul-deep differences over what the Republican party stands for. . . .

He ended the letter by challenging Goldwater to debate on the floor of the convention, saying that few people expected that Goldwater would accept and adding that the implication of the refusal would be that "you no longer have any regard for the opinions of uncommitted delegates or the American public."

Just about the time the letter was delivered Goldwater went upstairs from a reception by Southern states. The letter was handed to him. He was alone when he read it. Dean Burch, his deputy campaign manager, then appeared.

"Take a look at this," Goldwater said angrily. The Senator had noted that the typed and written signature read "William W. Scranton." In previous correspondence, the Governor had signed "Bill."

Goldwater and Burch called in Ed Nellor, Goldwater's public relations chief. Burch suggested a reply saying, "Some idiot is sending out letters over your name," but this idea was discarded. Other possibilities were discussed with Denison Kitchel, the campaign director; Karl Hess, a speech draftsman, Harry Jaffa, a former professor at Ohio State University, and Edward McCabe, a staff member. The mood of the Goldwater camp gradually changed from anger to good humor. At McCabe's suggestion, photographic copies of the letter were made and the original was stuffed into an envelope. Kitchel stepped outside and read the letter to newsmen.

Several hundred copies were delivered to the Republican committee's newsroom in the Hilton Hotel about 7:30 P.M. The letter's unusually caustic tone made it major news. Goldwater's staff ran off 4,000 more copies for distribution to all delegates and copies were also sent to each of about 200 major Republican figures with a covering memorandum from Goldwater: "I am attaching a copy of a letter I received from Governor Scranton. I consider it an insult to every Republican in San Francisco. Barry."

The Scranton organization caught the backlash when a member of the Wisconsin delegation asked the Governor about the letter. Scranton said then and later that it had gone out without his reading it, but that he accepted full responsibility. On a television quiz program financed by his own organization, Scranton was asked, "Will you repudiate the letter?"

"No, I won't," he replied. "It is true I did not write it and did not see it and did not sign it. I do not disavow responsibility for that letter."

Was the language impulsive? he was asked.

"I don't think the language is impulsive," the Governor said, rejecting an adjective he had frequently used in criticizing Goldwater. He said the language was "perhaps too strong," but added that this sometimes happened in campaigns and, "You simply have to face the responsibility."

There were three immediate consequences of the letter. Scranton had not only denied himself his best issue—that Goldwater was reckless, irresponsible and "shot from the hip"—but turned the issue back on himself. Whatever thoughts anyone in San Francisco had entertained about Scranton's availability for the Vice Presidential spot or his acceptability to Goldwater were conclusively dispelled—which may well have been one of the conscious or unconscious intentions of the letter.

The episode set the tone for the convention itself—a tone of internecine bitterness.

On July 12, the day before the convention opened, Eisenhower, under contract as a television commentator for the American Broadcasting Company, arrived in San Francisco after a two-day train trip across the country with other Republican officials, including his brother, Milton, who was to nominate Scranton for President three days later. In his first public comment, on July 12, Eisenhower said an "open contest" over the Presidential nomination had not developed as he had been proposing for the last year. He implied it was now too late to stop Goldwater, and said, "Things did not develop as I had hoped," referring to the open convention idea.

The Goldwater forces employed two agents to communicate personally with Eisenhower in the weeks before the convention, George M. Humphrey, the President's former Secretary of the Treasury, and a former White House administrative aide, Edward McCabe. Both men had been working for Goldwater for some time, Humphrey raising campaign funds and McCabe doing a little bit of everything, speech writing, research and leg work. Both men told the General that in reality Goldwater was no more conservative on most issues than Eisenhower was; he just sounded that way. Probably more convincing was the argument that it was too late to oppose Goldwater anyway, and that Eisenhower should not risk his stature and prestige in a losing cause, as Truman had done for Averell Harriman in 1956. On July 13 Eisenhower further disheartened the moderates by expressing general approval of the Republican platform. If Goldwater campaigned on its declarations, he said, "I don't see how he can go far wrong."

The convention on its first day plunged immediately into a spirited floor fight, but the brief battle displayed Goldwater's grip on the delegates more than it raised the blood pressure of any of the combatants. The skirmish was over almost before it began; roaring with enthusiasm, the delegates, alternates and Goldwater-packed galleries shouted down a rules charge proposed by the Scranton forces. This motion, which would have barred delegates seated by discriminatory procedures, was designed to put Goldwater in the position of opposing the rights of Negroes. Scranton men contended afterward that the defeat was just what they had expected, showing, they said, that Goldwater was opposed to civil rights and was prepared to force his views on the convention. The Senator's acceptance of the challenge, and the power he showed in putting it down, assured the continuance of an acrimonious convention, and also a floor fight over the platform.

The Republican platform committee had turned out a document ringing with the ideas and phrases of Goldwater conservatism, and committee moderates were crushed in efforts to write in amendments. James Reston studied both the platform and the mood of the delegates, and noted that the Goldwater platform was a tangle of contradictions:

It favors, for example, both a more militant policy toward the Communists abroad, and reduced expenditures and taxes at home; a more unified North Atlantic Treaty Alliance and a militant policy toward the Communists, which is the last thing the allies want; equal rights for the Negroes, and ambiguous policies for securing those rights.

The danger in this is that everybody at home and abroad will read into all this much more than actually exists. There is really much less here than meets the eye. The Goldwater people have got control of things, but to conclude that the platform represents a serious consensus of Republican opinion, or that they would be able to enforce it if they won in November, ignores all the subjective elements that produced the platform in the first place. . . .

It does not follow from this, however, that the Republican party, which was founded on an antislavery program, and controlled the White House for 60 out of the first 100 years of its history, has now met here in San Francisco in solemn conference and carefully outlined a new program for the future.

In the first place, nothing could be more removed from the atmosphere of dependable and objective discussion and definition than a national American political convention.

The party meets primarily to pick a man. Its objective obviously is victory. It deals with these things in a noisy, exhausted air of stale cigars, contentious personal cliques, blaring electronic campaign music, and all this with inquisitive, competitive, jealous reporters outside the committee door.

There is one thing that unites everybody in this, and every other, political convention: All the delegates, all the possible candidates, all the television heroes and combative newspaper reporters and all the platform writers, are trapped by events beyond their control.

All are deadly serious. All are well-meaning, but all are caught up in the big political machine. Therefore, it is questionable, and maybe even silly, to pretend that the platform indicates something of high significance.

It is easy, of course, to reach momentous conclusions and write impressive articles, if you take the words of the platform at face value. But all you can really do with any assurance is to talk or write about tendencies or drifts of opinion reached in an exhausted atmosphere.

On this basis, there are probably two tendencies in the Republican platform worth serious consideration. The first is what the platform says about foreign policy, and the second is what went on behind the scenes on the question of racial equality.

On the first, the main thing is that the Republicans who traditionally were against foreign entanglements now insist on being much more involved in the world than the Democrats, and on the second it is clear that the G.O.P. had a terrible struggle about defending the recent civil rights bill passed by the Congress primarily with the aid of its own leaders.

All the rest of the platform is faithful to the Republican tradition. For a generation and more, the Republicans have differed with the Democrats about policy on taxation, welfare and farm programs, regulation of business and labor and foreign trade. And today's G.O.P. platform has followed these normal tendencies.

On the opening day of a convention, the keynote speaker defines the conviction of the majority of his fellow party members, and this Governor Mark O. Hatfield of Oregon did as he ripped into the Democrats and Johnson with calculated vigor. But Hatfield also rubbed the raw nerves of the contending forces at the convention when he spoke out against the John Birch Society. "There are bigots in this nation who spew forth their venom of hate," he said. "They parade under hundreds of labels, including the Communist party, the Ku Klux Klan, and the John Birch Society. They must be overcome." Fewer than half the delegates joined in the brief demonstration after these remarks, and the next day Hatfield received hundreds of telegrams and letters—almost all angrily critical.

On the second day of the convention, July 14, the fight over the platform erupted on the floor. With the Presidential nomination virtually assured for Goldwater, the Scranton forces centered their efforts more and more on the platform. The central issue of the platform fight was civil rights, a subject on which the Scranton men were proposing a detailed and lengthy amendment to what they called "the generalities of the civil rights plank" as drafted by the platform committee. There had been continuing civil rights protests—parades, demonstrations, sit-ins—in San Francisco and outside the Cow Palace for the last week in the anticipation of the nomination of Goldwater. After much discussion and even more confusion, the ill-organized Republican moderates also decided to offer platform amendments with an extremism plank, proposing that the convention condemn the John Birch Society by name, and a nuclear weapons control plank, stating that control should remain in the hands of the President.

The amendments—totally unacceptable to the Goldwater forces—were an attempt to probe theoretical Goldwater weak spots. Because Goldwater had voted against the civil rights bill in the Senate it had been imperative for the platform drafters to draw a vague and general civil rights plank, even though the majority of the Republicans in the House and the Senate had voted for the bill. Indeed, the victory for the measure in the Senate was due in part to the efforts of Dirksen, the Minority Leader, who later, to the surprise of many moderates who sought to dissuade him, declared for Goldwater and agreed to place his name in nomination at the convention. This should not have been such a surprise for it was Dirksen who championed the conservative element of the party in a dramatic moment of the 1952 convention in Chicago when, speaking for Taft in his losing fight for the nomination, he pointed his finger at Thomas E. Dewey, the man who lost to Truman in 1948 and who had been a leader of the Eisenhower forces, and thundered, "We followed you before and you took us down the path to defeat."

The extremism amendment, with its specific mention of the John Birch

Society, was an even more direct attempt to embarrass Goldwater since some of his most ardent admirers and vociferous supporters were known to be members of the society and other similar organizations. Goldwater could hardly condemn these people, embarrassing as their public support might be. On the other hand, the moderate forces calculated that Goldwater would not want to place himself on record as condoning extremism. This turned out to be simply one more miscalculation, but it was a big one and apparently helped provoke an extraordinary Goldwater response two nights later.

The nuclear weapons control amendment was an effort to hang upon Goldwater the labels of reckless, impulsive and dangerous. Even more serious, it was an attempt to raise the whole issue of the Senator's fitness to be President. And behind this issue was the implication that as President, Goldwater might—knowingly or unknowingly—lead the country and the world into an apocalyptic nuclear conflict. Neither Goldwater nor his supporters could be expected to tolerate such a charge without a strong reaction. The main, if unstated and feeble, hope of the Scranton group was that the Goldwater forces would respond at length and in heat, that there would be a debate on all three amendments before the convention (with a last opportunity to sway the delegates) and, even more important, before a national television audience.

It is unlikely that this strategy would have worked even if it had been well conceived, directed, presented and timed, but it was none of these, and the Goldwater forces so controlled the convention that there was only one roll call vote, and what passed for a debate on the three amendments did not even begin until after 8 P.M. San Francisco time (11 P.M. on the East Coast). Directly preceding the "debate" was a ninety-minute reading of the 8,500-word draft platform insisted upon by the Goldwater group—an exercise in national stupefaction matched only by a similar ploy by the Democrats in Atlantic City several weeks later.

Even before the reading of the platform, the convention managers had rescheduled the evening's festivities so that Eisenhower's speech, originally planned to end the session on a joyous, unified note, was inserted earlier as a harmless dampener to the anticipated explosions. By the evening of July 14, it had finally come clear to everyone (or almost everyone) in the Republican party and the nation that Eisenhower had absolutely no desire to thrust himself into the fray. In fact, if the General could be said to have indicated anything clearly at all, it was his desire to remain above the battle, to act only as a soothing, calming influence, a friend to all factions, a peacemaker. There was no question of the affectionate regard that the majority of the delegates held for him. He received standing ovations both before and after his speech, and the speech itself was interrupted forty times by applause.

In his speech Eisenhower asked his audience temporarily "to bank the fires of personally competitive intraparty politics . . . to have done with scurrilous and misleading labels . . . and to contemplate the whole of this big party," the things on which most Republicans agreed rather than upon the few matters on which they were divided. "We must learn that when any Republican concerns himself too much in condemning this or that faction of decent people in the party, he is hurting himself and the party," he warned.

The convention hall fairly exploded when the General told the delegates that they should not let themselves be divided by "those outside our family, including sensation-seeking columnists and commentators . . . who couldn't care less about the good of our party." There was a deafening roar of boos directed at the press stands flanking the speaker's platform and many on the convention floor jumped up and shook their fists at those in the glassed-in television booths.

As Eisenhower departed, the platform fight began in earnest and in the open. It was not a polite fight; the Goldwater supporters were in full control of the convention and they showed it—sometimes in disrespectful ways. When the three Scranton amendments to the platform came up for debate and vote, Rockefeller arose to speak for the first of them, the one condemning extremism. As the Governor was introduced, a brief demonstration for him was drowned in a swelling chant of "We want Barry" from the galleries. Rockefeller smiled and waited, while the chanters built up volume and a bass drum joined in with a decisive thump.

Senator Thruston B. Morton of Kentucky, the chairman, gaveled the demonstration to a close with some difficulty. But as Rockefeller moved firmly into his speech, the thunder of the booing and the thump of the drum interrupted him constantly. On two occasions, Morton quieted hostile demonstrations with the gavel, and once added: "Now, look. The Governor has been up here ten minutes and he's only had a chance to talk about four."

Rockefeller admonished the demonstrators at one point, "It's still a free country, ladies and gentlemen." Mostly he stood mute, sometimes smiling, but it was a forced smile. Finally, he snapped, "Some of you don't like to hear it, ladies and gentlemen—but it's the truth!" That only brought more boos.

When the speaking ended, the delegates easily defeated the amendment, by a standing vote and a thunderous "no." Romney then came forward with another, milder amendment that would have condemned extremism without mentioning any organization by name. That, too, was shouted down. Debate on both the civil rights and nuclear weapons control amendments was desultory. The spark obviously went out of the minority effort for amendments after the reception given Rockefeller, although the Scranton men carried their fight through to the end.

The roll call vote on the civil rights question was 897 to 409, with delegates from twenty-six states and territories voting solidly against the broadening amendment. The delegates supporting Goldwater stayed in their seats past midnight to defeat the third proposal, which would have reaffirmed the principle of Presidential control of nuclear weapons.

The defeat of the Eastern liberal leaders and their followers was total and ignominious. Behind all the noise there were movements and concerns discernible to James Reston, who wrote in The Times:

The saddest figures in this convention are the Eastern moderates, who have dominated every other Republican convention since 1940. General Eisenhower is a television commentator; Richard Nixon is an outsider, and Governors Rockefeller and Scranton and Ambassador Henry Cabot Lodge are regarded almost as agents of the Democratic opposition.

When the G.O.P. met here in 1956 to nominate General Eisenhower, Len Hall opened the proceedings by shouting: "Is everybody happy?" Nobody tried that one today. For the party is deeply split on handling the race issue and the Communists, and it is embarking on a "Southern strategy" against its own traditions. . . .

Purely aside from the moral aspects of the question, the political problem of winning in the South is a tough one for the Republicans. It is not easy for the South to switch political allegiance, especially with a Southerner at the top of the Democratic ticket. Also, the Negro vote is rising in the South, and nothing that is happening here is likely to swing that vote to the Republicans.

July 15, the day of Goldwater nomination, dawned with an expression of pain from Eisenhower, who condemned the tactics of Goldwater delegates in rejecting efforts to strengthen the civil rights plank and to add one on extremism. Eisenhower said that it appeared that a majority of the delegates had "to some extent abandoned their reason" and had agreed in advance "not to tolerate" any changes in the Goldwater-oriented platform. To adopt in advance "that kind of a rigid position, is really not the democratic method as I see it," the former President said. "This is like you have got to vote yes or no, and that is very bad." While the General supported the proposals of the moderates the measured tones with which he spoke indicated a disinterested acceptance of the inevitable defeat. His manner prompted a former aide to remark, "I guess old soldiers do fade away after all."

Meanwhile, back on Nob Hill a television reporter caught Goldwater on his way to a service elevator in the Mark Hopkins Hotel after addressing a "captive nations" rally organized by persons with national origins in countries now in the Communist bloc. Such an audience was considered by his managers a natural for the Senator, because it would respond to his insistence on some day "freeing" these "captives."

The reporter asked the Senator if the convention's refusal to strengthen its civil rights plank would not give the Democrats a good issue in the campaign. The Senator's head snapped around. With an edge of scorn in his voice, he said: "After Lyndon Johnson—the biggest faker in the United States? He opposed civil rights until this year. Let them make an issue of it. I'll recite the thousands of words he has spoken down the years against abolishing the poll tax and F.E.P.C. He's the phoniest individual who ever came around."

It took seven hours of speeches and demonstrations to nominate eight Republican candidates for the President of the United States. In all there were thirty-three nominating and seconding speeches—for Goldwater, Scranton, Rockefeller, Romney, Margaret Chase Smith, Senator Hiram Fong of Hawaii, former Representative Walter H. Judd of Minnesota, and Lodge—before the balloting could begin and the utter lack of suspense could be ended.

Senator Everett McKinley Dirksen, in a well-modulated and rumbling speech, placed Goldwater in nomination. He pictured Goldwater as a peddler's grandson who had based his political career on blazing courage. The Illinois Senator said: "It is the fashion of our critics to sneer at patriotism, to label positions of strength as extremism, to find other nations' points of view right more often than our own. Perhaps too long the bugles have sounded 'retreat' in our relations with other lands." Through firmness, he said, through the sure hand, Barry Goldwater, the grandson of that immigrant frontier peddler, could retrieve the self-respect of America. Dirksen described Goldwater's vote against the Civil Rights Act of 1964—of which Dirksen was a chief architect—as an example of "that quality of moral courage which has won him the admiration of the citizens of this land." As for the ideological swing of the Republican party to conservatism, Dirksen declared: "Delegates to this convention, the tide is turning! Let's give 190 million Americans the choice they have been waiting for!"

As the mellifluous Senator closed his remarks, the Cow Palace erupted in a bedlam of sound—cheering throngs, blaring bands, howling auto horns above the thump of bass drums. Through the aisles of the great halls a mob of Goldwater supporters jammed their way, inch by inch, holding placards aloft, screaming as if gone mad. Two demonstrators, carrying an eight-foot-high banner bearing the Senator's likeness, shoved their way through the mob. Another puffed on a huge brass sousaphone. No one but a Goldwater demonstrator could move on the floor. The passionate demonstration was a tribute to the zeal that Goldwater inspired in his admirers—a zeal that seemed in the Cow Palace to take on a messianic fervor.

Goldwater's nomination was seconded by Senator John G. Tower of Texas, former Senator William F. Knowland of California, Representative Charles A. Halleck of Indiana and former Representative Clare Boothe Luce of Connecticut. Each of their speeches was punctuated with the thunderous applause of the Goldwater delegates and the spectators in the galleries—obviously an area where the Senator was a hero.

Finally, the balloting began and one by one the states called their votes. A flashing-light scoreboard was keeping delegates abreast of the totals and a mighty roar went up when it was realized that the South Carolina delegation, solidly Goldwater, would give him the nomination. When the noise died away, the South Carolina chairman, in deepest Southern tones, declaimed: "Mr. Chairman, we are humbly grateful that we can do this for America. South Carolina casts sixteen votes for Senator Barry Goldwater."

What millions of American conservatives had hoped and worked toward for years had come true. Goldwater had 663 delegate votes—eight more than he needed for nomination. A mighty storm of cheering shook the Cow Palace. Goldwater placards flew into the air, drums thumped and horns squealed, and men stood on chairs and screamed at the top of their lungs. Goldwater had won the nomination—he had taken virtually every Southern delegate's vote and had swept most of the delegates from the states west of the Mississippi, and in Ohio, Illinois and Wisconsin. The count of the first ballot stood as follows for the two leading contenders:

Goldwater 883
Scranton 214

In his nearby trailer, Scranton stood up and, with Mrs. Scranton, began the walk to the arena and the speaker's platform. At the conclusion of the ballot Scranton appeared on the platform to move for the unanimous nomination of Goldwater while his daughter and son in the gallery shed unabashed tears. Scranton extended congratulations to Goldwater and pledged, "I shall work for and fully support the ticket chosen by this convention. . . . Let it be clearly understood," he said, "that this great Republican party is our historic house. This is our home. We have no intention of deserting it. We are still Republicans—and not very still ones either."

Before Scranton's motion for a unanimous vote could be acted upon, a number of states insisted on switching their votes to Goldwater. The switches became so hurried that they could not all be tabulated. The last big state to switch was New York, which asked for more time to caucus informally on the floor. Down on the floor the New York delegation was in a state of confusion; many delegates had already walked out during the demonstration following the nomination. Those who had stayed were sharply, bitterly divided about making the Goldwater nomination unanimous. Several Negro delegates absolutely refused to change their votes. Small men were standing on chairs shouting. Big men—Rockefeller, Senators Javits and Keating—were either sitting silently or were absent. Finally, Fred Young, the state chairman, grabbed the microphone and shouted that New York now voted eighty-seven for Goldwater and five abstentions. It was impossible to learn who were the five delegates abstaining, or if indeed there even were such abstentions.

James Reston saw the nomination this way:

Senator Barry Goldwater has not only won a spectacular victory. He has also shifted the whole American political battleground to the conservative right.

President Johnson, it can be said on good authority, will not follow him in emphasizing the widening ideological differences between the parties. He does not want to inflame or envenom the almost theological issues between Republicans and Democrats that have been dramatized here. He will undoubtedly move now to the right to capture the non-attached, non-ideological voters in the decisive center. . . .

A wholly new alignment of political forces in America is now forming, however, so new in fact that all the assumptions of the past about the parties are unreliable. . . .

There are deep historical and psychological tides running here. It would probably be a profound mistake to regard all this as a Goldwater triumph of personality, or as a cunning take-over by well-financed and well-organized conspiratorial forces winning over the disorganized noblesse oblige liberals.

Mr. Goldwater may attract all the ultras, and the antis—the forces that are anti-Negro, antilabor, antiforeigner, anti-intellectual—but he also attracts something else that is precisely the opposite of these vicious and negative forces.

Mr. Goldwater touches the deep feeling of regret in American life: regret over the loss of simplicity and fidelity; regret over the loss of the frontier spirit of pugnacious individuality; regret, in sort, over the loss of America's innocent and idealistic youth.

It is easy to scoff at all this, and to demonstrate that the effect of Mr. Goldwater's policies on the Negro revolution and the Communist problem are reckless, but in this complicated and baffling era it is not surprising that many people put the family before the community, the community before the state, the state before the nation and the nation before the world.

All this has been fairly obvious in San Francisco, not perhaps on the clamorous floor of the Cow Palace, or on the television screen, but in the private conversations on the fringe, and even in the savage outcry against the newspaper columnists and the television commentators on the floor.

There is a bitter paradox in the Republican party between its respectability and its frustrations. It knows instinctively that the most vicious elements in our national life, from the Birchers and Ku Kluxers to the protectionists and the isolationists, are supporting Mr. Goldwater, but it is so frustrated and so genuinely opposed to the trend of modern life that it seems to be willing to use any means to oppose what it believes to be the wicked ends of a planned, international, interdependent, coexistence policy.

All this has come out here, even occasionally on the convention floor. The delegates are so involved in the game of politics that they do not listen, but the speeches are full of laments for our innocent past, of longings for the character of a more austere age, of disillusion with the consequences of success and prosperity.

Somehow, along the way, all these frustrations have been transferred into political terms, and the true Republican believer—not the extremists in the party but many of the most moderate and respectable Republicans—have come to identify the Democrats with everything from the decline of individual responsibility, to unemployment, racial tension, international confusion, and juvenile deliquency.

The liberals, in this present Republican mood, have become responsible for the destruction of authority and tradition. The threats and seductions of the radical innovators have produced, as they see it, moral confusion. The license of liberal doctrine has created a conflict in their minds between faith and reason, and produced a kind of intellectual and moral bankruptcy for which the Democrats, as they see it, are responsible.

This is what explains at least part of the revivalist atmosphere of the convention here. The Goldwater-controlled convention would concede nothing, not even to those who were trying to compromise with them. The Democrats, the liberal Republicans, the sophisticated and "decadent" East, the wicked, debased internationalist Eastern press—all were the enemies, not only of victory for the "right" here in San Francisco, and in Cuba, and in Vietnam, but also the enemies of the true objectives of the American dream.

No doubt there was an element of expediency and revenge in this atmosphere in the Cow Palace. Many delegates merely felt that Barry would help them in their own district to win in November. Many more were getting even for the liberal victories in the conventions from 1940 to 1960. Quite a few were still resentful about the Eisenhower triumph over Robert A. Taft in the convention of 1952, and wanted to score over Henry Cabot Lodge and Christian A. Herter, who led the Eisenhower campaign in that convention.

But back of all this is the deep feeling that is seldom reported: That the nation, in many Republican minds, has drifted into attitudes and policies that debase and weaken the American character, and threaten the security of the nation.

This thesis—right or wrong—is the "sleeper" in this election, and Mr. Goldwater is its symbol. It is surprising, therefore, that the Goldwater forces did not support on the convention floor the efforts to condemn the Birch Society and the other extremists, for Mr. Goldwater does not agree with them. Besides, they would vote for him even if he repudiated them.

Also, it is surprising that he opposed the moderate civil rights compromise put forward by Gov. George Romney of Michigan, who made the most moving appeal of the whole convention. For Mr. Goldwater's main hope in this election, as at least some observers here see it, lies, not in winning the South or the vote of the extremists on the far right, but in convincing the uncommitted and troubled voters in the middle that there is something basically wrong with the trend of our national life.

Mr. Goldwater's dilemma now is quite clear. On the one hand, he is arguing for the New Morality, but on the other he is supporting a racial policy that seems to many deeply immoral and attracts the most negative forces in the nation. On one side, he is arguing for allied unity, but on the other he is proclaiming policies that will clearly split the Western Alliance.

The convention has insisted after protracted debate on defending the right of dissent by the John Birch Society, but it has violently booed the right of dissent by the American press.

It has argued for a more militant policy toward the Communists one minute and called for a cut in expenditures and taxes in the next. It has asked for the cooperation of the liberals in the election campaign, but has refused even to grant them a few vague compromises in the platform that would ease their obvious embarrassment.

Accordingly, Mr. Goldwater is facing the most militant and ideological election campaign of the century with a divided party, and although he can undoubtedly force President Johnson to the right, he has to win in the center, where Mr. Johnson feels more comfortable than any place else.

The next morning Goldwater made official what had been unofficially expected in San Francisco. He selected Representative William E. Miller, the Republican National Chairman, as his Vice Presidential running mate. The selection, as much as Goldwater's nomination, symbolized the humiliating rout of the Eastern Republican establishment, for, although Miller had represented an upstate New York constituency in the House of Representatives for fourteen years, he had absolutely nothing in common with Rockefeller or Keating and Javits. On the surface, it was an attempt to balance the ticket; Miller was from the East and he was a Catholic. More important, Miller— both on the basis of his voting record and hard-hitting partisan oratory— was an orthodox conservative and that was essentially why Goldwater chose him.

What was left was Goldwater's acceptance speech. Nixon, the man some of the delegates to the convention believed "blew" the 1960 election, introduced "the next President of the United States." The place went wild again; hundreds of balloons tumbled from the ceiling, almost inundating "the next President" and his wife, and the noise of their popping rattled like rifle fire.

A Presidential candidate's acceptance speech is automatically an important campaign document, for not only are the basic issues set forth for the coming months but also the candidate's style, his manner, his point of view are on full display. Goldwater had never been noted as a particularly forceful or inspiring orator, nor had his prose style been admired for precision or clarity. Still, a newly nominated Presidential candidate can be expected to be gracious, holding out the olive branch to his opponents for politicians believe that party unity is essential to victory. But Goldwater was as uncompromising in his acceptance speech as he was during the fight. As he appeared in the Cow Palace, the band played "The Battle Hymn of the Republic."

He stated his theme early in the speech: "The good Lord raised this mighty Republic to be a home for the brave and to flourish as the land of the free —not to stagnate in the swampland of collectivism, not to cringe before the bullying of Communism."

Goldwater continued:

Now my fellow Americans, the tide has been running against freedom. Our people have followed false prophets. We must, and we shall, return to proven ways—not because they are old, but because they are true.

We must, and we shall, set the tide running again in the cause of freedom. And this party, with its every action, every word, every breath and every heart beat, has but a single resolve, and that is freedom.

Freedom made orderly for this nation by our constitutional government. Freedom under a government limited by laws of nature and of nature's God. Freedom balanced so that order lacking liberty will not become the slavery of the prison cell; balanced so that liberty lacking order will not become the license of the mob and of the jungle.

He called to his party "to free our people and light the way for liberty throughout the world." Communism, he said, must be made to "give way to the forces of freedom." Although he never once mentioned the word Negro or the phrase civil rights, Goldwater did say that "the sanctity of private property is the only durable foundation for constitutional government in a free society." Toward the end, Goldwater brought his audience to its feet with these extraordinary words:

Anyone who joins us in all sincerity we welcome. Those, those who do not care for our cause, we don't expect to enter our ranks in any case. And let our Republicanism so focused and so dedicated not be made fuzzy and futile by unthinking and stupid labels.

I would remind you that extremism in the defense of liberty is no vice!

And let me remind you also that moderation in the pursuit of justice is no virtue!

As Goldwater ended his speech, Senator Keating of New York, a somber look on his face, arose and walked from the hall in the center of the nation's television screen. It seemed as if he were literally turning his back on his party's Presidential nominee, but Keating explained that he had left to "avoid the rush." The next day, he explained further that he had hurried from the hall to return to his hotel to have a sore throat treated. Somewhat to his surprise, Keating found himself a hero for his action, whether or not intended as a rebuff to Goldwater; he immediately received many congratulatory telegrams and pledges of support for his own campaign.

Not only the moderate Republicans, but also many in the nation and indeed the world were shocked by Goldwater's final sentences—which were heavily underlined in the prepared text. Eisenhower (to whom "the passage conjured up a philosophy that the end justifies the means and that vigilantes and nightriders are entirely acceptable if their purpose is 'the defense of liberty' or 'the pursuit of justice' "), Scranton, Lodge and Rockefeller thought and said the passage was "dangerous," "irresponsible" and "frightening." Nixon called the speech "childish." Arthur Krock commented in The Times:

> With two sentences in his speech of acceptance, Senator Goldwater reopened the wounds inflicted on the Republican party by the contests over its platform and Presidential nomination during the national convention of 1964 that former Vice President Nixon and Governor Scranton of Pennsylvania had sought to bandage and to heal. . . .
>
> Why Senator Goldwater, on the instant of assuming his roles as Presidential nominee and national party leader, deliberately chose language which was bound to reopen and intensify the most acute cleavage among the Republicans must await development by the fuller explanation department. . . .
>
> Since it was obvious also that these two sentences in the speech of acceptance would rub salt into the sores of the defeated liberal faction in the convention, they virtually invited the angry and amazed reaction of which Governor Rockefeller's explosion was typical. Therefore, for the time being logic is on the side of the politicians here who read into these sentences a decision by Goldwater that to win the Presidency he must create a distinct national cleavage on the conservative-liberal line; and could do this without fear of a Republican bolt of proportions anything like as serious as that led in 1912 by Theodore Roosevelt on the independent Bull Moose ticket.

7

"Just Poopin' Along":
How Goldwater Did It

"Let's grow up, conservatives. Let's, if we want to take this party back—and I think we can some day—let's get to work."

With those words at the Republican National Convention on July 27, 1960, Barry Goldwater cast the first stone in what was to become a conservative avalanche four years later. The Senator from Arizona had received ten of the Louisiana delegation's twenty-six votes on the first ballot for the Presidential nomination; Nixon, 1,321. Goldwater then made a dramatic appearance in Chicago's International Amphitheater. Mounting the rostrum, he lectured party conservatives sternly on their future and asked that the votes for him be withdrawn and that Nixon be nominated unanimously.

"We have lost election after election in this country in the last several years because conservative Republicans got mad and stayed home," he said. "Now I implore you. Forget it." He congratulated his fellow conservatives on their splendid showing at the convention, told them that he, as a good Republican, would devote all his time to electing Republicans in November and urged them to do the same. It was their duty to unite behind Nixon, he said, to defeat "the blueprint for socialism presented by the Democrats."

Many viewed Goldwater's speech as the last gasp of the Republican Old Guard, but he did not. Neither did Arthur Krock of The Times, who was sufficiently impressed to describe Goldwater as "the sudden new hero of the right wing." He wrote, "Though the Republican conservatives knew very little of the Arizona Senator until Chicago, now their hearts belong to Barry."

Later that year Leo Egan of The Times looked ahead to 1964 for the G.O.P.:

Senator Goldwater could also be very much in the running. As the leading spokesman for the conservative cause in the Senate, he has a national following that ordinarily would not accrue to the representative of a state with only four electoral votes.

Goldwater had provided significant, but for the most part overlooked,

72

clues to his political philosophy even before the 1960 convention, by writing: "Over the years, the terms 'liberal' and 'conservative' have become so confused as to be almost meaningless. . . . The conservative believes that man is, in part, an economic creature with spiritual needs and spiritual desires. What is more, these needs and desires reflect the superior side of man's nature, and thus take precedence over his economic wants."

He had also called on the Republican party to seize the opportunity to present positive, proven ideals to the people by espousing conservative principles. "Reduced Federal debt and a balanced budget head the list of accomplishments we can achieve under conservative Republicanism," he said. "The corollary to this is reduced taxes. This becomes more than campaign talk when we implement measures such as removal of the Government from agricultural control, an item that costs the taxpayer $6,000,000,000 a year. This must, of course, be done gradually. But it is necessary that it be done and that we stop tampering with the laws of nature."

He continued: "Conservative Republicanism can take an important positive step by returning to the states that sovereignty which is guaranteed by the Constitution. We must further assure individual freedom by keeping the Federal Government out of education and medicine. And as demonstrated in the first session of this Congress with the enactment of the Landrum-Griffin labor reform bill, there is an urgency to return to the public that balance of power in labor-management relations which now leans toward labor."

The ears of some industry leaders (particularly small industrialists) turned up; those of labor turned red. These were warlike words, not heard from any prominent political figure for many years. The Republican political establishment—the moderates, the Easterners, the Wall Street money men and many corporation executives—however, shrugged its collective shoulders and decided to let Goldwater use his mounting popularity in the effort to put Nixon in the White House in 1960.

When Nixon lost to Kennedy, the Republican leadership was in disarray, its members discouraged and disheartened. One Goldwater disciple said, "The Eastern Establishment is powerful, rich—and senile." The men who had put Willkie, Dewey, Eisenhower and Nixon in nomination thought otherwise, despite the 1960 defeat. They still did not take Goldwater seriously; they underestimated the nature, vigor and direction of his appeal. To them, Goldwater was a bush-leaguer with a following of "nuts and kooks."

But Goldwater—pilot, businessman, family man, outdoorsman—had a far broader base of support than the Easterners suspected. Tom Wicker wrote in The Times:

He had the nuts and kooks, all right (like the man with burning eyes who inquired of him at Clear Lake, Calif., last spring: "Barry, how we going to drive all these Communists out of the country?"), but they were a small, if vocal, part of his troops.

There was a greater army of the discontented and frustrated—men and women

angry and disenchanted with the Cold War, Big Government, Big Unions, even
with Big Business. They writhed under Government restraints on their "initiative,"
muttered angrily about high taxes to support foreign "give-aways" and costly
welfare "handouts"; they complained at the dominance of the cities with their
"hyphenated-American" minority groups.

These ardent followers of a new order fiercely proclaimed the superiority
of all things American and were convinced that most of these things were
being sold out to the Communists. The Supreme Court's decisions on civil
liberties and rights were viewed as a Communist plot to destroy America;
they opposed the approaching reality of Negroes' moving into previously
white neighborhoods, restaurants, swimming pools, jobs and schools. Most
did not regard themselves as "out of the mainstream." They saw themselves
as the heralds of a new and stronger allegiance to the American ideas of
free men and free enterprise.

Goldwater, at the 1960 convention, and before and after, had appealed
to the sizable existing flock of arch-conservatives who believed the Federal
Government was an ever-growing, threatening monster. They were convinced, as Goldwater said, that the graduated income tax robbed the citizen
who managed by sweat and brains to achieve a little property. They were
convinced, as Goldwater insisted, that government could be restored to the
people at the local level first and at the state level second, leaving only a
necessary minimum for the Federal Government.

In sum, the arch-conservatives, joined by solid businessmen and many
from the old Taft school—barely edged out by the Eisenhower forces in
1952—viewed Goldwater as a handsome, courageous knight, fighting almost
alone, providing answers for the complex problems that oppressed them. The
image was spread across the land when the Senator became chairman in 1955
of the G.O.P. Senatorial Campaign Committee. The post, unusual for a freshman Senator, carried him all over the country and into close contact with
Republicans of all levels, most significantly the grass-roots levels. Wherever
he went he tirelessly called for a more conservative course for the party, and
he reported that he sensed a smouldering passion for a break from Eisenhower moderation.

Goldwater proved himself a good, unity-minded Republican. He campaigned against Kennedy and Johnson in Texas, in Oregon, in Indiana, in
Tennessee, in Florida, in New York, wherever he was sent or called. His battle
cry against the New Frontier: "What's wrong with the old frontier of the
Constitution, the Bill of Rights and the free enterprise system?"

With the narrow defeat of Nixon, he became even more aggressive in
pursuing his conservative theme, blaming the loss on "me-too-ism." Three
days after the election, he said in Phoenix:

Those who believe in the traditional philosophy of government, which is clearly
identified with the conservative cause, might very well decide the nation would
benefit from a realignment of the party and a more frank disclosure of the
philosophy of each group.

We who are conservatives will stoutly maintain that 1960 was a repeat performance of 1944 and 1948, when we offered the voters insufficient choice with a me-too candidate.

Asked about 1964, he replied: "I want to figure in 1964, not necessarily as the top candidate. But I don't want Rockefeller in that spot."

The Senate provided Goldwater with a good forum for his ideological exhortations—charge of weakness in defense and foreign policy, attacks on Adlai Stevenson at the United Nations, criticism of a pro-labor society led by a mushrooming government (although he always denied that he was anti-labor). Everything the Arizonan said in the Senate—and he raised some troublesome questions—he said again and again at banquet tables across the country. In 1961, he filled 225 speaking engagements. In the first eight and a half months of 1962, he filled 200 engagements.

Not unexpectedly, the Senator's enthusiasm and exposition of his consevative vision excited open intraparty dissension. His was not the only voice in the Republican party; this became clear when a high-level group of Republicans gathered early in July, 1962, on Eisenhower's Pennsylvania farm to eat fried chicken. Goldwater refused to attend, finding reason to make a speech out West. The party leaders endorsed a plan for an All-Republican Conference of leaders in and out of office to strive for unity and coordinate a drive to win control of the House of Representatives in the fall elections. Eisenhower gave his blessings to a second organization repugnant to Goldwater—a National Citizens Committee of prominent Republicans. Tom Wicker wrote in The Times:

The All-Republican Conference and others to follow, as well as the citizens committee, were basically the plans of the party's "modern Republicans." General Eisenhower, who coined that term, rebutted Senator Goldwater later in the week [on his forecast of defeat and destruction] and prime movers in the plan had been men like Senators Jacob K. Javits and Kenneth Keating of New York and Hugh Scott of Pennsylvania, Governor Rockefeller of New York and General Eisenhower himself.

It was the view of these strategists that the party indeed needed a voice more appealing than that of Ev and Charlie [Everett McKinley Dirksen and Charles Halleck, Republican leaders of the Senate and House] and an appearance more effective than that of Congressional obstruction [to Kennedy programs]. And, though they invited Republicans of all description and disclaimed any intention to "set policy," the power of the Eastern, internationalist, urban forces plainly was beginning to mobilize itself for the quadrennial struggle.

The clash of interior Republican forces may be sharper in 1964 than it has been since 1952.

Goldwater could bear it no longer and lashed out. He wrote to G.O.P. National Chairman Miller, an active sponsor of the All-Republican Conference, "It is unthinkable that the same leaders who caused most of our present party troubles . . . should be given another opportunity to lead us down the path to political destruction." On the surface, at least, this 1962 period was not one of Goldwater's best. Although Goldwater worked tirelessly in the fall elections as chairman of the Senate Campaign Committee, the party lost four Senate seats. As the prophet of the right wing he could count few victories, but he had further consolidated his popularity with the semi-amateurs who dominated Republican state politics. They liked his "guts" and directness, and, above all, he drew the crowds to fund-raising dinners that made it possible for scores of party finance chairmen to meet their goals.

Moreover, little noticed apostles of conservatism, particularly in the South, Midwest and West, were fired up by Goldwater and a few others like Senator John G. Tower of Texas. They believed their time had come, the time for conservative control of the Republican party—and the nation. They formed a "new breed." Who were they?

Those with the most exposure were the conservative intellectuals, such as William Buckley and Russell Kirk, who articulated the ideology. Not so well known to the public were other conservative thinkers like Dr. Milton Friedman, University of Chicago economist, and Gerhardt Niemeyer, Notre Dame political scientist, who provided behind the scenes advice. There were the new, and generally young, Southern Republicans who successfully set out to oust the inept, often corrupt, "Post Office Republicans" who had long ruled an inoperative party machinery. To a man the Southern conservatives were strongly attracted to Goldwater. Many conservative Congressmen, particularly in the Midwest, were friendly and useful to the cause—but cautious about total commitment. The backbone of the movement was made up of Republican figures at the state and local level, many of whom had never sought public office for themselves, but who had long dominated fund-raising and intraparty politics. An Associated Press poll, for instance, showed that about 80 per cent of county chairmen liked Barry best. It was essentially an apolitical force, seeking a political outlet for its profound desire to cut the encroaching, binding Big Brother—Government—down to size.

All of these were, in the main, people without national reputation. They were propelled relentlessly by mixed motives: A firm belief in the conservative philosophies of Goldwater, a thirst for power, and a delight in the efficiency of the new politics. Among them were:

F. Clifton White, of New York, an old Dewey lieutenant, the organizational genius of the Goldwater campaign for the nomination, who was to become co-director of field operations; Peter O'Donnell Jr., of Dallas, a millionaire and the Texas Republican chairman; Richard Kleindienst, of Phoenix, a lawyer who became co-director with White and later Republican candidate for Governor; Denison Kitchel, of Phoenix, a corporation lawyer and Goldwater's closest confidant, who was to become national campaign director; Dean Burch, of Tucson, a lawyer, one of the "Arizona Mafia," destined to become Kitchel's deputy and eventually G.O.P. National Chairman; William A. Rusher, a conservative intellectual who publishes *National Review* and who had his eye on Goldwater back in 1955; Roger Allan Moore, of Boston, a prominent lawyer, who became the new breed's parliamentarian; William Middendorf, a Wall Street broker, who specialized in fund-raising; Mrs. Judy Fernald of Montclair, New Jersey, an organization Republican who proved invaluable in setting up women's auxiliaries; John Grenier, of Birmingham, a lawyer and Alabama Republican chairman, who became Goldwater's chief Southern agent; and Representative John M. Ashbrook, of Ohio.

There were many others, of course, representing an amorphous movement of right-wing organizations and groups with widely, sometimes wildly, different aims and values. While Goldwater gained an individualist's reputation with his insistent call for conservatism, they began to weave their web, silently, efficiently and strongly. They prepared themselves to hand over eventually to candidate Goldwater a going, thriving organization, zeroed-in on San Francisco in 1964.

The inside story on the activities that finally launched the Presidential candidacy of Barry Goldwater was provided after the fact by a member of the original group. "In the early months of 1961," Rusher wrote, "it became apparent that the time was ripe for a new initiative—perhaps even a conservative one." He explained that a group of relatively young and conservative professionals began private conversations during the summer of 1961. For the most part, they were old friends. He continued: "Many of them had worked and politicked together during the preceding decade in the Young Republican National Federation. Some were now Republican state chairmen; others were in Congress; many held no party office whatever. All were influential at some level of their states' Republican politics, and they shared a common conviction that it was time for the Republican party to turn to the right—away from the aggressive liberalism of Rockefeller, away from the calculated and empty platitudes of Nixon, and toward the conservative principles and personalities which had begun to make themselves felt on the national scene in the latter half of the nineteen fifties."

The ground-layers—twenty-two from sixteen states—held their first formal discussion at the Avenue Motel in Chicago on Sunday, October 8, 1961, the day of the fourth game of the World Series between the New York Yankees and the Cincinnati Reds. Nobody discussed baseball. They concentrated on making themselves into an *ad hoc* committee dedicated to turning the G.O.P. toward conservatism.

White, as chairman, was authorized to draw a plan of organization and action. He was also instructed to inform Goldwater of the formation of the committee and its goals before the next meeting two months later. "Perhaps the best evidence of the maturity of the group," Rusher wrote, "was its decision not to become, then and there, at the very outset of its existence, merely a Goldwater-for-President Committee. After all, 1964 was still more than two years away; much could happen in the interval—and besides, many of the men around the conference table in the Avenue Motel were in no position to commit either their states or themselves to a specific candidate, however attractive, so far in advance of the convention." However, all agreed that the Arizonan was the best-known and best-liked spokesman of conservative Republicanism. White drove up Capitol Hill late in November to see Goldwater, who expressed delight that he was being joined in his struggle. But there was no commitment on anyone's candidacy.

On December 10, the committee reconvened at the Avenue Motel, with its membership increased to thirty-two, although five were kept away by bad flying weather. White was asked to establish and take charge of a small, full-time office in New York to coordinate the work. The country was divided into nine regions, each under a part-time director assigned to organize the conservative Republicans. This marked the first step in the kind of meticulous, methodical organization work that followed when Goldwater officially joined the contest. A finance committee was set up to raise funds and a 1962 budget of $60,000 was approved.

As 1961 ended, White closed down his own business and rented a two-room suite on the thirty-fifth floor of the Chanin Building at the corner of Lexington Avenue and Forty-second Street in midtown Manhattan. On February 1, 1962, he started full-time operations on behalf of the nameless committee. On the frosted door of the office in the skyscraper was merely the number of the suite: 3505. "With White from the outset, as secretary and Girl Friday, was a woman whose name deserves to be more widely and gratefully known among American conservatives: Rita Bree, a career business-woman who left her own secure position in the insurance field to help White in his new and crucial assignment," Rusher wrote. "For fourteen months, those two people were to be the entire full-time staff of the movement that launched the draft of the first conservative Republican Presidential nominee in modern times."

Comparisons between the tiny, crowded, two-employe operation of the conservatives and the elaborate five-story town house from which the Presidential ambitions of Rockefeller were being promoted were irresistible. Rockefeller, smooth, cool, wealthy, already had in his employ a staff of speech-writers, researchers, promoters and big-time political operators.

During the winter and early spring of 1962, White, traveling widely, conferred with political leaders on the state and regional levels and with anyone of value who would listen to him. Then the committee was called together on April 13, this time in a lodge in the frozen, snow-covered forests of central Minnesota. The purpose: To get to know one another in an informal atmosphere, to find out how each thought and acted, how deep their convictions ran. It was agreed that the committee would lie low through the fall elections and meet again in December. Meanwhile, White and Miss Bree kept the tiny New York office going, continuing the organization work.

By the time the group met again, Nixon had suffered his crushing defeat in the gubernatorial race in California, where the former Vice President had so badly needed to build a base from which to operate for 1964. In addition the Republicans had shown surprising strength in the South. Thus, despite the secrecy and cloak-and-dagger airs, it was a confident and optimistic group that came to Chicago in ones and twos in bracing, pleasant weather on

December 2, 1962, for its fourth meeting. Fifty-five persons attended, from almost every major state. The 1964 convention was now just a year and a half away, and the conservative group saw plainly that the time had come when they had to act to support a particular candidate. No one doubted who the candidate had to be. Rusher later related: "White was instructed to call upon Senator Goldwater and tell him: (1) that the committee proposed to launch, on or about March 1, 1963, a public movement to draft him for the nomination; (2) that no consent or approval for this move, on his part, was requested or expected; and (3) that the committee only asked that, if questioned about it, the Senator would refrain from a final repudiation of all possibility of his candidacy."

Before White could see Goldwater, word of the meeting leaked out—the last thing the group desired. The Times reported from Washington:

The Republican National Committee will meet here Friday to conduct a post-mortem on its electoral disappointments last month and to confront a rising tide of factionalism within the party.

The most recent instance of splintering occurred in Chicago yesterday when a group of prominent Republicans, many of them from the South, held a secret opening of a "Goldwater for President" drive. Reports of the meeting were first published today. They indicated that from 30 to 50 persons describing themselves as "conservatives" established an initial campaign fund of $250,000 to assure the Arizona Senator's nomination by the Republican convention in 1964.

Most participants in the movement, according to reports, declined to discuss the meeting in detail. A partial list of those present, however, included Republican state and national committeemen from four Southern states; two former national chairmen of the Young Republicans; a member of Congress from Ohio, and two New York financiers.

The Times quoted Goldwater from Phoenix: "I don't know a thing about it. I don't know who the group was, where they met or what it's all about. I did see or hear something about it today, but I don't know a thing."

White finally caught up with the Arizona Senator in his Capitol Hill office on January 14. Sprightly and confident that morning, he trudged down the Hill that afternoon "looking for a job," as he confided to a friend. The publicity about the Chicago meeting, flatly suggesting a Goldwater candidacy, had irritated the Senator, but it was only one of many causes for his antagonism. Goldwater believed he had little chance for election against Kennedy, and he did not want to throw away his Senate seat on a gamble. He was also upset that day about Congressional committee assignments that rubbed him the wrong way. In essence, White had to report that Goldwater would not declare his availability and would not permit a draft movement of any kind.

In February, analyses of the potential strength of a conservative Republican candidate against Kennedy, particularly in the South, appeared. The Chicago committee decided to proceed to draft Goldwater, with or without his consent. One step in the strategy was to name O'Donnell as chairman of the National Draft Goldwater Committee, the calculation being that the Arizonan would not be eager to repudiate a group headed by the party chairman of one of the largest and most conservative states, Texas. Thus the Chicago group rounded out its organization, with White as national director, and officially launched itself on April 8, with headquarters in Washington.

Meanwhile, Goldwater, abandoning his semi-obscurity in February of 1963, began to scold the Democratic Administration at every opportunity. He dusted off his tuxedo and took to the banquet circuit again with increased energy. He accused the Kennedy regime of everything from trying to socialize medicine through Social Security to black deals with Khrushchev. A Times article later recalled:

Perhaps not so clearly then, but in retrospect one can see him running for President on a test basis at least, synchronizing his driving energies with those of his draft-minded admirers.

He charmed Republican audiences from coast to coast, in obscure towns and large cities, with daring sallies against the Kennedy Administration.

The partisan crowds loved him for his handsomeness, his smile, and the total absence of stuffiness in his bearing.

During this period, however, Goldwater was saying publicly: "I don't want the nomination. I'm not looking for it. I haven't authorized anybody to look for it for me." But, he added, "Who can tell what will happen a year from now?"

Many moderate Republicans discounted both Goldwater and Rockefeller. They were looking for a third choice, and they were confident some logical candidate would turn up and get the nomination. But, as James Reston was to point out later, "Nixon, Scranton and Lodge all temporized at critical moments in the campaign, and it is hard to escape the conclusion that they all, in different ways, put personal interest ahead of party and national interests."

Meanwhile, the Goldwater boom went booming along. On May 9, the party faithful paid $1,000 a plate to honor the Senator for his fund-raising services. On July 4, the Draft Goldwater organization put on its biggest show, a rally in Washington that drew 6,000 or more people. Goldwater, still an unavowed candidate, was there only in spirit. Nothing would be easier to misunderstand than Goldwater's relationship with the Draft Goldwater committee. He never let it control him, or even get too close. When he finally made his decision to run, he filled all of the most important campaign posts with personal Arizona friends. Cliff White, originally hired as an assistant to Kleindienst, did rise on merit to the head of field operations, but men like Rusher, Buckley, O'Donnell and others were always kept at arm's length. In the end it was not they who manipulated Goldwater, but Goldwater who manipulated them.

The unofficial campaign seemed well on the track and continued that way —"just poopin' along," in Goldwater's words, even after Rockefeller announced his candidacy. When, on January 3, 1964, Goldwater finally came out and announced his candidacy, it was the signal for his organization to move above ground with a smooth, efficient operation reminiscent of the blitz of Kennedy's "Irish Mafia" four years earlier. Ahead were the state conventions and the seven primaries Goldwater chose to enter to obtain the 655 delegates needed at San Francisco.

The techniques of the behind the scenes campaign were outlined by Kleindienst later: In a state where a convention was coming up, the Goldwater men would have their initial correspondence with the state chairman perhaps two or three months prior to the convention. They would try to get from him a preliminary estimate of the probability of getting delegates for Goldwater. They sought information from him about his precinct organization, visited his state to give him the benefit of their knowledge, and suggested to him that they start urging at the grass-roots level, among the precinct committeemen and the county chairmen, the selection of delegates to the state convention who would be friendly to the candidacy of Goldwater.

Two or three weeks before the convention the Goldwater team revisited the state chairman and went over with him all the mechanics and details of a political convention: Who's going to be chairman of the nominating committee? . . . who's going to be chairman of the resolutions committee? . . . the credentials committee? . . . where's the convention going to be? . . . what arrangement had he made to be sure that the delegates, selected at the grass-roots level, were going to be present at the convention? . . . what was his strategy about the composition of the delegation? . . . would there be a floor fight? . . . if there was a floor fight, was he organized for it? . . . what could they do to get a resolution passed by the convention committing the delegates in advance to the candidacy of Goldwater?

On the day of the convention, either White or Kleindienst, together with a regional director—John Grenier in the South, Dick Herman in the Great Plains states, Wayne Hood in the Great Lakes states, Steve Shadegg in the Western states—would be there. In most instances, they requested the right to speak to the delegates for Goldwater. They caucused in the back rooms of hotels with their key leaders; they brought campaign materials and issued statements, buttons, bumper stickers.

They followed the book of rules for hard work and organization that all candidates know about, but few carry out. Like Kennedy in 1960, the Goldwater team went out and worked hard. The liberal and moderate Republicans fought among themselves, could not agree on a man to stop Goldwater and, just as important, neglected the basic rule of politics, which calls for cultivating the grass roots.

8

The Senator
and the "Arizona Mafia"

"I'm not one of those baby-kissing, handshaking, blintz-eating candidates," Barry Morris Goldwater once said, with typical disdain for the styles of the men of the East who he believed had too long dominated the Republican party and the nation in general. The West shaped the personality of the man who turned the Republican party of Lincoln inside out in 1964—a man of burning enthusiasm, great fortitude, capricious, determined and ruggedly individualistic.

Despite his silvery hair and his fifty-five years, Goldwater at the time of his nomination had an almost boyish bearing. In contrast to the cartoonists' caricatures of a dour, withered man, he was one of the most disarming figures in public life. That charm often allowed him to escape the penalties that sometimes follow intemperate remarks. When a crowd chanted, "We want Barry!" for ten minutes at a rally in Madison Square Garden, he shouted impatiently, "You'll get him if you'll just be quiet!" No one was offended. His followers loved him the more. To them, the Arizonan was like the hero of the western film—straightforward, honest and fearless. They even praised him when he stumbled onto hazardous ground because of his extemporaneous remarks. Once, when asked if he actually had made a comment attributed to him, he retorted, "Not in my most lucid moments." He escaped then as he did the time he was quoted as having said that he wasn't sure he had "the brains to be President." Asked about the remark, he shot back: "I've done all right in my life. I don't have a Phi Beta Kappa key, but I hire them."

Goldwater's grandfather, Michel Goldwasser, could have hired them, too, if he'd known what Phi Beta Kappa was. The grandfather was raised in Konin in the province of Poznan, in what was then Russian Poland, a member of a Jewish family of Russian background. He emigrated first to France in 1837 at the age of fifteen, but in 1848, when the French government collapsed, he fled to London. Two years later, he married Sarah Nathan and they, with Michel's brother, came to the United States in 1852. They crossed America—in part by horse-drawn wagon—to California, to the gold-mining town of Sonora, where Michel ran a saloon. His wife was not entirely happy there; the town once had twelve murders in six months. So Michel, having changed his name to Goldwater and acquired the nickname of Big Mike, took his wife and two sons, Morris and Baron, and moved first to Los Angeles, then across the Colorado River and set up an adobe trading post in the Arizona territory.

He transferred his business to Prescott, the territorial capital, in 1875, eventually becoming so prosperous a merchant that he was able to retire to California in 1885 and leave his sons in charge of the business. Ten years later Baron, a small and elegant man, moved to Phoenix to start a branch store. There he met and married Josephine Williams of Nebraska, a nurse who had gone to Arizona with what she thought to be an incurable case of tuberculosis. Barry Morris Goldwater, their first child, was born on New Year's Day, 1909. Other children were Robert and Carolyn, now Mrs. Bernard Erskine of Scottsdale, Arizona. Baron Goldwater died in 1929, when Barry was twenty years old. Josephine, thought to be dying at an early age, was nearly ninety years old at the time of her son's nomination.

Uncle Morris, who stayed in Prescott, had a strong influence on young Barry. He was Mayor of Prescott for twenty-six years and was instrumental in founding the Democratic party in Arizona—on Jeffersonian principles, true to his laissez-faire individualism. He helped write the state's Constitution in 1910 and was elected to the Arizona Legislature, serving terms both as House Speaker and Senate President.

But his mother was to be the strongest influence on Barry. Josephine was a devout Episcopalian (Baron adopted that faith when they were married) and Barry was christened in Trinity Cathedral in Phoenix. He wrote many years later: "I'm proud of my Jewish father and grandfather. I've inherited some of the characteristics of the Jewish people and that has been a great advantage to me. They are warmhearted, understanding people who make friends easily. And I've never been discriminated against because I am part Jewish." (But at other times, he would say, "I know what it is to be discriminated against.") The religious Josephine was adept with a rifle and shotgun and at a poker table. When he brought friends home for a card game, Goldwater recalls, she would sit down and the next thing you knew, she had all the money.

As a student, young Barry's academic record was poor. He did so badly in his freshman year at high school that he was packed off to the rigid discipline of Staunton Military Academy in Virginia. He was graduated from there and entered the University of Arizona, where he was still largely indifferent to classes. He finally quit after his freshman year to work in the Goldwater department store in Phoenix, turning into an ingenious merchandiser who developed desert fashions. One celebrated item designed by him was men's underwear printed with red ants. He referred to them as "antsy pants" and they achieved a measure of national fame when he advertised them in *The New Yorker.*

He developed a reputation among his associates for his ability to think up something the other merchants didn't have. Not all his ideas paid off. One that went sour was the stocking of fine china with Indian motifs made expressly for his store. Hoyt Pinaire, treasurer of the Goldwater stores, said the venture "cost us a young fortune." But the main thrust of the Goldwater business and investments was upward. The single store in downtown Phoenix did about $700,000 annual business when Barry went to work as a sales clerk at the age of twenty. In twelve years, it reached $1,000,000 a year and by 1952 the business (then a chain) amounted to more than $2,000,000 a year. Today, the Goldwater stores do an annual business of nearly $10,000,000.

The store in which Goldwater began his business career was eventually closed. In its place today there is a chain, consisting of a women's specialty and gift shop in a Phoenix shopping center, a men's shop in the same center, a women's specialty shop in suburban Scottsdale, and a women's shop in Prescott. In 1962, the business, of which Goldwater had become president and general manager in 1936, was sold to the Associated Dry Goods Corporation of New York. The deal brought the Goldwater family—Barry, his mother, his brother and his sister—$2,200,000 in Associated stock, and Associated assumed $2,000,000 in debts on the Goldwaters' books.

In 1964, Walter Bimson, chairman of the board of the National Bank of Phoenix, which held in a trust fund most of the Senator's financial assets, described Goldwater's holdings as those of a modest millionaire—with assets worth $1,700,000, mainly in stocks. In 1963, Goldwater said his annual income was about $65,000.

In 1934, Goldwater married Margaret Johnson of Muncie, Indiana, the wealthy daughter of R. P. Johnson, a founder of the Borg-Warner Corporation. A rival suitor for Margaret's hand was G. Mennen Williams, who later became the Democratic Governor of Michigan and Assistant Secretary of State for African Affairs. The Goldwaters have four children—Joanne, married to Dr. Thomas Ross of Torrance, California; Barry Jr. of Los Angeles; Michael of Phoenix, and Peggy, who married Richard Arlen Holt of Los Angeles as her father was driving toward the 1964 nomination.

It was Mrs. Goldwater who, years later, described how her husband had given so much of himself to the Goldwater business that he worked himself into two "nervous breakdowns"—a phrase she later said might have been inaccurate. An article in *Good Housekeeping* told of the two episodes: "One crisis occurred in 1937 when, after a period of intense work in the store, Barry suffered a nervous breakdown. After a lengthy rest, he went back to work. But two years later, when he went to Prescott, Arizona, to help open a new branch of the store, and spent five days and nights without sleep, he cracked again. 'His nerves broke completely,' says Mrs. Goldwater. 'He couldn't sleep nights. He was very nervous. I immediately said we were going to get away to Honolulu. He was seasick all the way. But then he relaxed on the beach and just rested.' The change of pace was, apparently, all he needed."

Mrs. Goldwater said in another interview: "I think possibly my choice of words was wrong. He has never had a nervous breakdown." She described his having worked overtime in the Prescott store and added that when he returned to Phoenix, "it was just complete exhaustion from overworking." She said: "And that was all there was to it. And there was certainly never any mental breakdown at all."

However, the Senator joked about the subject during the primary campaigns. He told a New Hampshire storekeeper that taxes and regulations were so annoying that he had had two nervous breakdowns trying to run a department store. On another occasion, he said that politics was an easier life than business, adding with a smile, "I had two nervous breakdowns running a business." Within a few weeks, Goldwater was describing the incidents as cases of exhaustion or collapse brought on by worry or overwork. His friends tended to minimize the difficulties, saying that he was merely "all tired out" because of business pressure.

Throughout the Presidential campaign, he exuded an aura of vigorous good health seen usually in considerably younger men. Six feet tall and weighing a firm 185 to 190 pounds, he kept in trim with such activities as swimming, golfing and hiking. Even during the hectic, tiring hours of the campaign, his health remained excellent. He underwent minor surgery to remove a bone spur from his right foot shortly before formally entering the Presidential race. Prior to that he had been treated by John F. Kennedy's physician, Dr. Janet Travell, for pains in the back; it "worked out very well; it was never a major problem," she said.

Goldwater does not smoke, drink coffee and rarely touches bread, potatoes or dessert. His menus usually include such high-protein, low-calorie dishes as steak and broiled lamb chops. His favorite alcoholic beverages are beer, bourbon with water and dry martinis.

A devoted ham radio operator, he has elaborate equipment in his Phoenix home, his Washington apartment and his sports car. Ham operators have become accustomed to hearing his voice: "The handle here is Barry—Baker, Adam, Roger, Roger, Yankee—it sure is a pleasure to work you." He developed so many contacts that he had one secretary in his Senate office doing nothing but sending out "QSL" postcards, used by hams to confirm radio contact.

Goldwater learned to fly an airplane as a young man, getting his pilot's license when he was twenty-one years old. Nothing relaxes him more than to be at the controls of his own Beechcraft Bonanza twin-engine plane. Despite problems of age and poor eyesight, he turned this hobby into a wartime occupation, successfully pressing Senators Carl Hayden and Ernest McFarland of Arizona into helping him wangle his way to active duty and flight status in the Army Air Corps in World War II. He did not see combat but ferried bombers and fighters to India. After the war, he helped form the Arizona Air National Guard—which he maintains he also helped desegregate —and remained an enthusiastic member of the Air Force Reserve, with the rank of major general, commanding a special squadron made up of Congressmen and their administrative assistants.

Goldwater is an expert mechanic. At his home in Phoenix he designed a flagpole that automatically raises Old Glory when the dawn's early light strikes a photoelectric cell, but he has had difficulty keeping it in working order. He also is an unusually gifted amateur photographer and has accumulated a massive library emphasizing Arizona and Western history. He is a member of the "Smoki," a group of Arizona white men who have learned authentic Indian snake dances and who put on a ceremonial performance in full Indian garb and war paint every year for the benefit of the Indian museum at Prescott. On the heel of his left hand Goldwater has four tattoo marks symbolizing his participation in the dances. He is reportedly known among Indians as "Barry One Salt," "Curley Head" and "Barry Sundust."

Like his brother and sister, Goldwater is devoted to practical jokes. At one time, one of them received a cake for a birthday and, instead of eating it, put it in the freezer and then ceremoniously delivered it back when the next birthday of a member of the family came around. The cake was transferred back and forth for several months in this way. Goldwater likes to lie on the bottom of his swimming pool, held down by weights and breathing air from a compressor through a rubber pipe. He once told some photographers that he sometimes stayed down for hours, but they never did find out whether he was joking. On another occasion, Goldwater and a friend, a dentist, during one convivial evening, got the idea of pulling a tooth and replacing it with a gold one in the mouth of Goldwater's bulldog, Cyclone. The story may be apocryphal, but Cyclone does have a gold tooth.

After the war, spurred on by business associates who urged him to turn his incessant talk of politics into action, Goldwater teamed up with Harry Rosenzweig and others to organize the bipartisan Phoenix Charter Government Committee. In the elections of 1949, the group ousted the city administration, and Goldwater led the ticket in the City Council races. Although active in the bipartisan committee, Goldwater was definitely a Republican, having decided at the age of twenty-one to so register, despite the state's Democratic complexion and his close ties to Uncle Morris.

Looking to the 1950 elections, Goldwater and another Republican, Howard Pyle, a well-known radio commentator, developed a plan to challenge the Democrats in Arizona. Goldwater was to run for Governor in 1950, with Pyle's support, and then in 1952, Goldwater would help his friend win election to the United States Senate. However, the radio announcer made such an impressive, impassioned speech before a group of Young Republicans early in 1950 that the group endorsed him for Governor. Goldwater joined in and managed the successful Pyle campaign, logging more than 50,000 miles in his private plane as he visited every part of the state.

Enjoying the taste of the competition, Goldwater decided to run for the Senate in 1952 against McFarland, a moderately conservative Democrat. Mc-Farland was a dull campaigner and Goldwater struck hard. His first problem came in a question at his first rally, "What kind of a Republican are you?" The answer that followed set the tone for the years ahead: "Well, I am not a me-too Republican . . . I am a Republican opposed to the superstate and to gigantic, bureaucratic, centralized authority." He won with 51.3 per cent of the vote, but gave the credit to Eisenhower, who swept into the Presidency with many Republicans riding his coattails. In 1958, he won again (with 56.1 per cent)—and again over McFarland, who had made a comeback by defeating Pyle for the governorship in 1954 and winning re-election in 1956.

Despite the ride on Eisenhower's coattails, Goldwater, once in office, showed himself to be a maverick and a conservative just as knife-tongued against Eisenhower's accommodations to liberalism as against the Democratic enemy. Such phrases as "dime-store New Deal" and "one Eisenhower in a generation is enough" were never forgotten by the General. But Goldwater seemed unperturbed as he rode Western-style over many of the Senatorial and Washingtonian don'ts. He had listeners for his criticisms of "big government," coexistence and high spending, and they loved his hell-for-leather way of stating them. In his role as chairman of the Republican Senatorial Campaign Committee he became one of the best-known Republicans among state and county chairmen and party contributors. He estimates that the fund-raising dinners he addressed before his entry into the Presidential race raised $6,000,000 for the party. Tom Wicker described Goldwater's effect on people as follows:

Handsome, informal, friendly, a man without pomp, Barry Goldwater earned the instant liking—even adulation—of men already favorably disposed to his way of thinking. To the inhabitants of small-town America, he seemed like a man who was "one of us."

But in Senate work itself, Goldwater's career was not marked by legislative accomplishment, for real success in the intricate work of the Senate depends on compromise. "Barry doesn't know what compromise means," according to one colleague. His career was notable for the raising of a strong voice of dissent. When his fellow Republicans united in party opposition to the Democrats, he almost always was with them. When his fellow Republicans united with the Democrats on major issues such as the civil rights bill, the tax cut and the nuclear test ban treaty, he left the party. Charles Mohr of The Times observed:

Mr. Goldwater made his reputation on the very fact that, in more than eleven years of service in the Senate, he showed a total disregard for the political "don'ts" of those who aspire to the White House. He traveled around the country saying exactly what he liked, with total disregard for those he might offend. By so doing, he captured the hearts of conservatives as a "man of courage and principle."

The very innermost circle of his advisors were his old Arizona friends. The hard core was motivated as much by friendship and respect for Goldwater as from conservative political convictions. Others were more professional and saw the candidate as the means to an end, the chance to translate right-wing beliefs into action nationally. Some had been associated with Republican party politics and rightist causes for years. The men around Goldwater when he began his drive for the nomination were for the most part the amateurs and the unknowns. After success at San Francisco, those same men, with a few additions, ran the Goldwater campaign and Republican national politics, for the most part ignoring the regular professional Republican politicians and those who had directed previous Republican campaigns. Charles Mohr wrote in The Times about this inner group and its relationship with the candidate:

To the Arizonan, friendship is a powerful consideration and he will work neither closely nor well with men unless he can relax with them. Being an adviser to this candidate can be difficult. Goldwater is courteous and receptive to ideas, but he can be stubborn. For weeks his staff could not even get him to have his speeches typed in large, easy-to-read print.

So rather than attempting to change his philosophy and style, Goldwater's advisers have adapted themselves to his views. Much of their energy goes to polishing his instinctive and extemporaneous conservative expressions and to the basic rudiments of political action—precinct work. And they struggle with an extreme individualist who sometimes wants to avoid crowds. . . .

Developed and toughened in preconvention battles, the Goldwater amateurs are probably the most disciplined group in either party in recent history. Now they bring the principles of good communications, firm discipline and detailed planning to a national Presidential campaign.

The man nearest the center of the "Arizona Mafia" was Denison Kitchel, a fifty-six-year-old Phoenix corporation lawyer. He was policy adviser, traveling companion and closest confidant of Goldwater, not so much a dedicated conservative as a dedicated friend of the Senator. It was doubtful that he would have displayed much interest in national politics if Goldwater had not been the candidate. They respected each other so much that Goldwater usually would listen only to Kitchel, while closing his ears to more seasoned professionals. It was Kitchel who was credited with helping to moderate and change the Senator's view that the government should play no role in enforcing the Supreme Court's school desegregation decision. His moderating influence was clearly shown one morning during the California primary when Goldwater was about to chew out a press aide for having made public the ingredients of his breakfast. Kitchel stepped in with the words: "They expect this sort of information, Barry. You're a Presidential candidate now." Another time, Kitchel was heard to say, "Dammit, Barry, you're a national figure," as Goldwater angrily demanded an explanation for the unscheduled appearance of an unusually fervent crowd. Ironically, Kitchel was a product of that Eastern Establishment so distasteful to the Republican candidate. In 1929, he fell in love with the desert country during a visit to a friend's ranch after his junior year at Yale, and after graduation from Harvard Law School ignored his father's admonitions ("What are you going to practice on out there—cows?")

and moved to Arizona. An introverted, quiet man, he developed into one of the region's outstanding lawyers, representing the powerful Phelps Dodge copper mining interests.

Another inside member of the team was Dean Burch, a thirty-seven-year-old Tucson lawyer with no previous background in national politics who looked so young he was sometimes mistaken for an office boy. Handpicked by the Senator to be chairman of the Republican National Committee after the convention, he took firm control and loaded the organization with stanch Goldwater adherents. Burch, who was administrative assistant to the Senator from 1955 until 1959, is genial but tough, a practical man who says he likes to carry out orders and get things done. He, too, was an important adviser on basic policy and seemed more moderate than ultraconservative. Like many other members of Goldwater's inner ring, he is wryly humorous and able to endure with a smile the kind of criticism that would enrage most politicians.

The organizational genius of the primary campaign, who was something of an outsider in the Goldwater circle and not personally close to the Senator, was Clifton White, forty-six, of Rye, New York. As an adviser versed and experienced in national politics, he directed field operations prior to San Francisco, controlled the floor strategy during the convention from a sealed trailer just outside the Cow Palace and, more than any other man, was responsible for the steamroller that drove to the overwhelming first-ballot nomination. A tall, slim man who wears bow ties, he is a master of detail and of disciplined, effective work. White, who became executive director of Citizens for Goldwater-Miller, was sometimes mistaken for a moderate Republican because he had worked for Eisenhower's nomination in 1952 and was director of organization of Citizens for Nixon-Lodge in 1960. But he had also been a political consultant to the Richardson Foundation, Inc., which contributed to right-wing groups and had been a strong supporter of conservative causes. White was known to advocate the destruction of the traditionally heterogeneous party structure, whereby both parties had liberal and conservative elements, in favor of a strong ideological foundation under American politics. "I want to see the Republican party become an instrument of conservatism in national politics," he said.

The liaison man between Goldwater and the Republican moderates was Edward A. McCabe, a forty-seven-year-old Washington lawyer who was once administrative assistant to President Eisenhower. Charles Mohr wrote of him as follows:

Director of research and an important policy adviser to Goldwater since last October, the Irish-born McCabe played a key role in the Senator's decision to seek harmony at the Republican "Unity Conference" at Hershey, Pa., after the convention. During the convention period, McCabe was a major representative in drafting the Republican platform. A persuasive, practical politician (he once handled Congressional liaison for Eisenhower) as well as an idea man, McCabe's important influence on the Goldwater campaign often escapes notice.

McCabe was shy and soft-spoken, a wispy six-footer whom nobody paid much attention to, but he was sometimes able to use his job as director of research for the Republican National Committee to edge the Republican candidate toward more moderate positions, hopefully to win back some of the frightened liberals and moderates.

The importance of the Southern campaign to the Goldwater forces gave extra stature to John E. Grenier, a thirty-three-year-old Birmingham lawyer who became executive director of the Republican National Committee. The emergence of a strong, militantly conservative, "lily-white" Republican party in the South was, in large measure, his work. He denied that he was a segregationist, but he opposed integration of rural schools in the South for the near future because it "will ruin the school system in rural areas." He was accused of manipulating the race issue to build a powerful Republican organization by attracting segregationist Democrats into his party. Grenier, regarded by some as an utterly ruthless man in politics, viewed Goldwater as "the catalyst of a new political system in the South." He carried out aggressive campaigns in Alabama, driving out the lethargic "post-office Republicans" who were once in control. His candidate Jim Martin, nearly defeated veteran Senator Lister Hill in 1962.

Another cog in the Goldwater machine was also a man with strong regional ties—Wayne J. Hood of La Crosse, Wisconsin, executive vice president of the Trane Company, and a long-time Republican politician who made something of a comeback in 1964 as director of field organization for the Goldwater campaign. Charles Mohr wrote of him:

In the late nineteen forties and early fifties, during part of which he served as chairman of the Wisconsin Republican party and executive director of the National Committee, Hood, a stanch conservative, was a close friend and supporter of the late Senator Joseph R. McCarthy. When the McCarthy era ended, Hood retired from active politics, returning this year as pre-convention Midwestern director for Senator Goldwater. Most Republicans know little about Hood and he likes it that way, for he prefers anonymity.

The lanky, white-haired, fifty-one-year-old business executive was motivated in Goldwater's behalf by the feeling that "too many party candidates have reflected the Eastern Establishment." He said, "The Midwest is sick of supporting your big cities in the East."

One of Goldwater's principal advisers was William J. Baroody, a personal friend, who in 1962 became president of the American Enterprise Institute for Public Policy Research, an organization dedicated to combat socialism by educational means. A behind the scenes adviser for years, Baroody had ready access to Goldwater's strictly guarded fifteenth floor headquarters at the Mark Hopkins in San Francisco and was one of those who worked with McCabe on platform matters and on the acceptance speech. A forty-eight-year-old New Hampshire native, Baroody talked the down to earth language that Goldwater understood, even though the message he brought was the same as the right-wing intellectuals'.

One of Baroody's associates who worked his way into the inside as sort of an adopted member of the inner circle was Karl Hess, a forty-one-year-old right-wing intellectual and writer. He joined the Goldwater group in March of 1964, virtually new to politics himself, but with a relaxed manner and ribald sense of humor that quickly won him a favored place among the Senator's adviser-friends, but who alienated many of the Republican regulars. Most of the major speeches delivered by Goldwater came from the typewriter of Hess, a round, cheerful man described as "Buddha-like" (Goldwater called him "the Brain"). Hess was a dedicated right-wing ideologue, even more conservative than the Senator. He was a leading contributor to *National Review, The American Mercury, Counterattack* and other arch-conservative publications and a consultant to a number of conservative foundations. Hess's close relationship to Goldwater could be seen in many of the candidate's most popular or most controversial remarks. The increased emphasis on nuclear preparedness, just before and just after the convention, came from Hess, for the most part. Goldwater's controversial acceptance speech—"extremism in the defense of liberty is no vice"—bore the Hess trademark, although it was also attributed to Professor Harry Jaffa, formerly of Ohio State University and now at Claremont Men's College in California. Hess refused to identify the author, insisting it was a joint effort. He, at least, typed out the draft manuscript on green paper.

Another man with a history of close relations with Goldwater—at least for a time—was fifty-five-year-old Stephen Shadegg. Once ranked as the closest of all associates and the most important of all advisers, he fell out of that high position when he ignored the Senator's wishes and ran unsuccessfully in a Republican Senatorial primary in Arizona. The case typified Goldwater's sensitivity to anything that might be regarded as disloyalty, for unquestioned fidelity rated far higher in his eyes than political astuteness. It is also thought that Goldwater did not want to be involved, through Shadegg, in a bitter factional fight in the Arizona Republican party over which he held benevolent and undisputed sway. If it had not been for their quarrel in 1962 Shadegg would undoubtedly have been named Goldwater's national campaign manager in the Presidential race. As it was, he was given no job when the campaign began in January. Gradually, he did enter the lists as a liaison man in the Oregon primary and finally as a field worker in the Western states. He came under attack for a controversial book entitled *How to Win Elections*, in which he said he had adopted some of the techniques of Mao Tse-tung while managing Senate campaigns in Arizona for Goldwater. The Senator never gave any sign that he personally disapproved of the book. He and Shadegg effected a partial rapprochement and the aide took over the general campaign in the Western states.

Charles Mohr of The Times, who covered the Goldwater campaign from beginning to the end, described Goldwater and his staff as usually pleasant company. "They are not right-wing ogres," he said. "And they show more intellectual tolerance than any men in politics that I have ever met. They can be joked with and joked about without losing their tempers."

However, to professional Republican politicians and those who had worked on previous campaigns, Goldwater's men seemed a bunch of amateurs, running an amateurish campaign despite their successes in the primaries.

9

William Edward Miller: "He Drives Johnson Nuts"

To the general astonishment of the American people, if not himself, William Edward Miller, a short, dark, intense, sharp-tongued fifty-year-old lawyer from Lockport, New York, became the Republican party's nominee for Vice President of the United States. Rarely in the modern Presidential era had a practicing politician so little known to the great mass of voters emerged so suddenly from the wings into the spotlight of national and international prominence.

For a broadly orthodox Republican, Miller achieved the signal honor of national candidacy in about the most unorthodox manner possible. He had, in fact, by his 1964 success—nomination, if not election—blazed a new if narrow trail through the wilderness of national politics, establishing a hitherto unexplored route for party advancement. Most politicians who achieve national prominence begin with strong local support and then move through increasing positions of power and responsibility in their party's state organization, ultimately arriving at its national councils.

From early in his career, however, Miller ignored this traditional approach, paying diminishing attention to his district and shunning any role in the New York State Republican organization in favor of a frontal assault on national politics. As a freshman and sophomore Congressman, Miller clashed directly with Governor Thomas E. Dewey over one of the most critical state issues of the early nineteen fifties: Public versus private development of power. In 1959, when Rockefeller was seriously weighing a campaign for the Republican Presidential nomination and relying on the solid loyalty of his state organization, Miller dealt him a stinging snub by publicly endorsing Vice President Nixon.

Thus at almost continuous odds with Republican leaders in his home state, the young Representative found other party figures to cultivate, men like Nixon, Representative Charles A. Halleck of Indiana and Senator Goldwater. These men could not help Miller advance his political career through the conventional channels of running for the Senate or for Governor at home. But they could be exceedingly helpful along the unusual path he chose: Advancing through the administrative apparatus of the party. In 1959 Miller was in the forefront of the group of House Republicans that deposed former Speaker Joseph W. Martin Jr. as minority leader and elevated Halleck in his place. A year later, the chairmanship of the Republican Congressional Campaign Committee opened up. The Halleck forces put forward the name of Miller, while Speaker Martin and his allies favored the veteran Ohioan, Representative William M. McCulloch.

As party leader, Halleck was officially neutral, but his supporters pressed the fight. McCulloch ultimately withdrew, charging that "a great deal of pressure has been put on many of my friends and on the members of this committee and on other members of the House to throw their support to other persons." A key figure in rounding up Miller support for the campaign spot was Vice President Nixon, by this time virtually assured of winning the Republican Presidential nomination later in the year and, accordingly, a formidable ally.

With Miller at the campaign helm, Republican House candidates in 1960 gained a net of twenty-one seats. This was considered a remarkable achievement in a Presidential year in which the party lost the national election. It was this campaign that first brought Miller into close personal contact with Goldwater, then his opposite number as the chairman of the Senate Campaign Committee. "The morning after I was elected campaign chairman," Miller has said, "Barry called me up and said we should get together. We had breakfast at the Congressional Hotel, and from then on we saw quite a bit of each other."

Only eighteen months later in 1961, Senator Morton of Kentucky, facing a taxing re-election campaign, resigned as Republican National Chairman. Miller's record with the Congressional committee automatically put him high on the list of potential successors. With the 1964 Presidential election on the horizon, a party chairman acceptable to the potential candidates was essential. Goldwater's approval of Miller was clear, based on their campaign association and a growing identity of political views. The other leading candidate, Rockefeller, cleared Miller for the post despite their past differences. The Governor reportedly concluded that a conservative from New York was better than a conservative from the Middle West or elsewhere.

As national chairman, Miller became known for his caustic tongue and a dedication to conservatism. Many Republicans called him "a gut fighter," a term of approbation from political friends and of both scorn and admiration from enemies. The day after Miller became Republican National Chairman, he turned his sharp tongue on President Kennedy, who was meeting Premier Khrushchev in Vienna. "I can only hope and pray," Miller said, "that it wasn't to negotiate some under-the-table deal in order to increase his prestige, which was lowered as a result of the Cuban incident." He once labeled former President Truman a "hatchet man" and on another occasion accused Kennedy of putting on "a smoothly rehearsed crybaby performance" over the defeat in the Senate of the Administration's bill on medical care for the aged.

One of the jobs of the party's national chairman is to needle the opposition party, often with a sharper point and deeper thrust than elective candidates find it prudent to use. Miller carried out the assignment with relish. He once remarked that the Democrats had improved two businesses, anyway, "the seat belt business in Texas and the paint business in Washington to white-wash investigations." This was a gibe at President Johnson's driving and what Miller tartly described as a whitewash of the investigation of Bobby Baker.

The giant step from national chairman to national candidate was the longest for Miller. National chairmen of both parties traditionally—almost inescapably—make the nasty charges so that the candidates can avoid them. They do so because they are never national candidates themselves, never intend to be and thus don't have to worry about personal popularity. Consider the Republican National Chairmen who preceded Morton for the previous dozen years: Carroll E. Reese, Hugh Scott, Guy George Gabrielson, Arthur E. Summerfield, Wesley Roberts, Leonard W. Hall, Meade Alcorn—some artful and canny politicians but not a national candidate among them. How did Miller make the remarkable jump across the political chess board from the national chairmanship to the Vice Presidential nomination? After his selection in July, 1964, his critics in both parties freely intimated that there was a deal: Miller helped win the nomination for Goldwater in return for second place on the ticket.

The bulk of the best evidence runs against this conspiratorial theory. Those closest to Goldwater—including Miller himself—were convinced until shortly before the convention that Scranton would emerge as the Vice Presidential candidate. "I didn't know if Scranton would go for it," a leading pro-Miller Republican said, "but it simply made the most sense. I wasn't sure Barry would buy it—he's an odd duck, too, you know—but it was definitely in the cards."

If Miller ran the national committee in furtherance of the Goldwater cause, most political observers agree, he did it so adroitly and imperceptibly as to qualify for his master politician's rating on the spot. Miller was keenly aware of the perils of partisanship in the pre-convention days and freely admonished his critics. "There's no way I can avoid charges of partisanship unless I go into hibernation," he said in October, 1962. "If I say I think Goldwater is ahead at this time, they say I'm pro-Goldwater. If I say Goldwater doesn't have the nomination locked up yet, they say I'm anti-Goldwater."

For a long time there was grumbling from the Rockefeller forces that primary information they provided the national committee as a courtesy somehow wound up in Goldwater headquarters. There were also reports that Miller shared the congratulations from party leaders the day after Goldwater's nomination. But there was no evidence Goldwater had any firm arrangement with Miller, either personally or through intermediaries, until a few days before the formal selection of the G.O.P. Vice Presidential candidate.

That did not mean that the Niagara County Representative had not viewed the prospect of second place on the national ticket with interest for some time. In 1960, when Nixon's running mate was still very much in doubt, Republicans in Miller's home town of Lockport turned out 1,000 strong for a dance in his honor and climaxed it by unveiling an eighty-foot banner reading "Miller for Vice President." In 1963, long before Goldwater's nomination was in any way assured, a far-sighted reporter quoted a "high Republican official" as listing three potential Goldwater running mates: Scranton, Representative Gerald Ford of Michigan and Miller. The "official" was Miller.

The New Yorker had been approached tentatively by Goldwater agents in late June and early July, but his name began to figure importantly in the speculation regarding a Goldwater running mate only after Scranton, who was generally believed to be Goldwater's first choice, had become the focus of the stop-Goldwater efforts. In June, several California Congressmen adopted a resolution proposing Miller for the Vice Presidential nomination. While he was flattered, Miller scoffed at the idea, privately and publicly and perhaps a shade too loudly, until a week before the convention, when mutual friends confided that Goldwater had said, in effect, "Bill Miller is the man."

Scranton's attacks on Goldwater, a poll of Republican Congressmen, and a series of related events were involved in the Goldwater decision. The poll was in the June 18 issue of *Roll Call*, a weekly newspaper for Congressmen and Capitol Hill employes. It showed that Miller was preferred two to one over Scranton by eighty-six Republican Senators and Representatives answering a questionnaire. As Scranton stepped up his attacks on Goldwater, individual national committee members wrote or telephoned the Senator urging him to consider Miller. Two weeks before the convention, Governor Tim M. Babcock of Montana issued a statement to that effect. The Utah delegation passed a resolution endorsing a Goldwater-Miller ticket. So did several Southern delegations.

On the Monday that the Republican National Convention opened, "Miller for Vice President" buttons and posters began to appear in San Francisco. The next day, Representative John R. Pillon of New York opened a campaign headquarters to promote Miller. And a committee of twenty Congressmen called a news conference to announce a "grass-roots demand from delegates across the country" that Miller be nominated for Vice President.

Miller, himself, was delighted but still mildly skeptical. No one had told him anything officially. And when the word came to him, it came by inadvertence, from Richard Kleindienst, the co-director of Goldwater's campaign operations. Kleindienst sought out Miller to suggest that he invite Governor Paul Fannin of Arizona to make one of the seconding speeches for Miller's nomination for the Vice Presidential candidacy. "Tell Barry that is a must," Miller answered deadpan to the implied news of his selection. But it was not until July 15, the Wednesday of convention week, the day before the balloting for President was to begin, that he heard from the Senator in person.

Goldwater telephoned Miller in his hotel suite and said: "Bill, I'm going to be walking down a long, lonely road. I wondered if you'd like to come along?" Miller said yes, Goldwater said thanks, and that was it. Actually, it was not until a meeting of Republican state chairmen the following morning that Miller heard the Senator flatly say that he was to be the Vice Presidential nominee. At the same meeting, Goldwater said that "one reason I chose Miller is that he drives Johnson nuts."

Months later Goldwater told a group of Republican leaders that many people had asked him why he picked Miller. "This was not, as you might say, a ouija board job," he replied, "it wasn't something done overnight." All during the primaries when he was wondering whether he himself was going to get the nomination, Goldwater went on, he turned people over in his mind. He didn't say precisely when he did make up his mind—although some believe that it was when Scranton, the natural choice for Vice President, sent his challenging letter to Goldwater on the eve of the convention. But he did go on to make the following explanation of why Miller was picked:

"I have worked with Bill Miller for the last eight years in this Republican effort of raising money, promoting candidates, getting candidates across the country. Bill is a tough fighter, not that we are going to wage that kind of campaign, but we can expect from the opposition certainly a lot of it. And I wanted a man with me who could return the fire, so to speak. He is very experienced in Congressional matters. He is a lawyer, which offsets my lack of legal training. He has a very, very charming wife and family. And, too, he comes from New York and I come from the Far West. I still believe that this geographic balance is a good one. If you have an Easterner, you must have a Westerner, and vice versa. And I think this solves that problem."

Goldwater's explanation left out one salient fact: Miller was a Roman Catholic and the Republicans hoped by putting a Catholic on the ticket to regain some of the votes lost when Kennedy defeated Nixon in 1960.

If one thing was clear from Miller's record in Congress, it was that his attraction to government had never been as compelling by half as his attraction to politics. Although he held public office almost continuously since his graduation from law school, with the exception of Army duty, he never really seemed to enjoy it; he was more interested in the visceral aspects of successful precinct politics than the philosophical concerns of government or the moral niceties of public responsibility.

His career in Congress, in fact, had been regularly punctuated by a series of decisions to resign, all later reconsidered. When a vacancy opened in his Congressional district in 1950, he first said he wasn't interested, then moved for the Republican nomination. In 1953, he said flatly he would not run again because he was sick and tired of continuous exposure to Capitol Hill pressure groups. In 1957, he said he was considering retiring because he was homesick for the practice of law. Again in 1959, he considered leaving the House but stayed. After his 1961 election as national chairman, he said he might give up his seat in Congress if he couldn't handle both jobs. In 1962, he decided he could. Finally, in May of 1963, after barely surviving the previous fall's election, he made firm and final his political retirement—only to relent in favor of the Vice Presidential nomination.

While his political achievements were considerable, Miller's legislative record had shown a discernible lack of enthusiasm. He himself lists only two major bills for his fourteen-year career in the House: The Niagara power compromise and authorization of a new Lake Erie-Lake Ontario canal east of the Niagara River. The tide of seniority raised Miller to second-ranking Republican in the House Judiciary Committee, but he played little part in the committee's deliberations and rarely sponsored any of its important products. In his years in the House, Miller compiled a voting record that was firmly conservative but still measurably to the left of his running mate. For example, he consistently voted for foreign aid bills, which Goldwater always opposed. Miller supported President Kennedy's trade bill in 1962, the income tax cut in 1963 and the 1964 civil rights bill. Goldwater opposed all of them. By and large, however, the voting profiles of the two Republican national candidates were fairly similar. Miller's attendance record in Congress, measured by the frequency with which he answered roll-call votes, was undistinguished. From 1951 through 1962 he was recorded on 75 per cent of the roll calls, compared to 87 per cent for the average House member. In 1963, as Republican National Chairman in a pre-convention year, his average dropped to 49 per cent, the second worst record in the House.

Chief among the Congressional issues that Miller contemplated was this question: Should New York State's untapped hydroelectric power be developed by a public agency or by private utilities? Through most of the nineteen fifties this issue produced sharp struggles both between the major parties and within Republican ranks. Of all his Congressional activities, Miller is best remembered for the role he played in this conflict and its ultimate resolution. In the first instance, he sponsored with Senator Homer E. Capehart of Indiana a bill that would have authorized five private New York State utilities to develop unused power at Niagara Falls and sell it to their customers all across the state. In the summer of 1953, the Capehart-Miller bill was approved by the House after a move to authorize state development had been crushed. Only a dramatic personal appearance by New York's Governor Thomas E. Dewey on Capitol Hill blocked final passage by the Senate.

Then public opinion began to shift. By 1956 Senator Herbert H. Lehman, a Democrat, won approval in the Senate of his bill to assign Niagara power development to the New York State Power Authority, a public agency. This Senate bill came before the House Rules Committee, which was tightly controlled by a coalition of Southern Democrats and conservative Republicans. Without this committee's approval, no bill could reach the floor. At the same time, the Eisenhower Administration was pushing a civil rights bill. Originating in the House Judiciary Committee, it was co-sponsored by Miller and included some amendments he had proposed in committee. He voted for it in subcommittee and signed the report that sent the bill to the floor. But when the civil rights measure came up for debate, Miller moved to recommit it or kill it, to the shocked surprise of his colleagues—or most of them. His motion was defeated but the bill never recovered, and neither did the Republicans who saw his move as an act of political treachery.

The Niagara power bill Miller opposed never emerged from the Rules Committee. Its chairman, Representative Howard W. Smith of Virginia, was one of the House's most adamant opponents of civil rights legislation. Miller insisted that the common fate of the two pieces of 1956 legislation was co-incidental and that his opposition to the rights bill was legal rather than philosophical. At the time, he called the measure "a legal monstrosity I could not accept as a lawyer." In all other instances, Miller voted for major civil rights legislation before the House, including the bills of 1957, 1960 and 1964. The Representative's protests that no deal was involved in bottling up the public power measure were not entirely successful. A *Buffalo Evening News* reporter in a 1957 interview touching on the issue wrote, "Always a realist in politics, Miller says it would be useless to explain that no 'deal' was involved."

The Niagara Mohawk Power Corporation, largest of the upstate utilities, dropped its opposition to government generation of power at Niagara Falls in 1957 when a landslide destroyed its existing plant there. A compromise plan was reached under which the State Power Authority would generate the bulk of the power and sell it to the private utilities at Nigara Falls. Then the utilities would distribute and sell it. Miller backed this bill, which was enacted in 1957.

The Representative recalled—accurately by the accounts of impartial neighbors—that his position for private power was the popular one in his district and throughout western New York at the time. The advent of public power, it was feared, would increase local taxes by taking utility property off the rolls and endanger the bargaining rights of utility workers, who would then become government employees. "Why, even the State Federation of Labor was with me on that one," Miller said, with the incredulity of a politician who has rarely found himself in such company.

How close had Miller been to the power company? His Democratic opponent in 1962, E. Dent Lackey, now the Mayor of Niagara Falls, believed he was very close indeed. "Miller espoused the point of view of Niagara Mohawk and the public utilities consistently and without exception," Lackey said recently. "He followed the public utility line and not his own party line during his terms in Congress. Niagara Mohawk supported him in his election contests. Generally the people of this district think of Mr. Miller as the voice of Niagara Mohawk in western New York. His relations with Niagara Mohawk were most intimate."

There was no record of any financial contribution by Niagara Mohawk to Miller's political campaigns. Miller contended that neither he nor his law firm had ever been employed by Niagara Mohawk. The same went for two other corporations in his district with which he had close personal associations: the Wurlitzer Company and the Bell Aerospace Corporation, formerly Bell Aircraft. Not all of Miller's political opponents faulted him for his adherence to the cause of private power at Niagara Falls. "I think you have to admit," one area Democratic leader said, "that his position was one any Representative from his district would have taken. Besides, if you're going to start closing in on every politician who's worked with the power lobby, the floor is going to be covered with heads."

The Republican Vice Presidential candidate was born March 22, 1914 in Lockport, a city of 18,000 on the western end of the Erie Canal to which remarkably little has happened in the last fifty years. The town was about as different from the urban, industrial centers of the East as a farm village in Kansas. His father was a janitor at the Harrison Radiator Company, now a division of General Motors. His mother ran a millinery store with her sister. He was an only child. Both his parents were Democrats at one time, "but they saw the light long before they died," according to Miller. He added, "I am sure for that reason they are in heaven."

By the seventh grade he had decided to become a lawyer. At Notre Dame, he majored in economics and was remembered by the class of 1935 as a crack debater and the school pocket billiards champion. At Albany Law School he was in the upper half of his class of 1938 and won the mock trial competition. A professor recalled that he could have been at the top of his class if he had spent more time on his books and less on poker and pool. "The only time he ever went into the library was to borrow money," a classmate said.

Back in Lockport as a member of the bar in 1938, Miller got his first political job almost at once. The senior Federal judge in the district, a Republican, appointed him a United States Commissioner, a sort of justice of the peace to arraign and set bail for Federal offenders. As he remembers it, the young lawyer earned about $220 in fees, the only compensation for the job, during the four years he held it. From his earliest days, Miller had excellent political sponsorship in Niagara County Republican circles. One of his closest friends from boyhood was Raymond J. Lee, now president of the Lockport Felt Company and a member of the State Athletic Commission by appointment of Governor Rockefeller. Lee's father, former State Senator William Lee, and Supreme Court Justice William A. Gold, the Senator's brother-in-law, were Republican leaders in Niagara County in those days, and they took the ambitious young lawyer under their joint wing.

In 1942 Miller became engaged to Stephanie Wagner, a striking brunette whom he had met when she was a witness in one of his early cases and courted assiduously while she was completing high school. They were married in 1943 after he had entered the Army. There are four Miller children: Elizabeth Ann, known as Libby, twenty at the time of the campaign; Mary Karen, seventeen; William E. Jr., five and Stephanie, two and a half.

Miller spent most of his Army service as an enlisted man in the United

States. After three years in military intelligence in Richmond, Virginia, he was selected in 1945 for Judge Advocate General's officer training and commissioned a first lieutenant. Assigned to the war crimes office in Washington, he was sent to Nuremberg for four months in the fall of 1945. His official biography reported, "In August, 1945, Miller was named an assistant prosecutor to the late Supreme Court justice, Robert A. Jackson, and played a major role in the prosecution of Nazi war criminals during the famous trials at Nuremberg, Germany." But Senator Thomas J. Dodd, Democrat of Connecticut, who served as a staff aide during the trials, denies that Miller participated in courtroom work. He said: "I knew every assistant prosecutor; there were only a few of them, and Bill Miller was not one. I'm sure of this because it was my job to plan with Justice Jackson who was to do what at which trials. Miller was over there only a short time and, I believe, had something to do with documentation of evidence." A military service report issued by the Pentagon states that William Edward Miller served with the War Crimes Office in Europe four months, from August 31, 1945, to December 29, 1945. This indicates he was there only one and a half months during the court proceedings, since the trials began November 14, 1945.

Lieutenant Miller returned to the United States at the end of 1945, was discharged the following February and resumed his Lockport law practice. Almost immediately, a vacancy opened up for an assistant district attorney in Niagara County. Miller's friends in the local Republican leadership put him up for the job, and the party executive committee voted him in. In 1948 the district attorney moved up to county judge, and Governor Dewey named Miller district attorney. That fall he was elected to a full term in the then solidly Republican county.

In Miller's two years as county prosecutor, the outstanding event was the four-month strike of the United Automobile Workers against the Bell Aircraft Corporation in 1959 and the major controversy was the role he played in that long, bitter and unruly strike. At one point, the strikers marched into the plant for what they called a "tour of inspection" but which management considered an invasion. District Attorney Miller flew into the struck plant—in a Bell helicopter—and talked with the non-striking workers. He asserted later that his only purpose was to take affidavits from those who had been injured during the "tour of inspection," but while he was there, he made a controversial speech.

"I told them I would do my level best to see they were protected," he explained afterwards. "Their morale was low. They were afraid of reprisals from the strikers. I urged them to avoid violence. I told them I couldn't be on their side if they were guilty of violence too."

The union considered the district attorney's acts in the plant a hostile intrusion into a labor-management controversy by a public official who should have been neutral. Labor criticism was scarcely stilled when Miller prosecuted twenty-three of the strikers for riot and conspiracy. All the criminal convictions he obtained were reversed by higher courts. The Court

Top:
"The dream of equal rights for all Americans, whatever
their race or color." The President signs the 1964 Civil Rights Bill.
(The New York Times photo)

Bottom:
A Harlem protest rally erupted into violence and rioting;
wild disorder spread.... Politically, the riots seemed to be dynamite.
(Associated Press photo)

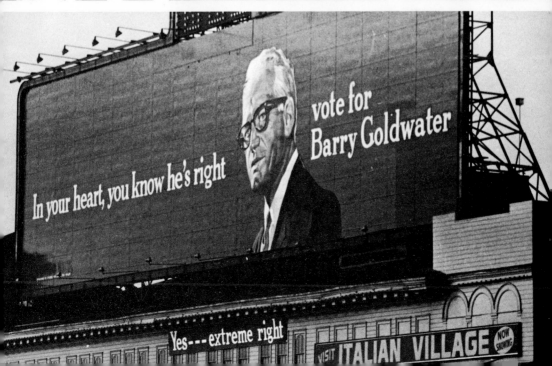

Left:
"When I think of President Kennedy,
I think of those lines from Shakespeare..."
(Associated Press photo)

Right:
"I think in all my life that I have never taken
any decision more seriously than picking Humphrey."
(George Tames, The New York Times)

Top:
The President preparing to address the nation
on the incidents in the Gulf of Tonkin
and the United States' retaliatory air strikes.
August 5, 1964.
(photo by George Tames, The New York Times)

Bottom:
"He may not have the answers..."
(photo by George Tames, The New York Times)

of Appeals specifically criticized the District Attorney for making an improper opening statement at the trial. In the eyes of the union, Miller's action colored all his subsequent political career, including his national candidacy. "At that time," one union leader said, "Miller used the powers of his office to help this private company carry out its program, which was exceedingly anti-labor in character. Nothing he has done since as a Congressman would lead one to conclude he would behave any differently as Vice President. There is every reason to believe he would use the powers of his office in behalf of the big corporations."

That was not the only assessment of Miller's role in the strike. When he was running for Congress in 1950, *The Niagara Falls Gazette* observed editorially that "his independence in thought and action . . . was strikingly illustrated in the Bell strike riot trials, which he prosecuted vigorously, despite strong political pressures." By 1964, however, that same newspaper, the only daily published in the Congressman's home county, found itself unable to support him editorially for the Vice Presidency, despite a measure of pride in the national prominence of a local boy. It was Goldwater that *The Gazette* was primarily unwilling to back.

Miller's career as a prosecutor proved short. In 1950 Representative William L. Pfeiffer decided to retire from Congress to devote himself to the Republican state chairmanship, creating another vacancy. The Niagara Congressional district included all of that county with some Buffalo suburbs in Erie County, which were much smaller in area but almost as large in population. Traditionally, the two counties passed the Congressional nomination back and forth, and in 1950 it was Niagara's turn. Once again Miller's solid position with the county Republican leaders served him well. Despite only two years in public office and no legislative experience, he was chosen for the Congressional nomination. In his first campaign, Miller won handily by 23,000 votes. His margin held steady between 30,000 and 43,000 for ten years. Then in 1960 he sagged to a 19,800 majority, and in 1962 he barely escaped defeat.

Western New York politicians ascribed the drop in Miller's local popularity to three factors: An economic decline in his home county over which he had essentially no control but which tended steadily to increase Democratic power there; a demonstrably diminishing interest by the Congressman in his district, as national political concerns occupied more and more of his time; and Miller's caustic attacks, as national chairman, on President Kennedy, a tactic that found little favor among his many Roman Catholic coreligionists in the district.

At first meeting, Miller suggests speed and intensity. He talks fast, thinks fast, learns fast, reacts fast. Even his friends concede that his sharp tongue would sometimes be better accompanied by a slower mind and more sense of deliberation. "Bill is a likable fellow, but not lovable," one of his oldest home county associates said. "He sometimes speaks too quickly, and people don't forget what he says. I guess you could say he's better at making enemies than friends—he's got plenty of both." His political allies in New York, whose enthusiasm was unwavering, admired his articulate advocacy of a cause and how he addressed problems head-on, forthrightly. They also summed up his command of governmental and political facts with the respectful phrase: "He does his homework."

A compact, active five foot, seven inches tall, Miller is aggressive not only in his speech and his politics but also in his recreation. He is a fierce competitor at golf, pool, poker and bridge, a man whose strong instinct to win sharpens his surface skills. Like many men under average height, Miller tends to be something of a dandy, leaning to monogrammed shirts, bold cufflinks and velvet-collared overcoats. In recent years, his advisers have protested in vain when he campaigned through rural areas with a Cadillac convertible, a pearl-grey Homburg and a cigarette holder. He favors Scotch whisky, enjoys professional football and baseball as a spectator and appears to lack only two of the minor social graces: He can neither swim nor carry a tune.

At the time of his nomination in 1964, he was senior partner in the Buffalo law firm of Miller, Farmelo & Stenger, which he helped set up three years earlier with the intention of participating full time after his planned retirement from the House. His partners, Republicans too, were Neil R. Farmelo, a former United States Attorney for the Western District of New York, and John H. Stenger, a former Assistant United States Attorney. Stenger became, in October, 1963, an aide in Miller's Congressional office at a salary of $13,742 a year, an appointment that raised a minor issue a year later, when it became known. Democrats, of course, criticized the propriety of such an appointment. Miller replied: "He's done a good job. He's earned his money and I'd do it again." Miller reported he had not drawn any income from the law firm since its establishment, being an inactive member.

During most of his service in the House, Miller had been able to supplement his Congressional salary with a retainer from the Lockport Felt Company that began at $7,500 a year in 1950. Eventually he became an officer and director of the company, the president of which was Raymond Lee, his closest friend. He also owned $27,500 worth of stock in Lockport Holdings Ltd., a Canadian corporation that was technically independent of the Lockport Felt Company but interrelated to the extent that its prosperity would be likely to reflect increased prosperity of the felt company. He said during the campaign that he did not own any stock in Lockport Felt, other than the single share required of a director.

During the campaign his association with Lockport Felt aroused many questions. On at least three occasions, Miller interceded in Congress on behalf of Lockport Felt. Twice he stood on the floor of the House of Representatives to speak against a bill that would have directly affected the company, without mentioning his personal relationship with the company. The first occasion was in 1956, when a bill was proposed to suspend import duties on certain coarse wool and hair fibers used by carpet and paper-makers' felt manufacturers. During the debate, Miller spoke against the bill, which was defeated. It was reintroduced in 1958 and once again Miller took to the floor to oppose it. He said it would make a ghost town in his district, but others described his arguments as "phony." The bill was adopted.

In September, 1964, former Democratic Representative Frank E. Smith of Mississippi published a book called *Congressman from Mississippi,* in which he reported that once on the floor of the House he had been approached by another member and offered a job as public relations man for a felt company. Smith, questioned about it, identified the man as Miller and said that Miller had told him that Lockport Felt had a plant in Mississippi and was willing to pay $350 to $500 a month for a publicity man. At the time Smith was a member of the House Public Works Committee considering the Niagara Power bill. According to Smith, he asked Miller if any Congressional activity on his part would be involved and Miller replied: "No, not at all. This is simply a matter of good business for the company in the South." In his book, Smith said, "It took quite some time for the idea to sink in that this had been some very direct lobbying." Nothing came of the offer. When the episode became public during the Presidential campaign, Miller commented, "I may only say at this time that I didn't offer Mr. Smith five dollars or five cents to act as a public relations officer for the Lockport Felt Company, nor have I ever talked to him about being retained by the company."

Although this sort of conflict-of-interest question continued to trouble Republican leaders and disturb voters during the Miller campaign, it never appeared to concern the candidate himself. Miller counducted his race for the Vice Presidency much as a student of his background would have expected him to do. He ran as a quick, shrewd, small-town lawyer, defensive of his friends and contemptuous of his opponents, arousing applause, cheers and shouts from his normally receptive audiences and a few worries from others about his fitness as the man "a heartbeat" from the Presidency, if elected.

10

Atlantic City:
"Not a Convention,
but an Appreciation"

The gods bumbled when they sent the Republicans to San Francisco and the Democrats to Atlantic City, wrote The Times's Anthony Lewis from the scene of the Democratic convention:

Atlantic City would really have fitted the nostalgic mood that everyone sensed at the Republican convention—the yearning for old-fashioned ways, uncomplicated by the tensions of an urbanized, international society. This town is yesterday's pleasure dome, bearing faded witness to a time when politicians did not have to worry about Negroes or Russians or nuclear incineration.

The hotels have names like the Marlborough-Blenheim. In some, one can see a grossly inflated version of the Long Island shingled mansion of 1920 where Jay Gatsby's guests danced away the night. Others are Moorish palaces à la Warren G. Harding.

Not even the most hardened Goldwater believer in property rights untouched by Government regulation could find a hint of planning or Socialism along Atlantic City's Boardwalk. A cacophony of commercialism assaults the senses. The stroller can hardly see the sea for the signs advertising salt water taffy "cut to fit the mouth."

The victory of good old-fashioned commerce is symbolized by the benches for tired delegates. They face away from the ocean, toward the taffy and souvenir and pretzel stands.

There is even a relic of colonialism. An outdoor restaurant on the Boardwalk has Negro waiters who wear pith helmets. The image of the pukka sahib is a bit confused, but the nostalgic flavor is unmistakable.

Inside the Convention Hall itself there is an organ that could have been built for the Roxy or one of the other great movie houses of that period. It is said to be the world's largest organ. On the wall above it are what must be the world's two largest pictures of Lyndon B. Johnson.

The President's likeness is everywhere, in the hall and along the Boardwalk and on the souvenir programs. At San Francisco there was an occasional Scranton picture, but here the prospect is unrelieved Johnson—at least until the President makes known his choice of a running mate.

The Democratic convention contained even fewer unknowns than the Republican. It was quite clear that Johnson would be renominated; it was equally clear that the platform would endorse the policies of Kennedy and Johnson and call for more of the same for the next four years. There were really only two questions to be answered: Who would be the Vice Presidential candidate (all logic pointed to Humphrey, but everyone knew that the candidate would be Johnson's choice, logical or not) and would there be a fight about seating the delegation from Mississippi?

The convention activities got under way the week before the convention actually met with the platform committee conducting hearings at the Sheraton-Park Hotel in Washington. More than 200 witnesses were heard before the committee settled down to write a document that was divided into two parts: (1) foreign policy and national security and (2) domestic affairs. A preamble, entitled "An Accounting of Stewardship," amounted to a lengthy recital of national accomplishments during the Kennedy and Johnson Administrations. The platform itself was drawn with a keen awareness of the major areas of friction among Republicans at their San Francisco convention—control of nuclear weapons, civil rights and extremism.

The Democrats sharply diverged from the Republicans on the issue of Presidential control of nuclear weapons, writing into the plank words that the Goldwater forces had rejected in San Francisco, "Control of the use of nuclear weapons must remain solely with the highest elected official in the country—the President of the United States."

On civil rights, the language was moderate because of the need to avoid further problems with the already splintering South. Referring to the recently enacted Civil Rights Act, it pledged "full observance . . . and fair, effective enforcement if there is any default." The Republicans had vowed full implementation and faithful execution, rejecting moves for fuller endorsement.

In the bitter area of extremism, the Democrats also found use for the words their rivals had rejected, "We condemn extremism, whether from the right or left, including the extreme tactics of such organizations as the Communist party, the Ku Klux Klan and the John Birch Society."

Another area of distinct difference with the Republican platform was disarmament. The G.O.P. spoke skeptically of the nuclear test ban treaty, the disarmament negotiations and the hot line between Washington and Moscow. The Democratic platform hailed the test ban, saying that "already the air we and our children breathe is freer of nuclear contamination," and it pledged to "continue all-out efforts through fully enforceable measures to halt and reverse the arms race." The foreign policy plank also pledged firm resistance to Communist aggression around the world, at the same time striving to present an appearance of restraint in contrast to the more aggressive tone of the Republican platform and candidate. The phrasing was obviously designed to reinforce the picture of a "reckless" Goldwater.

The section on domestic policy offered liberal planks on labor, urban

affairs, immigration, education, Congressional procedures and other subjects. In sum, an aura of harmony marked the platform deliberations for
the better part of a week. As one committee member remarked, "There's no
unhappiness about anything."

With that background, the Democrats gathered in Atlantic City on August
24 for the thirty-fourth in a line of conventions that began in 1832, when
Andrew Jackson and Martin Van Buren were nominated. Outwardly the
5,260 delegates and alternates were confident, but inwardly they were
jittery as they prepared for four rumbling days inside mammoth oceanside
Convention Hall—air-conditioned with Federal aid and ironically situated
on a Boardwalk bounded by Mississippi and Georgia Avenues. Their activities were to be recorded by more than 6,000 reporters and broadcasters
and their myriad technicians, and 5,000 or more spectators were to watch
from the galleries. The hall was bedecked with 87,000 circuit miles of
broadcasting cable, 3,000 telephones, 19,700 feet of video cable, and 250
teletype machines.

The delegates were in an odd mood. They were supposed to be unbeatable,
but they were uneasy. They talked big in public, but privately they worried.
They were not so excited about Johnson as they were afraid of Goldwater—
genuinely afraid that his policies were bad for the country, but somehow
fearful the country might not quite see it that way.

James Reston remarked in The Times:

All politicians, of course, hope vaguely and fear precisely, Barry Goldwater
included; but no party ever had so many backers and so many doubts as the
Democratic party at this moment.
This is more than the prudent political tactic of "running scared." Uncertainty
is the rule of the day. Kennedy, the unexpected hero, is now a tragic but persistent memory. The pollsters, who are a consolation, have been too wrong
recently for comfort. The unions, who were a decisive force when they were poor,
are now rich and divided. The powerful Big City bosses are not so powerful, and
the "Solid South" is not so solid.

On the opening day, the convention found itself embroiled again in that
traditional fight among Democrats, the loyalty oath. Back in 1948, liberals
led by Humphrey had demanded a loyalty oath; Southerners walked out and
ran a Dixiecrat candidate, Strom Thurmond, against the Democratic nominee,
President Truman. Now once again, a loyalty oath proposal spelled danger
for Johnson—the danger of spreading racial feelings among Southern
white politicians, Negroes, or both, and the possibility of more defections.

The dispute concerned the credentials of the delegations from Mississippi
and Alabama. Both delegations were strongly anti-Johnson, and the controversy narrowed to a question of whether they should be barred unless they
pledged support for the Democratic ticket in November. The Alabama delegation was challenged because of a statute enacted by the state legislature at the
insistence of Governor George C. Wallace providing for a slate of unpledged
electors, who had no other obligation in casting their votes in the Electoral

College than to vote for a Democrat. In the case of Mississippi, a pre-dominantly Negro Freedom party delegation challenged the regular delega-tion as illegal because Negroes were systematically barred from party activity.

The wrangle went on in the credentials committee, with the White House calling the tune. To the nation's television audience, this fight, at times, dwarfed the real business of the convention. The nation saw and heard tales of beatings and arrests from Negroes who had tried to register and failed. A stream of testimony came from witnesses, ranging from the wife of a Negro sharecropper, who told how she had been jailed and beaten for attempting to register other Negroes, to the Rev. Dr. Martin Luther King Jr. who said, "You cannot imagine the anguish and suffering they have gone through to get to this point."

Despite these very real agonies, the upshot was a compromise that the convention adopted quickly by voice vote. It called on the two delegations to sign pledges of support for the party ticket and, despite rejection of this compromise by the Freedom Democrats, seated two of that party's members as delegates at large. Only eleven of the thirty-eight Alabamians and four of the twenty-four Mississippians signed the loyalty pledges; the rest went home. Anthony Lewis wrote in The Times:

> The problem for the Freedom Democrats in their credentials fight was that in strictly legal terms they did not have much of a case. They were more a protest movement than a political party.
>
> Their strength was moral. It was apparent that the law of Mississippi did not give them fair access to the political processes—that they could not, realistically, express themselves politically under the rules of Mississippi.
>
> The lawyer for the Freedom party, Joseph L. Rauh Jr. of Washington, recognized that he had a moral and an emotional case to present, not a legal one. His parade of witnesses before the credentials committee who had been beaten and tortured by those sworn to uphold the law in Mississippi made it impossible for Demo-cratic leaders to brush the group aside.
>
> The fact is that the Freedom party's claims would have been brushed aside at any previous convention because of their legal insubstantiality. But this country has become much more sensitive to the cruelties of racism, and the convention reflected this change.
>
> Seen in this framework, the credentials committee compromise appeared a remarkable victory for the Freedom group.

The convention also planted the seed for a major political realignment in the South. It decided that in 1968 all delegations would be required to "assure" all voters opportunity to participate in party affairs and vote in Presidential elections "regardless of race, color, creed or national origin." That would require a fundamental transformation of the party in the South —and would certainly drive a substantial number of white Southerners to the Republicans or to a third party.

The Johnson forces, steered by Humphrey to the relatively safe compro-mise ground, were relieved that the dispute had evaporated without an open floor fight, much less a Southern walkout such as occurred in 1948—when a younger Humphrey had led the civil rights fight. The fact remained, however, that Alabama and Mississippi presumably now could be written off by the Democrats in November, along with a few other hard-core Southern states.

The credentials compromise was another display of Johnsonian power. Facing a mutinous Alabama and Mississippi, he knew, as Truman had proved, that the Dixiecrats were expendable. The labor vote of the big industrial states, the steadily increasing Negro vote, the vote of the liberals captured by Roosevelt and regained by Kennedy, the Democratic fraction of the farm vote—these could not be ignored. Johnson, therefore, confronted the dissident Southerners with the frank statement that the Democrats would be happy to proceed without them if necessary.

With that minor conflict behind him, and building momentum toward unification, Johnson turned with great relish and aplomb to his favorite theme, "Happy Days Are Here Again." The biggest billboard in town had been purchased by the Republicans for $10,000 in order to say to the multitude: "In your heart you know he's right—vote for Barry Goldwater" (and under it Democrats placed a small sign reading, "Yes—extreme right," until Republican protests forced it down). But no mere billboard could detract from the stellar personal performance in absentia of the man from Texas. That performance prompted Russell Baker to write in The Times, "What the Democrats are staging here is not a convention, but an Appreciation." He went on:

The distinction is illustrated by the party's mercenary policy on LBJ buttons. People who have been to conventions will find it hard to believe, but the only way to get an LBJ button here is to pay for it.
Such pinch-penny tactics are unheard of at genuine conventions, and the only explanation is that the Democrats believe the nation is not merely ready to appreciate Mr. Johnson but is willing to pay for the privilege. . . .
The general presumption has it that Mr. Johnson, sitting in Washington, decides everything down to such issues as which delegates get the hotel rooms without baths. In a sense, Mr. Johnson is the convention. And the convention itself is a family party staged for television.
The object is to leave the television audience with that good warm feeling that used to result from watching "I Remember Mama." Appropriately, the old patriarch in the White House has all his family gathered at the seashore, eating fudge and butter crunch, riding the ferris wheel and playing skee ball.

Johnson, determined to make himself the unifying factor in his national party, was unquestionably the stage manager, director and, in the end, the star. Except for a fired-up keynote speech by Senator John Pastore of Rhode Island, little happened on the floor to command attention. The TV cameras focused on the peripheral quarrel in the wings involving race. That was the kind of attention Johnson didn't want.

At times it seemed to the nation's television audience as if the major business of the convention was at the doors where barred Negro delegates were trying to get in and being held out and where civil rights pickets constantly paraded and held press conferences. But Johnson was able to prevent any serious blow-ups on the convention floor (there was not one roll-call vote) and when it was time for nominations, he stepped onstage and the show became a rousing spectacle.

There was no question of what the convention would do. Tom Wicker reported from Convention Hall in the early hours of Thursday, August 27:

Lyndon Baines Johnson of Texas, the man who took over the Presidency last Nov. 22 in the shattering hour of John F. Kennedy's assassination, was nominated for a term of his own last night by the 34th Democratic National Convention.

Then Mr. Johnson did what he loves to do. He smashed precedent by going before a turbulent and happy gathering of more than 5,000 delegates and alternates to name Senator Hubert H. Humphrey of Minnesota as his choice for the Vice Presidential nomination.

The happy Democrats, and thousands of spectators jammed into Convention Hall, cheered wildly for both Mr. Johnson's nomination and his choice of Mr. Humphrey.

Both men were nominated by acclamation, Johnson's having come after the Alabama delegation yielded to Texas so that Governor John B. Connally could place the Johnson name in nomination, as he had done at the Chicago convention in 1956. Governor Brown of California shared the nominating process and was followed by seven seconding speakers. The Convention Hall went wild, with balloons and marching, music and dancing.

Arthur Krock of The Times viewed the events this way:

A dull Democratic National Convention is a flat contradiction in terms. But when, as this year, its major decisions are prefabricated, even a Democratic convention can be dull. And the party gathering of 1964 would have belonged in this rare category if President Johnson had not dramatized it with a stellar personal performance for which American political history provides no parallel.

The advent of electronics partly accounts for this, because it enabled the President to play his unexampled leading role simultaneously on two stages—Washington during the first phase of the convention; Atlantic City for the final sessions. And twice he shuttled between the two in the course of 24 hours.

But the effectiveness of the President's performance derived chiefly from his brilliant virtuosity in the technique of politics, from his audacious disregard of the traditions by which his predecessors have been bound in similar circumstances and from his creative instinct in the field of public relations.

Indeed any success achieved by the Atlantic City convention belonged to Johnson. The platform reflected all his ideas on the social and economic responsibilities of government. Johnson swept to his coronation with the assurance and dexterity of a master politician, and the controlled drama leading to the words Hubert Humphrey left unquestioned the choice of the Minnesota Senator as the Vice Presidential candidate. James Reston wrote:

It is remarkable how quickly President Johnson has taken command of this party. Most of the Vice Presidents who took over the White House in the nineteenth century after the death of a President had trouble assuring their own nomination at the next election, and even in this century, Teddy Roosevelt, Calvin Coolidge and Harry S. Truman, while assured of their own nominations, did not get the Vice President of their choice, whether because the man they wanted would not accept or the convention would not approve.

The closest Johnson came to losing the spotlight through the convention week was during an emotional tribute to John F. Kennedy that centered on the controversial Attorney General and brother of the late President, Robert F. Kennedy, who had been scissored from the list of Vice Presidential possibilities by Johnson. The tribute had been carefully scheduled to follow the nominations of both President and Vice President to neutralize any impact the expected emotional outpouring might have on the delegates. After both Johnson and Humphrey had been nominated, Kennedy went to the enormous Convention Hall to introduce a memorial film about his brother.

He mounted the rostrum dressed in a black suit and black tie he had worn on public occasions since his brother's assassination. A surge of applause rose from the standing delegates and spectators, but there was no shouting, no music, no parading and only modest waving of state placards. Kennedy stood impassively before the massive arena for sixteen minutes of thunderous tribute, only a suggestion of a smile on his face, before he began to speak in a small, boyish voice, thanking the delegates for all they had done for his brother.

Admonishing them not to look to the past, he called on them to give the same dedication to the convention's candidates that they had given to John F. Kennedy. "When I think of President Kennedy," he said, "I think of these lines from Shakespeare:

> When he shall die,
> Take him and cut him out
> in little stars,
> And he will make the face
> of heaven so fine
> That all the world will be
> in love with night,
> And pay no worship to the
> garish sun.

The slain President's widow also received the delegates' tribute at a hotel reception with her brother-in-law and sisters-in-law. So many appeared to greet Mrs. Kennedy and to hear the reading of her husbands favorite selections of poetry and prose that they had to be accommodated in shifts throughout the afternoon. Mrs. Kennedy did not go near the Convention Hall, but she drew enormous crowds hoping to catch a glimpse of her.

Otherwise, the theme up and down the Boardwalk was "Hello, Lyndon!" joyously sung, or shouted, to the tune of "Hello, Dolly!" The song's strains were even used in the rain-soaked welcome of Lady Bird Johnson on nomination day, in which the First Lady and daughter Lynda were almost swept off their feet by a drenched mob. And those strains filled the skies as Atlantic City celebrated Johnson's fifty-sixth birthday in a ball on the Texas scale. Outside the ballroom in Convention Hall, thousands of party faithful from all levels pushed, shoved and shouted in honor of the President.

On that last night of the convention, Johnson accepted the nomination with a pledge of answers, not retreats, unity, not division, hope, not fear or smear. It was a speech carefully designed to answer again and again the challenges laid down by Goldwater. "We do offer the people a choice," the President said. "A choice of continuing on the courageous and compassionate course that has made this nation the strongest and the freest and the most prosperous and the most peaceful nation in the history of mankind." To what he said was his opponent's call for brinkmanship abroad, he replied, "The true courage of this nuclear age lies in the quest for peace." To Goldwater's charge that individual freedom was being curtailed, Johnson replied, "Americans tonight are freer to live as they want to live, to pursue their ambitions, to meet their desires, to raise their families than at any time in all our glorious history."

In an obvious reference to the Goldwater campaign slogan, he added, "And every American knows in his heart that this is right."

11

H. H. H.:
"If You and I
Just Apply Ourselves"

"I weighed this decision about the Vice Presidency very carefully—not long, but carefully," Hubert Humphrey said the day before his inauguration. "If there's one quality I do not have, it's reluctance."

But Lyndon Johnson's method of picking a running mate was both careful and long. The delay in naming Humphrey was planned and purposeful. Johnson had no doubts about Humphrey's qualifications, but he wanted the widest possible support for him within the Democratic party, and he got it before making his decision at 3 o'clock on Wednesday, the day the nominations were to be made in Atlantic City. Also, the President wanted to make sure at the end that he and Humphrey agreed on their concept of the Vice Presidency. When Humphrey flew in to Washington that afternoon, they had a long talk and agreed on the following things:

The Vice President, if the Democrats won in November, should have important executive responsibilities and should supervise the Johnson Administration's policies on space, disarmament, the antipoverty program, health, education and welfare and other fields within Humphrey's special competence.

The Vice President should take on a great deal of responsiblity in the field of foreign affairs and should represent the President abroad on special missions and assume many of the ceremonial duties that Johnson had to carry alone in the previous nine months. For this purpose, the President made it clear that he intended to ask the Congress to provide an official residence for the Vice President in Washington.

"I picked Humphrey because, in my judgment, and after checking with leaders all over the country, I was convinced that he would be the best man to be President if anything happened to me," the President said the night before going to Convention Hall.

Having reached a decision on the principle of picking a possible President, Johnson then wanted to be certain that he did everything he could to gain acceptance for his choice. The President's theory was that only under the last-minute pressures of the convention was it possible to know where the last pockets of serious resistance to a candidate lay. His job, he felt, was to listen to the end and let everybody have a chance to persuade him, and also to give himself the opportunity to persuade the doubters. He was up at 5:30 that Wednesday morning, for example, and spoke to more than fifty people all over the country. These included Governors, Mayors, prominent Senators and educators, newspaper owners and editors, and members of his own staff, in Washington and at the convention in Atlantic City.

The President was apparently particularly impressed by the warm support he got for Humphrey from three key members of his staff—Secretary of State Dean Rusk, Secretary of Defense Robert S. McNamara, and McGeorge Bundy, the principal White House aide on foreign policy. He kept pressing them to tell him who, in their judgment, could provide leadership for the nation and for the non-Communist world "in case I fell out of an airplane tomorrow morning." Each told him that in his judgment Humphrey was the man.

While Johnson seriously considered a great many men and "let the pot boil" to see who would come to the top, Humphrey bobbed up so often after Kennedy had been eliminated that he was always safely in the lead. The President made a special point of talking to Kennedy the day of the nomination to make sure that he had no last-minute doubts about Humphrey. Kennedy had none. In the end, the decision was made in favor of Humphrey primarily because of his long experience and particularly because the President felt that he was not only well informed in the field of domestic policy but had also been a leader, as a member of the Senate Foreign Relations Committee, in the field of foreign policy. "I wanted somebody," Johnson said, "who could if necessary speak for our country on equal terms with the Erhards, the Homes and the de Gaulles."

The story of what went on before the selection is even more complicated. Johnson had scarcely assumed office after the assassination of President Kennedy, when the Vice Presidential speculation began. The new President steadfastly refused to discuss it at his news conferences, and was seldom willing to talk privately about it, but that did not stop the guessing. In the earliest stages, the speculation centered on Humphrey, because of his eminence in the party and his liberal record; on Eugene McCarthy because of his friendship with Johnson and his general eligibility, and on Bobby Kennedy, because of his name. There were many in Washington, however, who never believed Johnson would be willing to run with Kennedy. They based this conclusion less on the idea that Johnson and Kennedy did not get along together than on the conviction that the President would want to win the election in his own right without any debt to the Kennedy name and glamor.

In addition, the Attorney General appeared to be the only possible rival for power in the Democratic party, and it was doubted that Johnson would willingly make such a rival his second in command. In the first months of

Johnson's Presidency, any small signs of his favor were enough to catapult a Democrat with a clean record into the Vice Presidential picture. When Mayor Wagner of New York was invited to sit in Mrs. Johnson's box at the President's first address to a joint session of Congress, Wagner's name was promptly entered in the race—at least by the press. When Johnson announced that Sargent Shriver, the director of the Peace Corps, would carry a letter for him to Pope Paul VI, and when Shriver was later placed in charge of developing the President's antipoverty program, he, too, became a subject of speculation. Adlai E. Stevenson, twice the Democrats' Presidential candidate, scored well in several polls and was added to the list. All governors of major states were looked upon as potential national candidates.

Johnson's known liking for the Senate and the kind of experience it imparted made a number of Democratic Senators seem like possibilities. These included Edmund S. Muskie of Maine and Senators Ribicoff, Dodd and Pastore. All these men appeared to have either geographical or religious qualifications, or both, that commended them as Vice Presidential prospects. Johnson frequently warned visitors, however, not to overlook the House of Representatives as a source of a candidate. He also dropped frequent hints that he had a college president in mind, and on one occasion actually mentioned Clark Kerr, president of the University of California.

Humphrey watched all this speculation carefully. He knew the President intimately and at first was hopeful that he would be chosen without any efforts of his own. But as time went on and others began maneuvering for the job, he came to believe that he had to promote his chances without pressing or irritating the President. Starting in February, Humphrey's closest friends began holding meetings to try to determine what they could do to support the Senator for Vice President. The word from White House aides, and from the President himself, was: "Don't press the President publicly. And don't fight Robert Kennedy directly."

Most of the weekly and biweekly meetings were held at the home of Max Kampelman, a close friend, on Highland Place in the Cleveland Park section of Washington. Other meetings took place at the homes of Oscar Chapman, Secretary of the Interior under President Truman; Dr. Evron Kirkpatrick, executive director of the American Political Science Association, long an intimate of Humphrey, and William J. Connell, another Humphrey friend and supporter. Among the people who participated in the meetings in Washington were Marvin Rosenberg, a New York businessman; Joseph L. Rauh Jr., a Washington lawyer and vice chairman of Americans for Democratic Action; Kirkpatrick, and several supporters from Minnesota. Humphrey himself never attended these meetings but kept in close contact.

Faced with the problem of not being able to promote his cause directly, the Senator's supporters set up private meetings, mostly in New York, with business groups, labor officials and politicians. However, Humphrey avoided putting public pressure on the President. The Senator, for instance, flatly rejected an offer by friends in Oregon to organize a "spontaneous" write-in campaign in that state's primary. Meanwhile, influential figures like Walter P. Reuther, president of the United Automobile Workers; Alex Rose, chairman of the Liberal party in New York, and Supreme Court Justice Arthur J. Goldberg backed Humphrey in private talks with the President.

In March, Kampelman and others began to mail material favorable to the Senator, such as news articles, editorials and public opinion polls, to party officials, labor leaders and other interested persons. A list was compiled showing significant individuals known to be favorable to Humphrey. In May, Louis Bean was commissioned to take a public opinion poll when the President was reportedly disturbed by several surveys that showed Kennedy to be the leading contender. Bean's nationwide poll the last week in May found Humphrey leading Kennedy by about two points. After the President received the findings, he called Humphrey to report the news. In June, Humphrey supporters commissioned Elmo Wilson, an old friend of the Senator's, to do two polls; they showed Humphrey to be the overwhelming favorite among labor and farm leaders, and these were shown to the President.

Humphrey forces began to spread a report in July that Johnson had reduced the field to McNamara and the Senator, and at the moment favored McNamara. Humphrey was particularly concerned with impressing labor and other Democratic leaders that the President was indeed serious about considering McNamara, former president of the Ford Motor Company. That apparently had some effect. George Meany, president of the American Federation of Labor and Congress of Industrial Organizations, Reuther and other Humphrey supporters brought their case against McNamara to the President.

After Johnson publicly eliminated all Cabinet members including Kennedy and McNamara, a White House aide told Humphrey to start getting "exposure" and to drum up public support. Humphrey went quickly to work, making speeches, attending banquets and generally putting himself in the public eye. Thereafter, his campaign kept growing, until the President got word that the Senator was opening headquarters at the Shelburne Hotel in Atlantic City. Johnson was perturbed, and reportedly told Humphrey through an intermediary to "take it easy." So Humphrey's headquarters was reduced to one switchboard, which he shared with his rival, Gene McCarthy, until McCarthy withdrew from the race.

Kennedy went through various periods of depression and hope during a long campaign. When the Attorney General began emerging in late January from the worst phase of his agony after the death of his brother, some of his friends started to encourage the idea of the Vice Presidency. His first reaction, and really his fundamental belief most of the time, was that it was absurd—that Johnson would never want him and that they were temperamentally incompatible. He said privately, in fact, that he would not take the Vice Presidency if it were offered. In the spring there was a flurry of newspaper reports about a "feud," most of them no more than a sensational treatment of the long-standing differences in temperament between the two men. It was at this time that the idea of Kennedy's running for the Senate in New York was first seriously considered. Then there was a period of seeming good feeling. Kennedy mentioned Johnson warmly in speeches, as he had been psychologically unable to do earlier. At the time of the Republican National Convention in San Francisco, there was a scene of public reconciliation between the two in Washington, when Johnson praised Kennedy as a great Attorney General. Speculation about Kennedy for Vice President flourished again, and Kennedy began to be persuaded that he really had a chance. That probably explains his shock at the moment when Johnson told him the Vice Presidency was not for him.

The famous session when Johnson broke the news seems to have had all the irony of Pirandello's view of "truth"—that it was entirely relative, each person involved in an event believing altogether sincerely in his version of it. Johnson felt he was being pressured; Kennedy insisted that he never thought of pressure. The President said he gave Kennedy an honorable way to drop out of the race himself; the Kennedy account was that nothing of this was mentioned until McGeorge Bundy called him and suggested that he remove himself by a leak to the press.

The Johnson-Kennedy story, so far as it can be pieced together, was as follows: The Attorney General seemed to get an early lift in January when Johnson sent him on a special mission to Indonesia. Many other envoys were available, and the President's action was thought to have given Kennedy a deliberate push forward. The President later denied that he intended either the Indonesian mission for Kennedy or the mission to the Pope for Shriver as trial balloons. In the case of Kennedy, the President told friends he was trying to help the Attorney General get back into circulation after the shock of his brother's murder. In the case of Shriver, Johnson was merely taking advantage of the fact that he was going abroad anyway and could deliver the message to the Pope directly rather than having it go through more formal channels.

The first firm development in the Vice Presidential situation came early in March, in the New Hampshire primary. A few days before the voting on March 10, it became known that New Hampshire Democrats were waging an active campaign to have Kennedy's name written in as that state's choice for Vice President. Since most Democrats there were taking it for granted that Johnson would be the Presidential nominee, there was no campaign to write in his name. The distinct possibility arose, therefore, that Kennedy might receive more write-in votes for Vice President than Johnson for President. Neither man was officially on the ballot.

The origins of the Kennedy write-in drive are still somewhat obscure. At least some of the activity was started by Paul Corbin, a Democratic National Committee worker close to Kennedy. But Corbin was not regarded as an important enough figure to have been given the assignment of organizing such an effort, had it been deliberate on Kennedy's part. At any rate, Governor John W. King of New Hampshire first opposed, then swung around to back the write-in plan, which spread rapidly. The New Hampshire Democratic party is heavily Roman Catholic, and the Kennedy name and record were popular with its members. King and other Democratic leaders decided to go along with, rather than oppose, the Kennedy appeal.

The Democratic National Committeeman, Hugh Bownes of Laconia, resisted it, however, and informed the White House of the danger that Kennedy might score more write-in votes than the President. Bownes felt strongly that New Hampshire should not participate in bringing such pressure on Johnson. Kennedy had already offered, through Kenneth P. O'Donnell, the White House appointments secretary and a close friend of the Kennedy family, to disown the write-in movement. O'Donnell informed the President of this fact. Johnson was reluctant, however, to appear to have pushed Kennedy out of the primary. There the matter stood until Bownes and press reports alarmed the White House about the possible primary results. At that point, Kennedy took a necessary step. He issued the following statement through a spokesman: "The Attorney General has said that the choice of the Democratic nominee for Vice President will be made and it should be made' by the Democratic Convention in August, guided by the wishes of President Johnson, and that President Johnson should be free to select his own running mate. The Attorney General therefore wishes to discourage any efforts in his behalf in New Hampshire and elsewhere."

King reacted promptly. "This write-in movement that is the product of spontaneous combustion has grown to such proportions that to try to stop it at this late date would be like trying to stop a forest fire in a matter of minutes," he said in Concord. But King and other Democrats began urging write-in votes for Johnson, too. The White House and Johnson's political agents also got busy promoting his write-in candidacy, and the Kennedy movement became, in effect, a Johnson-Kennedy movement. In addition, Johnson personally ordered Corbin dismissed from the Democratic National Committee.

According to one high source, when he informed the Attorney General of his decision, Kennedy demurred and said, "President Kennedy wouldn't approve of that." "But, Bobby," Johnson replied, in this version of the story, "I'm President now." (When this story appeared in The Times, Kennedy said that he did not recall the exchange).

When the New Hampshire returns were in, Johnson had 29,317 write-in votes for President to 25,094 for Kennedy for Vice President. Thus, the immediate danger of a serious embarrassment to Johnson and the possibility of strong pressure in Kennedy's behalf were averted. Many thought the relations of the two men were damaged by the incident, however, and that Johnson was permanently influenced in his belief that Kennedy intended to bring all possible pressure upon him for the Vice Presidential nomination.

Immediately after the primary, a Kennedy for Vice President movement sprang up in Wisconsin. The Attorney General quickly repudiated it and the organization never became a major factor. Nevertheless, Kennedy remained the central figure in the almost continuous Vice Presidential speculation that occupied Washington in the following months. At one point, it seemed that his followers and the "new men" surrounding the President might split the Administration virtually into two camps. Some Administration figures were passionately loyal to Kennedy, both for his own sake and because he seemed to them to be the true inheritor of his brother's particular appeal to a new generation of Americans. On the other hand, the men who came into power with Johnson resembled in many ways an older generation —almost a throwback to the New Deal years of the Democratic party. Johnson himself, who had said in 1960 that the nation needed a man with "a little gray in his hair," was prone to speak scornfully of some of "the kids" who had been influential in the Kennedy Administration.

As spring advanced into summer, a somewhat uneasy amnesty settled over the two camps, following the lead set at the top by Kennedy and Johnson. With the civil rights struggle at home and the war in Vietnam becoming increasingly difficult problems, the President and his Attorney General, both of whom were personally interested in the two crises, were drawn together in handling them. In addition, at the urging of some friends, among them Assistant Secretary of State Frederick G. Dutton, Kennedy sought out Johnson and the two had a long talk that lessened their strained relations. At about the same time, Johnson held a particularly moving memorial service for President Kennedy, on what would have been Kennedy's forty-seventh birthday. Then Johnson and his wife were invited to a dinner on behalf of the Kennedy Library, an activity from which they had been largely excluded. These friendlier relations were significant within the Administration, but they were not related to the selection of a Vice President by Johnson. He was going about that matter on a totally different basis.

For months before his choice was finally announced, Johnson conducted one of the most searching interrogations of his party and its leaders in modern times. His instruments were polls, telephone calls, personal conversations, conferences, long talkative luncheons in the private dining room of the White House—any means by which he could find out what others were thinking about the Vice Presidency and how others would react to his own choice.

Sometimes the results surprised Johnson, as when one of the best-known Democratic machine politicians in the nation told him that he would like to have the Vice Presidency himself. More often, the President heard what he probably expected—as, for instance, when Meany, in conversation after conversation, advocated the choice of Humphrey. Johnson placed considerable reliance on the various polls taken for him. One showed, for instance, that any potential Vice Presidential candidate would probably hurt the ticket, not help it. That was because the real issue was Johnson and his Administration. When almost anyone else was coupled with him, the person added political liabilities—say, Humphrey's weakness in the South, or McCarthy's lack of a national reputation. Thus, the President's polls convinced him that, to some extent, his problem was to find the candidate who would hurt him the least, rather than one who would help him the most.

The President was much interested by one nationwide poll with a very large sampling, showing that Stevenson was regarded as the most capable man to take over the Presidency, among those generally mentioned for Johnson's running mate. The same poll, however, indicated that Kennedy would be the best vote-getter on a national basis. Even more significantly, however, the poll showed that Stevenson ran badly as a vote-getter and Kennedy was not widely regarded as well qualified to take over the Presidency. In significant contrast, Humphrey placed a strong second in both divisions of the poll.

Among other things Johnson learned the following: The strongest candidates in the South and the Border states would be McCarthy and McNamara; the weakest would be Kennedy. The main problem for the Democratic ticket would be to carry the big Middle Western states—Illinois, Indiana, Ohio, Minnesota, and others—and there Humphrey and McCarthy would run strongly. Among business leaders of both parties, moderates of both parties, and conservative Democrats, McNamara attracted a wide following but Kennedy was strongly rejected.

Johnson was particularly concerned at the opposition to Kennedy among business leaders, moderate Republicans, and independents. He hoped to attract many of these to his support, particularly in view of their suspicions of Goldwater, but he found that most of them would not consider voting Democratic if they were putting Kennedy within one remove of the Presidency. Much of this opposition stemmed from Kennedy's action in the steel price crisis of 1962, particularly his use of the Federal Bureau of Investigation to obtain information.

As Johnson came to the conclusion that he could not choose Kennedy for his running mate, it was beginning to be strongly believed in the White House—perhaps even by the President himself—that Kennedy's followers would attempt to stampede the convention for the Attorney General by playing upon the emotions that had arisen from his brother's assassination. A part of this scheme, it was felt, would involve having Mrs. John F. Kennedy attend the convention in Atlantic City—although it had been announced that she would not do so—and receive a demonstration that would be of assistance to Kennedy.

Thus, at least by Monday, July 27, Johnson had determined not to select Kennedy, to inform him of the decision, and to make it public. He asked the Attorney General to call on him at the White House the next day. Kennedy had a meeting of the Kennedy Library to attend in New York, however, and requested that the conference with the President be delayed until Wednesday. Johnson agreed. When the Attorney General finally arrived at the White House, Johnson informed him that he had a high regard for his capabilities, that he believed Kennedy could some day "lead the country," that he —Johnson—would not stand in his way in that ambition. But, he said, "this is not the year and the Vice Presidency is not the route."

Johnson told the Attorney General he had enjoyed being Vice President, although there had been times, he added, when President Kennedy had suggested that the job might not be challenging enough. But he had known what he was getting into, Johnson went on, and he doubted that the Attorney General really knew what was involved. Johnson said he felt that the Attorney General was capable of handling just about any job. The President did not promise to remove any Cabinet official to make way for Kennedy, but anything available would be his for the asking. Then, he posed a question: What did the Attorney General want?

Kennedy, swallowing hard, replied that he did not know, except that he wanted to help the President in the campaign in any way possible. Fine, Johnson said. He wanted the Attorney General to help run the campaign organization, along with O'Brien, O'Donnell and James Rowe, just as soon as the Democratic convention was over and Congress was out of town. Kennedy asked if that would not mean he would have to resign as Attorney General. Johnson assured him he could do both jobs. Then the President said that his sole aim was to get President Kennedy's program through, and that he thought this was the Attorney General's aim, too. Kennedy agreed.

Only one point was left: How would the President handle the announcement? Johnson gave Kennedy a choice: He could announce he had withdrawn or that he had been asked to withdraw. (Kennedy's friends question this version.) Nevertheless, according to the White House story, Kennedy said he wanted to think it over, and with that he left.

White House reporters gathered for a news conference in Johnson's office on Thursday and badgered him for nearly an hour on his choice for the Vice Presidency. Johnson evaded all questions but did give this description of the man he was looking for:

"I think that we want the person that is equipped to handle the duties of the Vice Presidency and the Presidency if that awesome responsibility should ever fall upon him. I think he should be a man that is well received in all the states of the Union, among all of our people. I would like to see a man that is experienced in foreign relations and domestic affairs. I would like for him to be a man of the people who felt a compassionate concern for their welfare and who enjoyed public service and was dedicated to it.

"I would like for him to be attractive, prudent and progressive. I would like for him to be one who would work cooperatively with the Congress and with the Cabinet and with the President. I would expect him to be one that would meet with overwhelming approval of the delegates who have the responsibility for passing upon him."

The main result of the news conference, however, was to convince Johnson even more strongly that he had to make public his action with regard to Kennedy, that he had to stop or limit public speculation on the matter before it became farcical. He asked O'Donnell, who had lunched with Kennedy, what the Attorney General planned to do. When O'Donnell said he did not know, Johnson made a proposal that he would eliminate the entire Cabinet and dictated the statement to that effect. O'Donnell, speaking for Kennedy, approved the idea and the statement.

In addition to individual considerations, Johnson believed the involvement of Cabinet members in political speculation would increase their difficulties in dealing with Congress. Beyond all these considerations, however, was the question of Kennedy. The White House believed that the real issue was whether the President could choose his own running mate. Thus when word reached the White House on the afternoon after Johnson had talked with the Attorney General that Mrs. John F. Kennedy had changed her mind and would attend the convention, and a reporter asked for White House comment, there was none. But it was regarded by some of Johnson's associates as a "counter-attack" and that an attempt to influence the convention might still be made.

Shortly after 6 P.M. that day, Johnson strode into the Fish Room of the White House, faced newsreel cameras, and made the following announcement:

"With reference to the selection of the candidate for Vice President on the Democratic ticket, I have reached the conclusion that it would be inadvisable for me to recommend to the convention any member of my Cabinet or any of those who meet regularly with the Cabinet.

"In this regard, because their names have been mentioned in the press, I have personally informed the Secretary of State, Mr. Rusk; the Secretary of Defense, Mr. McNamara; the Attorney General, Mr. Kennedy; and the Secretary of Agriculture, Mr. Freeman, of my decision. I have communicated this to the United States Ambassador to the United Nations, Mr. Stevenson, and to the head of the Peace Corps, Mr. Shriver. In this manner, the list has been narrowed. I shall continue to give the most thoughtful consideration to the choice of the man who I will recommend and I shall make my decision known in due course."

That was all. Johnson accepted no questions. Within an hour, Kennedy's office issued a response, terse and to the point: "As I have always said, it is the President's responsibility to make known his choice for the Vice Presidency. It is in the interest of all of us who were associated with President Kennedy to continue the effort to advance the programs and ideals to which he devoted his life and which President Johnson is carrying forward."

Newspaper stories the next day about Johnson's action agreed that the two leading contenders for the Vice Presidency seemed, as a result, to be Humphrey and McCarthy, the Minnesota twins.

While almost every observer in the nation was convinced the President would name Humphrey, not even Johnson's closest associates knew for certain what he intended to do by the time they reached the national convention in Atlantic City. The night before the nomination, one of them said that it might be Humphrey, but the President really felt Humphrey was so energetic and well-informed he could conceivably create another center of political power in Washington without intending to do so. This aide was still speculating that Pastore, on the basis of his keynote speech, might in the end be the man. Even after McCarthy sent a telegram to the President withdrawing and urging Humphrey as the Vice Presidential nominee, the President was not only saying that he had not made up his mind but, walking around the White House lawn with reporters, he was also mulling over the decision.

In the long history of the Presidency, there had seldom been so much speculation about a Vice Presidential running mate. Johnson played it out to the end, but he kept control of the situation. He eliminated early the men he did not want, particularly Kennedy, and let the others simmer in the pot until the party seemed to have reached general agreement.

Hubert Horatio Humphrey, the man whom Johnson—and the party— turned to was born on May 27, 1911, in an apartment over his father's drugstore in Wallace, South Dakota. His father, a Republican turned Democrat by the oratory of William Jennings Bryan and the idealism of Woodrow Wilson, later moved to Huron, South Dakota.

In 1929 Humphrey entered the University of Minnesota, but the depression forced him out in his sophomore year, and he went back to help his father tend store. In 1932–33 he took a six-month course in the Denver School of Pharmacy.

In 1935, while on a vacation in Washington, he wrote to his fiancée, Muriel Buck, back in Huron: "Maybe I seem foolish to have such vain hopes and plans, but, Bucky, I can see how someday, if you and I just apply ourselves and make up our minds to work for better things, we can live here in Washington and probably be in government, politics or service. I set my aim at Congress. Don't laugh at me. Maybe it does sound rather egotistical and beyond reason, but, Muriel, I know others have succeeded." They were married in 1936.

A year later—after a six-year hiatus—he resumed his studies at the University of Minnesota. Mrs. Humphrey helped by working as a biller in a utility company. Three months before he graduated *magna cum laude,* the first child, Nancy, was born. While he worked for his master's degree in political science and taught at the University of Louisiana, Mrs. Humphrey supplemented his stipend by typing and making sandwiches for Hubert to sell for ten cents to equally poor graduate students. Back in Minnesota, Humphrey taught political science, first at the University of Minnesota, and then at Macalester College in St. Paul. Then, as other children came along—Hubert, Robert and Douglas—he decided to quit teaching and make a career of government and politics.

During World War II, Humphrey worked in the Minnesota branch of the War Production Administration. Several times he tried to enlist in the Navy but was turned down because of color blindness and a hernia. He was called up for Army induction in 1945, but rejected.

He made his first venture into politics in 1943, running for mayor of Minneapolis and losing. He then set about uniting the Democratic and Farmer-Labor parties and two years later again ran for mayor, but this time with united support he won. In 1947, he was re-elected. Although he had been an ardent supporter of Henry A. Wallace for Vice President in 1944, Humphrey waged war against the Wallace followers, who, supported by Communist sympathizers, tried to take over the Democratic-Farmer-Labor party in Minnesota. In 1947, he became one of the co-founders of Americans for Democratic Action, a liberal anti-Communist organization and remained active in it. In 1948, he ran as the Democratic-Farmer-Labor candidate for the United States Senate and, in addition to winning, helped swing his party to Truman rather than Wallace, the candidate of the newly formed Progressive party.

In his political career Humphrey has been the darling of the liberals because he was not afraid to commit himself to causes and rarely played it safe when his convictions were involved. Thus at the Democratic convention of 1948 when Philadelphia was swathed in moist heat, a young man, dressed only in his underwear, sat on the edge of a rumpled bed in his hotel room. His broad, smiling face—too broad for the puckish nose and mouth—gave him a winning, beamish-boy expression. The room was crowded with other men, young, eager-eyed, talking and laughing. But the man on the edge of the bed talked the most. He never stopped. He talked above and through all the other talk. Plainly he was the commander of this youthful force. They had much to talk and gloat over.

The night before, on his first venture into the national political scene, Humphrey, at thirty-seven a candidate for the United States Senate, had carried to the floor of the Democratic convention a fight over a civil rights plank tougher than the Truman Administration favored. He had won the fight, driven out all the Mississippi delegation and half that of Alabama (while the band played "Dixie"), and burned enough bridges across the Mason-Dixon Line to cost Truman thirty-nine Southern electoral votes.

That was 1948. In sixteen years, Humphrey had grown a little in girth and much in public stature. His energy was unimpaired but somewhat more controlled. In Atlantic City in August, 1964, Humphrey, waiting for Johnson's decision, played middle man for the White House in an effort to reach agreement on a formula that would ease the dispute over the Mississippi and Alabama delegations. Admittedly there was historic irony there. Increasingly of late years the Senator had been the patient, dogged Hubert searching for reasonable compromise rather than the derring-do Horatio who was the hero of the Americans for Democratic Action.

This led to a spate of articles (encouraged, it must be admitted, by the Senator) asserting that "Hubert has mellowed." The business community was assured that the "brash" young man had calmed down and could be trusted not to overturn the established order. There was some truth in this portrait, but it was a surface truth. It was the Senator, for example, who insisted at the convention that if the Mississippi and Alabama delegates were to be seated, they must first pledge loyalty to the ticket. He also insisted that in the future it must be made plain that discrimination in the affairs of the party would be a warrant for unseating a state delegation at the convention.

Of course, the Senator had changed. He recalled with chagrin how he was given the "club chill" when, not long after he entered the Senate, he had the temerity to criticize the venerable Harry F. Byrd of Virginia. But long ago he had found out the secret of the Senate. "In the Senate," he said, "you learn manners. You have to have manners without sacrificing convictions."

In the winter and spring of 1964, Humphrey, the majority whip, waited out the Southerners on the civil rights bill for eighty-three days. One day he had to quell eight threatened revolts, temper-tantrums and near-fisticuffs among his impatient liberal brethren. But the Senator from Minnesota did not blush to recall the first bill he introduced in 1949. It was a bill to provide hospital care for the aged under Social Security.

Now the taste of the nomination was welcome after two disappointments— the loss of the Vice Presidential nomination in 1956, and the collapse of his hopes for the Presidential nomination on that night of May 11, 1960, when he and his wife heard the primary returns in Charleston, West Virginia. But sweeter by far was the vindication of his labors supplied by the legislative record of the Eighty-seventh and Eighty-eighth Congress. The nuclear test ban treaty, the Peace Corps abroad and at home, food for peace, urban renewal, Federal aid for education, the wilderness bill—all had been pressed by Humphrey long before the Kennedy-Johnson Administration took them up. Yet none of these measures bore his name, for he found that the best way to get a project through the Senate was to turn active sponsorship over to other members.

Day in and day out before the 1964 campaign actually started, Humphrey was called off the floor or out of his office to speak to groups of school-children. He never refused, and anyone who ever heard him give an hour to a group of twelve-year-olds on the need for an education will never forget it, for this was a glimpse into the boyhood of a man, showing how deeply the man still associated poverty and educational starvation.

But he has been the despair of the doctrinaire liberals by departing from the norm that they so much admire. Humphrey has learned to temper his liberalism with pragmatism and leaven it with understanding of the prejudices and problems of colleagues. In doing so, he gained the affection and admiration of moderate colleagues, one of whom said, "I don't mind liberalism, it's the liberals I can't abide." But Humphrey is not universally liked. He still is viewed with suspicion as a radical by some, as a talking machine by others. He has a lively sense of humor, even about his own long-windedness. Once, after a lengthy speech, he commented, "And some of it even made sense."

Of his own nomination following Johnson's speech at Atlantic City, Humphrey said later, "It was the greatest speech he ever made, and I responded."

12

L. B. J.

Within hours after the Democratic convention ended on August 28, Johnson, with that restless, overpowering energy of his, plunged into campaign strategy talks with Humphrey on a three-hour flight from Atlantic City to Bergstrom Air Force Base near Austin, Texas. Whether the President continued the discussion on the fifty-five-mile helicopter trip to his LBJ Ranch in Johnson City is not certain. But once they were sitting in the shade of the live oaks on the banks of the Pedernales, as the President had promised the convention, the two men resumed mapping out the broad details of the campaign.

To Johnson, this warm hill country was home, where he felt at ease, where he did not have to worry whether he was being "corny" or too sentimental, where his rough edges were no rougher than those of his friends and neighbors, where he belonged. Johnson's return to the home of his forebears symbolized the essential difference between him and Kennedy. The late President, urbane and sophisticated, was at home everywhere—Palm Beach, Hyannis Port, the White House—and yet was never at home in the same fashion that Johnson was as he ranged his 438 sprawling acres under the "scattered Texas sky" in his cream-colored Lincoln Continental.

The ranch had not always been his; the President had bought it from an aunt in 1951. But his family had lived in that Central Texas area for one hundred years, after migrating there from Georgia. When the then-Senator Johnson took over the spread (not a large one as Texas ranches go), the house was shabby, the land arid and eroded. Today the earth is rich and green (damming the Pedernales and installing three irrigation pumps were a major factor), the stone and frame house attractive and made comfortable by additions. There is a swimming pool, television in virtually every room, a herd of breeding stock, other herds of goats and sheep. There is even a landing strip that cost Johnson $25,000, and is the municipal airport of Johnson City (a fact that had aroused some grumbling by critics who maintained that it was used primarily by the President).

All in all, the ranch is profitable, and a credit to Johnson's assiduous attention to the smallest detail, but it is not the principal source of the family's wealth. There are other ranches, a cattle company, and the Texas Broadcasting Corporation, which owns Station KTBC-TV, the only television station in Austin, and a radio station. The corporation also owns, directly or indirectly, partial interests in radio and television stations in Waco, Bryan and Victoria, Texas, and Ardmore, Oklahoma. It has the Muzak franchise in Austin, and the proliferation of Muzak speakers on the LBJ Ranch brings the piped music to all corners of the property virtually all day.

Many critics blamed Johnson's political influence extending over many years for the inability of others to establish a rival television station in Austin. Since the broadcasting interests constituted the cornerstone of the family's wealth, the Republicans throughout the campaign attempted to create the impression that there was something unethical about the accumulation of his fortune. Even before the Democratic convention began, Johnson, as Goldwater had, issued a report on the family's financial holdings. The Times carried this story by Eileen Shanahan:

WASHINGTON, Aug. 20—President Johnson and his immediate family own property and liquid assets valued at slightly less than $3.5 million, an independent accounting firm certified today. The audit of the family's financial holdings was made public at the President's direction.

It showed that Mr. Johnson, his wife and daughters had received income in excess of $1.8 million in the last 10 years. The income figure includes expense allowances Mr. Johnson has received for running his various offices and capital gains the family has realized from the sale of property.

The Johnsons paid $365,955 in Federal income taxes during the 10-year period.

The family's holdings have more than quadrupled in value since 1954, when they were valued at $737,730. The bulk of the increase is traceable to the earning of the radio and television properties owned by Mrs. Johnson and the two Johnson daughters, Lynda Bird and Luci Baines.

In arriving at the valuation of $3.5 million, Haskins & Sells, the accounting firm, relied essentially on the original cost of real estate and stocks.

The method of valuation of the Johnson family holdings was immediately attacked by Dean Burch, the chairman of the Republican National Committee.

He said that the estimate was "incredibly low," somewhat "like the city of New York listing the value of Manhattan Island at $24," the price paid, according to legend, to its original Indian residents by the first white settlers.

The Arizona bank that acts as trustee for Senator Barry Goldwater, the Republican Presidential nominee, has revealed that the Senator and his wife have assets worth $1.7 million, consisting almost entirely of stocks. This report was made on the basis of the current market value of the stocks.

Whatever the worth of the President's holdings, $3,500,000 as the audit reported, or as high as $14,000,000 as some Republicans contended, it was a tidy sum for a one-time farm boy to have amassed. Yet, to Johnson, one achievement had seemed beyond his grasp. Once he told a reporter: "I don't think anyone from the South will be nominated [for the Presidency] in my lifetime. If so, I don't think he will be elected." Kennedy apparently shared that view. In appraising the Democratic Presidential possibilities before the 1960 convention, Kennedy had said, "I think I'm as well qualified as any of the others—except Lyndon, and he doesn't have a chance." No candidate from a Southern state had won in 116 years—not since Zachary Taylor of Louisiana and the last successful Whig ticket in 1848.

Lyndon Baines Johnson was born on August 27, 1908, in a small farm house amid the pecan trees and the sycamores near the Pedernales River. His grandfather, Sam Ealy Johnson, was elated—"a United States Senator was born tonight!" he exclaimed. When young Johnson discovered politics in the early nineteen-thirties, he set off on a career that was to make him successively a legislative clerk on Capitol Hill, National Youth Administrator for Texas, a member of the House of Representatives, a Senator, Senate Majority Leader, Vice President and then President.

At the age of nine, when most boys his age were hunting squirrels, he was shining shoes in Johnson City's lone barber shop. The President delights in recalling incidents from his boyhood and one of his favorites, which came to his mind when Chancellor Ludwig Erhard of West Germany visited the ranch in the closing days of 1963, involved a recitation contest. He was about ten years old, and he and Walter Peter, the son of German immigrants (many of whom had migrated to the hill country in the mid-nineteenth century), were representing the tiny Stonewall community.

"My mother had been an elocution teacher," the President said, "and she felt sorry for Walter because he spoke broken English. She took him in and coached us both. I was still feeling sorry for Walter [when the competition began] because he had that broken German accent and she couldn't get it out of his speech. So I be damn if they didn't bring in first place for Walter Peter. Those judges were German too."

Here the President hesitated a moment, for effect, before continuing: "That ran through my mind when I had Erhard out here. I told him I didn't want to see him run against me over in Fredericksburg or Stonewall."

Johnson finished high school at fifteen and went to work on a road-building gang. He worked his way to California, doing odd jobs as an elevator operator, a car washer and a handyman in a cafe. Finding California little to his liking, he returned home to his road job. But by this time, as he noted later, "it became increasingly apparent to me that there was something to this idea of higher education." He hitchhiked to San Marcos and entered Southwest Texas State Teachers College, in an era when admission to college was considerably simpler than it is today. He got a part-time job as a janitor at the college, sold hosiery door-to-door and worked as a secretary to the president of the college. Nevertheless, money ran short and he had to drop out for almost a year. During this time he taught school in Cotulla, a small South Texas town. When he was twenty-two Johnson received his Bachelor of Science degree and, for two years, taught public speaking and debating in a Houston high school. Then came the first taste of politics that was to last a lifetime—the job of secretary to Representative Richard M. Kleberg of Texas.

It was during this period that he met his wife-to-be, Claudia Alta (nicknamed Lady Bird by a Negro nurse) Taylor, daughter of a wealthy Marshall, Texas, rancher. He married her on November 17, 1934 after a whirlwind six-week courtship and took her back to Washington. Their two daughters, Lynda Bird and Luci Baines, also have the same LBJ initials, reflecting an ingenuous vanity (akin to his pride in showing off his ranch and his possessions to visitors) that is a Johnson characteristic. His initials adorn all his possessions, from cuff links to the ranch. The President is a member of the Christian Church; his wife and daughters, however, are Episcopalians, and he sometimes attends the National Cathedral or All Saints Episcopal Church with them in Washington.

In 1935, Johnson was appointed to the post of Texas state administrator for the National Youth Administration. He resigned after two years to run for the Congressional seat made vacant by the death of James P. Buchanan of Brenham. There were nine other candidates in the race (Kennedy, by coincidence, faced a similar number of opponents in his first primary for a House seat).

A recent article in The Times Magazine by Ben. H. Bagdikian told what happened:

At the time, Roosevelt's Court-packing plan was creating serious desertions from Democratic ranks, none worse than the Texas delegation's. In Texas it was thought political suicide to be for the Court plan. But Lyndon Johnson ran on a platform of total support for F.D.R., Court plan and all. (Like much of Johnson's behavior, this was courage mixed with prudence and profit: he has always had an instinct to get close to power and F.D.R.'s was the ultimate power in 1937. Against a field of nine, where the others were against the Court plan, the minority of one could carry the election, as Johnson did.)

Roosevelt happened to be fishing off the Texas coast at the time. [Thomas G.] Corcoran recalled recently, "The Old Man had heard of this kid carrying the flag out there in Texas so he said he wanted to see this boy. Lyndon was invited to the boat at Galveston. When he got back to Washington, the Old Man issued orders to me, to Ben Cohen, Harold Ickes and Fred Vinson: 'Take care of this boy.'"

When the U.S. entered World War II in 1941, Johnson was thirty-three years old and a lieutenant commander in the Naval Reserve. After the Japanese bombed Pearl Harbor on December 7, he stayed around the House long enough to vote for declarations of war against Japan on December 8 and against Germany on December 11. He then obtained consent of the House for a leave of absence and became the first member of Congress to enter active duty. It was, however, anything but active duty that he saw in the beginning and, tiring of desk jobs, he appealed directly to Roosevelt to be assigned to a war theater. The President sent the young Texan to Australia on an inspection trip. In the course of that assignment Johnson received permission (without orders) to fly on a bombing mission on June 9 over New Guinea. Johnson took the risk so that he could ascertain for himself what bombing missions were like. It was the high point of his war career, and accounts of it were conflicting. Much later, Foster Hailey of The Times reported the following about the mission:

Mr. Johnson made the mission in a plane piloted by Lieut. Walter Greer of Russelville, Ark., who later was killed in a bomber crash in the States in 1944. Its crew had named the B-26 the "Heckling Hare."

Accounts of the mission vary somewhat. A dispatch of June 10 to The New York Times from Byron Darnton, its correspondent who later in 1942 was killed in action off New Guinea, indicated that Mr. Johnson's plane was not involved in a battle with a group of Japanese Zero fighter planes over Salamaua and Lae.

The long dispatch, printed on June 12, reported on the fight engaged in by the other planes on the flight. Mr. Darnton wrote:

"The plane [in which Mr. Johnson was riding] developed mechanical trouble and was forced to return without reaching its target. But the Representative got a good first-hand idea of the troubles and problems confronting our airmen and declared himself impressed by the skill and courage of the bomber crews and fighter pilots."

Mr. Darnton's dispatch passed through censorship, and some passages may have been cut or altered.

Other versions differ, especially that in a book entitled *The Mission* by Martin Caidin and Edward Hymoff, which was based on recollections of members of the bomber group, including some who flew with Johnson in the *Heckling Hare*. The men of that plane recalled that it had been attacked by eight Zeros, that it had been hit repeatedly by cannon and machine-gun fire, but had returned safely to base with no one injured. The Texan, they said, had displayed no signs of panic and had calmly climbed up to look out of the navigator's bubble during the battle.

Whichever version matched reality, Johnson was awarded the Silver Star, the third highest decoration for valor of the United States; it was presented to him by General of the Army Douglas MacArthur. On July 1, 1942, President Roosevelt issued a directive calling on all members of Congress in the armed forces to return to Capitol Hill. Johnson, on his way back to Washington before the order was issued, but detained in Suva in the Fiji Islands by an attack of pneumonia, reached the city in mid-July.

After five successive terms in the House, and one bid for the Senate that failed, Johnson was elected to the upper chamber in 1948. He defeated the conservative Texas Governor, Coke Stevenson, by eighty-seven votes in a primary tantamount to election (a victory that his opponents charged was tainted by rigged ballots). Six years later, he was re-elected by an overwhelming majority. Shortly after his arrival in the Senate, he became, with the support of Richard B. Russell of Georgia, the powerful Southern Senator, the Democratic whip or assistant leader. When the Democratic leader, Ernest McFarland of Arizona, lost his Senate seat in 1952 to Barry Goldwater, Johnson took over the post. At forty-four years of age, he was the youngest Senate leader in history.

In 1956 his name was entered as Texas's favorite-son candidate for the Presidential nomination at the Democratic National Convention and four years later, despite his misgivings about the chances of a Southerner for victory, he contested Kennedy for the Presidential nomination. He lost on the first ballot, 806 to 409, and accepted the Vice Presidential offer. His selection was a surprise; he had attacked Kennedy sharply in the fight for the nomination, criticizing his wealth, his record on McCarthyism and the pre-war attitude of Kennedy's father toward Hitlerism. Now, though, the election was foremost in Kennedy's thoughts and Johnson obviously was a man who could help the ticket in the South. Bobby Kennedy conveyed the offer to Johnson, who said, "If Jack wants me, I'm willing to make a fight for it." When Kennedy made the announcement that Johnson would be his running mate, there were gasps of surprise from the reporters. But just before the convention, when Johnson had been asked if he would settle for second place, he replied, "I have been prepared throughout my adult life to serve my country in any capacity where my country thought my services were essential."

Thus, most of Johnson's life has truly been spent in politics or, as he would say, the service of his country. In his company, one becomes aware of it forcefully—primarily for two reasons, as The Times noted:

One is the depth and variety of his political experience. He is always recalling incidents, stories, men and events, the impact of which will guide and caution him.

The other quality of the President that makes visitors aware of Mr. Johnson's political nature is the sense he imparts of a vast and unillusioned knowledge of human nature, of what men will do and will not do, to what stimuli they will respond, to what influences they are immune.

Undoubtedly, the greatest influences on Johnson were President Roosevelt and Sam Rayburn of Texas, long-time Speaker of the House of Representatives, with both of whom he worked closely. When Roosevelt died in 1945, Johnson, with tears in his eyes, said: "He was like a daddy to me always; he always talked to me just that way. He was the one person I ever knew— anywhere—who was never afraid. Whatever you talked to him about, whatever you asked him for, like projects for your district, there was just one way to figure it with him. I know some of them called it demagoguery; they can call it anything they want but you could be damn sure that the only test he had was this: Was it good for the folks?"

Rayburn, a colleague in the Texas Legislature of Johnson's father, was for years one of Johnson's best friends and his mentor in Washington. Without detracting from the President's skill as a legislator, there was little doubt that the influence of the powerful Speaker aided Johnson in his rapid rise in Congress. Even in 1960, Johnson still would not accept Kennedy's Vice Presidential offer without consulting Rayburn.

Johnson's nine months in the White House convinced adherents and critics alike of one thing: His legendary ability to deal with Congress remained with him. He lacked Kennedy's style, he might offend the Ivy League with his "cornpone" mannerisms and orations, with his habit of occasionally speaking with the voice and manner of a red-gallus politician of the South, but he could

get his bills through Congress. James Reston explained the Johnsonian relationship with Congress this way:

President Johnson's ability to get his program through the Congress is recognized
by both political parties, but there is still much confusion about how he does it.

One explanation, to use Tommy Corcoran's phrase, is that the President "knows
the deck." He knows the value of every card. He knows the player intimately.
And he works at it night and day.

All the popular notions of Johnson the "arm twister" and the "wheeler dealer,"
while partly true, debase and distort a much more intricate, delicate and positive
art.

The problem is to know where the wires of power lie, who are the key men,
what one group wants that another opposing group can be persuaded to accept
and a third group is likely to tolerate, however unwillingly.

This involves a whole lot more than "twisting arms" and "knocking heads together," though these political gymnastics help. It involves mastery of the details
of a vast variety of bills. It requires great knowledge of every parliamentary rule
and trick in the book. It demands an intuitive understanding of human nature and
enough experience to know what arguments will move one man but not another,
and precisely when to speak or be quiet.

John Kennedy did not "know the deck" and, frankly, he did not like the
Executive-Congressional game. It irritated him to spend hours wheedling votes
out of the proud and powerful chairmen of the committees. He was not really an
insider in the "club" even when he was a member of the House and Senate.
He was a back-bencher, who never quite lost the new boy's deference for the
elders of the Congress.

Johnson, in contrast, was an insider in the Congress almost from the first. For
nearly 30 years he has been talking and drinking with the senior members,
campaigning for them in their districts, visiting with them and their families.

Unlike Kennedy, he loves "the game." It is not a part of his life—it is his
whole life, his work and his sport. He doesn't separate politics from policy or
even from family.

Ironically, even Johnson's success in getting things done perpetuates the illusion that he is a political manipulator who somehow lacks interest in things
of the mind. Yet the intellectual requirements of mastering the political art are
enormous.

He not only has to master legislation and men, but he has to know their districts and states, their strengths and weaknesses, their supporters and opponents
back home, their ambitions and their fears.

The President himself frequently offered a glimpse of his way of doing
things by telling a story stemming from his early days as a Texas politician.
A prolific story-teller—in contrast to the quip humor of Kennedy—Johnson
particularly liked this one:

"One time when I got in a fight with a head of a power company that
wouldn't let me build a little REA [Rural Electrification Administration] line
in my country district in Texas, I said, 'As far as I am concerned, you can
take a running jump and go straight to——' and everybody applauded me,
and the Board of Directors thought I was brave and great. One old man,
though, the general counsel, who had been a lawyer a long time, and mightly
wise, and had been in a lot of fights, he didn't applaud. He looked serious.
He was an ex-Senator.

"I said, 'Senator, what did you think of my speech?' He said, 'Come by my office, and I will tell you.' I went by his office and I said, 'Senator, what did you think of my speech?' He said, 'Young man, you are just in public life, you are just starting. I hope you are in it a long time. I hope you go a long way. I am going to try to help you, but the first thing you have to learn is this: Telling a man to go to hell and then making him go is two different propositions.' He said, 'First of all, it is hot down there and the average fellow doesn't want to go, and when you tell him he has to go, he just bristles up and he is a lot less likely to go than if you hadn't told him anything. What you better do is get out the good book that your mama used to read to you and go back to the prophet Isaiah and read what he said. He said, 'Come now, let us reason together.' "

Johnson did just that, "reason together," all through his public life. To friends he was the "Great Persuader;" to critics, the "Great Wheeler Dealer." The Times quoted two men who should know on this subject:

Senator Harry F. Byrd of Virginia once confessed he had never won an argument from him [Johnson]. Senator Richard B. Russell of Georgia summed him up this way, in his Senate days:
"He doesn't have the best mind on the Democratic side of the Senate; he isn't the best orator; he isn't the best parliamentarian. But he's the best combination of all those qualities."

Some critics, and even some admirers, thought that Johnson was essentially a pragmatic man, a man who did the best he could with the conflicting men and interests around him; in short, without deep-seated beliefs of his own, a man who could persuade others to a consensus. But Johnson himself believed that he conducted himself consistently with the ideals he expressed in an article entitled "My Political Philosophy" that appeared in *The Texas Quarterly* in 1958. In it, he wrote that he was "a free man, an American, a United States Senator, and a Democrat, in that order" and went on, "I am also a liberal, a conservative, a Texan, a taxpayer, a rancher, a businessman, a consumer, a parent, a voter, and not as young as I used to be nor as old as I expect to be—and I am all these things in no fixed order." He continued:

First, I believe every American has something to say and, under our system, a right to an audience.
Second, I believe there is always a national answer to each national problem, and, believing this, I do not believe that there are necessarily two sides to every question.
Third, I regard achievement of the full potential of our resources—physical, human and otherwise—to be the highest purpose of governmental policies next to the protection of those rights we regard as inalienable.
Fourth, I regard waste as the continuing enemy of our society and the prevention of waste—waste of resources, waste of lives or waste of opportunity—to be the most dynamic of the responsibilities of our government.

A graphic representation of Johnson's life, like that of most men, would show some distinct peaks and valleys. His campaign for the Presidency in 1960 was ill-conceived and late-starting and disclosed his weaknesses as a national candidate. Then in his nearly three years in the Vice Presidency, he dropped almost completely from the national political limelight. "What ever happened to Lyndon Johnson?" became a frequent question around Washington. Indeed, up to the moment of Kennedy's murder, there had been much speculation that the Texan would be dropped as a running mate in 1964. The fact was, however, that by training, Johnson was superbly equipped for that moment in Dallas. Apart from his vast experience in Congress, he had in his thirty-four months as Vice President as intensive a course in the Presidency as was possible for any man not actually serving in that office.

President Kennedy had insisted that Johnson attend all Cabinet meetings and participate actively in the administration of the executive branch as well as in the formulation of policy. The Vice President played an important role in the development of the Kennedy civil rights bill—perhaps the most important measure of the Administration. He attended all but one of the meetings of the executive committee of the National Security Council during the week of the Cuban missile crisis in 1962. In the Berlin crisis of the summer of 1961, the Texan had been consulted and had given advice and finally represented Kennedy on a mission to the beleaguered city. His practical political knowledge also was regarded as a valuable commodity by Kennedy, and he was frequently asked for advice. Those close to the Kennedy White House circles contended there never was substance to the persistent "dumping" rumors.

As Vice President, Johnson was named chairman of the National Aeronautics and Space Council and made responsible for setting up of the President's Committee on Equal Employment Opportunity. It was also Kennedy's belief that his Vice President should become better known abroad as well as at home. Thus, Johnson became the President's special emissary. He went around the world on a goodwill tour in 1961 on an itinerary that included battle-scarred South Vietnam. Later he visited the Middle East on a fact-finding mission for the President. Another tour included a visit to the Scandinavian countries and a look at the capitals of the European Economic Community.

Truman was excluded so completely as Vice President from affairs of the Presidency and its official family that he remarked a few years after assuming the highest office that he was the worst prepared man for the responsibilities since Andrew Johnson succeeded Abraham Lincoln. In contrast, Lyndon Johnson, who had viewed the Vice Presidency in a traditional sense—that of presiding over the Senate and furthering the Administration's legislative program while increasing his knowledge of federal affairs at the highest level— may have been the best prepared Vice Presidential successor in history. This preparation bore fruits almost from the day of Kennedy's death. The Times, in assessing Johnson's Presidency at the time of his nomination, had this to say:

His program so far has been an amalgam of those of Mr. Kennedy (in taxation and civil rights, notably) and those of the New Deal (in the so-called war on poverty). He has gone further than any Democratic President since Grover Cleveland in seeking the support of business leaders and he has given frequent indication that his interest is in making the present constitutional system work rather than in reforming it.

History, taking the long view of his Presidency to date, may consider Mr. Johnson's greatest achievement to have been the smooth, sure way in which he kept that Government functioning and imbued the world with a sufficient confidence in his own leadership.

Other achievements of his nine months in office are considerable, however: the passage of the tax reduction and civil rights bills devised by Mr. Kennedy; the revitalization of the legislative-executive relationship that had seemed so nearly frozen just before he took office; the settlement of a threatened rail strike by determined White House pressure; the declaration of "war on poverty" and the initial legislation to prosecute it; the swift and effective response to the North Vietnamese patrol boat attacks in the Gulf of Tonkin; the maintenance of prosperity and price stability while unemployment was falling below 5 per cent; the reduction of the Federal budget for 1965 and the sizable economies in Government upon which he insisted.

There was another side to the picture: A sometimes fumbling touch in foreign affairs, particularly in the handling of the long controversy with Panama over the Canal Zone Treaty; an at least peripheral involvement in the tangled business affairs of his former protegé, Bobby Baker, and an impression of covering up some of the facts of that case; uncautious hints that the United States might be preparing to expand the war in South Vietnam; and a hypersensitivity to criticism, both from the press and opposing politicians.

The one thing that had become clear to the public after watching Johnson in action for nine months was his appearance as a dynamo of energy. There appeared to be no limit to the hours he worked, to the people he saw and talked to on the phone. He brought the expansive and gregarious manner of the West into the White House more forcibly than anyone since Andrew Jackson.

It would have been an astonishing performance for a man with a record of perfect health. Johnson did not have such a record. On July 3, 1955, The Times had carried this report on the front page:

WASHINGTON, July 2—Senator Lyndon B. Johnson, Majority Leader of the Senate, suffered a moderately severe heart attack today. He will be unable to return to active duty at this Congress session.

An aide, George R. Reedy, said the Democratic Senator of Texas was stricken while visiting a friend in Middleburg, Va., this afternoon.

The Senator was at the home of George R. Brown, Texas contractor, when he began to suffer from pains around the heart, Mr. Reedy said.

After an examination by a local physician, Mr. Johnson was transferred to the Naval Medical Center at Bethesda, Md. Mr. Johnson is 46 years old.

There was, therefore, frequently expressed concern over the President's health. He was aware of it and he often volunteered to friends and newsmen the latest electrocardiogram on the state of his heart or other medical testimony on his physical fitness. If he had any problems, one of the most apparent was weight. Before he suffered the heart attack, his weight ranged between 205 and 220 pounds, more on the high side than the low. He delighted in steak and potatoes and rich, creamy desserts. The heart attack, a coronary occlusion, changed all that. He was put on a 2,000 calorie-a-day diet that trimmed his weight and battled to keep it around 205 pounds. He gave up cigarette smoking at physicians' insistence, tried cigars for a while but put them behind, too. He was advised to exercise regularly and moderately. He followed this advice, walking around the White House grounds and swimming before lunch and dinner in the White House pool. His hours still ran as long as ever, although he broke away from his office during the afternoon for a nap.

Johnson's close associates appeared divided at times on whether he maintained a pace too fast for good health. A prominent Democrat observed in the middle of the 1964 campaign that he would start to worry about the President when the President started to worry. "Of course, he's a bundle of nervous energy," the Democrat went on. "But he works it off by going over problems out loud and sounding out people. Not long ago he attended a party at a hotel. It broke up about midnight. As so and so and I reached the curb, Lyndon was getting into his car. He called to us to come on and join him. We wound up at the White House for a snack and a drink and a long discussion of some Congressional problems. Now, we were dead tired but he seemed to be fresh as a daisy. That's the way he keeps fresh, airing problems and not letting them fester inside."

Kennedy had brought into the White House with him a group from Massachusetts, many Irish Catholics who had worked with him for a long time. When Johnson took over, he mixed in a smaller group, mostly Texas Protestants, who had worked with him for some time. Johnson asked the Kennedy men to stay on.

"I need you more than he did," he told them.

But he needed his own men, too, and the "Irish Mafia" was merged with the "Texas Mafia." While the staff lines never were drawn very clearly in the Johnson White House, it soon became apparent who, in general terms, was doing what. The Kennedy men held on for a while, but within a few months the exodus began—Theodore Sorensen, Arthur Schlesinger Jr., Pierre Salinger, Timothy J. Reardon. McGeorge Bundy, the late President's national security affairs adviser, remained in that key role under Johnson. Lawrence O'Brien stayed on as Congressional liaison aide. And when Sorensen left his post as Special Counsel, Johnson asked Myer C. Feldman, a Kennedy man, to take over the duties, if not the title. Kenneth O'Donnell, the Appointments Secretary for Kennedy, remained for a while longer, handling fewer day-to-day appointment chores and more political tasks. Of the team that Johnson brought into the White House, three, at this time, were closest to the throne—Bill (not William) D. Moyers, Jack J. Valenti and Walter W. Jenkins.

Moyers first came to the attention of Johnson when he spent his vacation from the University of Texas working in the Senator's office. He went back to Austin, worked for the Johnson-owned television station, later entered the Southwestern Baptist Theological Seminary at Fort Worth and was ordained a minister in 1959. He never planned to be a minister, however, and during the 1960 campaign he served as a key Johnson aide. He became a deputy director of the Peace Corps, and technically held on to that job, even after Johnson called him over to the White House on the weekend of the Kennedy assassination. In the President's words, Moyers was about the "most unusual twenty-nine-year-old I ever saw." His duties were concentrated on, but not confined to, appointments and scheduling of trips and appearances. Perhaps more than any other Johnson man, Moyers seemed able to speak in the President's name. Tom Wicker wrote of Moyers: "He has one vitally important, if unofficial, function: As both an authentic Johnson man and an authentic New Frontiersman, he has the confidence of everybody on the White House staff and is a useful linchpin holding Kennedy and Johnson men together. His ability is conceded and his devotion to Mr. Johnson's interest remarkable." Moyers is married and has two children, but the President said of him that "when other people go home at 6, Bill stays until 9 because I stay until 9."

A procession of three cars bounced across a lonely cattle range near Johnson City one sunny afternoon. A few cattle, goats and sheep scattered before the automobiles; in the first car rode the President of the United States. The car stopped suddenly. A small dark man wearing a golfer's cap and white buck shoes got out and trotted up the road ahead. "Now, there," said Johnson, "goes a valuable hunk of humanity. He can do anything for you and do it fast."

A few yards ahead Jack Valenti, forty-two, Harvard School of Business, picked up a soft-drink bottle from the road—scarcely more than two tracks across the grassland—and threw it aside. "That could have cut somebody's tire," the President said. Then he turned to a passenger and said of Valenti: "He's a Harvard man. He's got more Harvard degrees than Mac Bundy." (Bundy has only a Yale degree.)

The "valuable hunk of humanity" first came to national attention in photographs of Johnson being sworn into office on the Presidential plane, *Air Force 1,* shortly after Kennedy's death. The President sent for him with this order, "You stay with me." For months afterwards, Valenti remained the man who saw him most. He and Moyers frequently dined with the President and remained on to talk business. It was usually Valenti who briefed the President, often not yet out of his pajamas, in the morning. He was the aide de camp and more. He got the necessary papers into and out of the President's hands. Using his background as a Houston advertising man, he advised Johnson on how to handle himself at news conferences and before television cameras. He worked on speeches, and his sense of humor appealed to the President.

A White House aide said of one aspect of Valenti's activities: "He's the choreographer. He's the arranger of events as to the degree of the President's participation—whether he'll make a speech, whether it will be on television or whether he'll maybe just drop in and shake hands."

The grandson of Italian immigrants who came to Galveston in the eighteen eighties, Valenti grew up in Houston where his father held clerical jobs with the city and county governments. He graduated from high school at the age of fifteen, began going to the University of Houston at night and got a job as an office boy for the Humble Oil Company. After World War II service, during which he flew fifty-one B-25 bomber missions, he was graduated from the university. He went on to the Harvard Business School for two years, returned to Texas, joined the advertising department at Humble and then, in 1952, started his own advertising company. Some time in 1954 he began to write a weekly essay column for *The Houston Post.* In one of the essays he wrote that if Henry Clay could be called the Great Compromiser, and Oliver Wendell Holmes the Great Dissenter, then "Lyndon Johnson is the Great Persuader."

His advertising firm in 1960 handled the Kennedy-Johnson account in Texas. And, more importantly, Valenti married Mary Margaret Wiley, Johnson's pretty secretary, in June, 1962, at a wedding in Houston at which the Vice President gave away the bride. It was during Valenti's courting of his future wife during 1961 and 1962 that his friendship with Johnson took firm hold.

The personal tragedy of the Walter Jenkins case was epitomized best by a statement issued by Johnson the day after the arrest of his aide on October 14, 1964. In it, the President said: "Walter Jenkins has worked with me faithfully for twenty-five years. No man I know has given more personal dedication, devotion and tireless labor. Until late yesterday no information or report of any kind to me had ever raised a question with respect to his personal conduct. Mr. Jenkins is now in the care of his physician and his many friends will join in praying for his early recovery. For myself and Mrs. Johnson I want to say that our hearts go out with the deepest compassion for him and for his wife and six children—and they have our love and prayers."

The morals charge on which he was arrested, and the disclosure of a similar incident in 1959, brought to an abrupt and unhappy end Jenkins' devoted service to the President since 1939. Born on March 23, 1918 in Jolly, Texas, he had spent more than half his life working for Johnson, with time out for Army service in World War II and one unsuccessful run of his own for Congress. Jenkins, a rather chunky man, florid of face and with dark, graying hair, was a key man on the White House staff. The Times described his duties this way:

He was general manager of the White House, for one thing, in charge of personnel and the payroll there. Some of the recruiting of officials for the rest of the Government went past his eyes also.

Walter Jenkins was one of the few persons in the White House authorized to sign Mr. Johnson's name to letters. He generally reviewed letters and statements that required the President's signature.

His long years with the President inevitably gave him special political responsibilities. He usually dealt with the influential Texas delegation at the Capitol. He often talked to big political contributors and representatives of interest groups.

He was a general detail man for the President who followed up decisions to make sure they were carried out. In this capacity he was as close to a Cabinet secretary as anyone to Mr. Johnson.

He sat in on Cabinet meetings and took notes, and he sent out advisories on general Administration policy. His last such message [before his resignation] ironically, was a warning to all Government agencies to tighten up security procedures so as to avoid hasty appointments without adequate investigation.

Jenkins' name earlier had cropped up in the Bobby Baker case, and The Times recalled it:

Mr. Jenkins played a part in Mrs. Johnson's business enterprises as well as in her husband's governmental life. He was treasurer of the family corporation until last winter, when the White House disclosed that he had resigned.

In this connection his name came into the Senate hearings on Robert G. Baker, the former Senate majority secretary, last winter. An insurance salesman, Don B. Reynolds, charged that Mr. Jenkins had suggested he buy advertising on the Johnson television station in Austin, Tex., after he sold Mr. Johnson a policy in 1957.

The story was denied by Mr. Jenkins in a sworn affidavit submitted to the Senate committee investigating the case. The committee voted on party lines not to call him as a witness.

A little removed from the center of power, but still important cogs in the White House staff, were George E. Reedy, Elizabeth Carpenter and Horace Busby. The only non-Texan among the Johnson men, Reedy had been with the President for a dozen years before replacing Salinger as press secretary. A large, rumpled man of forty-six whose ponderous approach sometimes obscures a well-stocked and active mind, Reedy often gives the impression of a professor. "You ask him what tree is over there," Johnson once said, "and he'll tell you who first brought it to this country and talk half an hour before he tells you what you wanted to know in the first place. But he knows what he's talking about."

Reedy was born in East Chicago, Indiana, the son of a newspaperman. He was graduated from the University of Chicago and worked for *The Philadelphia Inquirer* and for the then United Press. He covered the Senate from 1939 until 1951, when he joined the Johnson staff (and adopted Austin as his home).

Mrs. Carpenter, an energetic and astute former Texas newspaperwoman, doubles as special aide to the President and press secretary to his wife. She and her husband, Les Carpenter, opened a news bureau in Washington during the war. Eventually, they had newspaper clients in four states—Arkansas, Oklahoma, Louisiana and Texas. When she was named Mrs. Johnson's press secretary in 1960, she left newspaper work. Later, she was appointed an assistant to the President and it was said that she dared to talk back to him. Her job in the White House was to advise Johnson on the problems of women in government and, by her own definition, to be his all-around trouble shooter.

Busby, a long-time associate of the President and a former Texas newspaperman and business newswriter, helped with the speech-writing chores. He also had considerable knowledge of national security and space affairs. Two others on the White House staff were Douglass Cater, a Washington newspaperman and editor, who was brought in to replace Schlesinger in what had been a position of something akin to "chief intellectual," and Eric Goldman, a Princeton historian, who was there on a part-time basis.

Another who belonged in the staff lineup, although technically not a White House employe, was Clifton F. Carter, the President's eyes and ears at the Democratic National Committee. Carter, who as a teen-ager in 1937 campaigned for Johnson and who was running his office in Austin at the time of the Kennedy assassination, helped coordinate Presidential and party activities and planning. Still another Texan, but one whose association with the President was confined mainly to his business interests in Texas, is Judge A. W. Moursund of Johnson City, to whom the President entrusted the care of his interests entirely. The Judge, or A. W. as he is known in the hill country, is an old and much-admired friend of Johnson's. His success in business, his knowledge of ranching, his formidable cow-trading talents were among the reasons for that admiration and for the fact that Moursund was Johnson's business trustee. Among the other members of inner circle of advisers are two old Texas friends, Governor John B. Connally and William S. White, the syndicated newspaper columnist and former Times correspondent.

At the outset of his Presidency, Johnson often turned to outsiders in Washington such as Abe Fortas and James H. Rowe, Jr., attorneys and old New Dealers; Dean Acheson, former Secretary of State, and Clark M. Clifford, another attorney who held the top White House staff post under Truman. However, as his Administration moved along, the outsiders seemed to decline in influence and the White House channels became somewhat clearer. Still, the nature of the operation continued to defy any neat organization chart. One observer, for example, likened Johnson men such as Valenti, Moyers, Reedy and Busby to soldiers standing at attention. As jobs came up for action, the President beckoned to one or another. The man stepped forward and did the job, and it might or might not be in some field already staked out for him—or in a field previously staked out for someone else. Tom Wicker noted in The Times: "Sometimes confusion results from the seeming formlessness of the Johnson administrative system. One old Kennedy hand recalls that on a single day he was called by Mr. Valenti, Mr. Moyers and Gen. Chester V. Clifton, the military aide; all gave him the same instructions from the President."

No list of Johnson advisers would be complete without Lady Bird Johnson's name, perhaps at the top of the list. Before they came to the White House, she managed their business enterprises. Now she acts as his eyes and ears on her trips and takes part in many of the informal political chats and decisions.

It was clearly more difficult in a Johnson White House to find out who might be handling, or be knowledgeable about, a particular problem. None, at least at the outset, was identifiably more expert in foreign than domestic affairs, or vice versa. This was in distinct contrast to the Kennedy staff, which at its full development was well-balanced between old government hands, political professionals and academics. Few of the Johnson men fell comfortably into any of these categories. They were of the Capitol Hill variety, for the most part, a different breed of cat from the "downtown" bureaucrat. For the President, however, the system worked. The Times noted that the staff "more nearly discloses a reflection of the man himself—constantly in motion, serving with remarkable dedication and energy, frequently entangled in detail and procedure, but getting results." He is considered to be a hard man to work for, a boss who has no consideration for the hours of his employes, their sensibilities or their private lives.

Presidential decision-making is a mysterious process. Johnson's way is to absorb the opinion around him, let it percolate inside in some instinctual way and come to a decision when it is ready. One close friend, quoted in an article in The Times Magazine, said: "I don't think he really expects answers from his friends most of the time. He uses his friends as sounding boards, letting his thoughts come out and bounce off them. He doesn't put things down on paper, pro and con, like a lawyer. He talks things out. This is how he formulates decisions. The chief function of his friends is to let him talk."

13

The New Mathematics:
The Republican Strategy

After their triumph at San Francisco, anything seemed possible to the Goldwater forces. Even the most experienced among them, men who knew the long road that lay ahead, were encouraged by the ease with which they had swept through the convention and by the great surge of enthusiasm from the delegates. Perhaps, as they had hoped but hardly dared believe, they really were riding the crest of a new wave of political thought that could sweep the country.

The new mathematics of the campaign—assembling 270 electoral votes—did not seem so awesome to the strategists who had readily mastered the old mathematics of the convention—655 delegates. The general outline of their plan had been clear for many months. The strategy involved virtually writing off the big states that most candidates had traditionally contested most fiercely in the past: New York, New Jersey, Pennsylvania and Michigan. It depended upon making up for these big losses in electoral votes by cutting heavily into the South. One formula suggested that the Middle West without Michigan and Minnesota, the Border States without West Virginia and the South without Arkansas, Georgia or Texas would produce 257 likely Goldwater electoral votes. Then the Republican would only have to carry either California or Texas to win without the vote of a single Eastern state. This strategy recognized that Goldwater's philosophy was unlikely to make much headway in the East, which conservatives regarded as lost to liberalism. It held out the hope that his philosophy would find a broad audience in the rest of the country, for his was essentially an appeal to the dwindling rural, Protestant, anti-urban America which had always been suspicious of cities and their minorities—this at a time when the nation was being transformed more and more into a network of connected cities. Some of the elements that would make up that audience were well known to the Goldwater high command: The young campus conservatives, the segregationists in the South, the anti-Negro property owners in the North, the people who hated Communism at home and the people who feared it abroad, all of these plus the "little old ladies in tennis shoes" who had become the half-proud, half-derisive symbol of the radical right.

But Goldwater knew that a coalition of these dissident, disaffected groups would not be enough. They would presumably bring with them seriously conservative elements of the Democratic party, but that would not be enough either. The candidate had to count heavily on two other sources of support: One was the regular Republican state organizations, manned by loyal party workers who would support the Republican Presidential candidate because he was just that, the Republican Presidential candidate; the other potential power source was what had come to be called "the silent vote." It had become an article of faith with conservatives that there were millions of Americans who had not voted for any Presidential candidate for years because they were awaiting the arrival of a Real Conservative. Some of these people had been waiting, it was said, since Calvin Coolidge ran in 1924. Demonstrably, there were millions of eligible voters who did not participate in Presidential elections. Untold numbers of these voters, right-wing theorists stoutly maintained, would turn out when they heard the appealing call of Barry Goldwater.

That same belief underlay much of the financial planning for the Goldwater campaign. While there were a number of weathy conservatives who could be counted on for large contributions, the Republicans were convinced that they could amass a really sizable operating fund from $5 to $25 gifts from hundreds of thousands of partisans. Approaching the question realistically, the G.O.P. fiscal experts thought they might be able to raise through small donations about a third of the $14,000,000 the party had tentatively scheduled for the national campaign.

Early in August, Ralph J. Cordiner, retired chairman of the General Electric Company, was named chairman of the Republican National Finance Committee, i.e., the chief fund-raiser. Nominally, his committee was to produce $3,000,000, its legal limit; in fact, he would be responsible for many times that amount. Politicians agreed generally that the total campaign expense to both parties, before the massive effort was concluded, might well exceed the $175,000,000, taking into consideration spending at the state and local level, that had been expended in 1960.

Goldwater had to proceed on the theory that he would get about the same amount of Republican organization support as any other candidate—at least in the states most important to his strategy. After all, he had campaigned strenuously for years through these states for Republican candidates, not all of whom were in agreement with his views. He felt he had earned the right to draw on this accumulated loyalty now—just as he himself in the 1960 convention had pledged support to Nixon and had worked hard to elect him.

Already, in the days just after the nomination, the cracks began to appear in the usually solid Republican alliance. Governor Romney of Michigan indicated he would not ally himself with the Presidential candidate in his own re-election campaign. Governor Rockefeller of New York pledged his support but found himself talking about the top of the ticket in his speeches; the name Barry Goldwater seemed to stick in his throat. Both of New York's Republican Senators, Kenneth Keating, who was up for re-election, and Jacob Javits, flatly refused to endorse Goldwater. Senator Hugh Scott of Pennsylvania, who was also running, said he was supporting Goldwater—but that was about all he said. There were rumblings from other Republican candidates across the country of what they called independence and the Goldwater staff called disloyalty.

Campaign issues are generally thought of as means of winning over the independent, undecided voter, but they can be just as important in galvanizing a shaken party into combat unity. Thus, it was important for Goldwater to develop as rapidly as possible issues that would make uncertain Republicans support him. Such an issue, Goldwater himself was convinced, was morality in government. In its early stages, the morality issue was wrapped up in a series of inferences that the Republicans felt the American people should draw. The Republicans could not attribute any wrong-doing to Johnson directly, but they could fire off demands that he explain:

Why the lucrative contract for an experimental fighter plane, the TFX, had gone to General Dynamics, of Forth Worth, although Boeing, based in Seattle, had submitted a lower bid?

How had Billie Sol Estes, a Texas wheeler and dealer and an acquaintance of Johnson, managed to dupe the United States Agricultural Department—along with a lot of other people—so successfully?

Was it not likely that Bobby Baker, a Johnson protegé on the Senate staff whom the President now virtually disowned, had bartered high political influence while amassing a million-dollar fortune on a $20,000 salary?

Did or did not the bulk of the Johnson family's fortune come from a television station that enjoyed a big-city monopoly created and preserved by a Federal regulatory agency?

Questions like these never got any answers from the Democrats—or from the Republicans who asked them—but they persuaded a lot of Republicans who had questioned other Goldwater policies that the Presidential candidate was on the right track, after all. So did his persistent efforts to capitalize on dissatisfaction with the inconclusive war in Vietnam and his protests that a policy of accommodation toward the Soviet Union had weakened rather than strengthened the nation's international position.

But Goldwater's civil rights policy remained divisive, not only in the country, but within his own party. In 1961 he had told a group of Georgia Republicans, "We're not going to get the Negro vote as a bloc in 1964 or 1968, so we ought to go hunting where the ducks are." And in 1960 in *The Conscience of a Conservative* he had written: "It so happens that I believe it is both wise and just for Negro children to attend the same schools as whites, and that to deny them this opportunity carries with it strong implications of inferiority. I am not prepared, however, to impose that judgment of mine on the people of Mississippi or South Carolina."

There was not much question where these statements had placed Goldwater in the eyes of Americans concerned with the civil rights cause, politically or morally or both. If you did not intend to try to win Negro votes, these people argued, then you were going to win anti-Negro votes. If you claimed a belief in the principle of equal educational opportunity but refused to endorse it where such opportunity was the most unequal, then your claim was only pretense. For those who interpreted the Republican candidate's record this way, his vote against the Civil Rights Act of 1964 merely underlined his stance, no matter how loudly he insisted that his opposition was a matter of Constitutional principle. Without much doubt, Goldwater's civil rights posture was probably more responsible for driving liberal Republicans away from his standard than any other aspect of his philosophy. In purely political terms, this was a calculated risk. Goldwater strategists, who were less concerned with principle than their candidate, hoped that his position would attract enough Southern segregationists and nervous Northerners to make up for the Republicans who could not accept it.

For Goldwater, the month and a half between his nomination and the formal campaign kickoff was to be a period of consolidation and reconciliation, but it certainly did not open that way. His selection of Miller as his running mate and his defense of extremism in his acceptance speech had not been calculated to assuage his Republican opponents. As the convention closed, and the new candidate took over the organization, The Times reported:

SAN FRANCISCO, July 17—Senator Barry Goldwater moved today to insure conservative control of the Republican National Committee. He assured its members that he would work "with and through that body" and no other.

At a meeting at the St. Francis Hotel, the committee approved the Senator's choice for the national chairmanship, Dean Burch of Arizona.

Mr. Burch announced that John Grenier of Alabama, the Southern Regional Director of the Goldwater campaign, would become his special assistant.

Other appointments gave little if any more comfort to the moderate forces from whom the Goldwater conservatives had wrested control of the party. There was an undercurrent of resentment among those moderates at what they felt was the militant opposition Senator Goldwater and his followers were showing them.

Goldwater had decided that the national committee staff was to be his campaign organization. Unlike a number of Republican Presidential candidates who had set up their own campaign staffs and left the national committee alone, the Arizonan decided to convert the existing organization—and convert it he did. He moved his own headquarters down from Capitol Hill to the committee offices. Then his chief lieutenants, Burch and Grenier, began cleaning house ruthlessly, replacing the staff who had worked under Miller and Senator Thurston Morton with a hand-picked group loyal only to Goldwater. By the time the campaign formally opened, there was just one important professional left on the national committee staff who had been there before Burch arrived, and he was forbidden to talk to the press. Even at the secretarial level, committee workers with years of experience were transferred to outlying annexes and given menial assignments, clearing the way for replacements. Burch could not replace dissident members of the national committee itself, for they were elected by their state organizations. But he could and did shake up the executive committee, through which the national group functions between meetings, dropping members like George L. Hinman of New York, Rockefeller's political chief of staff, and filling many of the vacancies with Goldwater men.

One major political roadblock in Goldwater's path was removed immediately. Four days after the Republican convention ended, Governor George C. Wallace of Alabama went on television and withdrew as a Presidential candidate. Wallace had threatened to run on a third-party ticket and an outright segregationist platform in sixteen states, including virtually all of the South. Had he done so, he would almost certainly have split the conservative opposition to Johnson, endangering Goldwater's chances of carrying Southern states. In withdrawing, Wallace said that his primary mission had been accomplished with the nomination of a conservative candidate by the Republicans. He denied, however, that his retreat had been the result of any deal with Goldwater. Acknowledging Wallace's own excuse that he did not need to run since there was a conservative candidate in the field, Claude Sitton of The Times maintained that this was not the only factor. He wrote:

> But many politicians feel that the Governor's decision was reluctant. They feel that Mr. Wallace was impelled toward withdrawal by the prospect of an embarrassing defeat at the polls in his own home state and by an abrupt loss of financial support for his campaign.
> The Goldwater nomination, they note, all but wiped out what popular support there was for the protest campaign being waged by Mr. Wallace. Observers said there had been a very real question whether the Alabama Democratic Presidential electors, who were committed to the Governor although technically unpledged, could have defeated those pledged to Mr. Goldwater.
> Some of the largest contributors in Alabama to the Governor's campaign were Republicans. With the Goldwater nomination, hope ended that they would back the 16-state campaign planned by Mr. Wallace.

As the Goldwater Southern strategy was being thus preserved, outside events rapidly seemed to underscore its potential value. In New York City a white off-duty police lieutenant shot a fifteen-year-old Negro boy to death. The policeman said he had been threatened with a knife; Negroes who came to the boy's defense maintained the killing had been without justification. A Harlem protest rally erupted into violence and rioting; wild disorder spread on successive nights to a Negro section of Brooklyn and to lower Manhattan. Then the rioting moved to Negro communities in other cities—to Rochester, New York, to Paterson, Elizabeth and Jersey City, to Philadelphia and to Chicago. In almost all cases, the episodes involved deep Negro grievances but they also involved looting and other destructive lawlessness by young Negroes who were more concerned with vandalism than racial equality.

Politically, the riots seemed to be dynamite. Despite their general feeling of confidence, Democrats openly expressed fear that continued outbursts would consolidate the white backlash into a very real campaign factor. Goldwater, too, was troubled by the violence, despite the political profit he might reap from it, and readily accepted proposals for a bipartisan attempt to discourage further disturbances. On July 24, at the President's invitation, Goldwater came to the White House and talked with Johnson for sixteen minutes about the problem. Later, a statement to which both men had agreed was issued. It said: "The President met with Senator Goldwater and reviewed the steps he had taken to avoid the incitement of racial tension. Senator Goldwater expressed his opinion, which was that racial tension should be avoided. Both agreed on this position."

Both men knew that civil rights and all the issue's implications could not be kept out of the campaign. Goldwater acknowledged that some of his supporters could not be stopped from trying to capitalize on the Negro rioting "unless you lock them up in a room and throw the key away." Johnson, two hours after the Goldwater meeting, said they had differences on civil rights and "there will, of course, be discussion. And I intend to carry on some of it, if I am a candidate."

Within a few days, the leadership of the major Negro national organizations, which were solidly if unofficially behind Johnson, stepped in to try to lend a hand. At the behest of Dr. Martin Luther King Jr., the Southern Christian Leadership Conference, the National Association for the Advancement of Colored People, the Urban League and the Negro American Labor Council joined to call for a broad curtailment if not total moratorium on mass civil rights demonstrations until after the election. The chances of rioting could be greatly reduced, the reasoning went, if the demonstrations that assembled large groups of protestors could be eliminated, for the time being. Two more militant Negro groups, the Congress of Racial Equality and the Student Non-violent Coordinating Council, refused to join in the appeal, but it proved nevertheless to be broadly effective.

In late July, with the Democratic National Convention on the horizon, Goldwater began his first—and, as it developed, almost his only—efforts at reconciliation with the moderate—once called liberal—wing of the Republican party. He named two of the party's most respected professionals, Leonard Hall of New York and Ray Bliss of Ohio, to advisory posts on the national committee's campaign staff. Neither man had a public anti-Goldwater record, and both were from states where the Senator badly needed support. As it developed, these were purely propaganda appointments; Hall and Bliss were never admitted to the innermost councils of the campaign nor was their advice taken on matters of really major importance. Hall, a former chairman of the Republican National Committee, and the man who had directed Nixon's 1960 campaign, came down to Washington to be helpful and was all but completely rebuffed. Not even an office was provided for him.

The Washington headquarters of the national committee was organized with

Kitchel as Goldwater's personal representative, while Burch, the young chairman of the national committee, directed its operations. Neither liked or trusted any of the practical politicians who had had experience in previous campaigns, although some were invited to the weekly strategy sessions, held at 2 P.M. every Sunday in Burch's office. Among those who attended, in addition to Kitchel and Burch, were Cliff White, Wayne Hood, John Grenier, Hall, Bliss, L. Richard Guylay, who was director of publicity for the committee; Edward McCabe, Ralph Cordiner, and William S. Warner, Miller's campaign director. Goldwater promised that he or Miller would attend each strategy meeting, if they were in Washington.

On the tactical level, Goldwater instructed his tour managers to arrange short campaign swings, no longer than five or six days at a time. "I want to sleep in my own bed at least once a week," he told one of his associates.

In August, as the Republicans were making their plans, they got a swift and dramatic lesson in the difficulty of countering a President politically when a foreign policy crisis arises. On August 2, an American destroyer, the *Maddox,* was attacked in international waters off Vietnam by North Vietnamese gunboats. Two days later, there was another attack, and Johnson decided to authorize a counter strike against the gunboat bases. Before he announced this decision on television, he consulted Goldwater (who at first refused to accept the President's call, but then decided he simply had to listen to the President). The Republican supported the President's action—he seemed to have little choice—but this did not prevent him from arguing later that Johnson had endangered the United States air raid by his television report while the strike was still in progress. The public opinion polls indicated, however, that Johnson's resolution in time of crisis had won him new friends, in a situation over which his opponent was almost completely powerless.

For a time in early August, Goldwater made a major effort to establish himself as the candidate of all Republicans. On August 6 he attended a top-level strategy conference at Gettysburg, the home of the Republican party's greatest unifier, and publicly rejected immoderate support. Charles Mohr wrote in The Times:

GETTYSBURG, Pa., Aug. 6—Senator Barry Goldwater and his Vice Presidential running mate, Representative William E. Miller, met here today with former President Dwight D. Eisenhower and Richard M. Nixon and solicited their advice on the coming campaign.

In an informal conference after the meeting, Mr. Goldwater firmly repudiated the Ku Klux Klan and said he did not want the support of organizations bearing that name.

In rejecting support of the Klan, Mr. Goldwater seemed to have overruled both Mr. Miller and the new Republican National Chairman, Dean Burch. In recent days, both of them have said that the Republicans would not reject the support of Klansmen.

In breakfast meetings with Republican Congressmen the day of the Gettysburg conference and the morning after, Goldwater exhibited more confidence in his election prospects than ever before. He said that his election would be assured if he carried California, Illinois, Texas, Indiana and Ohio. It was a big order, but he seemed to feel it could be done and it had to be done if he were to win.

It developed later that one of the main purposes of the Gettysburg meeting had been the drafting of a speech for Goldwater to deliver at his one major party harmony effort, a Republican unity conference he had called for Hershey, Pennsylvania, six days later. While Eisenhower outlined issues on which he thought Goldwater might profitably provide the American people with clarifications, two of the General's former aides, Bryce Harlow and Edward McCabe, took notes. McCabe, who was then serving as research director of the Goldwater campaign, supplanted the regular Goldwater speech writer, Karl Hess, for this assignment. Eisenhower, Nixon, fourteen Republican Governors and fourteen candidates for Governor attended the Hershey meeting.

In Hershey, Goldwater faced the problem of how to disassociate himself from the lunatic right-wing fringe without losing whatever legitimate voting power that might accrue to him. At one point he said, "I seek the support of no extremist, of the left or of the right." Another time he said, "We repudiate the character assassins, vigilantes, Communists and any group such as the Ku Klux Klan which seeks to impose its views through terror or threat or violence." But this did not satisfy Rockefeller, who asked why Goldwater could not make "a forthright statement saying you and the candidates completely reject the support of all those who encourage or resort to lawlessness, conspiracy, racism and violence."

"Didn't you get that out of what he said?" Eisenhower asked.

"Well, you could if you were a lawyer, but when you are one of the fellows on the lower level, it does not quite say that," Rockefeller persisted. After raising the question of the Republican party image, and the dangers of losing in the industrial states, Rockefeller went on, "I think, from my own point of view, I must continue to vigorously oppose any and all efforts that would make our party appear to be a party of lawlessness, a party of racism, or a war party."

"I don't know how I can say it any more candidly or more clearly than I have said it," Goldwater replied.

Before the conference ended, Rockefeller returned to the subject of extremists. "You don't seek their support, but you don't reject their support," he said. It was clear that the two men were politely disagreeing on this issue, but in general the Republicans who attended found themselves in agreement on other differences—at least for the campaign. Charles Mohr reported:

HERSHEY, Pa., Aug. 12—Senator Barry Goldwater offered to Republican leaders today a sweeping set of political reassurances including a promise to consult former President Dwight Eisenhower on the appointments of Secretaries of State and Defense.

In a speech to a unity conference of party leaders, Mr. Goldwater made what observers considered to be a distinct shift toward the middle of the road.

The Republican Presidential candidate repudiated extremist groups and "character assassins." He expressed support of the United Nations, which he has often criticized and of the Social Security program. He promised not to shirk Federal responsibility in the field of civil rights.

Afterwards, Eisenhower pronounced himself satisfied with Goldwater, although the candidate himself refused to admit he had been conciliatory or made concessions. In general, reaction among the Republican leaders—except for Rockefeller and Romney—was good. Some of them felt for the first time that this was a candidate with whom and for whom they could campaign with honor and without risk. The Hershey declaration was the high-water mark of Republican unity in a campaign that was not to open formally for another three weeks.

Just after the Hershey meeting, there was encouraging news from the South. At a meeting of Democratic Governors in New Orleans, three of them —Wallace of Alabama, Johnson of Mississippi and Faubus of Arkansas— reported they were planning to endorse Goldwater during the campaign. A fourth, McKeithen of Louisiana, was understood to be holding back only because he did not believe the Republican would win.

On August 19, Goldwater set out on his first campaign trip since the convention. In Springfield, Illinois, he told 15,000 people at the State Fair that Johnson had endangered the lives of American pilots by giving the North Vietnamese warning that their patrol boat installations were about to be bombed, in retaliation for the attack on the *Maddox*. He also drew loud applause with attacks on lawlessness and violence in the nation.

But Goldwater disturbed many observers who had become fond of him by his increasingly open use of the white backlash issue. Reporters referred to it as his "anti-rape" speech, in which he virtually accused the Democrats of responsibility for molestations of women. He said that dishonesty and cynicism in high places had led to increased crime of all sorts. "Every wife and mother, yes, every woman and girl, knows what I mean, knows what I am talking about," he said.

A week later he told a veterans' convention in Cleveland that small conventional nuclear weapons should be allocated to the North Atlantic Treaty Organization, one of a series of speeches that seemed designed to downgrade the seriousness of atomic weapons and their custody. At both appearances, the Republican was warmly received as he spoke but caused little stir otherwise.

Then Goldwater flew west for a six-day yachting vacation off the Southern California coast. He made sporadic news there by radiophoning his views on the Democratic National Convention, Vietnam and race rioting to his press secretary on shore. He made a quick trip to Washington to vote against the medical care for the aged bill on the Senate floor, and finally returned to Phoenix for the formal opening of the Republican campaign.

What kind of a campaign would it be? James Reston had expressed the hope that the deep differences between the candidates would lead the parties to a more fundamental examination than had featured national elections in the past. He wrote:

It will not do . . . for the Democrats merely to debate the Senator's voting record and ignore his philosophy, to denounce his allies and scoff at his moral yearnings. For he is at least talking about the essentially human ends of political life, and even if you think he is often talking nonsense, somehow he has inspired an emotional personal following that no other active figure in America can equal. . . .

A savage conflict between the parties on ideological grounds cannot be avoided now, but it can have some advantages. Ideally, the purpose of an election is to clarify and not to confuse the issues, to destroy and not to perpetuate illusion, to make a little clearer what we are and where we are.

Senator Goldwater has set the stage for this. He has offered his choice. He has arrested the attention of the nation. He may not have the answers, but at least he has raised some good questions, and the Democrats, if they are wise, will stop moaning about Barry and his allies, and start dealing with his arguments.

14

The Middle Ground:
The Democratic Strategy

At the LBJ Ranch that weekend after the nomination, Lyndon Johnson and Hubert Humphrey chased cows, joked with reporters, looked at the house where Johnson was born, the family graveyard and the home of the ranch foreman. "Yahoo! Yahoo!" yelled Humphrey as he rode after some cows. "He's good at relaxing," the President said.

There was, however, no relaxation that weekend for the Democratic party strategists. Looking to the formal opening of the campaign on Labor Day a little more than a week away, they tried to match up their marked advantages against the usual "run scared" worries of a candidate widely assumed to be way out in front. They had known for months who their nominee would be and had already spent months preparing a campaign cut to his specifications.

It was clear to all that Johnson himself was the master strategist of the Johnson campaign. He kept a tight hand on every detail; he called all the shots. Some of the men who worked in the inner circles of the White House knew that the President was frequently criticized as corny; but they also recognized that he knew the people wanted simple, unsophisticated answers to their questions and fears. He remembered that Adlai Stevenson, for example, in his campaigns of 1952 and 1956, had spoken over the heads of his audiences and even though he had won the plaudits of the intellectuals, he had lost votes. Moreover, sophistication just didn't fit the image of the country boy from Texas. Sincerely and with a straight face, the President, when he wanted to plead for unity, could get his message across even at the risk of triteness by reciting such homilies as "United we stand, divided we fall."

Another factor that helped shape Johnson's strategy was his oft-expressed desire for victory in his own right, for an overwhelming mandate. Some more cynical observers felt that his compulsion to win big was an outgrowth of his own ego, a manifestation of his desire to be well liked. A gregarious man, who liked people and wanted to be liked, Johnson's way of expressing this was that he wanted to be "President of all the people."

There was yet another determinant in Johnson's political makeup: A deep-seated fear, not of Goldwater himself, but of the men who supported him. He believed they were dangerous men; he called them the bomb throwers. In private conversation, he would tick off their names one by one, and, on the memorandum pad on which he habitually makes marks and doodles, he would emphatically make a check as he called off each name. He equated them with insidious forces in American political life, such as the Ku Klux Klan, and he said he hoped they would be beaten and repudiated once and for all.

Johnson firmly believed that the American people possessed a strong sense of their times and that they would respond to a candidate who gave reasoned answers to the questions uppermost in their minds. These questions, he felt, could be reduced to two: Peace or war and future well-being. Moreover, he felt that the nation had come through a violent upheaval in the assassination of President Kennedy and that it could not face another major change in its government in less than a year, given, of course, the premise that the country was at peace and relatively prosperous and wanted to remain so.

In his conception of what the campaign would be, Johnson turned the normal pattern 180 degrees around: Usually campaigns start out with a high moral tone and discussion of the issues, then degenerate into personalities, but the Johnsonian concept was to keep himself on a high "let's discuss the issues" level throughout the campaign. At the beginning, his aides would attempt to pin warmonger, irresponsible, extremist and right-winger tags on Goldwater, thus putting him, they hoped, on the defensive; as the campaign drew to a close, all the Democrats would turn their attention to issues, dismissing low personal attacks as gutter politics. In short, the Democrats hoped to build early in the campaign an image of Goldwater as a man who could not be trusted with the lives of the American people while picturing Johnson as the man above petty politics, always willing to talk sense to the voters.

Under the direct guidance of Johnson, the Democratic National Committee had already been converted into an integrated campaign organization with a blend of Kennedy men and Johnson men at the top. John M. Bailey had been picked to run the campaign in his capacity as chairman of the Democratic National Committee, reflecting a Johnson decision to use the committee as the vehicle for his race rather than a separate personal organization (in the last three Democratic campaigns, separate organizations had largely bypassed the national committee). To share responsibility with Bailey, the President sent over Clifton C. Carter, a rangy, taciturn Texan, who had helped Johnson in every election since 1937 and had served as a full-time administrative assistant since he became Vice President. Known as the President's man at the committee, Carter took on the job of campaign coordinator. At the White House, Walter Jenkins was Johnson's chief liaison man to the committee; he came with instructions from Johnson and when he spoke everybody understood that it was Johnson speaking.

In addition, the Democrats set up an electronic network unlike anything used in previous campaigns. Central headquarters in Washington was connected around the clock with each state coordinator by high-speed telecommunications circuits. These would be used for urgent committee messages and to transmit important news releases for simultaneous distribution in all parts of the country. A crew in Washington was organized to monitor all network news programs and receive telephone reports from twenty cities on the top political articles and editorials in the local newspapers. As before, the Democrats tried to generate steam behind a drive to register new voters, particularly in the traditionally Democratic counties and districts of the ten or twelve largest states. The 1964 Democratic campaign manual had told workers that the majority of "unregistered persons are likely to vote Democratic and that the Democratic party's platform, policies and candidates will have more appeal to new voters." It was not just a coincidence that the Post Office Department issued a Register and Vote stamp for 1964.

Even before Kennedy's assassination the Democrats had opened a massive registration drive called the Voter Identification Program. In the major urban areas of twelve key states, where the bulk of the electoral votes lay, the Democrats picked out precincts that normally voted 60 per cent Democratic. Using special telephone directories that listed subscribers by street and house and voting registers, volunteer workers called every person not registered, urged them to register and sent other volunteers to their doorsteps to make sure they did get out to the registration booths. It was a sign of the economic growth of the country that the telephone was no longer a mark of relative affluence and, therefore, of a leaning toward the Republicans; nobody worried that using telephone directories for lists of names might distort the political picture, as *The Literary Digest* did in 1936 when it predicted the election of Landon by a straw poll of telephone subscribers.

Goldwater, in his effort to win his party's primaries and its nomination, had been forced to reveal earlier in the year much of the hand he intended to play during the campaign. With so many Goldwater cards face up on the table, Democratic strategists had learned early what kind of game to expect. As Cliff Carter put it shortly before Labor Day: "The big issue, I think, is peace —peace or war. I think what most people want to know is whose hand is next to that nuclear panic button. We are going to stress responsibility versus irresponsibility in high office."

Thus, even before the campaign had its formal start, Democrats were pointing at the challenger and saying, Do you want this man's finger on the button? They had decided to fight fear with fear, to counter Goldwater's fear of moral decline at home and of loss of honor abroad by raising the fear that his policies would produce war abroad and depression at home.

On the basis of what they knew about Goldwater's views, Democrats decided to try to convince working class voters that the Republican nominee was anti-labor, might tinker and tamper with the Social Security benefits and possibly jeopardize gains made by workers since the nineteen thirties. They would point to the seeming contradictions in some Goldwater statements, try to picture him as a man of snap judgments and raise the question of whether he actually knew his own mind.

On foreign affairs, Democrats also worked out their answers to Goldwater's oft-expressed opinion that military power could prevail if the United States had the courage to build it and demonstrated a determination to use it. The Democrats planned to stress the need for such power and, at the same time, to cite the grave danger of indiscriminate use of it.

The strategists came up with this advice: Point to the withdrawal of Soviet missiles from Cuba in the 1962 crisis and to the Johnson-ordered air attack on North Vietnam after the Gulf of Tonkin incidents as examples of Democratic strength; emphasize that victory depends on how strength is used, on the ability of an Administration to gauge the trend of world affairs and on the experience to take advantage of that trend by peaceful means. Putting the best possible face on deteriorating situations, they also suggested noting that American strength—including that at the bargaining table—had been used to prevent a take-over in Laos, to buy time in Vietnam and the Congo, to puncture the Iron Curtain that so long insulated Eastern Europe from Western contact, and to take modest steps toward the limitation of the arms race. The idea of brinkmanship in foreign affairs or using tactics on the verge of open warfare to force Communist nations to back down from their policies, they said, was both risky and unrealistic for the nuclear age.

The Democrats knew they had one supreme advantage. Their man was, after all, the President of the United States and in most campaigns that usually was enough. The three Vice Presidents who moved into the White House in this century on the death of the President—Teddy Roosevelt, Coolidge and Truman—were all elected in their own right at the next election. The only Presidents defeated in this century for re-election were Taft in 1912 because the Republican party split with Teddy Roosevelt and the Bull Moosers, and Hoover in 1932, blamed for a depression not of his making.

The single week before Labor Day illustrated the immense advantages of a White House incumbency. At a gathering at Stonewall, Texas, Johnson stood near a hundred foot barbecue pit, and gave his neighbors a folksy lecture on foreign affairs that included a defense of his policies in Vietnam and Cuba. When Castro turned off the water at the United States naval base at Guantanamo, Johnson said, he had received a lot of advice. "I had some generals here and there," the President said, "who hollered at me to send in the Marines. I saw no reason to send the Marines, so I sent in an admiral instead"—who set up a new water supply system. Such comments, of course, enhanced the image of quiet responsibility the Democratic strategists had long ago decided to project.

Another tremendous advantage that the Johnson forces enjoyed as a result of their candidate's incumbency was the power to raise campaign funds. The Democratic National Committee had estimated, in a rather off-hand way, that it expected the 1964 campaign to cost somewhat more than the $10,000,000 spent four years before. Actually, neither of these figures came close to real overall expenditures, but everyone knew that the financial problem was going to be challenging. Behind Johnson, in addition to the usual collection of general and special committees, was a relatively new medium, the President's Club. This assemblage of Americans who had each contributed a minimum of $1,000 a year to the party was regularly called on for more. The Democrats also could rely on the lion's share of the collection of the A.F.L.-C.I.O.'s Committee on Political Education, a substantial fund-raiser for years. Finally, as the favorite, Johnson was sure to fall heir to contributions from individuals and groups that wanted to be on record as having supported the winner.

After appearing on the front pages of the nation's newspapers lecturing neighbors, chasing cows and riding horses during the weekend at the ranch, Johnson flew back to Washington. There at a White House ceremony he signed the wilderness bill and a measure for Federal aid for nurses' training, calling both achievements in the interest of all the people. Then he used a little direct persuasion on Capitol Hill to win passage of the $4,100,000,000 food for peace program without some proposed restrictions that had been suggested for limiting Presidential authority. One member of Congress said he had become convinced overnight that the restriction was unwise. He did not deny that he had received a phone call from the President.

Johnson deftly sidestepped a potential embarrassment when the Bobby Baker case reared up again. Senator John J. Williams, Republican of Delaware, charged that Baker had conspired to divert $25,000 from a public stadium contract in Washington to the 1960 Kennedy-Johnson campaign. Johnson decided to send the whole matter to the Federal Bureau of Investigation.

He passed out some more ammunition to support his Administration in its running quarrel with Goldwater about the pace of new weapons development. Again he didn't refer to his rival's charge of military lethargy, but he hailed as new and significant the navy's continuing experiments with improved submarine-borne nuclear missiles and with more efficient nuclear power plants for future aircraft carriers. He also talked about advances in the Polaris A-3 missile.

The President had done this before, and it led Russell Baker to observe:

President Johnson has developed an odd habit. Whenever he comes under political attack, he hits back with news bulletins from the wonderful world of hardware.

The hardware rebuttal seems to have been used for the first time last February when Republicans were nagging the President about Robert Baker. While everyone wondered how the President would retaliate, he called a news conference and announced the "development" of the new flying machine called A-11. Or was it SR-71?

In any case, it was a flying machine. Actually, it may have been that the A-11 or the SR-71 had just been "improved," made "operational," or "deployed." The curious thing about exciting new hardware news is how rapidly it rolls off the memory. It is like Chinese food—exciting to the taste, but doesn't stay with you.

Well, after the news of the development, improvement or deployment of the A-11 or SR-71, Republicans kept sniping at the President, and the President returned a steady barrage of hardware news.

With metronomic regularity, we were all urged to exult at news that the Pentagon would develop Redeye, or Walleye, or Shillelagh, all of which, when improved and deployed, would shoot the bejeebers out of something or other.

Last month, when Bobby Baker was re-entering the news sphere, Mr. Johnson announced "speedy development" of a new plane for anti-guerrilla warfare. A fortnight later, he reported the latest on ocean-going hardware: The A-3 missile, "a new and significantly improved" advance over the old A-1, had just been deployed on a Polaris submarine. It represented a 60 per cent improvement over the old A-1. Or was it a 40 per cent improvement over the old SR-11?

The early strategy, including all that talk of military hardware, seemed to be working. Editorial support in the nation's newspapers began to mount. *The Kansas City Star*, for instance, endorsing a Democratic Presidential candidate for the first time since Grover Cleveland ran in 1892, came out for Johnson, saying "it would be safer to keep his finger on the nuclear treaty than to place the awesome responsibility on Senator Goldwater." Also during that pre-Labor Day week, the A.F.L.-C.I.O., to the surprise of no one, decided it also liked Johnson better than his opponent. At a meeting in Washington, it endorsed the Johnson-Humphrey ticket, calling Goldwater "basically an impulsive man"; it voted to spend $2,000,000 on political education.

The business reaction, however, did contain some surprises. In line with Democratic strategy to woo Republicans antipathetic to Goldwater, the White House announced just before Labor Day that the President had received broad backing from an influential group of the nation's business and financial leaders—three-fourths of them Republican. The support came at an organizational meeting in the White House of the National Independent Committee for President Johnson and Senator Humphrey. Among those attending were Marion B. Folsom and Robert B. Anderson, both Eisenhower Cabinet officers, Henry Ford 2d, and Edgar F. Kaiser, chairman of Kaiser Aluminum and Chemical Corporation. (The Goldwater forces also had organized a business committee of 450, led by George M. Humphrey, Eisenhower's Secretary of the Treasury, and Vivien Kellems, the Connecticut businesswoman whose opposition to the income tax had brought her into well-publicized conflict with the Government.) An earlier Times article by M. J. Rossant described why businessmen seemed to be going to Johnson:

Whether or not businessmen follow the example of Henry Ford 2d and vote for President Johnson next November, it is clear that they have confidence in him and his policies. The mood in the business and investment community is brighter than at any time since the early years of President Eisenhower's "Businessman's" Administration.

It did not take a major shift in policy to win the confidence of businessmen. They were surprised and impressed by Mr. Johnson's decision to cut back on Government spending, which helped to gain speedy passage of tax reductions. Since he declared that businessmen and Government were partners, they have had the feeling that they now have a friend in the White House.

The President's policies are pretty much a continuation of those set by his predecessor. At the same time, he inherited an economy that was in remarkably good shape. But he is being hailed as "probusiness" while President Kennedy was labeled "antibusiness."

Economic historians cannot yet make any decisive judgments. But style seems to be the main difference between Mr. Johnson and Mr. Kennedy.

The business community was suspicious of President Kennedy's intellect and his reformist approach. It was annoyed at his attack on business myths even though few businessmen were prepared to defend them.

In contrast, businessmen feel at home with President Johnson. They know that he is disposed to use the power of his office as fully as Mr. Kennedy, but they understand his way of operating. He may be even more firmly committed to the price-wage guidelines that business dislikes, but this does not seem to matter either. There is continuity, but with a difference.

In effect, Johnson and his aides had decided, ironically, to try to win much of the ordinarily conservative Republican vote by asking the nation to conserve—conserve the comparative peace and prosperity they enjoyed under the Johnson Administration, maintain stability in national government, and reject the radical pleas to turn out an incumbent by electing a man who would be the third different President in fourteen months.

There was a conscious effort on the part of the Johnson strategists to reap political advantage from Goldwater's defense of extremism in his speech accepting the nomination. The opening was there: Picture the Goldwater followers as "kooks and nuts" and try to lure moderate Republicans into the Democratic fold; talk about the capture of the Republican party by a faction; convince the moderates, in short, that Goldwater had abandoned the wide middle road of American politics where most of the nation stood. In support of this strategy, Johnson condemned clandestine hate organizations. Asked if he referred to the Ku Klux Klan and the John Birch Society, he replied: "I refer to all hate organizations by whatever name they make. I am not one who believes that the end justifies the means."

Johnson and his aides realized that Goldwater's policies, particularly his "no" vote on civil rights, would go a long way to help the Republican nominee capture the 128 electoral votes of the Old Confederacy. Even before his nomination, the President was said by The Times to believe that the Goldwater civil rights stand would insure victory for the Senator in Mississippi and Alabama. The President also believed then that Virginia and Florida had so nearly become Republican states in national elections that they would be likely to go Republican in any case. Elsewhere in the South, the President's view was that with a strong effort he could carry Georgia, North Carolina, Arkansas and Texas. Tennessee, South Carolina and Louisiana he regarded as states on the fence. Later Administration strategy would pit the farm pocketbook against the civil rights issue. "We hope," one campaign planner said, "that we can get through to the voters who are wavering and produce some thoughts that perhaps economics should be weighed fairly against civil rights."

The idea was to gear the Southern pocketbook strategy not only to the larger urban centers that depend on agriculture but also to the somewhat isolated backwoods rural areas of small cotton producers and local merchants who carried them on credit. The appeal would reach into areas benefiting from the Federal rural electrification program; the Tennessee Valley Authority, which Goldwater had suggesting selling, extended deep into the heart of Dixie, with dependent rural electric co-ops in Tennessee, Kentucky, Georgia, Alabama and Mississippi. The Authority's lines intertwined with city and private systems throughout the South.

Another hope was that the success of the Negro registration drive in the South might help offset some pro-Goldwater sentiment, for polls showed early in the race that the President might receive as much as 97 per cent of the Negro vote. For the ten-year period ended in 1962, the number of Negroes registered in the eleven-state region had only increased from a little over 1,000,000 to about 1,390,000; in two subsequent years, owing to drives by civil rights organizations and pressures brought by the Federal Government and the courts, it shot up to an estimated total of 2,165,000.

In the North, the Negro vote would be even more substantial, but the Administration found new worries created by the continuing civil rights demonstrations and violence there. The first major evidence of Northern white resentment—the so-called backlash—had come in the Wisconsin Presidential primary in April when Governor George C. Wallace of Alabama received 266,136 votes, or about one third the total; Governor John W. Reynolds, who was running as a favorite son, won with 522,405 votes. Then on May 5 the Alabama segregationist had done it again. In the Indiana primary he received 172,646 votes, or nearly 30 per cent of the Democratic total, while running against Governor Matthew E. Welsh, a stand-in for Johnson. This vote was especially significant because Wallace carried Lake County, which includes Gary, where the civil rights movement was more militant than any other place in the state. Two weeks later Wallace ran up his greatest primary total, winning 43 per cent of the vote in Maryland against Senator Daniel B. Brewster. Wallace would have won the primary but for a heavy turnout from urban Negro districts and middle-class suburbs of Baltimore and Washington. The final tally was Wallace 214,837 and Brewster 267,104.

There were various explanations: Wallace's opponents were not outstanding candidates and had not waged aggressive campaigns. In each state, it was said, there were factors other than race involved. It was also emphasized that Wallace had lost each of the primaries. Nevertheless, the Governor had proved his point: That the white backlash extended to the North. How widespread it might become remained to be seen. But Democratic leaders in the last week of August were hoping the backlash could be reduced if new racial explosions could be averted.

For his part, Johnson began talking of a poll showing a marked "frontlash"—the Republican voter defections stemming from distrust of Goldwater policies. Just before Johnson left for his ranch that post-nomination weekend, The Times reported his pep talk to some members of the Democratic National Committee:

For every backlash we Democrats lose, we will pick up three frontlash. Of course, it's disappointing to realize that the one you lose is because someone doesn't believe in equal treatment for all Americans. But the three you gain, do believe in equal treatment.

But the Democratic party is open to all people, the humble and the proud, the wealthy and the poor, the weak and the strong. . . .

So we will welcome the backlash to come back and the frontlash to come forward.

The President believed that his stand on the major issues, his stance in the political center, his de-emphasis of party, his repeated appeals to moderate Republicans, would do much to offset what white backlash might exist in the North. Moreover, he clearly felt, along with his campaign planners, that he stood to gain more out of such issues as social legislation, including medical care for the aged, than Goldwater would with his attacks on big government.

The favorable polls, meanwhile, continued to roll in. The President, as The Times reported shortly before Labor Day, watched them carefully:

It is known that the President is scrutinizing a wide variety of political polls, some private and some public. Many of them are so lopsided, including one that shows margins of up to 79 per cent in his favor in New England, that he regards them with disbelief and is having them rechecked.

The President, it is learned, will use the polls in campaign strategy meetings, as guides to the scheduling of his campaign appearances.

While he is heartened by the polls, he regards them with enough skepticism to realize that the wide margin currently apparent may narrow as the campaign proceeds.

Nevertheless, the President is reliably reported to be unworried that topheavy poll reports now will develop into voter apathy that might damage him in November. He is known to feel that voters do not go to the ballot box or stay away because they believe the outcome of an election is a foregone conclusion.

He has expressed this view to confidants by equating it with the reasons people join the army—not, he says, because it is a big army, or well trained or physically fit, but because they want to do their duty. The President is convinced that citizens cast their votes for the same reason.

In this entire century only Franklin Delano Roosevelt among the winning Democrats got a majority of the total national vote—not Kennedy, nor Truman, nor Wilson. There were still enough imponderables to cause worry among some strategists—the extent of the white backlash, the strength of the Goldwater type of conservatism, the wave of longing by Americans for the simpler times Goldwater talked of, the cry for order in the streets.

As Labor Day approached, the Democratic strategists got out their pencils for a little electoral vote calculations. If they wrote off part of the Old Confederacy, their forecast showed the President should still have enough states elsewhere to carry the election, maybe even carry it big. Few Democratic planners lost any sleep worrying about the Northeast—Connecticut, Delaware, Massachusetts, New Jersey, New York, Pennsylvania and Rhode Island alone would give the President 118 electoral votes out of the 270 needed to win.

But in the Middle West, the highest Democratic hopes were to carry Michigan, Illinois and Minnesota again (all three had gone to the Democrats in

1960). These fifty-seven votes would give Johnson a total of 175. Labor, strong in Michigan, was all for Johnson; Minnesota, the home state of the Vice Presidential nominee, should be no problem; and the farm vote downstate and the city vote of Chicago might well turn the trick in Illinois. With Iowa in the farm belt and West Virginia in the Border states, the President would have a total of 191. The Democratic planners, now seventy-nine electoral votes short, believed they could wrap it up with four more states—Texas, with twenty-five; California, forty; Oregon, six; and Washington, nine, for an over-the-top total of 271. If California, despite the big Democratic edge in registration, went awry, they counted on perhaps Ohio and a few of the Mountain and Border states to make up the difference.

The strategists were not worried about the Goldwater campaign particularly but they knew that external events could conceivably affect the race. Along with the advantages of the Presidency went the responsibilities for failure. Among these possibilities were an expanded war in Vietnam, a major Soviet thrust, the beginnings of an economic collapse in this country and, more pointedly, another heart attack for Johnson.

One week before Labor Day, The Times reported, "After a week of exchanging views and attending private campaign briefings conducted in Atlantic City by national organization experts, Democratic party leaders have returned to their fifty states confident that President Johnson will be elected by a landslide."

15

"I Possibly Do Shoot from the Hip"

On the morning of September 3, Goldwater drove to Skyharbor Airport in Phoenix to make the short flight to Prescott, Arizona, where he was to open his campaign formally. The Senator and his wife were posing for pictures on the tarmac before boarding their plane when he winked at Charles Mohr of The Times. Mohr asked if Goldwater had any phrase or slogan to match President Truman's legendary 1948 remark, "I'm going to give 'em hell."

Goldwater tried to maintain a mock solemnity, but a grin crept out as he said, "I'm not allowed to use language like Harry Truman does." His wife, Peggy, overhearing this, turned her head in surprise—and laughed.

Nevertheless Goldwater's ungrammatical disclaimer was misleading. Although he talked softly on the campaign stump, he made some of the harshest charges in political history. Both he and his peppery running mate, Bill Miller, were going to give 'em hell, even if they did not use the nasty word itself. Goldwater was convinced that "subtle impulses," stemming from various dissatisfaction and discontent, were at work throughout the nation, and on them he based his hope for victory on November 3. To convert those feelings into votes for himself, he would have to stir a variety of passions among the voters, raise controversies and attract the uncommitted.

Thus as Goldwater spoke from the bunting-draped courthouse steps in Prescott, a town of 15,000 atop a mile-high plateau hugged by the Bradshaw and San Prieto Mountains, he talked tough, but also attempted to assuage fears about his views on the economy and foreign policy. It was a friendly home town area. The Senator could see in front of him Goldwater's, a branch of the family department store that had served the community since 1876. He had begun his Senate campaigns in 1952 and 1958 in the same courthouse square. The crowd of about 5,000, while far below the predicted turnout of 20,000 to 30,000, received the speech enthusiastically.

Goldwater promised to act compassionately and gradually in carrying out his conservative principles, and said present commitments to the public in the social welfare and economic fields must be honored. "Good faith requires that we not disappoint reasonable expectations based on those commitments," he said. On two other subjects, however, Goldwater bore down with the aggressiveness expected of him—the backlash issue and a new one, that of the military draft.

On the first, he contended that it was the responsibility of national leaders to enforce the law, not let it be abused or ignored. Although conceding that local laws were local problems, he elaborated: "It is a responsibility of the national leadership to make sure that it, and its spokesman and supporters, do not discourage the enforcement or incite the breaching of these laws. Choose the way of this present Administration, and you have the way of the mobs in the street, restrained only by the plea that they wait until after the election to ignite the violence again." This refrain, to be sounded again and again during the campaign, was taken by his listeners as indirect reference to the Negro civil rights fight and to white resentment engendered by it.

On the draft, he said: "This Administration uses the outmoded and unfair military draft system for social schemes as well as military objectives. Republicans will end the draft altogether, and as soon as possible! That I promise you!"

If Goldwater was raising a new campaign issue with his draft proposal, it was not a new idea, as the Pentagon was quick to point out the same day, reminding him—and the voters—that Johnson four months previously had ordered a study aimed at ending the draft as quickly as possible. The statement also recalled that President Eisenhower in 1956 had said that "the issue of our military draft is no matter of a technical point to be scored in a political debate."

The draft question brought Goldwater bold headlines across the country, but also considerable unfavorable editorial comment. James Reston replied this way to a "Goldwater lady from Indiana," who questioned what she termed the bias of the wicked left-wing Eastern press against her candidate:

We simply read what Barry and his spokesmen say, and then pass on the results. Or we compare what the Senator says one day with what he or his aides say on another, and the thing comes out anti-Goldwater almost every time. . . .

The Republican nominee's speech . . . today illustrates one side of the technique. It is an exercise in moral philosophy. It is full of the noble words of the English language—honor, hope, faith, vision and purpose.

It invites the voters to join him in "a good and noble cause," to clarify and purify our lives, to seek "greatness and purpose, to reject easy morals and uneasy ethics," to acquire "greatness of heart and self-restraint," and to follow men who will lead the way to these high ideals, meaning, of course, Goldwater and Miller.

. . . but alongside or underneath these eloquent yearnings in the Goldwater camp, there are other themes directed at less noble sentiments.

In the same speech, the Senator calls for more military strength, and "a slow-down in the expansion in Federal spending," and the end of the military draft— all within a few paragraphs of one another!

In one paragraph he condemns the Democrats for suggesting his policies might lead to war, and a few minutes later condemns the Democrats for drifting "closer to war on an ebbing tide of military strength."

It remained for Johnson to have the final word on the draft—at least for the moment. Two days later, at his press conference, he rejected the draft as a campaign issue and suggested that the reporters look up Goldwater's comments on a speech in 1956 by Adlai E. Stevenson, who had pledged to reduce the national debt and end the draft. Then Goldwater had observed that Stevenson had called for an adequate defense linked to the end of compulsory military service, and quipped, "If I were Adlai Stevenson, I'd take that platform and tear it up."

On the day of Johnson's reply on the draft, Goldwater flew 3,800 miles to give a speech that lasted only a few minutes and consisted primarily of carpetbagger jokes directed at Robert Kennedy, now Democratic candidate for the Senate from New York. It was a speech, however, that helped launch the second stage of the G.O.P. Presidential campaign—at Lockport, New York, Miller's home. Enroute to Lockport, Goldwater released a Labor Day statement that managed to draw a fair share of attention to himself without disrupting the rally. He said that, if elected President, he would propose to Congress "a regular program of automatic annual cuts in income taxes." It was a teaser statement, calculated to stir and hold interest until Goldwater spelled out the details in a later speech at Los Angeles, but it was understood that the proposal would depend on a series of balanced budgets.

Taxes, a perennial subject of paramount interest to the voters, dominated the Senator's activities for the next few days. He had been scheduled to amplify his views in a speech on Tuesday, September 8, at Dodger Stadium in Los Angeles, but his thinking on the issue was leaked by a key aide the day before. What Goldwater had in mind was an automatic tax cut of 25 per cent, spread over five years, with Federal expenditures stabilized at roughly present levels. The reduction would be in the amount of tax paid each year, not in the tax rate. The proposal was based on the theory that the gross national product would continue to rise steadily and generate more tax revenue.

Dr. Milton Friedman of the University of Chicago and Dr. Warren Nutter of the University of Virginia, both conservative and non-Keynesian economists, were regarded as the men mainly responsible for the Goldwater proposal, although they credited Dr. Arthur Burns, who had once been Eisenhower's chairman of the Council of Economic Advisers, with advancing the theory of a disposable, steady increase in revenue. It was anything but conservative. Secretary of the Treasury Douglas Dillon, in a talk to businessmen, said of the 25 per cent tax-cut plan, "No one with the slightest understanding of fiscal affairs . . . could countenance the prospect of blindly and irrevocably binding us to annual tax cuts for many years ahead regardless of the state of the economy." Dillon did not mention Goldwater in his speech, but his target was not difficult to pinpoint when he said, "In the conduct of economic policy, moderation is no vice—it is an absolute and virtuous necessity." M. J. Rossant in The Times said the plan made President Johnson look like the very model of a fiscal conservative.

The G.O.P. nominee finally made his tax speech at Dodger Stadium, where more than 51,000 persons paid a dollar each (something of a departure in political campaign rallies) to fill the huge arena. Their fervor and loyalty were deafening. Among the past and present Hollywood figures involved in the rally were Martha Tilton, Randolph Scott, Walter Brennan, Cesar Romero, Monte Montana and Ronald Reagan. Montana performed rope tricks for the crowd before Goldwater arrived, and Miss Tilton sang a new version of Gershwin's "Of Thee I Sing":

> Of thee we sing, Barry.
> You are our boy, Barry.
> You've got guts . . . you're what we need, Barry.

When Goldwater and his wife entered in a convertible from deep center field the stadium shook alarmingly as the spectators stamped their feet in unison. The crowd also roared "Charge!" in unison as an electric scoreboard winked the word on and off. The crowd cheered Goldwater more than the tax cut proposal—possibly because of the way the speech backed into this and many other subjects. Although he was proposing a huge tax cut himself, Goldwater called the Democratic tax cut of 1964 a "cynical scheme, impulsive, massive, politically-motivated tax cut gimmickery." He explained that he had voted against the tax cut bill because it was reckless and "designed to drug the economy into an artificial boom." He termed his own proposal honest and said it was primarily designed to "find ways to keep more money in your pocket."

If the candidate's reception at the stadium rally pleased him, he had received a more mixed greeting earlier that day in San Diego where he was heckled by civil rights groups who brandished such signs as "Thinking Americans Favor Civil Rights But Not Senator Goldwater" and "Bigots, Racists United For Goldwater." At one inopportune juncture, a false fire alarm was triggered by a heckler, lowering a steel firescape into the crowd surrounding his speaker's truck in front of the U.S. Grant Hotel. No one was injured and after the fire bells were stilled, Goldwater wisecracked, "I've made strong speeches, but never made one that strong."

It was in San Diego, too, that the Senator broke one of his campaign pledges—albeit a minor one. All year long he had been insisting that he was not a baby-kissing candidate, and his campaign manager, Denison Kitchel, had once jokingly threatened to resign if Goldwater ever reneged on this issue. But at Lindbergh Field, on his arrival in the city, he kissed a three-year-old girl on the cheek and flashed a defiant grin. Kitchel, averting his eyes, said, "I didn't see it and I don't believe it."

The Senator spent the next day touring the Pacific Coast, and it was a notable day in many respects. First, he returned to the campaigning style of the New Hampshire primary—rambling, informal talks that he had studiously avoided since his defeat there. He also plunged into handshaking and autographing sessions with the crowds, with less than his usual diffidence and

Yia Bi Kin is Navajo for House in the Sky.

(photo by Max Scheler, Black Star)

Following page:
"Of thee we sing, Barry.
"You are our boy, Barry.
"You've got guts...you're what we need, Barry."

(photo by Max Scheler, Black Star)

Before.

(photo by Dennis J. Cipnic)

After.

(photo by George Tames, The New York Times)

Miller came . . . as a sort of medical specialist,
called in on consultation.
(The New York Times photo)

discomfort at having to push himself at strangers. He was enjoying himself, and it showed. When a "Democrat for Goldwater" welcomed him in Sacramento, he said cheerfully, "I just managed to get my brother to switch this year," a reference to his younger brother, Robert, who had been a registered Democrat.

In an address at Seattle, Goldwater announced the formation of an advisory task force on foreign affairs, headed by Nixon. It was a significant announcement, one that would normally have captured top headlines for him. But advance copies of his speech had been distributed with customary restrictions on their use until shortly before delivery. The waiting period permitted Johnson in Washington to call a sudden news conference and disclose the appointment of sixteen distinguished citizens to consult with him on international policy. Since the members of the Johnson group were far better known nationally than those of Goldwater's, and since the President had shrewdly made his announcement first, Goldwater's attempt to dominate the news that day failed.

Goldwater managed to anger the Democrats that day. He charged that the Kennedy Administration had timed the Cuban missile crisis of 1962 for maximum domestic political effect in that election year and warned of a similar staged crisis in this election year. Contending that the Johnson Administration had protected American and allied interests abroad only when it would win votes for the President, he said: "If an element of foreign policy hurts Lyndon Johnson's election chances, forget it. If it helps his election chances, assign ten press agents to it." The reference to Kennedy, less than a year after his assassination, was a risky piece of campaign oratory, and it drew immediate reaction. Secretary of State Rusk accused Goldwater of a basic lack of understanding of Presidential responsibilities in foreign affairs and added, "If I could find a way to remove all the crises around the world between now and November, I would seize the opportunity to do so."

Then Johnson took the panting press on another walk around the White House backyard, this one for thirteen laps with his beagles, Him and Her, and Mrs. Johnson hand-in-hand for the last lap. Enroute, the President deplored by implication Goldwater's accusation that his Administration would juggle foreign crises for political advantage. He said he regretted that the Senator's statement would be noted by leaders of foreign nations, whose reactions could not be predicted.

James Reston in The Times also took Goldwater to task on the issue:

He continues to make serious charges, based on wildly inaccurate information, which open him up to counterattack and make him look ridiculous.

His charge yesterday that President Kennedy timed the missile crisis in Cuba for political reasons at home is a case in point.

The record on when the long-range missiles were first spotted in Cuba is available to him. It is precise, down to the exact minute when the photographs were taken, who took them and when and where.

If the Senator does not trust John McCone, the head of the C.I.A. and a prominent Republican, who was instructed by the President to brief him on such information, he can double-check the information with his friends in the Air Force, where he is a reserve officer.

Yet he has chosen instead to affront the memory of the late President by suggesting that Kennedy actually risked atomic war with the Soviets at a time calculated to pick up votes for the Democrats. . . .

Goldwater is certainly right on one thing: foreign policy, as he said this week, is an issue and should be debated, but he is not likely to benefit from that debate unless he gets the available facts and asks the right questions.

Goldwater returned to a familiar theme on September 10, a day spent flying from Boise, Idaho, to Great Falls, Montana, to Minneapolis in his chartered campaign jet, *Yia Bi Kin* (Navajo for "House in the Sky"). He condemned lawlessness and disorders on the streets of America and, for the first time, endeavored to relate this to liberal social welfare philosophies. "If it is entirely proper," he said, "for government to take from some to give to others, then won't some be led to believe that they can rightfully take from anyone who has more than they?" He also decried what he called the assumption by the state of the obligation to keep men in a style to which demagogues encourage them, and declared, "This can never again be truly a nation of law and order until it is again fully a nation of individual citizens."

To bolster his position, Goldwater cited a report by the Federal Bureau of Investigation that showed a 15 per cent rise in the crime rate in the first six months of 1964. He deplored "gang rape" in California, youth riots in New Hampshire and Oregon, the "degradation we see going on in the large cities of the East completely dominated by the Democratic party," and called Washington, the national capital, a crime-ridden city. "And throughout the year," he said, "men have gone into the streets to seek with violence what can only be found in understanding."

Goldwater's coupling of the civil rights movement and crime rate omitted one important statistic: Phoenix, Arizona, the city in which he served on the City Council, had one of the highest crime rates in the nation. The F.B.I. statistical comparisons, based on crimes for each 100,000 persons, showed Phoenix, with a population of 816,000, having 2,408 crimes per 100,000 residents, compared with 1,688 for the New York metropolitan area, with a population of 11,229,000. The murder rate was 6.4 in Phoenix to 5.2 in New York, forcible rape 18.6 to 8.0. Even in Washington, the "crime-ridden" city, the rape rate was 10.4, far below that of Phoenix.

If, as the Senator was wont to point out, the Democratic foreign policy was based on a crisis a week, it quickly became apparent that his own campaign produced a controversy a day. The following day, in a Chicago speech to the American Political Science Association, he criticized the Supreme Court as the branch of Government least faithful to the principles of the Constitution. Saying that he was weighing his words carefully, he charged that the court had abandoned the principle of "judicial restraint, with respect to acts of Congress with which it disagreed but which are founded on legitimate exercise of legislative power." In another portion of his address, Goldwater lashed out at the concept of a strong Presidency, accusing those who supported this belief of having a "totalitarian philosophy that the end justifies the means." The 2,200 members of the association constituted one of Goldwater's tougher audiences, since his support among the academic community was acknowledged to be limited. He was applauded twelve times, a lukewarm reception, and some of his remarks were met with derisive skepticism.

Goldwater provoked a violent reaction with his attack on the Supreme Court. Representative Emanuel Celler, the Brooklyn Democrat, charged him with demagoguery that "can only incite disrespect for law and order," and there were other comments of the same nature. Johnson, however, flatly rejected the injection of the court into the election campaign. He said he could see nothing to be gained by involving another branch of the Government in the political struggle. On the issue of Presidential power, Johnson remarked that he thought the powers of the office were adequate and had developed in orderly fashion through constitutional processes.

The end of the first full week of the campaign found Goldwater taking a breather in Washington, buoyed in spirit by large and enthusiastic crowds that had greeted him in the West and Middle West. He issued a statement reiterating his fears that the Democrats might be planning a foreign policy crisis. He specifically mentioned South Vietnam, saying that "if there is a solution brewing there, now is the time to tell the American people about it," instead of waiting for a politically opportune moment. Early the next morning the Senator had his answer. There was an attempted coup d'état in Saigon. The coup eventually collapsed, but it again aroused concern about the Administration's policy in South Vietnam and provided the Republicans with fresh campaign ammunition.

In this first week of campaigning, another kind of political warfare started —the war of the television commercial. Both parties embarked on elaborate and multi-million dollar programs that included spots and longer network time purchases.

The G.O.P. assault started with a five-minute spot seen in 187 cities. The theme: Republicans were the party of peace through strength. An announcer's voice told of failures at the wall of shame in Berlin and failures at the Bay of Pigs in Cuba and in Vietnam, then Goldwater appeared on the screen, asserting that Communism was the only great threat to peace: "Some distort this proper concern to make it appear we are preoccupied with war. There is no greater political lie. I am trying to carry to the American people this plain message. This entire nation and entire world risk war in our time unless free men remain strong enough to keep the peace."

It was mild and essentially defensive compared with his rivals' approach. One Democratic spot began with a little girl licking an ice cream cone, while a woman's voice, tender and protective, told her that people used to explode atomic bombs in the air and that radioactive fallout made children die. The voice recalled the treaty outlawing all but underground nuclear tests and said that a man who wanted to be President of the United States had voted against it. "His name is Barry Goldwater," the voice went on, "so if he's elected, they might start testing all over again." The ominous noise of Geiger-counter clicks almost drowned out her last words; then an authoritative male voice: "Vote for President Johnson on November third. The stakes are too high for you to stay home." Another Democratic spot along a similar vein showed a girl plucking daisy petals and concluded with a nuclear blast. The voice of Johnson then was heard: "These are the stakes: To make a world in which all of God's children can live, or go into the dark. We must either love each other or we must die."

The spots shocked even some loyal Democrats, who wrote to the national committee criticizing their brutality. Of course the Republicans were outraged. Dean Burch filed a formal complaint with the Fair Campaign Practices Committee: "This horror-type commercial is designed to arouse basic emotions and has no place in this campaign. I demand you call on the President to halt this smear attack on a United States Senator and the candidate of the Republican party for the Presidency." The Democrats contended that everything Goldwater had said and done on the subject of atomic weapons and their control was terrifying enough and that it was "extremely important that the American people understand what kind of man wants to be in the White House."

What Goldwater had said on the nuclear issue had been controversial for nearly a year. In October, 1963, at a press conference in Hartford, Connecticut, he suggested that the North Atlantic Treaty Organization supreme commander be allowed more freedom concerning the use of tactical nuclear weapons in case of any enemy attack. The German publication *Der Speigel,* in its issue of June 30, 1964, published an interview with Goldwater in which he repeated his position.

In another section of the *Der Speigel* interview, which was not printed in Germany but which became public in the United States on July 11, on the eve of the Republican National Convention, Goldwater made several controversial statements that the Democrats gleefully publicized. One of them was on the conduct of the war in Vietnam. Goldwater said our policy should be to win and then he added, "I would turn to my Joint Chiefs of Staff and say, 'Fellows, we made the decision to win, now it's your problem.' " Answering a question about his alleged impulsiveness, Goldwater admitted that "I possibly do shoot from the hip," and went on to explain that he had traveled and experienced more things that most members of Congress and had been exposed to problems "and I don't have to stop and think in detail about them."

The Senator was not alone in his belief that the United States should give its allies a share in the control of nuclear weapons, and that the President should not have the sole discretion in decisions concerning their use. Similar proposals had been made by members of both Democratic and Republican Administrations who feared NATO was being allowed to deteriorate because our allies, particularly France, were being denied a nuclear voice. This, it was maintained, weakened European confidence in Western defense.

More important, Goldwater, in answering a question on a television show on May 24, 1964, had become identified with a policy of using atomic bombs in Vietnam. Following is the colloquy:

QUESTION: Now a lot of supply lines seem to run in on the Laotian border, in any case, through jungles and along trails. How could you interdict those, with no good—
SENATOR GOLDWATER: Well, it is not as easy as it sounds, because these are not trails that are out in the open. I have been in these rain forests in Burma and South China. You are perfectly safe wandering through them as far as an enemy hurting you. There have been several suggestions made. I don't think we would use any of them. But defoliation of the forests by low yield atomic weapons could well be done. When you remove the foliage, you remove the cover. The major supply lines though I think would have to be interdicted where they leave Red China, which is the Red River Valley above North Vietnam and there, according to my studies of the geography, it would not be a difficult task to destroy those basic routes.

Two days later, he was questioned on the point in a press conference and said he did not favor using nuclear weapons in Southeast Asia for defoliation or other purposes.

"I outlined the low-yield defoliation idea which had been talked of and talked of and talked of by the highest levels in the Pentagon," he said. "This is nothing new, and I made it perfectly clear, I thought, that this was not a suggestion of mine."

This exchange followed:

QUESTION: You haven't meant the use of atomic bombs in a way that would kill people?
ANSWER: There has been a study of atomic devices as contrasted to weapons and the overwhelming advantage of a device is that you can use it in a way in which you don't kill people. You might kill off lot of monkeys and animals but you would do it at a time of day so it would not kill humans.
QUESTION: Are you saying this should be done or that it could be done?
ANSWER: It could be done but I don't think it should be done. If I had my choice I would go at the Red River Valley approaches in South China.
QUESTION: Do you favor action to cut supply lines in Red China itself?
ANSWER: It's not a suggestion now because I think we could accomplish the same end by interdiction of the supply lines in North Vietnam as the tracks approach the south. That would be the first step.
QUESTION: What are you advocating?
ANSWER: As of now, I think we can start with North Vietnam. I've merely said we should stop supplies coming into South Vietnam, period.

Then in staff conferences, one faction of Goldwater advisers, led by Denison Kitchel, repeatedly attempted to persuade him to stop his constant references to such subjects as nuclear weapons and mass destruction. In one speech he had mentioned such grim words twenty-six times in about as many minutes. But Goldwater and speech writer Karl Hess continued to argue that he should meet the issue—whether or not it disturbed voters and some Republican candidates.

The effect of the Goldwater candidacy on moderate Republicans seeking office had been a source of deep and brooding concern to party leaders even before his nomination. That concern now generated another blow to the Arizonan's hopes. In New York, a pivotal state where Senator Keating was running for re-election independent of the national ticket against a strong opponent, Bobby Kennedy, the Republican leadership reached the reluctant conclusion that a Johnson sweep was in prospect. To avoid complete disaster, G.O.P. candidates for the legislature were urged to divorce their campaign from Goldwater.

This latest in the series of dismal tidings was counteracted to some extent by the announcement by Senator Strom Thurmond, the South Carolina Democrat, that he was bolting the party to support the Republican nominee. Thurmond, who had bolted once previously, in 1948, when he became the States Rights party's nominee for President in protest against Truman's civil rights posture, gave this reason: "The Democratic party has abandoned the people. It has repudiated the Constitution of the United States. It is leading the evolution of our nation to a socialistic dictatorship." Goldwater welcomed the South Carolinan literally with open arms; the defection came, by no coincidence, as the Republican candidate began his second week of campaigning with a four-day pilgrimage through Southern and Border states. He expressed the hope that thousands of other conservative Southern Democrats would follow Thurmond's example.

In his Southern tour, Goldwater again displayed a propensity for saying, from a strictly political standpoint, the right things in the wrong places. His impassioned disciples expected him to be consistent in his opposition to the Tennessee Valley Authority, but not in the heart of the valley itself, so heavily dependent on the Federal power project for its well-being. They expected him to be scornful of the Administration's antipoverty war, but not in West Virginia, the prime example of deprivation in the country. They expected him to be against the Supreme Court decision ordering the reapportionment of state legislatures, but not in Atlanta, long a victim of rural domination. It was almost as if Goldwater's candor had become such an obsession that it amounted to a political death-wish.

In St. Petersburg, Florida, the Senator revived his law and order theme, devoting virtually his entire speech to it. He pledged to work to overturn a series of Supreme Court decisions on the rights of arrested criminals, saying they were being pampered and law and order were being sacrificed "just to give criminals a sporting chance to go free." To achieve his end, Goldwater said, he would, as President, first use his power of appointment to Federal courts to redress constitutional interpretations in favor of the public.

Then in the Tennessee Valley, he reiterated his belief in the desirability of selling the T.V.A. to private enterprise. This time, however, he said that a President did not have the authority to take such a step, and implied that Congress would not give it to him. His views on the T.V.A. were a definite liability in the South. In Memphis auto bumper stickers were seen that read: "Sell T.V.A.? I'd rather sell Arizona."

In New Orleans, Goldwater accused the Administration of attempting to conceal the Bobby Baker scandal until after Election Day. In North Carolina, he tried to persuade peanut farmers that he was no enemy of theirs: "I'm probably the most violent advocate of peanut butter in history. On a dare from one of my sons, I actually shaved with peanut butter and it wasn't bad, but it smells." He also denied that he would end Federal price supports for farmers. He would sit down with farmers crop by crop and seek solutions to their problems. But at a television news show later, he took a giant step backwards by saying that "in most crops, a return to the market, with sufficient time for it, would be a better choice."

On his final day in the South, Goldwater derided the antipoverty program and charged that Johnson was designing a Great Society in which there would be no penalty for failure and no reward for success. He chose to utter those remarks in West Virginia, one of the states of Appalachia, a region of persistent hard-core poverty and unemployment. Goldwater insisted that he believed in a compassionate society, but suggested that the President's billion-dollar program was conceived to maintain him in office: "Human misery is not to be trifled with just to get votes in an election."

Never once, in his four days below the Mason-Dixon Line, did Goldwater mention integration or the burning issue of racial equality. His strategy for victory in November put great emphasis on the role of the South, yet he had to win the South without alienating the North. As James Reston put it: "This may be why he sang 'Dixie' *pianissimo*. For while he needs the South, the South is not enough to win, and one day soon he must face the big electoral battalions in the North."

By the middle of September, a pattern had been set that endured for the rest of the campaign. Goldwater drew large, overflow crowds (often despite a ticket charge) to his major well-organized evening appearances. These crowds were composed of the fellow conservatives on whom Goldwater could count absolutely. But during the days he could not attract street crowds that came close to matching the throngs that turned out for President Johnson. In some cases, Goldwater could draw no street crowd at all—there seemed to be a lack of public interest in seeing him. Goldwater, always meticulously dressed in blue or grey suits, his wavy grey hair seldom ruffled, seemed isolated from the reality of this situation. He concentrated his attention on the good crowds and not on "the crowds that are not there," which, according to one of John F. Kennedy's axioms, were the only really important crowds in politics.

While the tone of his campaign speeches was aggressive and uncompromising in its advocacy of his conservative philosophy, Goldwater himself remained cool and aloof. Even on the Yia Bi Kin, which he shared with fifty-odd newsmen, Goldwater was socially isolated while being physically cramped. He almost never came into the press section to talk (at the same time that White House reporters literally could not hide from Johnson or avoid constant political chatting). Goldwater toyed with his ham radio, worked on speeches, dozed, took a hand at the aircraft controls, had a martini or bourbon. But he seldom talked to anyone who told him frankly where his political weaknesses lay.

In this period, another pattern was set that endured until the end of the campaign, a guarded attitude toward the press. Even though Goldwater liked and respected some individual reporters, he and his advisers knew that the only way to manage what he said was by restricting press conferences. Therefore, he held no formal press conferences at all until the end of the campaign. Reporters were even barred from the inner rooms of the Republican National Committee in Washington, a striking contrast to the treatment they received by the Democrats, who welcomed them and fed them more information than they could use. Texts of all Johnson speeches were immediately available at Democratic headquarters; rarely were newspapers able to get transcripts of Goldwater speeches. Even in his approach to the public, Goldwater, who exerted a real charm in small groups, kept aloof; he hardly ever spoke informally for fear that he would make mistakes.

The first nationwide poll conducted for Goldwater by Opinion Research Inc. of Princeton showed him with only 31 per cent of the vote, even after the undecideds had been allocated—a disheartening reckoning. Thus Goldwater's chances, despite his publicly voiced optimism—he was looking forward to "a real big boo-boo on November 3" on the part of the pollsters, he told one audience—still seemed poor; he trailed the President in all of the voter opinion polls. In mid-September, the Gallup Poll reported that Johnson was ahead of Goldwater by the largest margin any candidate had held that early in a Presidential race in the poll's twenty-nine-year history. Even in Arizona, Goldwater's home state, a poll taken by the state's largest newspaper, *The Arizona Republic,* showed the President ahead. The results were not published, but one report indicated the Senator trailed, 42 to 58 per cent. The *Republic's* publisher, Eugene C. Pulliam, a friend and stanch supporter of Goldwater, angrily denied that the poll had been suppressed, insisting it never had been intended for publication.

Earl Mazo in The Times analyzed the situation:

If the current election polls even nearly reflect voter opinion at this time, Senator Barry Goldwater needs to pick up more support during the next six weeks than any Presidential candidate in modern times.

Since professional voter polling was started in the 1936 Roosevelt-Landon election, the average change between a candidate's rating in early September polls and his showing in the November election has been about three percentage points.

The biggest swing—at the beginning of modern polling in 1936—was 12 percentage points.

In the Kennedy-Nixon race of 1960, the difference between the initial poll showings and the election result was less than 1 per cent.

This year, Mr. Goldwater's own confidential campaign-starting survey, conducted by the Opinion Research Corporation of Princeton, N.J., indicated he must gain more than 21 percentage points before Nov. 3 to achieve a bare popular-vote majority.

Another type of poll—The Times's surveys of voter opinion by states, sections, ethnic groups and other classifications of the population—began to appear now almost daily. All carried the same message:

Labor unions regarded Goldwater as the "perfect" candidate to oppose (one official said the Senator's "record is 100 per cent against labor").

Roman Catholics in New York City were overwhelmingly in favor of Johnson.

Negro G.O.P. leaders in the city were in open revolt against the Goldwater ticket ("We will not put up signs for Mr. Goldwater. We will not distribute literature for him. We will not make speeches for him. We will not invite him into our community.").

The city's increasingly important Puerto Rican voters favored Johnson by a landslide margin ("This Senator from Arizona. I never know where I stand with him. He never speaks clearly.").

Republican suburbanites in the San Francisco area were swinging in unusual numbers to the Johnson standard ("We can't take Goldwater." And "Johnson is the lesser of two evils.").

Farmers in the corn belt were turning more and more to the Democratic nominee ("If the Republicans had somebody a little more level-headed, I'd vote for him. I'm afraid of Goldwater. I don't know what he'd do if he got ahold of the nuclear trigger.").

Businessmen in the Northeast and Midwest, most of whom had voted Republican all their lives, voiced increasing support of Johnson ("It's perfectly respectable for a businessman to be for Johnson. Nobody is shocked. You don't lose anything socially.").

At least 95 per cent of the Jews were for the Democratic candidate ("It is difficult to conceive of a candidate the Republican party could have nominated who is less likely to receive votes from Jewish voters than Senator Goldwater.").

Three of the five bellwether counties in the nation that had backed the winning candidates for President in every election in this century, Laramie in Wyoming, Crook in Oregon, Palo Alto in Iowa, were decisively in favor of Johnson at this point. Later surveys of the two other bellwether areas, Coos and Strafford Counties, both in New Hampshire, disclosed a split: Coos for Johnson and Strafford for Goldwater. And an even later survey showed both for Johnson.

Because of the deep difference in the political views of the nominees, many newspapers and magazines announced their choices much earlier than usual —including The Times, which editorially supported Johnson. A number of Republican newspapers came out for a Democrat for the first time in their history; many Southern papers backed their first Republican. The big chains, like Hearst and Scripps-Howard, plumped for Johnson, a switch from their usual G.O.P. leanings. The rush of newspapers to get their endorsements on the record was made clear in a poll by *Editor & Publisher,* the trade publication, in mid-September. Of the 1,754 dailies in the nation, 828 responded to the magazine's survey with these results: 243 papers, circulation 12,618,721, backed Johnson; 250 papers, circulation 5,268,691, supported Goldwater; 335 papers, circulation 11,946,035, uncommitted.

A startling defection in the Republican ranks among magazines came when *The Saturday Evening Post,* which had never endorsed a Democrat as far as its history could be traced, came out for Johnson in an editorial that castigated the Senator. "Goldwater is a grotesque burlesque of the conservative he pretends to be," *The Post* declared. "He is a wild man, a stray, an unprincipled and ruthless jujitsu artist like Joe McCarthy."

As the opening phase of the campaign ended, what did Goldwater have to show for his efforts? Tom Wicker reported in a Times article:

Senator Barry Goldwater, not President Johnson and his record, is the central issue of the Presidential campaign. That paradoxical conclusion emerges from surveys made by The New York Times among various voter groups in recent weeks. These surveys disclosed a big lead for Mr. Johnson over Mr. Goldwater....

More significant was the fact that in virtually all The Times' surveys, the principal motive of the voters seemed to be whether he was for or against Mr. Goldwater.

The same surveys did not necessarily suggest overwhelming popularity for Mr. Johnson, great Democratic party allegiance, or deep admiration for the Kennedy-Johnson Administration and its programs. Nor did they disclose—except infrequently on the subject of civil rights—a deep-seated resentment or mistrust or fear of Mr. Johnson.

How widely shared the views expressed in The Times' surveys may be is difficult to tell. They do suggest, however, two paradoxes.

One is that the President of the United States, a year in office and a national figure for many years longer than Mr. Goldwater, is less firmly fixed in the public mind as representing a particular set of views than is his challenger. Thus, it is Mr. Goldwater who arouses strong emotions in this campaign, not Mr. Johnson.

The other paradox is that as a result of the first, there does not seem much public interest in or assessment of the accomplishments or shortcomings of the Johnson Administration. That sort of analytical interest is fixed rather on Barry Goldwater and his ideas. For that reason, the challenger's ability to challenge effectively seems to be reduced. His greater need is to defend himself.

16

"This Is What America Is Really All About"

On September 5, President Johnson held a Saturday afternoon press conference in his office, then took reporters on a leisurely five-lap walk around the White House grounds. His mood swung widely from brusque to jocular; in about two hours with the press there was more talking than walking. As the fourth lap ended, Mrs. Johnson appeared on the White House balcony and yoo-hooed at him to "come in, sit down and get something to eat." The President responded, "One more lap and I'll be up," but even when that was over he did not leave immediately, making certain, as he told reporters, "that you are all satisfied."

During the amble around the grounds he reminisced. One of the questions concerned his horsemanship, implying that it wasn't up to par because he had been pictured handling a horse with reins held separately in his two hands. Johnson replied that the writer was apparently ignorant of the fact that Tennessee walking horses were guided in that fashion, in contrast to cow ponies trained for neck-reining with the lines held together in the left hand. That answer characteristically reminded him of a story, but not before he said that he did not want to be known for his horsemanship and was glad when he found another way to make a living.

Some years ago, Johnson went on, during the old O.P.A. days, he was cutting calves out of a bunch on a Texas ranch, together with Paul Porter, former director of the agency. When Johnson turned a nimble calf deftly, the ranch foreman sitting on a log fence was heard to remark, "Ol' Lyndon shore has rode before." The calf ducked, Johnson's pony followed, the rider was nearly unseated, and the foreman added, "But not lately."

One of the answers at the indoor press conference earlier in the day offered strong evidence of the type of campaign Johnson had in mind:

QUESTION: He [Nixon] said the Republican party is now the party of the people. Would you agree with that?
ANSWER: I think the Democratic party and the Republican party both are trying to do what they think is best for all the country without regard to any specialized segment of the country. . . .

I think we can all work together . . . I think this nation's most important concern, as far as we can see ahead, is and should be the unity of this country.

Never in history has any people succeeded in building a free society on such a huge scale, and with the variety of such different religious denominations, ethnic stocks and races.

We have witnessed the complete destruction by inner conflict of many nations because they pitted race against race and religion against religion, group against group. What your question implies or suggests is class against class. That must not happen here in either party. . . .

So I want to suggest this morning that we proceed with our adventure in freedom, a part of which is the grand tradition of political campaigns with a firm commitment to law, a just and efficient enforcement of all laws, a faith that a people which has learned to triumph over prejudice will once more demonstrate the vitality of our most striking ideal: *E Pluribus Unum*, From Many, One. . . .

It was clear from all these remarks that Johnson intended to make national unity the basis of a broad and fervent appeal to the electorate. As President, he was in an ideal position to campaign as a non-campaigner. The odds were heavily in his favor—so heavily that even early in the campaign there was talk about overconfidence. The President tried to convince his followers that every vote counted with a typical Johnson story. He recalled the time when his wife, Lady Bird, was in an automobile that turned over just prior to an important election in which he was involved.

"What was your first thought when you came to?" she was asked.

"I wished I had voted absentee," she said.

In Cadillac Square in Detroit, the traditional Democratic opening site, on roughly the same spot where Kennedy had opened his campaign in 1960 and which had been renamed John F. Kennedy Plaza, Johnson delivered the Labor Day address that inaugurated his drive for office in his own right. Labor, in the form of Walter Reuther and his giant United Automobile Workers, had long been a decisive factor in Michigan politics, and the union-oriented Democratic party was fully aware of this. In addition, the state's twenty electoral votes barely went to Kennedy in 1960 and its Republican Governor, George Romney, was trying to disassociate himself from Goldwater. Detroit, therefore, was fertile ground for the first seeds of the campaign.

A crowd of 100,000 listened to an almost evangelistic speech. Johnson's voice resounded stridently over the loudspeakers dotting the square. He flailed the air and pounded the lectern, speaking principally in lofty abstractions, but his carefully chosen words, his attempt to picture himself as the leader for all the people, were too nonpartisan for his pro-Democratic labor audience, and brought only perfunctory applause. The President devoted nearly half of his formal speech to the need for peace, emphasizing national unity and the submergence of conflicting interests while pursuing prosperity, justice and peace. He did not mention his Republican opponent by name, but he struck hard at Goldwater's stand on August 25 that "a way must be developed to provide NATO with its own stock of small, tactical, nuclear battlefield weapons—what may truly be called, and ultimately will be called, conventional weapons." The word conventional marked the preliminary round in one of the few major campaign issues that would seize the imagination of the voters—that of the control over nuclear weapons.

"Make no mistake," Johnson declared. "There is no such thing as a conventional nuclear weapon. For nineteen peril-filled years, no nation has loosed the atom against another. To do so now is a political decision of the highest order, and it would lead us down an uncertain path of blows and counterblows whose outcome none may know. No President of the United States of America can divest himself of the responsibility for such a decision."

Here again was another key word—responsibility. Since the days of the New Hampshire primary campaign, Goldwater's responsibility had been questioned not only by Democrats but also by members of his own party. Johnson was too astute a politician to miss the opportunity to hammer away at that point.

The President's audience was apathetic, however, and he sensed it. In a long epilogue (some contended it was not spontaneous and had been prepared for him by a speech writer, Richard Goodwin), he told of his boyish dream for the nation under "the scattered Texas sky." (A bit of phrase making that almost matched his famous line in Culpeper, Virginia, in 1960, "What did Richard Nixon ever do for Culpeper?") That dream concerned "the simple wants of people, but this is what America is really all about. Reality rarely matches dream, but only dreams give nobility to purpose. This is the star I hope to follow."

The epilogue aroused the throng much more than his bland address. There were enthusiastic cries of "Yeah! Yeah!" much like the shouts of "Amen!" at revival meetings. Johnson left the platform and plunged toward the crowd as sweating policemen tried to hold back the press of people at the barricades. He strode half the distance around the huge square amidst cheers and squeals. He shook hands until the back of his neck was damp with sweat and the little finger of his left hand bloodied at the nail. It was only then that Johnson—the political campaigner, for a few moments not the lofty President of all the people—was satisfied and flew back to Washington.

There was something symbolic—perhaps an urge to break another Kennedy precedent—in his flight to and from Detroit. He made the trip in a plane that did not carry his doctor or the military officer bearing the top-secret codes needed in the event of a national security emergency, which were routine precautions during the Kennedy Administration.

In The Times, James Reston offered this estimate of Johnson's speech:

President Johnson did not excite this crowd as much as his backers would have liked. Maybe this was merely because it is difficult to be jubilant in a sweating mob under a noonday sun, but there is something about the President that somehow discourages Beatleish screams from a crowd.

It is not that he does not impress them; quite the contrary—he overwhelms them. Seen for the first time in person, he seems larger and somehow more formidable than on the screen, and when he is unleashed in a crowd, striding ahead of a battalion of Secret Service fullbacks, he is an elemental and awesome figure.

On the platform he is obviously the head man, and when he is at his shouting best, arms waving like a helicopter, he not only commands but almost stuns his audience.

There is something contradictory about Lyndon Johnson's pacifying role on the one hand and his appearance and manner on the other. He is a healer in the garb of a warrior. He tells us to "reason together" at the top of his voice. He is a whirlwind who wants to calm the waves.

If the President chose to remain above the battle, his Democratic followers did not. Senator J. W. Fulbright of Arkansas, using language seldom heard on the Senate floor, denounced Goldwater for an aggressive new American foreign policy that could lead the nation by inadvertence into the disaster of nuclear war. Fulbright described the Arizonan's ideological view of the conflict with Communism as immature and said: "Goldwater Republicanism is the closest thing in American politics to an equivalent of Russian Stalinism. Each makes a religion of its ideology, the Stalinists of Communism, the Goldwaterites of their own special brand of 'freedom.' Each is convinced that there can be no peace in the world until its own ideology is universally practiced."

Fulbright's vehemence, which also included a stinging rebuke to the Republican Vice Presidential candidate for his attack on Humphrey's liberal voting record and his association with the Americans for Democratic Action, was an example of the bitterness in the opening days of the campaign—and fitted perfectly the Democratic strategy of early personal attacks on Goldwater by Democratic orators, but not Johnson himself. In this phase of the campaign, issues were rarely debated; only charges and countercharges were hurled. Few of the verbal spears penetrated deeply, but their flights were spectacular and captured the attention of the voters. Humphrey, whose role Johnson had elevated to a level never before enjoyed by a Vice Presidential nominee, was a prime target for the G.O.P., as was Miller for the Democrats, and Arthur Krock explained why:

If the furor engendered by Representative Miller's attack on Senator Humphrey's super-liberal voting record and group affiliations shall awaken the public to the importance of the choice for Vice President, it will have contributed something of value to this campaign which has been lacking since 1804. The adoption in that year of the Twelfth Amendment to the Constitution abolished the original provision that the runner-up in the contest for President would be the winner's Vice President.

But this year . . . the matter of their [running mates'] fitness for succession was a highly influential factor. This was a consequence of the assassination of President Kennedy, the current vacancy in the Vice Presidential office and the awareness of both Johnson and Goldwater of the physical strains that campaign would impose. These conditions have also aroused the American people to the realization that their votes on the party ballot they select are potentially for two Presidents instead of one.

Two events on September 9 proved cheering to Johnson. One was the settlement of the contract dispute between the United Automobile Workers Union and the Chrysler Corporation, giving the union nearly all its demands. The fact that a strike had been averted was regarded as a modest victory for the Administration from a political standpoint. Actually, the possibility of a strike had been remote, and even a short tieup would not have damaged Johnson's political image very much. As it turned out later, the U.A.W. did strike General Motors, but the national walkout lasted only ten days.

The second event was the request by the Democratic leadership of the Senate for the reopening of the investigation of the outside business activities of Bobby Baker. The earlier inquiry, which had ended in June after eight months of partisan wrangling, had exonerated Baker of illegal acts but accused him of many gross improprieties. By reopening the inquiry the Democrats hoped to mitigate the impact of Republican accusations, something the President's denial that Baker had been his protegé had failed to do. At the same time, it was highly unlikely that the investigation could accomplish anything of importance before Election Day.

On the following day, September 10, Johnson invaded Republican Pennsylvania, a state whose thirty-two electoral votes had been captured by Kennedy in 1960 and where an unhappy liberal Republican Senator, Hugh Scott, was attempting to shrug off the onus of sharing the ticket with Goldwater. The President molded his appeal for unity into a sharp denunciation of extremism, calling on voters of every political stripe to form around his banner in opposition to reckless factions that he said were abroad in this responsible land.

"They demand," he told his listeners in Harrisburg, "you choose a doctrine alien to America—a doctrine that would lead to a tragic convulsion in our foreign relations—a doctrine that flouts the unity of our society and searches for scapegoats among our people. It is a doctrine that invites extremism to take over our land. It is a doctrine that plays loosely with human destiny—and this generation of Americans will have no part of it." The President did not mention Goldwater by name; he did not have to.

Then another form of extremism—a nonpolitical natural disaster called Hurricane Dora—gave Johnson, the indefatigable non-campaigner, an opportunity to dominate the news without even trying on September 12. He toured the devasted shore from Jacksonville, Florida, to Brunswick, Georgia, walking through sodden resort areas, shaking hands with still-dazed survivors and voicing his warm concern. He was only doing what came naturally to him—being the President of all the people (in a section of the country supposedly a major base of Goldwater strength), with politics and votes ostensibly far from his thoughts.

After the first week of campaigning, it was apparent that Johnson, at least in this early stage, intended to follow the strategy of being the President of all the people. He did not need to fire up his adherents or find new issues; the issues were there for him in the record of his Administration and of Kennedy's. He could be expected, therefore, to limit his strictly political appearances for the immediate future and, at the same time, reinforce and exploit the image of a responsible President, a man of restraint, a healer of wounds.

On one of these early trips, as Johnson was driving from the White House to National Airport in Washington, he started to notice bumper stickers and then to count them. To his shock, he found thirteen Goldwater stickers, mostly reading "GOldwater in '64," and only one for himself. Johnson, who carefully kept his temper in public, exploded in private, demanded an explanation and ordered corrective steps to be taken. Thereafter, the Democratic National Committee shipped out thousands of stickers reading "L.B.J. for the U.S.A." whenever the President left Washington so that his eyes could feast upon them as his motorcade passed through any town along his route.

All four candidates were doing virtually all their campaigning in jet planes. They flew roughly 75,000 miles each. Johnson used an Air Force Lockheed Jetstar for short flights and a giant Boeing-707 on long hauls. Cost to the Democratic National Committee for political trips: $525 an hour for the Jetstar and $2,350 for the 707. Goldwater chartered a Boeing-727 from American Airlines; cost: $2,100 an hour. The new three-engine plane came fully equipped with crew and special modifications for berths and working space for his staff and the press. The total cost of the airliner was $280,000 and, under unusual rules, the press entourage footed all but $71,000 of the bill cash in advance—at $3,660 a seat. Miller used a modified Electra for his campaigning. Cost: about $3.50 a mile. Humphrey also chartered an Electra under a different arrangement—$1,500 an hour.

In the air, at least, the President and Goldwater had one thing in common. Both liked to fly, both could relax or work once aboard their planes. It was the one flight by Johnson over New Guinea during World War II that precipitated a campaign skirmish—a comparison of the military records of the two candidates. The Republicans, particularly Miller, lashed out at the fact that the President had served little more than seven months in service while Goldwater, "who really knows what war means," had been in uniform from before the outbreak of the war in 1941 until November, 1945, although he had never seen combat. Miller attempted to depict Johnson as a man who had chosen the safety of Capitol Hill over the dangers of the battlefronts. It was an issue, however, that did not generate much reaction among the voters.

The aggressive Republican Vice Presidential aspirant on September 15, before the Republican State Convention, in Austin, Texas, also accused Johnson of imposing anti-Negro restrictions on property he owned in the city. The delegates accorded Miller a standing ovation when he read from what he said was a certified copy of a deed from the President and Mrs. Johnson conveying seven lots on the outskirts of Austin. In 1938, when the Johnsons bought the property, Miller charged, it was free of restrictions against selling or renting it to anyone. In 1945, when the Johnsons sold a portion of it, Miller said, the deed contained this prohibition, "That no part of the above described premises shall ever be conveyed or in any way transferred, demised, leased or rented to any person or persons of African descent." The New York Congressman went on, amid whoops and cheers: "This shows the hypocrisy of Lyndon Johnson on the whole issue. It narrows down to this simple question: Do we want as President of the United States a man who has the courage of his convictions or a man who changes his convictions every month to suit the electorate so he can get elected?"

The White House immediately expressed regret if any such covenant had been placed on the property. George Reedy, Johnson's press secretary, said that the President had no recollection of deeds on property sold twenty years ago and that he was flatly opposed to any such restrictions and this was a matter of record. The minor flurry turned into a stand-off a few days later, when it was discovered that there had been a restrictive racial covenant in the deed of the $60,000 home Miller had purchased in Bethesda, Maryland, in 1958. Miller maintained that the situation was different in his case because the clause had been inserted in his property in 1946, whereas Johnson's restriction had been written in while he owned the land. The New Yorker explained that the restrictive clause on all the land in the area had been made totally invalid a full ten years "before I purchased my home by the 1948 Supreme Court decision on the subject." Technically, Miller was right, but for the general public the issue of restrictive covenants had no glamor. Miller himself was satisfied to forget he had ever mentioned the matter on that one triumphant afternoon in Austin.

Still another peripheral sensation cropped up at this point. On Sunday, September 13, the Very Reverend Francis B. Sayre Jr., Dean of the Protestant Episcopal Cathedral in Washington and the grandson of President Woodrow Wilson, delivered a sermon in which he indicted the American people for the nomination of the two men heading the national tickets. He said the selections reflected "the emptiness of our faith." Dean Sayre did not mention either Johnson or Goldwater by name, but his meaning was certainly clear: "This summer, we beheld a pair of gatherings at the summit of political power, each of which was completely dominated by a single man; the one a man of dangerous ignorance and devastating uncertainty, the other a man whose public house is splendid in its every appearance but whose private lack of ethics must inevitably introduce termites at the very foundation. The electorate of this mighty nation is left homeless, then, by such a pair of nominees. It knows not where to turn, it stares fascinated at the forces that have produced such a sterile choice—frustration and a federation of hostilities in one party; and, in the other, only a cynical manipulation of power."

The Dean was both highly praised and severely criticized. His polemic was regarded as more injurious to Johnson than to Goldwater because it riveted, with bitter, if subtle terminology, attention on the President's alleged use of public office to amass a private fortune. It stirred a latent uneasiness among many voters who were opposed to Goldwater on policy grounds but were equally unhappy about Johnson's ethics before his elevation to the Presidency.

Two days later Johnson, long regarded as without a peer in Capitol Hill strategy, suffered a double defeat. In the Senate he was set back on a compromise resolution that sought to resolve an emotional deadlock over apportionment of state legislatures. It was a decisive victory for a coalition of Southern Democrats and Republicans led by Senator Dirksen. In the House, Administration chiefs abandoned plans for a test vote on medical care for the aged under Social Security. By permitting the issue to go to a Senate-House conference without attempting to bind the House conferees, a majority of whom opposed the Administration plan, a Senate-approved medicare proposal was considered as good as dead.

On the same day of his legislative losses, Johnson flew to Miami Beach to address the national convention of the 900,000-member International Association of Machinists. He made a vigorous bid for labor's support—virtually his already, by default of his opponent—and cited the economic advantages working men had enjoyed since the Democrats took over in 1961. He pledged his wholehearted backing of medicare and a stronger Social Security program —two of labor's prime objectives. The President received a rousing ovation from the 1,400 delegates and 2,500 guests—his twenty-four-minute speech was interrupted thirty-five times with cheers, applause and cries of "Attaboy, LBJ." There was nothing startling about this; what was interesting was what had been inserted in and deleted from Johnson's address. According to the White House, the medicare and Social Security topics, which aroused the most enthusiasm, were inserted on the flight from Washington. Deleted was an extensive defense of the Administration's policy in Cuba. The reason: Union officials, told in advance of the content of the talk, had requested that it be altered to appeal more directly to labor interests.

On September 16, the President embarked on two days of stumping in four states of the Pacific Northwest, Montana, Washington, Oregon and California, which had given their electoral votes—fifty-one in all—to Nixon in 1960. Johnson skillfully blended his role as candidate and President, and received the inadvertent assistance of the Canadian Prime Minister, Lester B. Pearson. The two heads of state joined in ceremonies marking the implementation of the Columbia River Treaty. Pearson flew to Great Falls, Montana, to meet the President, and they then went by air to Vancouver, British Columbia (the first time Johnson had left the United States as President). From Vancouver, the two leaders drove to the marble International Peace Arch between Blaine, Washington, and Douglas, British Columbia, for the proclamation of the treaty.

In his Seattle remarks at a civic dinner, Johnson, still refusing to mention his opponent by name, assailed Goldwater's views on nuclear weapons. He told the country that his Administration "had taken every step man can devise to insure that neither a madman nor a malfunction could trigger nuclear war." He again voiced his belief that control over nuclear arms must remain with the President, but acknowledged that, despite the horror of atomic war, the use of such weapons might become necessary in defense of freedom. Then, playing on the fears of Goldwater's supposed recklessness, he promised:

"I will never let slip the engines of destruction because of a reckless and rash miscalculation about our adversaries. Every further step along the way —from decision to destruction—is governed by the two-man rule. Two or more men must independently decide the order has been given. They must independently take action.

"An elaborate system of checks and counter-checks, procedural and mechanical, guard against unauthorized nuclear bursts. In addition, since 1961, we have placed permissive-action links on several of our weapons. These are electromechanical locks which must be opened by a secret combination before action is possible. And we are extending the system."

It was the first time these devices, long known to scientists, had been made the substance of a Presidential policy statement. The next day in Sacramento, California, from the steps of the State Capitol, the President confided to his audience that the United States had developed two systems that could intercept and destroy armed satellites circling the earth in space. The weapons, he said, were in place and operationally ready, alert to protect the nation and the free world. The President also disclosed the production of over-the-horizon radar that could look around the curve of the earth and give warning of a missile attack within seconds. (Again, these were astonishing revelations to be made in the context of a basically political speech.) Finally, Johnson added, the United States had no intention of putting warheads into orbit in military satellites. "We have no reason to believe," he went on, "that any nation plans to put nuclear warheads into orbit."

The speech, before a tumultuous throng estimated at more than 70,000 (the largest in size and enthusiasm since the opening day of Johnson's campaign), was again a reply to Goldwater charges that the nation had failed to speed new weapons systems. The people's ardor gratified the President, and he moved into the crowd briefly after his talk. All in all, the day was a masterful demonstration of the Johnson astuteness in politicking—replete with color, humor, pathos and news. It began early in the morning when he was greeted at the Portland airport by Governor Mark Hatfield of Oregon, a Republican but not an ardent Goldwater follower. Hatfield had presented the President with a bowl full of "LBJ for USA" buttons, and dryly commented that he believed in giving practical gifts.

Once the breakfast was over, Johnson went out into the crowd, shaking hands with his familiar, rapid, two-handed motion. He waved to those he could not reach, a wave that was unusual in its stiffness of the right arm and the flat flapping of the hand from the wrist. It was a delicate, almost invisible gesture that one would not expect from so large a man. On leaving Portland he paid an impromptu visit to a Shrine hospital for crippled children, distributing pens and Presidential medallions. He told the children, "All of you take good care of yourself, now, and I know you will all be better."

Johnson attracted large and friendly crowds in the Northwest. If they did not jump and scream for him as they had for Kennedy, they at least screamed. His talks managed to hold their attention and drew appropriate cheers, but his style of delivery, slow and deliberate, did not tend to stir them to high pitches of emotion. They applauded, shouted and cheered because he was a celebrity—the President of the United States.

Fendall W. Yerxa of The Times, who had traveled with both candidates, noted a vast disproportion in the size and enthusiasm of the crowds that greeted them: "But one thing is certain—President Johnson sought the crowds, had them and proved he could stimulate enthusiasm; Senator Goldwater did not gather them and did not seek them out—and proved that he was willing to stand or fall with his hard core of believers."

17

The "Niagaran"
and "The Happy Warrior"

On any given day during two months of the fall of 1964, a voter in any one of forty of the fifty states might have looked up and found himself being addressed by a candidate for the Vice Presidency of the United States. For Senator Hubert H. Humphrey and Representative William E. Miller, it was just one speech after another—in city squares and at county fairs, from dawn until well after midnight, at airports and in stadiums, before teeming thousands and before lonely little clusters of the already convinced.

Miller came before these myriad audiences as a sort of medical specialist, called in on consultation. His manner as he came and left was efficient, brisk, sometimes even brusque, but his presentation was pointed and expert. Once he had fulfilled his function, he moved quickly on. Humphrey, on the other hand, spoke with the unhurried patience of the old family physician, the general practitioner who didn't mind being called out in the middle of the night and then lingered to chat, in no hurry to leave.

Miller delivered "the speech"—a set address that, like a child's construction toy, consisted of interlocking parts. It could handily be made shorter or longer; new pieces could readily be substituted for old; it could be assembled and adapted to suit any locale and audience; made to contain just the right number of charges, refutations, and instant visions. But Humphrey could not tolerate the monotony of one basic speech. He was happiest when a questioning audience, a news event or even the scenery let him depart from familiar patterns.

In one respect, however, the rival campaigners were much alike. Each was fond of the antiphonal effect of audience participation and each knew how to use it. At Atlantic City on August 27, Humphrey accepted the Democratic nomination for the Vice Presidency and set at least one pattern for the scores of speeches to follow—by making his audience a lusty chorus. "Most Democrats and most Republicans in the Senate voted last year for an expanded medical-education program," he declared adding, after a pause, *"But not Senator Goldwater!"* That became the cue, the raised baton.

Humphrey continued, "Most Democrats and most Republicans in the Senate voted for education legislation. . . ." Now the responsive audience boomed along with him, *"But . . . not . . . Senator . . . Goldwater!"*

A week later in Lockport, New York, at his campaign opening Miller also led a litany that would be heard again across the country in evolving forms. He told his hearers that Humphrey had been a founder, chairman, and vice chairman of Americans for Democratic Action, "unquestionably the most influential organization in our nation's capitol attempting to subvert and transform our government into a foreign socialistic totalitarianism." The Republican nominee asked, "Do we want a Vice President from the Americans for Democratic Action, which advocates diplomatic recognition of Red China . . . which advocates the admission of Red China to the United Nations?" After the chorus of "No! No!" had subsided, Miller added, *"Well— Lyndon Johnson does!"* That was Miller's raised baton. "Do we want a Vice President who says that the United States should turn over Berlin to the United Nations?" "No!" bellowed his audience, and then chanted along with him, *"Well—Lyndon Johnson does!"*

The role of the Vice Presidential candidates in 1964 was expected to be— and, indeed, proved to be—a grueling one. Johnson's early strategy called for him to appear to be above outright politicking, too concerned with world affairs to engage in common ordinary vote-seeking. He was to remain in the White House spotlight, while the Senator from Minnesota went out to all the states, speaking on subjects—the Republican nominees and their curious views—and in ways—scornful, shocked, challenging, mocking, derisive —that might seem undignified for a President. Goldwater, too, hoped to travel a relatively high road, leaving the less dignified path, the one that would permit Miller to "drive Johnson nuts," to the second man on the ticket.

How many voters might be converted by these tactics could not, of course, be known. James A. Farley, a veteran of many campaigns, is supposed to have said long ago that most people decide before Labor Day how they will vote in November. Farley would have been the first to add, however, that the side that relaxes may never get its friends into the voting booth. The ward leaders, the district captains and the city chairmen have to be kept active and combative, periodically re-inspired, prepared to assemble their troops. In many instances, these were the people whose resolve was being stiffened by Humphrey and Miller.

In both parties the Vice Presidential candidates were truly running mates. Coordination and communication were about as advanced as they had ever been in a national election. The Miller plane was equipped to talk or listen to the Goldwater plane when either or both were in flight. The Johnson-Humphrey campaign was tied just as closely—electronically, personally, philosophically. Once, on impulse, Johnson in Washington wanted to chat with Humphrey, who at that moment was riding in a motor caravan in New York. The President picked up the telephone and the Humphrey motorcade was brought to a halt in the middle of Brooklyn Bridge. Humphrey hustled out of his car back to the communications vehicle, and the door shut behind him to insure privacy for the White House call. Breathless with expectancy, Humphrey picked up the phone.

"How's everything coming along up there, Hubert?" the President asked.

Even before the campaign, Johnson had pointedly elevated the status of the Vice Presidential candidate by his painstaking canvassing of the possibilities and his personal nomination of Humphrey at the convention. In doing so, he made the nation remember again that Truman had taken over suddenly, startlingly, from Roosevelt; that Eisenhower had twice become seriously ill while President; that Johnson himself was in office only because of unforeseen tragedy. The campaign cliché about Vice Presidential nominees—men who stand "only a heartbeat" from the Presidency—had terrible relevance in 1964.

In 1960, for example, when Henry Cabot Lodge had the second spot on the Republican ticket, he flew around the country with a staff of eight or nine people, including political aides, secretaries, speech writers and public relations men. The Miller staff was nearly twice as large. The large plane normally carried four or five reporters. There were never fewer than a dozen on the Miller campaign—more, counting television crews. Lodge had chartered relatively small, propeller-driven planes, shifting from one to another every week or so. Miller had an Eastern Airlines turbo-jet Electra named "The Niagaran" permanently assigned to him, with two crews that worked on alternate weeks. Lodge was not used by Nixon to make news. (His big news break—calling for a Negro cabinet member while speaking in a Puerto Rican area of New York—was a jarring shock to his running mate.) Basically, Lodge delivered the same speech everywhere, preferring to stand as a handsome symbol of American resistance to international Communism. During each week of Miller's campaign there was a new charge of scandal, duplicity, or impending collectivism.

By the third week of the campaign, the Congressman from Lockport had developed his basic speech to a high polish. His major themes, in regular order of appearance, were: Hubert Horatio Humphrey, the radical; Lyndon Johnson, the good right arm of Bobby Baker; Barry Goldwater, the war hater and family man; and the low estate to which American foreign policy had fallen since 1960. "It is a speech," reported Warren Weaver Jr., of The Times, "that the candidate delivers with zest and a remarkable sense of timing." Weaver continued:

From a good, lively audience, the candidate can get as many as three dozen bursts of applause and cheers in the half hour the speech takes to deliver.

"Now Senator Goldwater and I have only been campaigning about three weeks," Mr. Miller begins, "and I think we are making a lot of progress. We have already reopened the Bobby Baker case [applause] and Hubert Horatio Humphrey [applause and then laughter] has resigned as vice chairman of the A.D.A." [applause].

Then, if the audience is conservative in tone, comes a list of the positions of the Americans for Democratic Action and a series of free-wheeling quotations of statements made over the years by the Democratic Vice Presidential candidate.

Now comes what Mr. Miller regards as one of the major issues of the campaign: A direct frontal attack on the Democratic contention that Senator Goldwater would be a trigger-happy, war-prone President.

"Now here we are, ladies and gentlemen, engaged in the campaign of 1964, and here we find ourselves being criticized by the Democrats as the war party," he says. "They say 'Keep a man of restraint in the White House. Keep the peace.' And this, from a party that has drawn this nation into war four times in this century.

"Senator Goldwater served his nation honorably in combat for four years during World War II. He is now a major general in the Air Force Reserve. He has a wife and four children whom he loves very much. He has four grandchildren whom he loves very much. He loves America deeply and has served it well, and no man in America hates or detests war more than Barry Goldwater of Arizona."

Along about here comes a series of questions as to whether American boys would be dying in South Vietnam if the Bay of Pigs invasion had been a success or the Berlin wall had never been built or the coalition government in Laos never formed. His audiences usually respond with shouts of "No!"

About 15 short sentences follow, all decrying the state of affairs in Cuba, Berlin, Laos, South Vietnam, Panama, Zanzibar, Cyprus, Pakistan and the Congo. Slowly building in speed and intensity, Mr. Miller concludes this itemization with:

"And, in the face of all this, Lyndon Johnson has the colossal nerve at Atlantic City to accept the nomination and go before the American people on television and say: 'Let us continue.'"

Then, as the applause echoes, it is back into the motorcade, and back to the airport and off to the next campaign stop for another go at "the speech."

While Miller clearly enjoyed stump speaking, he, like Goldwater, just as obviously did not take to handshaking. When crowds pressed up to the airport railings, it was his good-looking wife, Stephanie, who walked over immediately and greeted them personally. Miller usually trailed behind her, an uncomfortable, fixed, slightly toothy grin on his face. In motorcades, it was again the candidate's wife—not Miller—who seemed to make contact with the people on the sidewalks. But on the platform Miller was in full, almost effortless command; his audiences would applaud, cheer, stomp, shout, and laugh at the moments he chose. He could usually produce instant applause—compounded in varying degrees of vocabulary, intonation, inflection and rhythm, plus a sense of what people want to hear. Miller unfailingly evoked partisan derision by his enunciation of the full name of his Democratic opponent: Hu-bert Ho-rat-io Hum-ph-rey. He warned his audiences that "Walter Reuther may be appointed Secretary of Labor if President Johnson is elected," eliciting groans. Then he added that this would put Bobby Baker in line for Secretary of the Treasury [laughter] and that Billy Sol Estes would become Secretary of Agriculture [laughter, applause, even stomping]. In California, laughter and applause punctuated every sentence of two paragraphs added to "the speech" for local consumption: "It's wonderful to be here in California," he observed. "I've already been here longer than Pierre Salinger [laughter]. I'm not going to run for the Senate [more laughter] because I couldn't vote for myself [voice rising above the growing laughter] but Pierre can't vote for himself either." [Roars of laughter and cheers and applause while the candidate grins and takes a drink of water.]

Miller was popular with those who traveled with him on "The Niagaran" because of his refusal to take himself too seriously. In private conversations, he gave frank estimates of Republican chances in the election. Miller didn't think they were very good, but his campaign audiences never caught a hint of his professional political pessimism. To an unusual degree for a major politician, he shrugged off newspaper and magazine stories critical of him and never seemed to take any reports of his activities personally. One correspondent gave him a particularly hard time at a news conference, questioning him persistently on a fairly clear contradiction between various Goldwater statements on a key issue. Miller told him later, smiling, "Paul, you tax my ingenuity."

Miller never escaped—if he wanted to—the reputation he had built as national chairman, that of a "hatchet man." A partial list of the charges he made during the campaign showed that at the very least he was a hard-hitting, tenacious "gut fighter":

—He accused the President of "playing with the nation's security for political purposes."

—He suggested that there was a secret "deal" between the Administration and the Soviet Union to maintain the status quo in Cuba.

—He said that "maybe" a Communist agent had known about Walter Jenkins' arrest in 1959 on a morals charge, and added, "We all know how susceptible these people are to blackmail."

—He suggested that State Department security-risk files in twenty cities were being burned because officials of the Johnson Administration "may not want the Goldwater Administration to learn next January what is in those files."

—He backed Goldwater's allegations that Kennedy had "played politics" with the 1962 Cuban missile crisis, and that Johnson was preparing to turn the Vietnam struggle to his political advantage in the 1964 campaign.

Rarely is a Vice Presidential candidate a major drawing card. Miller's opening speech at Lockport attracted a crowd of about 12,000. From then on his crowds usually ranged between 700 and 4,000, and in a few instances were no more than a few hundred. By late October, reporters traveling with the Miller party began to sense a private air of resignation in the group. Wallace Turner of The Times reported on October 19:

Chins were out and upper lips were stiff, but there was an air of futility about the election as Representative William E. Miller's campaign entourage moved out of San Diego tonight for the final two-week drive. . . .

The atmosphere around the staff is glum. There are serious discussions in jocular tones about job opportunities, for example, from persons with several years' tenure in the Republican National Committee.

"I am looking around," one staff member said. "But whatever you do, don't use my name."

In the final week of the campaign, this note of resignation—with barbed political overtones—began creeping even into Miller's speeches. Repeatedly he told his audiences that "we know that if 51 per cent of the American people want to be Federally born and Federally housed and Federally educated and Federally subsidized in business and on the farm and finally buried in a Federal box, Barry and I will lose." Then in a more philosophical mood, Miller would counsel the crowds that they must accept the decision of the majority.

From the very start, Humphrey conducted an entirely different kind of campaign. A few days after he was nominated in August as the Democratic Vice Presidential candidate, Humphrey met with a small group of aides and academic supporters. Over dinner and afterward at the Carroll Arms Hotel near the Capitol, Humphrey and his guests discussed how they could give his campaign intellectual content. Humphrey insisted that he did not want to do what he said most Vice Presidential candidates had done—simply repeat their acceptance speech endlessly. He said that he wanted to educate and inform. He asserted that the voters had a right to know what kind of man he was and what he was likely to be for or against. From this discussion emerged major themes that the group agreed Humphrey should discuss.

Humphrey began to treat these themes in a series of speeches, mostly before university audiences. "To a degree," noted John D. Pomfret of The Times, "his views on key topics have been overshadowed by the color of his campaign and by the vividness of his denunciations of his Republican opponents:"

About the Presidency, the candidate says that if, according to Lord Acton's dictum, absolute power in Government can corrupt absolutely, the absence of power in Government can corrupt just as thoroughly. . . .

American society should not be a planned society, he thinks, but a continuously planning society. Government planning, he believes, is pragmatic and open-ended, and is an attempt to reach widely accepted goals by reasonable and fair methods.

Humphrey says the genius of American politics and the source of its true conservatism is that it has stayed close to the realities of life and has understood that life is larger than logic. It is the conservative, he maintains, who is the enemy of a utopian or an apocalyptic approach to political questions.

The Senator insists that the nation cannot tolerate poverty and has the means to eradicate it if it wants to. The luxuries of yesterday are the necessities of today, he says, and poverty is not just a matter of the purse, but of the spirit as well.

On metropolitan problems, he maintains that the traditional distinction between urban and rural life has disappeared and that between suburb and city it is fast being eroded. The Senator argues that to meet the problems of transportation, education, recreation and poverty in a metropolis there must be a cooperative effort of Federal, state and local governments and private groups and individuals.

The Senator contends that there are various ways of supplementing farm income without distorting market prices and normal channels of trade. Vigorous efforts to expand outlets for farm products at home and abroad seem to offer the brightest hope, he thinks, and farm cooperatives and other segments of the free enterprise system probably should perform many of the marketing functions now being performed by Federal agencies.

In a nuclear age, Senator Humphrey contends, the deliberate initiation of full scale nuclear war as an instrument of national policy has become an absurdity. The nuclear test-ban treaty, he says, was the first step to a more enduring peace, but the nation must seek additional measures to prevent war by miscalculation or accident.

In foreign affairs, Mr. Humphrey says, it is essential that a bipartisan policy be continued.

On the problems of youth, Senator Humphrey says, young people privileged to receive a fine college education bear an obligation to return to their communities and participate actively in bettering both it and their nation.

Humphrey had taught political science at the University of Minnesota and at Macalester College in St. Paul. His preoccupation with young people never left him, and he aroused unabashed enthusiasm on college campuses across the nation. At the University of Toledo, for example, he was met by 7,500 exuberant teen-agers and collegians, many of them carrying amateurishly lettered placards—"We Dig Hubert," "We Love Hubert," "Everyone Loves Hubert." The students mobbed him, stole the watch off his wrist, took cuff-links from his shirtsleeves, delayed his tight schedule while the girls insisted on kissing him goodbye. And—they listened to him. A Times report said:

Mr. Humphrey loves every minute of it. He seems to gain sustenance from the young crowds. He makes it obvious that he enjoys young audiences.

There is also an element of practical political calculation. In planning his trip to Kentucky, Mr. Humphrey asked for a university audience. "Remember, they vote at 18 there," he reminded an aide.

When Mr. Humphrey speaks at places such as the University of Southern California or in the Greek Amphitheater at the University of California at Berkeley, he does not have to remind himself that these young people will be voting— perhaps not in 1964, but at least by 1968 and 1972.

The latter year is one in which it is reasonable to expect that Mr. Humphrey, who is now 53 years old, may be running himself for the nation's highest office.

Mr. Humphrey has developed a stock of academically oriented political quips that he dusts off for every young audience.

He advises them to study ancient history, but not vote it. He says that had Senator Barry Goldwater, the Republican Presidential candidate, been in his political science course, he would have flunked him, or at least given him some "remedial reading."

"Politics should be fun," Humphrey insisted before his audiences. Some of it he supplied himself, by mocking his own long-windedness. "Glands," he would explain simply. Or he'd tell the audience that his wife, Muriel, often told him, "Don't forget that your speeches don't have to be eternal to be immortal." E. W. Kenworthy of The Times gathered some examples of Humphrey humor in a report in early October:

Senator Barry Goldwater, the Republican Presidential nominee, and William E. Miller, his running mate, have taken to referring to Mr. Humphrey by his middle name, Horatio.

Alluding to this the other night, the Senator gave them a stern warning:

"I am going to bring together all those people who have middle names they wish their parents had never heard of—that would be a majority vote."

After Mr. Goldwater accused President Johnson of being "soft on Communism,"

Mr. Humphrey said: "Lyndon may be a little soft on Republicans, but not on Communists."

At a conference of rural electrical cooperatives in Arkansas, Mr. Humphrey said he could offer only one reason for Senator Goldwater's votes against appropriations for the rural electrification program—"They have some kerosene lamps left in that department store in Phoenix they're trying to get rid of."

In Tifton, Ga., Mr. Humphrey quoted Mr. Goldwater as saying that he would get rid of farm price supports—"though it might take three to five years."

"He's saying he'll give you a few more years to decide where you want to be buried," Mr. Humphrey said, "but he'll be in office four years—he'll getcha."

After his speech at the University of Southern California two days ago, he said, "I think we have time for a few questions"—and then pointing to a young man whose heckling had been particularly vociferous—"and first from you over there on the far right."

At Fort Wayne, Ind., he was closely following his text detailing Mr. Goldwater's negative votes on a wide range of social welfare legislation, when he suddenly stopped and asked:

"And where was Mr. Goldwater—he was sitting under the no-no tree in the shade of his own indifference."

In a speech the other night in the Midwest, he was taking after Mr. Goldwater for being "impulsive."

"He's ultimatum happy," Mr. Humphrey cried in the tones of an Old Testament prophet. Then he paused and a smile spread over his sunburned face.

"You can't even bring up a family that way—much less run the world."

While he had no set speech, he did have a set theme—expressed best, perhaps, in a series of questions: What kind of Government do you think the founders intended? What was the spirit that animated them? What kind of country do you want this to be? What kind of people do we want to be? Humphrey gave his own answers. What made America different at its founding from any other nation and what gave it promise of success, he declared, was what John Adams called its spirit of "public happiness." This spirit, he said repeatedly, prevails despite all surface rancor and divisions, riots in the streets and any decline in private morals. And he is confident most of the people want this spirit to prevail.

"We don't see our America as weak, as confused, as immoral, as bad and as indifferent," he said in Fort Wayne, Indiana. Standing before the county courthouse in Terre Haute, he suddenly paused and said to a mixed crowd of townspeople, farmers and college students, "What a blessed land we have. What a blessed people we are—divinely blessed." He said this without any of the politician's sentimentality, but simply, matter of factly, as if he had suddenly discovered it.

As the campaign progressed, Humphrey charged in almost every speech that Goldwater had "a nervous trigger finger," that he could well be capable of "one rash act—and 100 million of us would be ashes by nuclear attack."

Early in September Humphrey had been telling his audiences that "what we are talking about in this election is life itself. The future of the planet. The salvation of the species." At the end of October, Miller conceded that the claims that Goldwater would risk nuclear war "had placed the Republicans on the defensive." He remarked, "We had to dedicate a considerable amount of time to setting the record straight."

Humphrey was able to be shocked by "shoddy and shabby Republican political talk" at the same time he himself plastered labels left and right—but mostly right—on his opponents. In one speech he called Goldwater and Miller "amateur," "radical," "irresponsible," and "extremist." He blithely ignored Goldwater's and Miller's assurances that they did not plan to sell T.V.A. or to end Social Security. From the first of his speeches to the last, he promised that he and the President would make certain that T.V.A. wouldn't be lost to the people and that Social Security would be broadened, not eliminated.

Humphrey's campaign—zesty, wide-ranging in subject, passionately partisan, professorial, corny, jovial, intensely knowledgeable—seemed to provide assurance to the nation. Somehow Humphrey managed to be reminiscent of Truman, Kennedy, Johnson, Adlai Stevenson, and even Franklin Roosevelt— without stealing attention from Johnson. He assured his audiences that Johnson was one of America's great Presidents, and would grow greater. He showed himself, in sum, to be a master politician.

18

A Choice not an Echo

At the National Plowing Contest on September 19 on Elmer Fraase's farm near Buffalo, North Dakota, Humphrey charged that Goldwater's election would seal a death sentence for agriculture. By the time Goldwater reached the Fraase farm, Humphrey had left and the crowd had increased to 50,000, somewhat below the attendance of previous years. In a solidly Republican area (North and South Dakota's eight electoral votes had not gone Democratic since 1936), Goldwater had a forum sympathetic to his views. He could therefore depart from the normal pattern, he reasoned, centering less than half his talk on farm policy, the rest on foreign affairs.

"Today we are at war as certainly as the sun sets in the west," he said, and this had resulted from "a policy of weakness, a policy of indecision, a policy of indirection." Goldwater said Johnson and his "curious crew" (an expression he was to use again and again during the campaign) had lost the peace inherited from Eisenhower because they believed there were good Communist leaders. He said his own foreign policy was based on one simple principle, "The best—the only—way to avoid use of force, is to have force to use."

Turning to farm policy, the Senator reaffirmed his belief in voluntary price supports, including payments in commodities to farmers from Government-owned surpluses (in 1960, Goldwater had termed the price support program absurd). Now, in a departure from his prepared text, he said he had no intention of stopping supports overnight. Goldwater had always prided himself on the courage of his convictions, on his political frankness, but here he was being more confusing than frank. He was sticking to his opinion that the farm subsidy program was wrong, while promising that he would not do anything to change it except with the greatest deliberation. At times he even suggested that the voters need not fear because Congress would not allow him to carry out his aims. Once again, many voters were left with a vague uncertainty as to just what Goldwater would do if elected.

At the plowing contest the stage was surrounded by fervent Goldwater supporters, many of them women in red, white and blue uniforms and young men carrying posters. As usual, the lung-power of their ovation was impressive but as Goldwater droned on in his matter of fact, unemotional style, the vast body of the crowd stretching in a great half-moon across the mud was greeting Goldwater's remarks with a stony and ominous silence.

That evening Goldwater appeared in St. Louis and the contrast could not have been more marked. Kiel Auditorium was jammed with adoring, rapt Goldwater supporters who cheered so loudly that the candidate looked genuinely startled. He had never regarded himself as the center of a cult but that night he looked pleased. He fiddled with his glasses and muttered "thank you, thank you, thank you" as the crowd cheered. In his speech, Goldwater said it was time an American President advised Khrushchev that he was wrong. "If Communism intends to bury us," Goldwater said, "let us tell the Communists loud and clear we're not going to hand them the shovel." Max Frankel in The Times commented:

> Thus was the issue joined. President Johnson has dwelt heavily not only on peace and preparedness, but on "prudence." Senator Goldwater has complained that survival depends above all on "purpose."
>
> As presented to the voters so far, these are not just slogans. Senator Goldwater's friends, like his opponents, seem persuaded that he means what he says about using the Presidency to offer militant resistance to Communism and to lead Americans as the "missionaries" of freedom "in a doubting world."
>
> This overriding issue of Mr. Goldwater's personality and philosophy has given new life and meaning to some otherwise familiar foreign policy questions. In vowing not to cringe before the bully of Communism, condemning such "failures" as the Berlin wall and the Bay of Pigs, linking the concept of disarmament with appeasement and lumping "failure" in Vietnam with "defeat" in Korea, the Senator has managed to persuade friend and foe that he would act upon his sense of mission. . . .
>
> Mr. Goldwater's discussion of foreign affairs, therefore, has been guided above all by a desire to make plain that this time the alternative is real. President Johnson, in turn, has been only too willing to grant the distinction, to proceed in the belief that the majority of Americans endorse the nation's postwar foreign policies and, indeed, to claim that his Administration is now the only representative of the foreign policy views of most Americans in both parties.

The second incident in the Gulf of Tonkin between United States warships and North Vietnam patrol craft provided Goldwater with the ammunition for another attack on the Administration's foreign policy. Again decrying the "lack of purpose, direction and even honesty," he said: "The Administration has tried to manage the news so that the incident is forgotten as quickly as possible. They cannot, however, sweep a war under the rug."

The day after issuing that statement, on Monday, September 21, Goldwater flew to Eisenhower's Gettysburg farm, for a political strategy session and then went on to Charlotte, his third visit in six days to North Carolina. Once unquestionably Democratic, North Carolina, with thirteen electoral votes, had given Republicans nearly half its popular votes in the previous two Presidential elections. With the potent civil rights issue as a lever, Goldwater was hoping to pry away enough lukewarm Democrats from the party to carry North Carolina as well as other Southern states.

Before 17,000 screaming, shouting Republicans in the Charlotte Coliseum, Goldwater challenged Johnson to stop avoiding the major issues of the campaign: "Can my opponent talk? What does my opponent have to say? I challenge my opponent, the interim President Lyndon Baines Johnson, to face the issues. I dare him to face me before the world. I demand of him, debate." (In the past he had voiced different views—on January 31, 1964, "I think it's kind of dangerous to subject a President of the United States to questioning and debate. . . ." On February 12: "I don't think a President of the United States should debate anybody. He . . . could very well disclose secrets that only he knows.")

Goldwater also contended that the Administration clung to the dangerous belief that government was master, not servant of the people, and insisted it operated through a centralized authority "that has even given you a number to replace your name." Then, returning to his persistent, almost mystical theme of a long-lost freedom, he said: "We want to give you your freedom and your names back again. We want to give the Government of this nation back to the people of the nation. An administration that understands, rather than one that tries to wreck the balance of constitutional power, can do the job."

On September 22, the thirtieth anniversary of his marriage, Goldwater and his wife sped through Oklahoma, Texas and New Mexico. In 1960, seven of Oklahoma's eight electoral votes were cast for Nixon and one for Byrd; Kennedy won Texas's twenty-four and New Mexico's four. Goldwater was aware that the week was crucial. His own polling information indicated that only a few disaffected Republicans were returning to his standard. It was good, but not good enough. The chief impediment to his campaign, he and his aides were convinced, was the all-important nuclear issue and its corollary image of an impulsive and reckless candidate.

It was imperative, therefore, that he fling the trigger happy charge back at the Democrats. Goldwater let it be known to the press, on his swing through the Southwest, that he believed military field commanders already possessed the power, without a specific order by the President, to employ nuclear arms in an emergency, that standby arrangements with the President, for use in extreme situations of open war, had long been in operation. Goldwater made it clear that he intended to exploit to the fullest what he now regarded as the fluid nuclear situation. "If I can be called trigger happy for suggesting it," he said, "what can you call the President for having already done it?"

Yet Goldwater was attempting to change the terms of the debate. What he had been advocating since 1963 was that small, battlefield tactical nuclear weapons be available for use by the NATO commander in case of a sudden, massive ground attack in Germany. There would be no question of the President of the United States being dead or out of communications with SHAPE (since the contingency Goldwater had in mind did not envision general war or an attack on Washington and Paris). Goldwater was asked about this—

sharply questioned, in fact—during a background briefing with newsmen. He simply refused to answer the questions clearly or to say what kind of contingency delegation of nuclear weapons he now had in mind.

In Washington, the Pentagon declined to comment on his nuclear opinions, but the assumption was growing that certain field commanders, particularly those responsible for defense against an attack, had long possessed Presidential authority to retaliate with nuclear arms in specific situations. The Administration's silence in itself was regarded as indicating Goldwater's position had some factual substance, although his original proposal had been vastly different from the contingency plans involving Presidential disability or a communications breakdown.

A taped TV program with Eisenhower was aired that night and that, too, attempted to picture the Senator in a softer light. The General termed the charge of warmongering against Goldwater as tommyrot. "No man who knows anything about the war is going to be reckless about this," the former President declared.

The nuclear theme also dominated the third day of Goldwater's tour. In Dallas, addressing the annual convention of the American Legion, he said the great, harsh fact of the world was the war against Communism. It was not necessary to look forward to a cold war that would last forever, he said, adding, "There is a rational solution to the problem which confronts us . . . nuclear destruction or take-over by a Communist dictator." What was the solution? The Senator answered, "The responsible use of power—to deter those with hostile intent—is not nearly so likely to provoke all-out war as it is to prevent war by keeping the aggressor within bounds." Goldwater insisted that to halt Communist inroads we must be stronger than the enemy, not just a little bit, but by far, and contended that Administration policy was based on false answers, that its theory of "let's be friends" had failed dismally.

A few hours earlier, in Forth Worth, Goldwater had accused Johnson of using tax returns to force support for his campaign, but had refused to elaborate further. It was the type of charge, strewn casually along the trail by Republicans and Democrats alike, that aroused Senator Karl E. Mundt to bemoan the "low-level schoolyard campaign" being waged by both parties. Mundt, a conservative South Dakota Republican, told the Senate that day that both candidates and their running mates were conducting a race that was an insult to the intelligence of the American voters. "What kind of madness has overtaken these candidates for office?" he asked. There was still time to restore some degree of dignity and decency to the campaign, he said, and he was echoing the concern of thousands of voters dismayed by the emotionalism and the absence of rational debate on the major issues.

The following day Goldwater ranged through Kansas, Iowa, Wisconsin and, for the first time, a state in the Northeast—Massachusetts. (Four years previously the three Midwestern states, with thirty electoral votes, went for Nixon; the Bay State gave its sixteen to Kennedy.) It was a bad day for Goldwater. He encountered resistance in Boston, which was expected, but he was jolted by heckling in Wisconsin and he left his farm listeners in Iowa cold. Only at an early morning rally in Wichita, Kansas, did he get the kind of rousing greeting that is a basic staple in any politician's diet.

In Iowa, a traditionally Republican state, Goldwater found "LBJ" signs prominently displayed at the Mason City airport. He told 5,000 listeners at the airport: "I know when a candidate comes into farm country he is supposed to make a farm speech. But I was given the biggest ear of corn I have ever seen—so it is obvious I can't tell you anything about farming." The jocularity did not please the Iowans. One party leader said later, "It would have been better not to talk about the farm program at all than to say that."

Opposition to Goldwater was raucous at Madison, Wisconsin. Classes at the University of Wisconsin were suspended for the noontime rally, and the state Capitol grounds abounded with students, many waving banners and signs that taunted the Senator. One, directly in front of the speaker's platform, said tartly, "Bring the Bomb—Back Barry." Another parodied his most pervasive slogan, "In Your Heart You Know He's Trite." Nevertheless, despite the throng's obstreperousness, despite repetitive cries of "We Want Lyndon," the majority of his listeners seemed inclined in his favor.

At this stage of his campaign Goldwater believed he had improved his chances in the South, had retained a hold on the Midwest, but was in desperate need of evidence that the Northeast was reacting to his message. But in Boston he found: The crowds in the streets were below expectations and were polite and restrained; a picket line of several hundred members of the Committee Against Political Extremism circled Fenway Park, scene of the rally; the crowd of 18,000 to 20,000 was well below capacity. But his followers in the ball park loved what he had to say and proved it with their lusty applause and shouts.

Goldwater, in his speech, emphasized crime in the streets and the Bobby Baker controversy. He blamed the bosses of the Democratic party for the lawlessness gripping the nation because they controlled the big cities, and on the Baker case, he reminded Bostonians that Matthew McCloskey, former Democratic treasurer and accused of a kickback deal with Baker, was the same Matt McCloskey who had built the Boston Veterans Hospital in the early nineteen fifties. The hospital was improperly constructed, Goldwater said, and action instituted to recover $4,000,000 from the McCloskey contractors. "But McCloskey hasn't paid up yet," said the Senator.

Three prominent Republicans appeared on the platform in Boston with him, Senator Leverett Saltonstall, who did not have an election to worry about in 1964, and who introduced him; former Governor John A. Volpe, making a political comeback, who was introduced but did not speak; and Howard Whitmore Jr., an investment broker with the unhappy task of attempting to unseat the injured Senatorial incumbent, Edward Kennedy, and who also took a bow without speaking. Two Republican nominees pleaded prior engagements and stayed away from the rally, Attorney General Edward W. Brooke, a Negro seeking re-election, who earlier had repudiated Goldwater, and Elliot L. Richardson, running for Lieutenant Governor.

On September 25 Goldwater finished his swing around the Northeast, touching Maine, New Hampshire and Vermont, before flying to Albany, New York. The three New England states, whose twelve electoral votes had gone to Nixon in 1960, displayed typical Yankee taciturnity. It was a bed-rock Republican section, and he was the Republican candidate, but Goldwater found it difficult to establish any rapport. In Portland, Maine, a sign in the airport crowd urging him to support civil rights brought forth his first direct reference to the problem: "This civil rights bill has been on the books for months and months, and it still hasn't solved the problem. I hope it will. I voted against it, but I hope it does the job. But it's not going to unless it's enforced, and the present Administration shows no inclination toward support- ing it—just as the last Attorney General [Robert F. Kennedy] showed no inclination of supporting the laws we have on the books—adequate laws—to give the people the right to vote, which is the only civil rights mentioned in the Constitution."

It was raining when Goldwater's plane landed in Albany. Rockefeller and his wife were there to greet the Senator and his wife. There was friendly chit-chat. The Senator apologized for being late. Rockefeller said, "We're just glad you're here," and Mrs. Rockefeller said, "Sorry you didn't get here in time to come to the house." Amenities finished, they went to the political rally, where Rockefeller introduced Goldwater as "one of the most dedicated, hard-working, courageous members of the Republican party." What he did not say—vote for Goldwater—was more important. Nevertheless, the Senator told the throng of about 5,000 that "all across this country, we look to this state with envy for the Governor you have." He even plumped for party unity by asking for the re-election of Senator Kenneth B. Keating (who still shunned the national ticket) in his fight against Bobby Kennedy. Rockefeller's arms-length rapprochement contributed heavily toward the apathy of New York. New York's electoral vote, reduced from forty-five in 1960 to forty-three, remained the largest single bloc in the nation, and Goldwater's chances of carrying it were negligible.

Goldwater ended his grueling week with a day-long tour of Michigan, and Governor Romney rewarded him with two rebuffs. Romney not only declined to support Goldwater, he also rejected the latter's offer of assistance in his own gubernatorial race. He made adroit use of the Arizonan's acceptance speech to say, "I subscribe wholeheartedly to his view that conformity does not create party strength."

Then still another setback jarred the Goldwater camp. A pamphlet de- picting the Senator as a personally dedicated and vigorous champion of Negro rights was summarily suppressed by the Republican National Com- mittee. The reason: Distribution at this time "might turn the backlash into a frontlash by falling into the wrong hands." The pamphlet had been designed to circulate among Negroes in Washington and, unfortunately, did fall into wrong hands—those of Democrats. Since the leaflet called the Senator a card-carrying member of the National Association for the Advancement of Colored People, and since it termed Johnson a racist and said he was solidly against Negro rights, the Democrats did the natural thing. They shipped the pamphlet into the one section where it could be calculated to damage Goldwater—the South.

The tone and style of the Goldwater and Johnson campaigns had hardened by this time. The two opponents differed as widely in style as they did on issues, except for a tendency to moralize. Goldwater called for repentance and uttered dire warnings of damnation; Johnson appealed for love and compassion in his sermons. In their public speeches, neither Goldwater nor Johnson could remotely be compared with the urbane and witty Kennedy. Both were colloquial and folksy. A favorite Goldwater tactic was to call Johnson by his full name, drawling and drawing out the word Baines in a tone of distaste. Johnson at this late stage had never mentioned Goldwater by name—or even referred to him as "my opponent." The Democratic nominee's arrival in most cities generated more excitement and filled more streets than Goldwater's did, but the latter was doing well in his formal nighttime appearances, organized by his supporters.

When Goldwater grounded his airliner for a five-day whistle stop train tour, it gave birth to an incident that Charles Mohr of The Times dubbed "The Spy Who Was Thrown Out Into the Cold." All the proper elements were there: A pretty girl, a cunning mastermind, furtive pre-dawn searches of the train and, at last, the triumph of justice—marred somewhat by a touch of Marx brothers slapstick. The trip began inauspiciously on the night of September 28 with a rally at Washington's Union Station Plaza.

Shortly after, the train started off toward Ohio, Indiana and Illinois. Goldwater's schedule called for thirty-six stops in an effort to hold Ohio's twenty-six electoral votes and Indiana's thirteen, and to recapture Illinois's twenty-six from the Democrats. Aboard the train and almost unnoticed among the press corps was Moira O'Conner of Chicago, a tall, pretty, twenty-three-year-old brunette, who said she was a free-lance writer and who had paid $225 for a roomette on the nineteen-car train. She wore a trench coat, carried a bulky leather handbag and a ticket to Room 7 in Car 12.

Copies of a newsletter, appropriately entitled *Whistlestop,* began to circulate almost before the train left the station, promising to keep everyone informed "and, with considerable assistance from the Senator himself, amused." After listing four traditionally Republican newspapers in Ohio that had endorsed Johnson, the newsletter casually reported that fluoride had not been added to the water on the train. The following day The Times carried this account by Charles Mohr of what then occurred:

What followed had the elements of an episode of an Ian Fleming or Eric Ambler thriller on the Orient Express rushing through the Balkan night.

There were soft footfalls in the darkened corridors as the gently rocking Goldwater Express went rushing through the West Virginia night. There was a swift and ruthless search of baggage. And then came the pre-dawn discovery and confrontation of Miss O'Conner by Senator Goldwater's assistant press secretary, Vic Gold.

She was caught silently slipping under compartment doors a new edition of "Whistlestop" contrasting the crowds Richard M. Nixon drew in Ohio in 1960 with what was expected for Mr. Goldwater today.

Mr. Gold's words to the pretty Democratic spy were: "I think you may have made your last delivery, my dear."

Miss O'Conner, given five minutes to pack, was thrust out into the cold of a damp morning in Parkersburg, West Virginia. A little later, the Goldwater staff put out a final train edition of *Whistlestop* under "new, stream-lined management," pointing out that Miss O'Conner's $225 was a Democratic contribution to the operation of the Goldwater campaign train. Miss O'Conner, as it developed, was a fashion copy writer and a volunteer worker at Democratic headquarters in Washington. The mastermind behind the prank was Richard Tuck, a forty-year-old Californian who took great delight in playing practical jokes on unsuspecting Republican candidates. In 1960, it was Tuck who donned a trainman's cap and signalled the engineer to start the train just as Nixon was beginning a speech. It was Tuck who created chaos in a tight Nixon schedule by the simple device of switching signs on two campaign buses. And it was Tuck, now a "researcher" on the Democratic payroll, who, along with Miss O'Conner, continued to follow the Goldwater train, handing out new issues of *Whistlestop* at each station until he tired of his sport in Toledo. The final broadside included this, "We wish we could say that Goldwater's speeches speak for themselves, but they don't."

The Senator was speaking for himself all through Ohio, at Marietta, Athens, Chillicothe, Blanchester and Cincinnati. At the earlier stops he usually spoke from the rear platform of the train and the crowds ranged from 3,000 to 6,000. At Athens, students from Ohio University subjected him to the worst booing and heckling of his campaign. In Cincinnati, Goldwater made what, in many ways, was the harshest and toughest address of the campaign and there, too, for the first time, he accused the Administration of being soft on Communism and the Democrats of being the party of "the corrupt, the power-mad and the radicals of the left." The auditorium was filled to its capacity of 16,500 and the Senator received a roaring ovation, one of the very best of his campaign. There was prolonged applause the four times he repeated his accusation of soft on Communism. The Republican nominee also singled out Humphrey as "this A.D.A. radical of the left," and asked why the Minnesotan wanted "so badly to be a heartbeat away from the Presidency—to drag our nation into the swampland of collectivism, to take hundreds of billions of dollars from your pockets to spend on silly Socialistic schemes?"

Ohio again occupied all of Goldwater's time the next day. It was sunny and the throngs at each stop were considerably larger than the day before. At Lima, the campaign train got lost. While Goldwater spoke downtown, the train was to be switched from one set of tracks to another, but no one could find it. Goldwater and a few aides started their own search for the train and a few newsmen asked advice as to where to find them. "Might try the D. T. and I. 'Y' crossing," said the Lima sage. The what? "The Detroit, Toledo and Irontown 'Y' crossing." A check showed that Goldwater had just left—for another crossing. There he was found, trapped against an anchor fence signing autographs and posing for pictures for a small army of Negro children, with no train in sight. For a change Goldwater seemed happy to have the company of reporters. They began to ask questions, especially why he had not followed up on the soft on Communism theme. This exchange took place:

"Oh," Goldwater replied, "that's not new, it's run all through the campaign. . . ."

"But not in so many words."

"No. Actually that attack was suggested by Nixon and Herbert Hoover Sr. We're going to wait and see what the reaction is before we push it."

Nixon later disavowed suggesting this tactic, and said there could be no question regarding the attitude of Johnson and Humphrey toward Communism. The ailing former President did not comment before his death on October 20. Johnson waited a few days before replying at a news conference:

QUESTION: Mr. President, can you give us your view on the suggestion that your Administration is soft on Communism?

ANSWER: I don't know that I want to reply in kind to the charge of that nature. I see in the papers—that is the only information that I have—the new and frightening voice of the Republican party is merely trying out this charge at the moment to see if it works. On that basis, my own advice would be to drop it.

I also saw it reported that he was advised along these lines by Mr. Hoover and Mr. Nixon, former President Hoover, but both President Hoover and Vice President Nixon are men I have known for many years and have worked with them, and I doubt very much that either of them would make such a suggestion about me or about my Cabinet or this Administration.

My own belief is that this sort of nonsense was the product of some third-string speech writer and accidentally got into the public print without prudent or careful screening. As far as I am concerned, I intend to ignore it. I think when the Republican candidate really has a chance to think about it and study it, he will stop it.

If Goldwater did study it, he did not stop it. He concentrated on South Vietnam at Columbus. He said the United States got into the guerrilla war by mistake, and blamed one of his favorite whipping boys, McNamara. The Defense Secretary "went there and told those boys to start shooting when they were only supposed to be instructing," he insisted. Asked if American troops should not have been allowed to fire back at the North Vietnamese, he said: "Not at all. Probably [that decision was] the only one you could have reached—what I am saying was it was taken without the proper kind of review procedures." Standing far above his crowd on the elevated terrace of an auditorium, Goldwater admitted that it was fair to ask what a Republican would do about Vietnam. His answer, stripped of the rhetoric: He would go on television and talk frankly to the American people.

The intrusion of Nixon's name into the campaign limelight coincided with the start of his month-long tour for Goldwater. The former Vice President, redeeming a pledge made to the G.O.P. convention, gave the first of about 150 addresses in thirty-six states for the Arizonan. He thus joined Scranton, another loser in the nomination struggle, in an attempt to re-establish party unity. Rockefeller, Romney and Lodge were giving lip service —no more and sometimes less—to the national ticket.

Ben A. Franklin of The Times described Scranton's turnabout as follows: "In his standard post-convention speech, Mr. Scranton invokes the image of Lincoln and urges Republicans to 'go forward and give us victories.' Between attacks on the Johnson Administration, he praises Senator Goldwater's 'broader point of view' as Presidential candidate." Two reasons were given by Scranton supporters for his switch: He hoped to keep moderates in the party by his example and, having made a pledge of party unity following the nomination, he felt he could do nothing else but respond to the national committee's call for campaign help. A third reason: If Scranton had any Presidential ambitions for 1968, they could best be served by working for the party—even if it meant working for Goldwater—in 1964.

Many of the same considerations motivated Nixon, who stumped long and hard for Goldwater. An overwhelming triumph for the Democrats might leave the G.O.P. so shattered that it would be years before the two-party system had any real significance in the nation. To avert this and make certain the Republicans elected a proportionate share of Senators and Representatives was probably the chief reason Nixon put aside his law prac-tice and took to the hustings for a candidate for whom he had no abiding affection. He also was looking forward to 1968.

Goldwater, continuing his Middle West tour, spent a day in Indiana, a state in which white industrial workers had shown resentment of Negro advances in civil rights by voting for Wallace in the Presidential primary. During the day, he concentrated on the struggle against the Communists, promising that no United States President—meaning himself—would in-tentionally start a war. In a speech at Indianapolis, he again pictured John-son as a cynical politician who was soft on Communism and interested only in winning votes.

On the final two days of his tour, the Arizonan crisscrossed Illinois. Again, soft on Communism; again, crime in the streets. And then the whistle stop tour, a rarity in the day of jet airliners, was over. On October 3, Russell Baker offered this analysis of it:

Senator Barry Goldwater's train tour of the Middle West this week has drama-tized the peculiar paradox of the electronic-nuclear age.

The closer the politicians get to the people, the harder it is to tell what's going on. The problem was illustrated the other day in Frankfort, Ind., a town of 15,000 persons that seemed to have turned out half its population to hear the Republican nominee for President.

As the Senator ran through a half-dozen of his stock campaign themes, the big crowd responded with the kind of cheers that warm a politician's heart. What the

Senator did not know, however, was that most of the cheering thousands could not have heard a word he said.

The public address system on the rear platform of his private car was too weak to project his voice more than 30 yards beyond the platform. And so, whatever else the bulk of the crowd may have been cheering, it could not possibly have been the message the Senator had brought to Frankfort. It was a small mystery, but it typified the larger quandary a Presidential candidate faces in the age of coast-to-coast television, scientific polling and mass-mind manipulation: Shall a candidate tie his fate to the electronic tube, the cosmetician, the opinion sample and the computer, or shall he rely on the old flesh-and-blood contacts?

All the evidence of the last week suggests that the intimate whistle stop campaign, which worked for Harry S. Truman in 1948, may be better for the candidate's morale than for anything else.

All polls tell Mr. Goldwater that he is in deep difficulty, but all through Ohio, Indiana and Illinois his trainside crowds have been big. Not enormous and not tumultuous, to be sure, but large enough and sympathetic enough to cheer a candidate with the suspicion that the polls might just possibly be wrong.

But do the crowds mean anything in terms of voting patterns? It is a mystery. . . .

And what of the unusually heavy heckling given Senator Goldwater through Ohio? Some of the anti-Goldwater signs that faced him from the crowds were more violent than anything a Presidential candidate has had to face in the last generation.

How seriously is the heckling to be taken? It is a mystery. . . .

The Senator himself is said to have enjoyed the week and to have found it relaxing. The flesh-and-blood contact seemed to give him a lift, and his rear-platform speeches frequently seemed so relaxed that the audience, which had come to hear him raise the hair on the back of its neck, stood along the tracks looking anesthetized.

His rhetoric runs to powerful statement, and in the newspapers he seems fierce as he accuses the President of arm twisting, blackmailing, lying and "softness on Communism"—four charges he repeated consistently all week.

His delivery, however, is so gentlemanly, so matter of fact, that he rarely stirs the powerful juices of crowd passion or evokes the animal roar that tells the politician he has hit the jugular. And when he introduces Mrs. Goldwater—"a grandmother I've been married to for 30 years"—the tableau of gentle domesticity gives the tiger image its coup de grace.

But Murray Schumach of The Times, trailing behind the train, found that the Presidential campaign had burned a swath of bitterness across Ohio, Indiana and Illinois and that some community leaders feared the effects might last beyond the election. "Supporters of Mr. Goldwater declared they could not discuss the campaign with Democrats on a rational basis," he reported. "Democrats said the Goldwaterites were too rabid for reason. Close relatives as well as friends appear to have declared a moratorium on political discussions until after the election."

The campaign, now at the halfway mark, had grown increasingly embittered. Goldwater's charges were harsher and wilder ("I charge this Administration has a foreign policy of drift, deception and defeat"). His prospects for victory, small at the start, seemed to be dwindling, and he futilely tried to goad Johnson into a debate ("Every time we ask an embarrassing question, Lyndon leaves town to dedicate a dam. Well, I want him to know, and you to know, that we have more questions than he has dams."). Pessimism about his chances had a solid foundation: Public opinion polls, surveys of the voters, a spreading defection of newspapers and magazines from the Republican camp. With few exceptions, The Times' surveys showed the tide running strongly against him:

Maine: There was a good chance the President would carry that die-hard G.O.P. state.

California: The elderly dependent on pensions and Social Security were for the Democrats in landslide numbers.

Pennsylvania: Republicans were in dire trouble over the national ticket.

Business leaders in the South were split; support for Goldwater was greater than in the past for a Republican, but not enough to offset the normal Democratic tradition.

Negro Republicans in five major cities—New York, Philadelphia, Chicago, Detroit and Cleveland—were turning to Johnson.

G.O.P. moderates in Oregon were refusing to aid Goldwater.

The outlook in Tennessee, where the Senator had once been far in the lead, was now viewed as a toss-up.

Nevada, which Kennedy barely carried by 2,500 votes, was believed safe for Johnson.

Cattle ranchers in the West were switching in surprising numbers to the Democratic side. (Typical comment: "I'm concerned about what happens to my kids and their kids. If I can do anything for them, I will, and I don't want any trigger happy jackrabbit around.")

White Protestants in New York City, mostly Republican, were swinging toward Johnson.

Goldwater was losing ground in Virginia, and there was a definite danger he might lose the state's twelve electoral votes.

Intraparty strife in Idaho was damaging the Senator's chances.

Only three of the surveys offered any encouragement to the Senator:

In Minnesota, the depressed iron mining region, normally two to one Democratic, was only grudgingly for Johnson.

In the South, large numbers of white workers were found ready to vote for the Senator in protest over the Civil Rights Act.

In the Midwest, suburban voters were undecided about supporting either candidate ("I'm undecided whether to vote for a kook or a crook").

The most discouraging survey of all appeared in The Times of October 6. Written by Tom Wicker, it said:

Exactly four weeks before Election Day, Nov. 3, Lyndon B. Johnson is the most overwhelming choice to win the Presidency since Thomas E. Dewey at the same stage of the 1948 campaign.

Therein may lie a warning to the Democrats. Yet, even Mr. Dewey never enjoyed the kind of lead that every reliable indicator now gives Mr. Johnson— and Mr. Dewey's upset by Harry S. Truman was a tame event compared with the shock that would hit political analysts, poll-takers and party officials if Senator Barry Goldwater were to manage a victory this year. . . .

Seventeen states and the District of Columbia, with a total of 252 electoral votes, only 18 short of the necessary majority, apparently are sure to go to Mr. Johnson; 14 others are leaning strongly toward him.

In eight states, including four in the South, the race is about even.

The public opinion polls, however, brought into focus what many voters considered the disturbing question of Johnson's ethics. A survey by Samuel Lubell disclosed a sharp increase in the number of voters made uneasy by suspicions of the President's "personal honesty and by how the Bobby Baker case has been handled." How widespread this feeling was, whether it could be caused to spread by the drumfire attacks by Goldwater and Miller on those two issues, remained to be seen. There seemed little doubt that the Republicans regarded the morality issue as Johnson's Achilles' heel.

An off-beat poll in the magazine *Fact* aroused a storm of protests. The magazine sent to 12,356 psychiatrists the following question, "Is Barry Goldwater psychologically fit to be President of the United States?" Full-page newspaper advertisements based on the question helped to publicize the survey and stir up the controversy. Of the 2,417 psychiatrists who replied to the question, 1,189 answered "no," 657 said "yes," and 571 said they did not know enough about the matter to answer. The poll was severely criticized by the American Psychiatric Association and the American Medical Association; the organizations termed it yellow journalism and said the magazine had printed a hodgepodge of the personal political opinions of psychiatrists.

The two endorsements of Johnson that provoked the widest comment came within a day of each other. The New York *Herald Tribune,* in its issue of October 4, supported a Democrat for the first time in its 124-year-old history:

For the Presidency: Lyndon B. Johnson.
Travail and torment go into those simple words, breaching as they do the political traditions of a long newspaper lifetime. But we find ourselves, as Americans, even as Republicans, with no other acceptable choice.
We hold no brief for the Democratic doctrine of ever-encroaching Federal authority; we fear a continued spending spree; we despise the traditional Democratic practice of buying votes by the bloc, with special interest legislation wrapped in compassionate slogans.
But in Mr. Johnson we are offered a man of vast experience and manifest competence.

Life, which since 1944 had supported Republican nominees, announced for Johnson, too. It was the first time any publication of Time, Inc., had backed a Democratic national ticket. One interesting aspect of the *Life* endorsement was that Luce's wife, Clare Boothe Luce, playwright and former Ambassador to Italy, was national co-chairman of Citizens for Goldwater.

Goldwater and his aides were still searching for some break or issue which would set fire to the campaign. He added a new twist to his Vietnam position, promising that if elected he would request Eisenhower "to go to South Vietnam and report back to me on the situation in Southeast Asia." The General would head up a group of qualified experts, Goldwater said, and the proposal inevitably recalled Eisenhower's dramatic campaign pledge in 1952 to go to Korea after his election and seek a truce, which he did.

Goldwater's idea was born at a staff meeting at which he was quoted as saying: "Why don't we say what we are going to do if elected? We just can't leave this Vietnam business just sitting there." Intimates of the General said immediately that the Senator had not discussed it with him. Eisenhower, they emphasized, was not committed to go to Southeast Asia no matter what the outcome of the election. A few days later the former President gently suggested he might be too old for the task. Goldwater let the idea quietly die.

The Goldwater forces, angered by the apathy of top Republican leaders in New York, now accused Rockefeller of withholding support from the national ticket. The rift that had been there all the time but not discussed, was thus brought into the open. The Governor attempted to make amends the next day by calling Goldwater "a man of courage and integrity who has not ducked the issues." In an address to G.O.P. candidates and party leaders in Albany, he said, "We are pledged to support our candidates, from Barry and Bill right down the line all the way, and that's what we're going to do." Rockefeller's words were the warmest of the campaign, but his usual coolness returned in short order; he refused to disclose whether he would vote for Goldwater, insisting this was a private matter.

Responsible G.O.P. officials admitted that only an unforeseeable break, or a spark that ignited the country, could turn the tide. But what spark could be transformed into a winning tactic, what break?

Goldwater indicated his own approach in an address to 350 editors and publishers at a United Press International conference in Washington. He told them he was prepared to devote the four remaining weeks of his campaign to the broad general issue of liberalism versus conservatism. "I don't have any desire or particular interest in getting down to what will make this particular district or that particular district respond to me," he said. "I want to deal with the problems that are recognized by people in all parts of the country. I know people are concerned with the basic issue, and we're going to continue our campaign, as we have, along those lines."

19

Some Non-Political Speeches

During an unexpected news conference in his office on September 21 (his twenty-eighth in ten months in office), President Johnson remarked that he expected to step up the pace of his campaign. "We think that people want to hear from us," he said. "They want to get our viewpoints on public questions, they want to know how we stand on issues, so we are going to be visiting all over this country."

The President walked restlessly around and around his green swivel chair in a counterclockwise direction as he continued: "I expect, myself, I will be in many, many states. I don't have any accurate poll on them, but to just pick a figure out of the air, I would think now, since I have been President, the ten months, and maybe eleven months by election time, that I will be in states that involve a population of 125,000,000, and probably more than thirty states."

The President was in a cheerful mood and, as usual, his pockets were bulging with polls showing him far ahead of Goldwater in most of the country; he was always ready to discuss them—at length, with figures. But those familiar with his thinking knew that he also believed that Goldwater had made a strong showing in the South the previous week, had drawn good crowds and was substantially ahead of him in Alabama and Mississippi.

The following day Johnson amply demonstrated that he meant it when he said he didn't believe in overconfidence. He flew in a helicopter to Atlantic City, landing in a parking lot with a light rain falling and high winds whipping the ocean breakers. In the same Convention Hall in which he had received the Democratic nomination, he made his most impassioned speech of the campaign to date, to the annual convention of the United Steelworkers of America. Again Goldwater was not mentioned by name, again the talk was classified as non-political. The 3,500 delegates, representing 828,000 Democratic-minded workers, showed their appreciation with the kind of ovation usually reserved for contract concessions.

"We will extend the helping hand of a just nation to the poor and to the helpless and the oppressed," the President said. "We will do all these things because we love people instead of hate them, because we have faith in America, not fear of the future, because you are strong men of vision, not frightened crybabies, because you know it takes a man who loves his country to build a house instead of a raving, ranting demagogue who wants to tear down one. Beware of those who fear and doubt and those who rave and rant about the dangers of progress."

He lashed out at the philosophy of the soup line (still an unwelcome depression memory to the older union men), denounced prejudice and bigotry and hatred and division, pledged a limitless future for a united and tolerant nation, and paraphrased an opposition slogan, "And you know in your heart that I am telling you the truth."

The President's reluctance to become involved in even an indirect personal attack against his opponent was accentuated a few hours later when the White House press office requested that the word demagogue in the official transcript be changed to the plural. The request was withdrawn after a recording check disclosed that Johnson had not uttered demagogues, but the singular. To the President, the distinction was important; to his listeners, to the nation, it could hardly have mattered less. He later confided, however, that he was not aiming so much at Goldwater as at the "bombthrowers" around him.

Another labor convention, that of the International Union of Electrical Workers, heard the Democratic nominee a day later at the Statler Hotel in Washington. Through closed-circuit television, his remarks and image were carried to gatherings of five other unions in New York, Miami Beach, Chicago, St. Paul and Kansas City. A festive spirit akin to New Year's Eve prevailed at the Washington meeting; confetti and paper streamers filled the air. Many of the 1,500 delegates jauntily wore red, white and blue paper caps bearing the legend, "LBJ and HHH for the U.S.A." They wanted nothing more than to hear the President tear into Goldwater the arch-conservative. They were disappointed. He came close to naming Goldwater, closer than ever before, and what he said was forceful, but his solemnity, his slow and measured delivery put a damper on their ardor.

"Americans are faced with a concerted bid for power by factions which oppose all that both parties have supported," he said. "It is a choice between the center and the fringe, between the responsible mainstream of American experience and the reckless and rejected extremism of American life." During the G.O.P. primaries, Rockefeller and other moderate Republicans had time and again characterized Goldwater as being outside the mainstream of American life. Now Dean Burch, the Republican National Chairman, sought to divert the Presidential fire in Humphrey's direction by saying, "I can only conclude that Johnson is referring to the radical and widely discredited Americans for Democratic Action."

The President, continuing his attack, said the factions he meant were united by "one determination—that your country shall not provide for the general welfare of its citizens." He cited their opposition to the broad range of social and welfare programs of the last thirty years, then began to inch toward an allusion to Goldwater. Some factions condemn social justice as the work of those bent on centralizing power in Washington, Johnson said, but they forget their history. "In many works of compassion, states have led the way. In 1914 the first old-age pension was established in a state where character has not been collectivized by compassion—the great state of Arizona." The sally aroused laughter—a rarity during that speech. He still had not directly mentioned the Arizona Senator, but he could go no closer to the water without falling in.

The next day the President returned to the Southwest where one hundred years ago the flooding Rio Grande had shifted its course between Mexico and the United States. The diversion of the river resulted in the arbitrary expropriation of about 600 acres of Mexican territory. An arid tract on which 5,600 persons lived, the area was covered by a desert weed from which it derived the name of El Chamizal. A settlement was reached, and on September 25, 1964 Johnson flew to El Paso, Texas, to meet with President Adolfo Lopez Mateos in a ceremony marking the return of 437 acres of territory. He took advantage of the occasion to make three other speeches, too—at the dedication of Eufaula Dam near Muskogee, Oklahoma, at the Oklahoma State Fair in Oklahoma City and at the dedication of the John F. Kennedy Square in Texarkana.

He was met by huge crowds and he reveled in them. At El Paso his route was lined for miles by crowds estimated between 100,000 and 250,000. His hands aching and scratched, the President nonetheless delightedly stopped his car ten times and plunged into the milling mobs. The Secret Service detail looked on impassively at what they could not prevent. Peace was on the President's mind at El Paso. He declared that the United States was not a government of ultimatum and would not frighten others into a nuclear war. On South Vietnam, he said, "We are not going to start another war and we are not going to run away from where we are." He told the large throng of Americans and Mexicans, "I pledge to you now that I will go to any remote corner of the world to meet anyone, any time, to promote freedom and peace."

At Texarkana, Johnson's remarks became more political. Speaking from almost the exact spot where Kennedy had in 1960, Johnson declared that "who leads America must speak what is deep in the hearts of Americans —and not what comes from the top of the head.

"There are voices in the land tonight that have a strange and brittle tone," the President went on. "They cry out that we are weak and soft and blind . . . insist the way to the future is the road back into the past . . . demand suspicion as the price of liberty and belligerence as the alternative to peace. They just can't seem to find anything right in our beloved country. All they find is wrong."

Texarkana is Southern, and the civil rights question was a sore subject. Nevertheless, he appealed to his audience: "Today, we ask for equality and justice for all citizens under our Constitution. The voices say this is wrong, but truth says it is right."

While the President spent the weekend at his ranch near Johnson City, one unusual aspect of the campaign, the role of the Johnson Cabinet, came in for some attention in a Times article by Jack Raymond:

Serving at the pleasure of the President, the members of the Cabinet—some of whom no doubt would like to continue serving him, in the event of President Johnson's election—have been unstinting in their public support of the President.

Even the leading Republican in the Cabinet, Secretary of the Treasury Douglas Dillon, spoke for the Kennedy and Johnson Administrations in reply to criticism by Senator Barry Goldwater, the Republican Presidential candidate, in an appearance in New York this week that the Democratic National Committee publicized.

The other nominal Republican in the Cabinet, Secretary of Defense Robert S. McNamara, appeared in place of the President before the American Legion in Dallas in opposition to Goldwater, who appeared before the same forum the next day . . .

Secretary McNamara has been prompt and vigorous in his retorts to Republican allegations. Secretary of State Dean Rusk has publicly questioned Senator Goldwater's capacity in international affairs. And there appears to be no precedent for the appearances of the Secretaries of State and Defense before political party Platform Committees such as Messrs. Rusk and McNamara made this year.

The Warren Commission report on the assassination of President Kennedy was issued on September 27, and for days the nation and the world were reminded of the death of the young President, the accession of Johnson to the Presidency and the dangers of fanatics. The central finding of the commission, that the assassination was the work of one man, Lee Harvey Oswald, and that there was no conspiracy, foreign or domestic, satisfied most Americans and most objective observers that the facts had indeed been told. The review of the events of November 22, 1963 brought to public attention once again the legacy of Kennedy, the training of Lyndon Johnson, the Vice President, and the uncertainties with which the American government and people face the future.

All that could only help Johnson, the candidate for election. For one thing, it spotlighted the comparison between Humphrey and Miller as potential Presidents and the advantage seemed to many overwhelmingly for Humphrey. For another, it drew attention to the central issue of the campaign, stripped of charges and allegations: Who was better fitted in a changing world to be President, Johnson or Goldwater? One other question was raised: Would the American people, having faced a violent upheaval in their government just a year before, voluntarily choose to change it again, or would they prefer the status quo, which after all, was peaceful and relatively prosperous?

The Warren report urgently advocated greater security precautions to protect a President, but Johnson, the very next day, blithely ignored its admonitions in a swing through five New England states. He set out with an almost grim determination to disprove the theory that the public had no real enthusiasm for him. The crowds, cooperating, were enormous and enthusiastic at each stop. He was welcomed by tens of thousands of roaring hand-fluttering admirers at Providence, Rhode Island. At the Providence Airport, when he walked along the fence shaking hands, he called a reporter over and said: "Look at this. I want you to see a crowd reaction." On his way into town, he stood in an open car waving repeatedly to the throngs and haranguing them through a bullhorn.

If this reckless exposure was not frightening enough to his bodyguards, still smarting—though they did not show it—under the criticism of the Secret Service in the Warren study, an incident occurred that, for a moment, brought back memories of that fateful November day in Dallas. Brown University, where Johnson was to speak on education at the bicentennial convocation, is situated at the top of a hill. The Presidential motorcade, crawling through the congested streets, finally reached the foot of the hill, far behind schedule. A Secret Service car, the fourth in line, burst into flames from an overheated motor. The word flashed back along the line that it was the President's car, there was a moment of breathlessness, then the doors of the press buses flew open, newsmen scrambled out, running into each other, swearing in the oppressive heat, clawing their way to the head of the motorcade, toward the column of smoke from the burning car. By the time they got there, the President's car, with Secret Service men abroad, had split off from the motorcade and roared up the hill out of reach of the excitement. A few moments later, Johnson, capped and gowned with dignity, took the stage and spoke, as calmly as though he had spent the last hour in academic contemplation.

The ovation in Providence differed little from those Johnson received elsewhere during the long day and night. In Hartford, Connecticut, the throngs in the streets seemed endless. The police said 50,000 persons, the largest crowd in the city's history, heard the President speak outside the Hartford Times building. Some spectators were injured in the crush; a few were literally pushed out of their shoes. Johnson made only a brief appearance at the airport at Burlington, Vermont, but 20,000 persons waited more than an hour for him. In Portland, Maine, although by now the President was two hours late, the streets were jammed and 25,000 heard his address at City Hall Plaza. He was the first President to visit the city since William Howard Taft in 1912. It was the same in New Hampshire. The President was so willing to indulge in handshaking that long before the day was over his hands were scratched and bruised.

There were as many people on hand at the Portland Airport late at night just to see Johnson off as there were to hear Goldwater's speech a few days before. It was an extraordinary reception in a traditionally strong Republican area. In 1960, Nixon swept Maine's five electoral votes (the state's total was cut to four in 1964), New Hampshire's four and Vermont's three; Kennedy won Rhode Island's four and Connecticut's eight.

As a result, Johnson switched tactics for New England. He did not attack Republicanism and Republican voters; he praised them. In Hartford he said, "I have more respect for the Republican party than some of those who have taken over its name this year." In Burlington, in a state that had never supported a Democratic Presidential nominee, he said: "One of our great parties has been captured by a faction of men who stand outside the whole range of common agreement and common principles which have brought us to the summit of success. These men have not just marched out of step with American progress; they have refused to march at all. If they gained control of our Government, they would not just change the direction of our march; they would halt it altogether. They have already said they do not intend to pass laws, but to repeal them. The philosophy that would tear down these programs does not represent the Republican party of America. They do not represent the view of responsible forward-looking men of any party."

Johnson's last scheduled stop of the tour was at Manchester, New Hampshire. It was there, speaking to a small group of editors of weekly newspapers in the state, that the President did what he had not done before in the campaign—he mentioned his opponent by name. It was a causal and non-critical reference, delivered in an off-the-cuff embellishment of his prepared text. He said the suggestion to carry the Vietnam war to the North had been advanced by Goldwater, among others, and added, "Before I start dropping bombs around the country, I would want to think about the consequences of getting American boys into a war with 700 million Chinese."

Deploring the mounting toll of American lives in Vietnam, which at that point had reached 190, the President said: "But it's not like the 190,000 we might lose the first month if we escalated that war. We're not going south and run out and let the Communists take over either."

Having finished a tough day, the President then stopped on his way back to Washington for a midnight visit to Senator Edward Kennedy at a Boston Hospital. This visit, coming as it did after his earlier solicitude for the ailing David O. McKay, the Mormon leader, in Salt Lake City, prompted the observation that if Albert Schweitzer should fall ill, the President would drop off in Africa to see him.

The President was highly elated by his New England venture, which was reported as a political triumph—and which had been carefully planned and organized by John Bailey. He returned to the White House, tired but ebullient, at 4 A.M. The next day, he took off on another non-political foray that produced still another political success.

He flew to Strategic Air Command headquarters at Omaha with Manlio Brosio, the secretary-general of the North Atlantic Treaty Organization, who was his White House guest for the day. The trip took him deep into presumed Republican territory in Nebraska. It gave him an opportunity to respond, merely by his presence at the SAC base, to charges by Goldwater that he was downgrading the role of manned bombers in the scheme of national defense. In this sense, it was a political trip, but it also had a valid non-political basis. It was an official military inspection by the commander-in-chief and an important foreign guest. It was an act of diplomacy, in that it afforded an opportunity to lend support to the entire Atlantic alliance—and it was another example of Johnson's skill at combining the functions of President and candidate.

James Reston was still worried about the President's free-wheeling style of campaigning:

The problem of assuring the health and safety of Presidents and potential Presidents of the United States is much broader than the Warren Commission's review of the subject this week.

The Commission, for example, acknowledges that a President can be made only as safe as he wants to be, and it implies that if he wants to be reckless with his own safety, nothing can be done about it. Yet there is nothing in the requirements of the Presidency or even in the requirements of political campaigning that obliges the Chief Executive to be as rash and careless of his health and safety as President Johnson was on his New England tour this week. He was not merely in touch with the crowd in Providence, Hartford, Burlington and elsewhere; he was in the middle of it. He was not the helpless victim of the disorder, but by constantly leaving his car he was the cause of the disorder, beyond the control of the Secret Service or anybody else.

All the sensible precautions proposed by the Warren Commission to check on subversives and police buildings along Presidential routes cannot possibly protect a President who insists, like President Johnson, on scrimmaging with every crowd, and shaking every outstretched hand.

He goes beyond the expectations of all Presidents in the past. Mr. Lincoln recognized that while it "would be safer for a President to live in a cage," no President could do business that way. President Johnson is fond of quoting that. He also likes to recall that, on the very day of the assassination, President Kennedy remarked to Kenny O'Donnell that anybody with a good rifle and a good perch in a high building could shoot a President.

Johnson apparently did not agree with this assessment, or with the advice. The next day he gave newsmen a private lecture on Presidential security, pointing out that he was much safer mingling and shaking hands than he was, for example, standing alone in full view of a throng where he presented a clear target to any sniper. He was disdainful of any personal peril and he seemed much more concerned that reporters might develop the security matter into a political issue that could hurt him by making him seem more reckless than he was about the kind of risk Reston had written about.

The President was concerned about the proliferation of right-wing paperback books, printed and distributed in the millions, written by ultraconservatives and all purporting to prove the Johnson Administration soft on Communism and the President a man of little principle. Despite an ostensible hands-off attitude on the part of the Republican National Committee, local Republican organizations jumped at the chance of putting such books— attacked as smear jobs by the Democrats—in the hands of as many voters as possible. They were also distributed by the John Birch Society and thousands of individual Goldwater supporters.

Stacked high on the tables and in showcases in Southwest Houston's supermarket-sized Republican campaign headquarters at this stage in the campaign, for example, were copies of J. Evetts Haley's *A Texan Looks at Lyndon;* on order were additional copies of John A. Stormer's *None Dare Call it Treason* and Phyllis Schlafly's *A Choice Not An Echo*. They were also on sale at many other Goldwater headquarters throughout the country, according to Donald Janson of The Times, who made a nationwide survey and reported that more than 16,000,000 copies of the books had been printed, with the Haley and the Stormer books accounting for more than 5,000,000 copies each. Janson wrote:

Avid Goldwater partisans express high hopes that the books disavowed as "smut" and right wing propaganda by some Republican leaders, will swing close states to the Republican banner.

Democrats concede that the books have been widely discussed but hope that exposure to analysis will win back by Election Day any voter who had strayed.

The Stormer book, described on its cover as "the carefully documented story of America's retreat from victory," carried the familiar right-wing message that the nation was perilously close to total subjugation because of its leaders' conspiratorial failure to deal with communism. But the National Committee for Civic Responsibility, a Cleveland nonpartisan organization, checked 818 references in the book and concluded that it was "at best an incredibly poor job of research and documentation and at worst a deliberate hoax and fraud." *A Texan Looks At Lyndon* was as sharply criticized as the Stormer book because of its reliance on rumor and innuendo; it was laced with phrases such as "Johnson is reported to have . . ." "It was rumored . . ." and "Many persons believe . . ." *A Choice Not An Echo* had as its theme that a small group of secret king makers in the Eastern liberal wing of the Republican party had selected the Republican nominee since 1936—but not in 1964.

All in all, there were about thirty-five separate titles of political paperbacks in circulation during the campaign, including at least one sharp anti-Goldwater book, *Barry Goldwater: Extremist on the Right,* by Fred J. Cook. Many of these were the normal puff books, Horatio Algerish biographies of the candidates, but it seemed that neither the pro nor the con books were having much effect on the electorate, except for the already convinced, who found in them ammunition for their own convictions.

Another feature of the campaign was the proliferation of specialized committees for Johnson or Goldwater. Lawyers, doctors, scientists, educators, actors—name your profession, its members were organized on one side or the other. There were Republicans for Johnson, Democrats for Goldwater, Republicans and Democrats for Johnson and Keating, Scientists and Engineers for Johnson-Humphrey, Independent Democrats-Republicans for Johnson, Fighting Aces for Goldwater, even Chiropractors for Goldwater and Veterinarians for Goldwater.

Since the President's wide margin over Goldwater showed no signs of diminishing, he now began to indicate that he was looking past November 3. The first evidence was a report, of the kind that could not materialize in print without some official basis in fact, that he planned a trip to Europe, if

elected, to begin an intensive personal effort to break down East-West antago-
nisms and ease international tensions. He based his hopes on the assumption
that the election results would sharply repudiate the diplomatic policies
espoused by Goldwater.

The second evidence of his preoccupation with the future was the disclosure
that eleven (later increased to thirteen) groups of distinguished intellectuals
and administrators had been working secretly for a month to prepare the
groundwork for Johnson's own four-year Administration, to mark the route
to the Great Society. Top talent from private business, the academic community and the government staffed the panels, which were concentrating on
domestic affairs. Because the White House, the State Department and other
specialized organizations constantly reviewed foreign policy, the President believed no study group was needed in this field.

On October 1, the Federal Communications Commission delivered a glanc-
ing blow to an incumbent President's ability to capitalize on his eminence of
office in an election campaign. The Federal agency ruled, four to three, that
any radio or television station carrying one of Johnson's news conferences in
full must grant equal time to all other Presidential candidates. The decision
did not affect a station's prerogative to broadcast excerpts from conferences
that constituted bona fide news. In effect, because there was no speedy and
practical way to edit news conferences as they occurred, the ruling ended
live broadcasts for this campaign—and for all campaigns, unless it was
modified.

Johnson took a baby-kissing stroll in Baltimore on his way to speak at
the Johns Hopkins University.

"The purpose of politics," he said in what developed into a largely impromptu address, "must be to make man's extinction improbable, and his
fulfillment inevitable. Your nation must always be prepared to have its
leader go anywhere, talk to anyone, make any plan that can honorably be
made to achieve understanding. The day and the time and the era for government by ultimatum was yesterday, and is gone forever. This age of knowledge
deserves and demands politics of understanding. Instinct and intuition are not
enough to rely on in directing our national destiny."

Again citing a statistic to emphasize the terrible consequences of a nuclear
war (this time it was the fact that the United States was capable of destroying
three hundred times as many lives as were lost in World War II), Johnson
urged politics of restraint and said Cuba and Vietnam both had tested that
restraint. Now he turned to his vision of the future and a touch of evangelistic
fervor again crept into his voice.

Americans, as the most affluent people, he said, must fulfill their obliga-
tions to the other peoples of the world "because the human beings of the
world are not going to endure always the lot that is theirs today." He went
on: "The ancient enemies of mankind—disease, intolerance, illiteracy and
ignorance—are not always going to prevail. There is going to be a revolution.
There is going to be a rising up and a throwing off of these chains. If a

peaceful improvement is not possible, if a peaceful revolution is not possible, a violent adjustment is inevitable." But Johnson the evangelist could not hold down Johnson the politician for long. After asking his audience for their help and prayers "because I need them so much in the days ahead," he left them laughing. "If I were in another setting, on another occasion, I might even ask you to give me something else," he said.

Congress's frenzied rush to adjourn on the weekend of October 3 pushed the political combatants into the background. Two bills with high Presidential priority—health care for the aged under Social Security and aid to the depressed Appalachian region—were lost as the legislators rushed to get home and campaign. Despite these setbacks, the Eighty-eighth Congress produced a remarkable volume of significant legislation, including the Civil Rights Act, a tax cut ranging upwards of $11,500,000,000 and a $950,000,-000 anti-poverty program. Much of the credit for these achievements, as The Times noted in an editorial, "was attributable to the remarkable skill in Congressional relations Mr. Johnson displayed in his year in the White House." The President could point with pride to that record—and he did.

The campaign was now at the halfway point between Labor Day and Election Day. Already Johnson had traveled 15,000 miles and made twenty appearances (Goldwater's statistics: 20,000 miles and sixty-seven stops). The Democratic nominee was striving, with some success, to create the impression of a busy President rather than a campaigner. National unity, continuity, and stability were still his watchwords. More and more he referred to his plans after November 3—the trip to Europe, a White House peace conference, a visit to the United Nations—almost as if his victory were ordained.

Yet the President's donning of the mantle of non-campaigner created a slight problem. Goldwater charged that Johnson was burning up taxpayer money a mile a minute, campaigning all over the country. Unquestionably, Johnson on the campaign trail could not—and would not—discard the appurtenances of his office. But when, with skill, he combined political trips and non-political trips, in a single tour, a single day or a single speech, the basis for the Republican's charge was easily discerned. Determining the cost ratio of those intertwined trips—so much to be paid by the Democratic National Committee, so much by the White House—was a complex accounting nightmare that could only be solved by Presidential dictum.

The issues took a back seat to personalities on October 5, when Lady Bird Johnson began a four-day tour of the Old Confederacy, accompanied by her daughter, Lynda Bird, about a hundred reporters and fifteen Southern girls in Breton straw hats, who served as hostesses, passing out balloons, peppermint taffy, buttons and pennants. On the day the train left, Mrs. Johnson's press secretary, Elizabeth Carpenter, tacked a welcome note to the train bulletin board that gave some idea of the hectic time in store:

A whistle will blow two minutes before the train starts moving. We hope we won't be scattering you over the country-side, but the train does not wait. In case you do get left, look for the advance man [the person who makes arrangements in advance at every campaign stop]. He can be easily identified as the happiest man at the depot because all of his problems have just left. See if he can work out your transportation to a nearby town. If he can't just take out residence, register and vote.

The nineteen-car "Lady Bird Special" began the 1,700-mile trip at the old-fashioned depot at Alexandria, Virginia, and the President was there to see his wife off. Speaking from the rear platform of the train with a scalloped red, white and blue awning, Mrs. Johnson told her well-wishers that the Civil Rights Act must be enforced. The President, standing behind her, nodded agreement.

"We are a nation of laws, not men, and our greatness is our ability to adjust to the national consensus," Mrs. Johnson went on. "I wanted to make this trip because I am proud of the South, and I am proud that I am part of the South."

But not all of the South shared her sentiments that first day. There were Goldwater adherents at each stop, shouting and heckling and waving banners that read, "Vote for Barry—brinkmanship is better than chickenship," or, "Fly away Lady Bird, here in Richmond Barry is the cat's meow." At Wilson, North Carolina, teen-agers' incessant chanting of "We want Barry," almost drowned out the cries of "We want Johnson." Somewhat flustered by the demonstration, the President's wife still managed to thank "all you young people" for their enthusiasm.

Mrs. Johnson made thirteen stops and thirteen speeches in Virginia and North Carolina on the first day, and the farther South she traveled the warmer became the weather and her welcome. Surprisingly, the crowds were larger than those that had shown up to greet her husband in 1960. "Gawd almighty, they weren't out like this for Lyndon last time," one observer noted.

That first night at Raleigh, the President rejoined the train and Mrs. Johnson listened to him speak in North Carolina State College's Reynolds Coliseum. The President was late in arriving, but the crowd of 15,000 greeted him with a great roar. On the platform as the President spoke were three opponents of the Civil Rights Act, Senator Sam Ervin, Representative Basil Whitener and Dan K. Moore, the Democratic candidate for governor. Their presence was certain indication that Johnson's prospects for carrying the state's thirteen electoral votes were greatly improved. The President did not touch on civil rights in his speech. He derided Goldwater's recurring complaint of a lost freedom: "Don't let anyone tell you that there's not more freedom in the world today than at any time during your lifetime."

The Johnson girls, Lynda Bird, twenty years old, and Luci Baines, seventeen, were already campaigning every weekend on their own. Under the auspices of the Young Citizens for Johnson, both girls presided at old-fashioned Texas barbecues; from California to New York, from the Canadian border to the Gulf of Mexico, they consumed no one knows how much pork ribs, fried chickens, hot dogs, chili, corn, biscuits, baked beans and potato salad.

With the Goldwater family, it was somewhat different. Mrs. Goldwater, a very shy woman, had accompanied the Senator on most of his trips from the beginning of the campaign, but had been loath to strike out on her own. She did not like crowds ("They can be frightening, these crowds, even though I know they mean well") and her subdued approach to politics led many to believe she was too reserved for a Presidential campaign. The Senator's wife, however, considered this appraisal incorrect, and scheduled her first solo effort since the Republican convention—a tour that would begin in Muncie, Indiana (a city where she was born and a state whose thirteen electoral votes had gone to Nixon in 1960) and end in New York City. Her trip would set a precedent in one respect; she would not make a single speech, although holding nonpolitical news conferences, or solicit a single vote for her husband. "I don't speak," she explained, "I don't really like speaking lessons." She shook as many hands as possible, making small talk and leaving the impression that she was deeply concerned by everything confided to her. She possessed a vital political ingredient—the knack of being able to look directly into the face of the person shaking hands with her.

Their two sons, Barry, Jr. twenty-six, and Michael, twenty-five, were much less reluctant about making speeches. They started out on the search for votes back in January, when their father first announced he was a candidate for the G.O.P. Presidential nomination. They had been at it ever since, stumping from coast to coast. After a while they teamed up with Libby Miller, twenty, and Mary Karen Miller, seventeen, the attractive daughters of the Vice Presidential nominee, in a new type of campaigning labeled, for want of a better name, jamborees. Obviously modeled after the Democratic barbecues, the affairs were sponsored by Young Americans for Goldwater and Miller. One of the features was a "Barry Burger," made from a recipe provided by Mrs. Goldwater.

More significant aspects of the campaign were disturbing James Reston:

In the first month of the Presidential election campaign the two candidates have told us what a terrible world this would be if the other fellow was elected. In the last month of the campaign, now starting, it would be helpful if they would define in more specific terms what they would do if they won.

Nineteen sixty-five is not likely to be a period of dramatic new initiatives in world politics. Some influential men here even go so far as to say that the United States should concentrate for the foreseeable future on its serious educational, agricultural and racial problems at home and worry less about foreign affairs.

There are, however, several serious problems overseas, including the possibility of a wider and more serious war in Vietnam, which may even overwhelm our domestic concerns if they are allowed to drift as they have been drifting during the campaign.

How do President Johnson and Senator Goldwater propose to achieve the allied unity they both want . . . ?

How do the candidates propose to avoid a major war in Southeast Asia . . . ?

All the indications now are that the new nations of Africa are going to be more unstable internally and more quarrelsome with their neighbors in the next four years than they have been in the last year. Yet the campaign is casting very little light on how the two candidates propose to approach these problems . . .

It is startling to compare the quality of the speeches delivered in this campaign even with the speeches of the Kennedy-Nixon campaign. And when they are compared with the Stevenson speeches of 1952 the contrast is almost ludicrous.

One by one, the major economic, political, foreign policy and even philosophic questions before the nation were discussed by Stevenson in that campaign twelve years ago, but it is difficult to point to a single distinguished speech by either President Johnson or Senator Goldwater since the battle started over a month ago.

20

The Other 495

There were two Kennedys (Bobby and Teddy) running for the Senate; a Rockefeller (Winthrop) was trying to become Governor of Arkansas; a Connecticut Lodge (John Davis) hoped to win a Senate seat; Howard Baker Jr., the son-in-law of Republican leader Everett Dirksen was asking voters in Tennessee to send him to the Senate; a former football coach at the University of Oklahoma, Bud Wilkinson, was in the field for the Senate from that state; a former Hollywood song-and-dance man, George Murphy, thought he would make a better Senator than the cigar-chomping former White House press secretary, Pierre Salinger; a Taft (Robert Jr.) was running for the Senate in Ohio; and for the first time in Texas history, Republican candidates stood for the House in every district in the state.

In all, besides the big one, there were 495 other elections of national interest—435 for members of the House, thirty-five for members of the Senate, and twenty-five for Governors. Moreover, there were thousands of local contests, ranging from garbage collector to city councilman. In Illinois, for example, Adlai Ewing Stevenson 3d, the thirty-four-year-old son of the United States Ambassador to the United Nations, and Earl D. Eisenhower, the sixty-six-year-old brother of the former President, were attempting political careers of their own by running for the state House of Representatives.

Hundreds of proposals were being submitted to the voters on matters affecting their states and local communities. A constitutional amendment outlawing the death penalty for first degree murder was before voters in Oregon. In North Dakota, voters debated whether to end the eighteen-year prohibition against serving food and liquor in the same public place. Before Arkansas voters was the question of whether to legalize gambling houses in the resort city of Hot Springs. And in Akron, Ohio, residents were to vote on whether to repeal one of the strongest antidiscrimination laws in the country dealing with real estate. The proposal attracting the most national attention was the one in California that would give residential property owners the absolute right to select or reject Negro tenants and buyers because they were Negroes. The housing proposal, backed by the California Real Estate Association, was aimed at nullifying the 1963 Rumford Act, which prohibited racial discrimination in about 60 per cent of California housing.

From coast to coast, the proposals and the races for House, Senate and Governors' mansions helped stir voters who found themselves unmoved by the Presidential contest. The sole question on the Presidential race seemed to be the size of the Johnson plurality. But many of the 495 other races were so close and interesting that a visitor to any one of a number of states was likely to hear more talk about Senatorial or gubernatorial contests than about Goldwater and Johnson. The Kennedy-Keating race in New York, Salinger-Murphy in California, Young-Taft in Ohio, Romney-Staebler in Michigan, Percy-Kerner in Illinois, all were prime examples.

No matter how enthusiastic Republicans across the country felt about their various candidates, they acknowledged that the prospect of their party capturing control of the Senate was almost statistically impossible and of the House slim. The lineup before Election Day in the House was 257 Democrats and 178 Republicans; with 218 needed for a majority, the G.O.P. had to keep all and pick up forty more. The most optimistic Republicans pointed to the Republican gain of eighty seats in 1938, but this was the first election after the 1936 Roosevelt sweep which had left only eighty-nine lonely Republicans in the House. Democrats had been in numerical control of both houses of Congress since 1932 except in the Eightieth Congress (1947-48) and the Eighty-third (1953-54). At best, Republicans in 1964 were hoping for a gain of perhaps ten House seats. For in only seven Congressional elections since 1932 had either party gained more than twenty-five.

Writing in The Times on July 18, just three days after the Goldwater nomination, Warren Weaver Jr. reported the thinking of Democratic leaders:

They believe that the nomination of Senator Barry Goldwater by the Republican National Convention has opened the door to a substantial increase in the Democratic membership of the House of Representatives.

More important, Democratic strategists foresee a measurable increase in Administration support in the House, even though some Democratic members may be lost along the way.

The hypothesis is that any Republican Representatives who ride into office on Mr. Goldwater's coattails are likely to replace Southern Democrats, most of whom only vote with the Administration when it suits them.

On the other hand, new Democrats elected to the House in a Johnson-Goldwater contest are likely to come from the cities and suburbs of the North, Middle West and West and hence entertain much more enthusiasm for President Johnson's programs than the Republicans they replaced.

Republicans tried to put a good face on their House prospects. Sixty-two Republican House members signed a full-page advertisement in The Times, saying in part that the Arizonan would rally the "forces of the Republican party in the mainstream of its traditional philosophies." They were convinced, they wrote, that the nomination of Goldwater by the Republican party would result in substantial increases in Republican membership in both houses of Congress. Many Republican candidates doubted it. The President would probably carry some Democratic candidates to victory on his coattails and it seemed entirely possible that Goldwater would drag some Republican candidates down to defeat.

Thus many Republican candidates found themselves in a quandary. Should they say they were for Barry Goldwater and, if so, how loud? Many G.O.P. candidates in definitely non-Goldwater territory actively promoted ticket-splitting by disassociating themselves in varying degrees from Goldwater. A few flatly announced they were not supporting him; others merely implied as much by disagreeing with the Senator's position on various issues and rarely mentioning his name. Times correspondents reported from the field that a typical stratagem was for a non-Goldwater Republican to say, when pressed for a statement on his Presidential preference, that he was support-ing the entire Republican ticket but conducting his own independent cam-paign on the issues as he saw them. Democrats in general were identifying themselves with Johnson and the policies of his Administration, and trying to pin Goldwater labels on all Republican opponents, particularly those re-luctant to wear them.

Both parties concentrated, as usual, on marginal Congressional districts, those won with less than 55 per cent of the total vote in the last election. Of eighty-one such districts, forty-one were held by Democrats and forty by Republicans. Political analysts generally agreed that between fifty and one hundred districts could be classified as vulnerable to turnover in party con-trol. At the beginning of October, with a little more than a month to go, John D. Morris wrote that the Republicans were confronted with the prospect of moderate to severe losses. By the end of the month, he wrote:

> While the Republicans have a long record of overestimating their party's poten-tial strength in Congressional elections, Democratic campaign officials usually are more realistic in their forecasts.
> Their current prediction is that Democrats will score what is described as a "rock-bottom minimum" gain of 12 to 15 House seats.
> Prospects of at least a 12-seat gain are borne out by independent soundings in the field by New York Times correspondents and reflect the apparent consensus of political experts here.

In the Senate, Republicans had long looked to 1964 as the year they could perhaps recoup the huge losses suffered in 1958, when the Democrats scored a seventeen-seat gain. But here, too, the major imponderable was: How badly would Goldwater harm various Republican candidates? The Senate before the election consisted of sixty-six Democrats and thirty-four Repub-licans (allowing for the late switch of South Carolina's Thurmond to the Republican party). Of the thirty-five seats being contested, twenty-six were held by Democrats and nine by Republicans. To achieve a well-nigh impossible majority, the Republicans needed to hold their own and gain seventeen seats. But of the twenty-six Democratic seats, six were in the South where Democrats usually win. And, of the remaining twenty, at least seven were held by well-entrenched Democrats. Even if the Republicans were to win the thirteen "possibles" they would still fall short of the fifty-one majority.

Just before the election, E. W. Kenworthy reported that Senate Democrats were expected to have the two-to-one majority in the next Congress that they had in the last. He said chances were fairly good that the Democrats even might increase their margin slightly:

Three things, it is generally agreed, have altered Republican prospects in the Senate.

First, there is the tremendous pulling power of the President's coattails, particularly in some Eastern states. Thus it is believed that if Mr. Kennedy wins in New York and Miss Blatt in Pennsylvania, they will owe their victories largely to Mr. Johnson—with an assist, of course, from confusion over ballot-splitting.

Second, there is the "front lash" against Mr. Goldwater, largely on the issue of "the bomb," which has hurt not only those who were closely identified with him but also those who have given him reluctant or pro forma support.

Third, in some states the Republicans nominated candidates who were undistinguished or not widely known. For example, in Indiana, D. Russell Bontrager, although a State Senator, is an unknown figure in much of the state. In Michigan, Elly M. Peterson, who had been former assistant chairman of the Republican National Committee, has had no legislative experience.

The most commanding Senatorial race was that between Kennedy and Keating, the thirty-eight-year-old former Attorney General and the sixty-four-year-old legislative veteran. It was almost a Hollywood situation: The jovial, aggressive silver-haired Senator, the first in the country to refuse to support Goldwater, running on his own record of twelve years in the House and six in the Senate, pitting his experience against the young, ambitious dynamo with the Kennedy name, who had been rejected by Johnson as his Vice Presidential candidate and who then moved in on the Empire State.

Keating quickly seized upon the carpetbagger issue. Kennedy, with homes in Massachusetts and Virginia (as well as a new one in New York), fought back with the reminder that he had been born in New York and had lived there many years. His constant pursuit of this theme brought a phone call from brother Ted, a Senator running for re-election in Massachusetts although bed-ridden from a plane crash earlier in the year: "If it's all the same to you, would you mind easing up on all those years we've been in New York?" Teddy said. "Now I'm a carpetbagger in Massachusetts."

On the point of qualifications for Senator, the Constitution reads as follows: "No person shall be a Senator who shall not have attained to the Age of thirty years, and been nine Years a Citizen of the United States, and who shall not, when elected, be an Inhabitant of that State for which he shall be chosen." Kennedy, who took a home on Long Island, met those qualifications. But in Keating's view, Kennedy was simply a politician from Massachusetts who wanted to use New York as a power base for higher office—the Presidency. This issue turned many Democrats, both prominent and humble, away from Kennedy.

Keating also belabored Kennedy for a decision made as Attorney General in a case involving a one-time German cartel, the General Aniline and Film Corporation, which had been seized as enemy property during World War

II. It seemed strange that a settlement of this case, reached in 1963 after years of litigation, could become an issue in the 1964 Senatorial race, but in a state with a large Jewish population any accusation that a decision favored former Nazis was sure to reverberate. Kennedy bitterly replied that Keating had hit a sorry new low in campaigning and the Justice and State Departments supported Kennedy's position in the settlement.

Then the white-haired Senator turned to ridiculing Kennedy for not discussing the issues. This point, developed into a challenge for a televised debate, eventually bordered on the ludicrous. Keating bought television time and "invited" his foe to a debate and ended up debating an empty chair, while Kennedy charged he had been blocked by Keating cohorts from entering the studio. They finally did come face to face on a late-night radio show, with questionable voter effect, but they never debated before the television cameras.

Kennedy had begun his campaign at dawn after the nominating convention with an appearance at the Fulton Fish Market. For several weeks, he seemed to try to play on the emotions of the huge crowds that went to see him, cheer him and paw him. He used his brother's name to the fullest and capitalized on what seemed his boyish shyness, being careful not to impugn Keating. "You can't get anywhere attacking Grandpa," one of his managers said. Another Democrat summed up the campaign: "The theory was that all he had to do was show the voters that he was a good guy and that would be that. Well, he went around the state, saying very little but letting everyone see that he didn't have horns and shaking about two million hands. There was plenty of enthusiasm, but it didn't show up in the polls."

A lot of the hands he shook were those of teen-agers. One day the former Attorney General discovered some youths calling off numbers when they shook his hand. One girl clasped his hand and said "nineteen." Later Kennedy found out he was being used in a game by the teen-agers to see who could reach him the most times. "And here I was," Kennedy said, "beginning to feel smug and full of myself and I'd shaken hands with the same kid nineteen times."

In mid-October, R. W. Apple Jr., wrote in The Times:

The tenor of Robert F. Kennedy's campaign for the Senate has changed radically in the last week and a half.

No longer does his campaign have the flavor of a personal-appearance tour by a movie star; no longer does he seem to be relying on glamour and nostalgia to win votes; no longer is he reluctant to comment on his opponent's record. In part, the change is a result of the natural evolution of any campaign, of its tendency to become more intense in the final stages. But it is also a result, according to Mr. Kennedy's intimates, of the realization that the old approach was not working. . . .

Perhaps the most remarkable change has been Mr. Kennedy's new-found willingness to attack . . . Keating.

Shifting gears, Kennedy hammered at Keating for what he said were votes against Federal aid to education, against legislation authorizing Government medical research, and against key measures in the housing field. Kennedy said, "I do not propose to be lectured . . . by an opponent who has consistently supported legislation to deprive criminal defendants of [their] rights."

Even the Fair Campaign Practices Committee, a nonpartisan privately-financed group, was brought into the rough campaign. Keating protested that his position favoring the nuclear test ban treaty was being distorted by his opponent. After examining the complaint, Bruce L. Felknor, the committee's executive director, wrote to Kennedy, charging that his attacks were "not only false and distorted, but also appeared to be either a deliberate cynical misrepresentation or the result of incredible carelessness." A few days later, Felknor and Charles P. Taft, chairman of the committee, withdrew the letter, saying it had been intended as a confidential communication to Kennedy, and further reporting that the committee had received additional material "which raises quite different issues of fact." Keating aides were bitter about the switch and some Republicans charged that political pressure had been brought to bear on the committee.

Keating continued to defend his record, one that had earned him a liberal reputation in both parties, but he faltered, as do so many when forced into the explainer's role. Early polls had shown him running ahead, although his crowds were consistently smaller than his rival's. Even Kennedy conceded Keating's edge in the polls. As Election Day drew near, however, the pollsters were less certain, and then, led by *The Daily News'* Straw Poll, they began to put Kennedy farther and farther ahead.

Carpetbagging also was the main Republican battle cry in another of the contests that gave life and color to 1964 politics—the California Senatorial race between Salinger and Murphy. It was not an unusual issue for the country's most populous state. Carpetbagging was a charge hurled at Richard M. Nixon in 1962, when after fifteen years in Washington he returned to his native state to run—unsuccessfully—for Governor. Now it was affixed to Salinger, who had resigned as White House press secretary in March to seek the seat held by the ailing Senator Clair Engle. The thirty-eight-year-old former newsman, who had served Presidents Kennedy and Johnson, was then a resident of Virginia, although a native of California. He won the nomination in the primary after the California courts ruled that long-standing state qualifications for Senatorship were transcended by the Federal Constitution's simple requirements. With the death of Engle, Salinger received a further boost in his contest with Murphy when Governor Brown appointed him an interim Senator.

Salinger and Murphy presented a sharp contrast in their barnstorming. The former Presidential aide is a chubby five-foot-seven, somewhat Santa Clausian, even in his expensive suits, a cigar-chewing exponent of the hard-sell. Murphy, a former dancer, dresses like the very model of a man of distinction and always looks fit. His campaign was conducted in a relatively sedate manner while Salinger used helicopter, automobile, airplane, an outmoded narrow-guage train, folk-singers and a jazz band. In Oakland at one point, Salinger's supporters conducted a "swinging affair with Pierre" at an old lakeside mansion. On the top floor was a group of folk singers, on the main floor a jazz band, in the basement a record player rocking with the Beatles and on the lawn a combo tooting some old favorites. Four bars were in operation. Murphy, meanwhile, used the soft-sell, talking quietly and mixing easily with crowds. He adroitly sidestepped identification with Goldwater, although he left no doubt of his conservative leanings.

Lawrence E. Davies of The Times captured the flavor of the campaign in the homestretch:

A soft-spoken, well tailored smiling man with a leisurely story for anyone who is willing to listen thrusts out a hand and says, "I'm George Murphy."

A less relaxed and chunkier opponent alternately autographs a campaign leaflet and shakes a hand while saying, "I'm Pierre Salinger." An ever present cigar accommodates itself to his words.

On any day somewhere in California, these two rivals for election to the United States Senate are bidding for support on a sidewalk, at a banquet table, on a university campus, on a television or radio program—in any corner where a stray vote may be lurking.

Mr. Murphy, the Republican nominee, who sang and danced his way into a place in the entertainment world, came up with a campaign innovation last week. He surprised early-morning commuters by boarding trains on the San Francisco peninsula and hopping off a few stations later after interrupting card games and the perusal of stock-market quotations.

"I'll bet you we've got 95 per cent of the votes on there," he said as he stepped off.

Mr. Salinger, the press secretary to two Presidents, replied the next day with plans to help cable-car operators turn a car around at the turntable at Powell and Market Streets in downtown San Francisco and campaign aboard it up to Nob Hill. The idea was promising but a cable broke earlier in the afternoon, throwing the whole system out of service.

Salinger started the race with what many experts had regarded as a substantial lead, but he began to slip in the polls as Election Day neared. First, Bobby Kennedy's entrance into the New York campaign heightened Californians' sensitivity to the thought that there was a power play in the works. After all, Ted Kennedy was running for another term in the Senate from Massachusetts, and other Kennedy allies—Salinger among them—were trying for key government positions. According to one Democratic analyst, Californians were beginning to feel they "didn't want California to be a tail on the Kennedy dog." Second, it seemed that many who had reservations about voting for Johnson but planned to vote for him anyhow over Goldwater might express their reservations by voting for the conservative Murphy. In addition, Salinger undoubtedly was losing votes because of his stand on Proposition Fourteen, the measure calling for repeal of the Rumford [Fair Housing] Act. Salinger was against repeal of the law; Murphy decided not to take a stand. Salinger also came off badly in a television debate with Murphy, not so much on substance but on appearance. Even a Democrat said: "Pierre would have been better off if the debate had been on radio only. Anybody who is heavy just doesn't look well on TV."

The Senatorial race in Ohio pitted a Democrat presumably in the twilight of his public life against a young Republican with historic political ancestry. The Democrat was seventy-five-year-old Stephen M. Young, a liberal in a Republican stronghold who rode a surprisingly powerful anti-Republican wave into the Senate in 1958. The Republican was Robert A. Taft Jr., forty-seven-year-old son of the late Senator Robert A. Taft of Ohio and grandson of the twenty-seventh President, William Howard Taft. After four terms in the Ohio House—one as majority leader—and a term as Ohio's Representative at Large in the Eighty-eighth Congress, Taft was considered on his way to a Senate career and perhaps more. Young stood squarely on the Kennedy-Johnson record, while Taft supported Goldwater, even though he disagreed with him on some points, such as the Civil Rights Act.

Another extremely close contest shaped up in Pennsylvania where Senator Hugh Scott, sixty-four, met a persistent challenge by a lively Democrat, Miss Genevieve Blatt, who at fifty-one had been Pennsylvania's Secretary of Internal Affairs for ten years. Close races were not unusual for Miss Blatt, for she had won the nomination over the state organization's choice, State Supreme Court Justice Michael A. Musmanno, by only 491 primary votes out of 921,731 cast. Scott, too, had party problems because of his fight against Goldwater's nomination at the Republican convention.

Additional sparks were added to the election fireworks by spirited contests for Governor. Experts anticipated some shifts, but the party balance, as in the House and Senate, was expected to remain heavily Democratic. The lineup before the election was thirty-four Democratic Governors to sixteen Republicans. Since 1952, the Democrats had been moving into the Governor's mansions of an unusually large number of traditionally Republican states. Of the twenty-five Governorships at stake in 1964, eighteen were currently held by the Democrats and seven by the Republicans.

Just before the election, Joseph Loftus reported:

Prime Republican sources see their candidates leading in six of the races for Governorships now held by Democrats.

Their fondest hopes would give them nine of these states.

The big prizes in which the Republicans claim leads are Illinois and Wisconsin.

The Republicans concede nine other states now held by Democrats. They do not concede any Governorships now held by a Republican. . . .

The tenuousness of the Republican hopes is evident in their own estimates. In the six contests that they claim to lead, these sources concede that five of them are close. Only in Indiana do they give their own candidate a safe margin.

The six Democratic-held states where the Republicans give themselves margins are Delaware, Illinois, Indiana, North Dakota, Washington and Wisconsin.

Three Democratic states that the Republicans consider toss-ups are Vermont, West Virginia and Massachusetts. The Democrats claim Vermont and agree that the two others are tight.

The Democrats hope to pick up five now held by the Republicans, although laying no claims to safe leads. These are Arizona, Michigan, Montana, Rhode Island and Utah.

The nine states conceded by the Republicans to the Democrats, who already

Top:
"I think you have made your last delivery, my dear."
(Associated Press photo)

Bottom:
"It is obvious I can't tell you anything about farming."
(photo by George Tames, The New York Times)

Opposite top left:
The Johnson girls campaigned
every weekend.
(photo by George Tames, The New York Times)

Opposite top right:
Stacked high on the tables
and in showcases
in Houston's supermarket-sized
Republican campaign headquarters...
(The New York Times photo)

Opposite bottom:
With the Goldwater family,
it was somewhat different.
(photo by George Tames, The New York Times)

A TEXAN LOOKS AT LYNDON

A Study In Illegitimate Power
by
J. Evetts Haley

"They didn't want California to be a tail
on the Kennedy dog."
(photo by Bob Martin)

Opposite top:
The Secret Service detail looked on impassively
at what they could not prevent.
(photo by Max Scheler, Black Star)

Opposite bottom:
"Gawd almighty, they weren't out like this
for Lyndon last time."
(United Press International photo)

Top:
"I'm George Murphy."
(photo by Phil Bath)

Bottom:
Salinger was undoubtedly losing votes
because of his stand on Proposition Fourteen,
the measure calling for repeal of the Rumford Act.
(The New York Times photo)

control the statehouses there, are Arkansas, Florida, Iowa, Missouri, Nebraska, New Hampshire, New Mexico, North Carolina and Texas.

Of all the races, two were being watched particularly closely because the Republican contenders, if elected, might be Presidential possibilities in 1968. These were in Illinois where Charles H. Percy, sometimes referred to as the boy wonder of business, was challenging Governor Otto J. Kerner, and in Michigan, where Governor George Romney, the Republican incumbent, was seeking a second term against Representative Neil Staebler.

The Romney-Staebler race was one of the most interesting, and in many ways, the most important gubernatorial race in the country. Romney had fought the Goldwater nomination and decided to hold the Senator at arm's length during the campaign. It was apparent that a successful Romney would almost certainly be called upon to help rebuild the Republican party if Goldwater lost. Romney, a handsome and supercharged former automobile executive who turned his persuasive sales techniques to politics, won his first term in 1962. The Governor, fifty-seven, a devout Mormon, was aided during the campaign by a wave of prosperity that reduced Michigan's unemployment to 2.9 per cent of the labor force, the lowest since 1955. The economic issue seemed to be hurting Staebler, who at fifty-nine had been a power behind Michigan's Democratic party for fifteen years and had managed G. Mennen Williams's five successful campaigns for the Governorship. Staebler accused Romney of having piled up a $57,000,000 surplus at the expense of adequate provision for the state's needs. The charge did not draw blood, and Staebler proved unable to pin the Goldwater label on Romney.

In Illinois, Percy had much going for him, although he was a moderate running in what was believed to be Goldwater country. The forty-five-year-old Republican—dynamic and handsome, chairman of Bell and Howell, the camera company—was a protegé of former President Eisenhower and had been chairman of the Republican Platform Committee in 1960. Like Romney, Percy did not view Goldwater as the man most likely to help him in his home state. He embraced the Republican Presidential nominee, but only reluctantly after a majority of Illinois delegates virtually made the decision for him. During his campaign, he said he supported the ticket, though he differed with Goldwater. The fence-straddling seemed to be losing him votes among both moderates and Goldwater backers as Election Day neared.

Everywhere, as November 3 grew nearer, local Republican candidates tried to disassociate themselves from Goldwater and what they viewed as his impending defeat, everywhere except in the South. In the Southern states, the Goldwater strategy was paying off, especially in Mississippi and Alabama, the two states where Negro agitation for rights was the strongest. The revolt of the Southern Democrats had gone so far in Alabama that Johnson's name wasn't even offered to the voters; they had a choice of Goldwater or unpledged electors. And in those states, Republicans running for the House of Representatives had a good chance of winning.

21

"Tell Mum
I'll Be Home
after the Election"

Goldwater made a one-day, hedge-hopping, helicopter swing through New Jersey on October 7, that pointed up his political problems. During fourteen hours in a state he had little hope of carrying, the Senator was heckled so severely he broke off a speech and applauded so thunderously that little of his speech could be heard. As he moved north up New Jersey, Goldwater made his stops in Republican territory, swinging around the Democratic strongholds in the metropolitan area. Even so, in Asbury Park, some 200 well-disciplined young Democrats succeeded in drowning him out repeatedly with a chant of "L.B.J., L.B.J." In an obvious allusion to the President's refusal to debate him, Goldwater told the hecklers good-naturedly, "I hope you have more luck in getting L.B.J. than I have, because he hides all the time." Then, when they kept up the noise, the candidate cut short his speech and left.

In West Orange, however, nearly 8,000 partisans jammed the armory to hear him, with hundreds shut outside pounding on the door. In Teaneck, it was the same; 10,000 others roared a welcome while still more clamored to get into the packed armory there. However, the state's popular Republican Senator, Clifford P. Case, did not accompany Goldwater on any part of the trip, continuing to sit out the campaign because of his disagreement with Goldwater on basic policies. The day before, in a quick trip through the suburbs of Philadelphia, Goldwater found another one of his nominal party allies unwilling to campaign with him. At all the rallies he paid tribute to Senator Hugh Scott, but the Pennsylvanian, facing a difficult race for re-election, never appeared once.

On the Pennsylvania swing, Goldwater made what seemed to some of his listeners an attempt to appeal to the white blacklash. In suburbs only a few miles from the scene of the Philadelphia race riots of the summer, the candidate declared that "unfortunately, in our Government over the past thirty years, excepting the eight years of the Eisenhower Administration, minority groups have run this country." He said he was speaking of "all minority groups, those who are able to put together an expensive lobby in Washington and make themselves heard," but the ugly phrase spelled "Negro" to many in his audiences. The next day, in New Jersey, he made the same charge, but about "special interest groups."

Despite buoyant crowds like these in the Jersey suburbs, pessimism was running strong among Goldwater strategists. There was a frank feeling on the part of some that "we are not going to win this way," but they were divided about what to do. Some thought that only an unforeseeable break could win for the Senator, perhaps a sharp foreign policy setback; others thought the key was a change in Goldwater's style; still others called for a switch in campaign tactics. Most staff members tended to agree with the Senator's view that the charges that he was trigger happy and might start a nuclear war constituted his greatest liability.

Tom Wicker in The Times analyzed the Goldwater impact this way:

In this strange, uneventful, yet fascinating Presidential campaign, it is Senator Barry Goldwater who has roused the strong emotions that probably decide most American elections.

On the one hand, Mr. Goldwater as the apostle of a new "conservatism" evokes a fanatical enthusiasm and a Messianic zeal in the hearts of his followers—convinced as they are that Big Government and "soft on Communism" foreign policy are despoiling the land of the free and home of the brave.

On the other hand, Mr. Goldwater, in his mild and unlikely way, arouses a powerful surge of fear in the hearts of many Americans—fear of diminished income, fear of damaged status, fear of rights denied, fear of the strange and unknown.

These frightened hearts do not necessarily throb with love for President Johnson. The evidence of most polls and surveys suggests that affection for Mr. Johnson personally does not run deep and that many voters are turning to him in spite of lukewarm or antagonistic feelings.

How could Goldwater turn these lukewarm feelings for Johnson into votes for himself? If he had his way, the campaign would have developed along different and more clear-cut ideological lines. The day after the New Jersey trip he wistfully interrupted a prepared speech to ad-lib to 11,000 cheering partisans in a Lubbock, Texas, auditorium: "Oh, I wish these two parties would fight this out on proper grounds. I wish the opposition party would accept the term Socialist party because, whether they know it or not, or like it or not, this is the road they are on. We are not calling these people something evil; we are merely calling them what they are."

On this tour through the familiar Southwest, Goldwater's strategy for the last half of the campaign became clear—stated simply, it was to make Johnson's personal integrity the "gut issue." That approach could be summed up by borrowing a question the Democrats had used against Nixon in 1960 and making it read, "Would you want to buy a used car from Lyndon?" The idea was to capitalize on the undercurrent of doubt about the President, to

shift Goldwater off the defensive and to make Johnson start answering the
questions. For many Americans, unquestionably, a suspicious mist of distrust
swirled about Johnson through the campaign. They had questions about the
President's wealth, the family-owned television station in Austin and the
Bobby Baker and Billie Sol Estes cases that had never been answered satis-
factorily. For Goldwater's purposes it would have been ideal if an impartial
voice could translate these doubts into votes against Johnson at the polls.
But many of the impartial who evidenced distrust of the President, like
Dean Sayre of the Episcopal National Cathedral in Washington, tended to
balance such criticism with doubts about Goldwater's extremist views.

But the most important change in the Goldwater tactics in this first week
of October was a decision to emphasize television speeches above all else,
even personal appearances. Both Goldwater and Miller had decided it was
absurd to tear around the country at a breakneck pace to speak to a relative
handful of voters when they could address millions by television. Moreover,
Goldwater, in his public appearances, was mainly speaking to the already
converted; he made few converts of the undecideds and even alienated some
of them. The response from Goldwater's first nationwide television talks were
uniformly good; many viewers had commented that he seemed sincere and
sensible. And so the Republicans set up fifteen half-hour programs on
nationwide television, much more on state television circuits, and numerous
one-, five-, and twenty-second spots. In most of these Goldwater himself
would talk, always relaxed and calm, always on tape so that his well-known
frankness would not get the better of his judgment.

Goldwater's third nationwide television appearance, on Friday, October
9, was typical. Sitting in a chair alone in a quiet room, he spoke directly
to the audience. "You have probably been reading and hearing about some of
the unorthodox things I have been doing," he said, with a sort of masochistic
satisfaction, and went on to list them—attacking the Administration's antipoverty program in impoverished Appalachia, medical care for the aged in
Florida retirement country, the T.V.A. in Tennessee and legislative reapportionment in under-represented cities. "I have done all these things deliberately," he said, "for a reason that is clear in my own mind. I will not
appeal to you as if you were simply pocketbooks surrounded on all sides by
self-serving concerns."

Charles Mohr's account of the Goldwater approach put it this way:

Mr. Goldwater has increasingly shown that he is running for President far
outside the boundaries of usual political activity in the United States.
He is not centering his arguments on the usual questions of governmental policy
or expenditure for specific programs. Instead he is arguing to the voters that he
will be able to reform American life and even morals.
Mr. Goldwater concedes that the nation is enjoying prosperity, and speaks
instead of such issues as the "deterioration of the home, the family and the
community, of law and order, of good morals and good manners."

He says that all of these things are in serious decline and that this is "the result of thirty years of unhealthy social climate. I refer to the philosophy of modern liberalism, the dominant philosophy of the opposition party."

As the Senator moved into California and up the coast he expounded his trickle-down theory—that morality must start at the top, in the White House, and filter down to the people. It was on Saturday, October 10, in the Mormon Tabernacle in Salt Lake City that Goldwater made the clearest presentation of his views. He began with the gloomy assessment that "the moral fiber of the American people is beset by rot and decay." Then he went into an attack on the United States Supreme Court for decisions that forbade state-written or state-prescribed prayers and religious exercises in public schools. Goldwater also appealed to the Mormons' piety by saying: "You will search in vain for reference to God or religion in the Democratic platform. This is a matter of even greater regret when we realize that this platform, with its utter disregard of God, was written to the exact specifications of Lyndon Johnson."

Just when Goldwater thought he had the issue outlined as simply and dramatically as possible, two developments in Congress set him back. A House subcommittee cleared the Administration of any wrong-doing in connection with the nefarious Billie Sol Estes. And the Senate Rules Committee, reinforcing its political role while nominally avoiding it, postponed any further hearings on the Baker case until after the election.

The latter move prompted Republican Chairman Burch to charge that it was perfectly obvious that orders from higher up had caused Senator B. Everett Jordan, the committee chairman, to delay further hearings. "This action is a shameful admission by the Johnson Administration that it is afraid to face the truth about this major Democratic scandal," Burch said. "It underscores the major issue in the Presidential campaign—the moral rot in Washington. In this same week, the Administration completed the whitewash job on the Billie Sol Estes case. Estes is telling intimates that he will never serve a day in prison, even though he has been tried, convicted and sentenced to twenty-three years in jail."

Someone slipped Goldwater a note about the postponement of the Baker hearings while he was speaking at a street corner in Des Moines. He dropped the flat, unemotional tone that characterized much of his speaking and his voice rose to a shout. He said the President was responsible for "twisting arms" to call off the investigation "that I am now convinced leads to the White House."

Actually Goldwater's attitude toward the issue of the President's ethics was ambivalent. Throughout the campaign he had openly questioned the President's integrity, and appeared to do so with relish. But in an interview he said it pained him to do it. He said he honestly felt that the Baker case was "hurting the President more than anything else," and that the mere mention of "Bobby Baker brings everything from mild applause to outright boos for the President, which I don't like to hear." He called it "difficult and distasteful to me to have a campaign where another man's well meaning or honesty is in question."

While Goldwater was fighting the pessimism in his ranks he himself was displaying some of it, scolding the public aggressively, as if he did not believe it would heed his call for a more moral America. He seemed to be warning voters that they could vote against him if they liked, but it would be a virtual admission of weakness on their part. Nevertheless, he felt he should try to raise the spirits of his followers, dampened by the surveys that showed him far behind Johnson.

An opportunity came with the results of a private poll taken for him by Opinion Research Inc. of Princeton, New Jersey. He interpreted the poll to show that he had at least 40 per cent of the voters in every state and that he could close the remaining gap fast enough to win on November 3. The polls also indicated that "defected Republicans" were returning at the rate of 6 to 8 per cent a week.

This poll was one of the few that attempted to measure the backlash vote—and it misled Goldwater completely. Because it was clear that no one would honestly answer a simple question tying voting to civil rights action, the poll takers devised an oblique question: "It has been said that some Goldwater supporters are not saying so to anyone for reasons of their own. In your personal experience have you heard of any?"

"Yes" was the answer of 37 per cent of a nationwide sampling. Goldwater strategists were thus reinforced in their belief that there was a large silent vote waiting for Goldwater's name to appear on the ballot. Two other polls, taken independently, came up with contradictory results. In California, the Field Research Corporation found that half the Democrats who said they would vote for Johnson also said they would vote for repeal of the Rumford [Fair Housing] Amendment, indicating that racial prejudice might be over-shadowed by other considerations. Another pollster, Oliver Quayle, found that the backlash factor was receding, but not dead.

A Louis Harris sampling taken about the same time gave Johnson 58 per cent to Goldwater's 34, with 8 per cent undecided. This was a gain of two percentage points for Goldwater over the Harris findings of a month before. The Harris poll also found that dissident Republicans were returning to the party, but at a rate of 5 per cent in two weeks, much more slowly than the Goldwater poll indicated.

With his usual frankness, Goldwater conceded that the charge that he was trigger happy had hurt him badly, but he insisted that it was being over-come by "just people stopping to think that no man, particularly no Ameri-can, is ever going to push that button." Besides, he said, he personally believed that "we will never engage in nuclear war, and even if we got into war, I don't think the Russians or ourselves would be stupid enough to devastate cities that we couldn't afford to rebuild."

The statement only pointed up a salient factor: The challenger was still on the defensive—with only three weeks remaining to turn the tide. Goldwater then decided on two moves—to step up his television appearances still further and to narrow the focus of his attack to just four issues. The decision to concentrate on four issues was outlined in this memorandum written by Goldwater's steering committee:

Brief—concise—the summation of our case. We charge the Administration has let the people down. We had great promises in 1960 but they have not been kept.

1. Instead, we have seen a shocking decline in political morality—moral decay—a national disgrace.

2. This has led to crime and violence in the streets—a breakdown of law and order—terrorizing our people.

3. Meanwhile in the world arena we have weakened ourselves and permitted our enemy to make gains all over. Our alliances are failing—the war in Vietnam persists. Cuba is a cancer spreading poison throughout the Americas—and the Johnson Administration plays politics with our defense. Communism is on the march and the Johnson Administration flounders.

4. And finally, our national leadership has failed to inspire us or the world. Is Johnson a true national or world leader? Or is he a selfish politician more interested in buying votes than in the welfare of our people and the future of our country?

He is a wheeler-dealer, not a leader. And his running mate is a creature of the A.D.A. which has goals dangerous to our best interests.

An unforeseen event then caused a crisis among the Democrats. On Wednesday, October 14, the newspapers and then the public learned that Walter W. Jenkins, a close friend and top assistant to Johnson, had twice been arrested on morals charges, once five years ago, once only a week before. The forty-six-year-old Jenkins had been an associate of Lyndon Johnson for twenty-five years. Soon after Johnson succeeded to the Presidency in 1963 he made Jenkins a Presidential aide and Jenkins rapidly became a top White House assistant. His duties were never precisely defined, but he seemed to serve both as official and personal aide to Johnson. He occasionally attended Cabinet meetings and sessions of the National Security Council. More important at the moment was the fact that Jenkins was the link between the White House and the Democratic National Committee. His close friendship with Johnson was reflected in the fact that one of his six children was named Lyndon.

The record of arrest came to light amid mystery and suspense that matched its explosive potentialities. On the evening of October 14, anonymous tipsters advised certain reporters to check the records of the Morals Division of the Washington police. There they discovered that Jenkins had been arrested October 7 in the Y.M.C.A., two blocks from the White House, for "disorderly conduct (indecent) gestures." Additional search of the records then disclosed that Jenkins had been arrested in 1959 in the same place for "disorderly conduct (pervert)."

Newspaper calls to the White House warned Jenkins that the story was about to break. He telephoned two of the President's legal advisers, Clark Clifford and Abe Fortas—both Democrats and former Democratic Administration officials—who called on some editors in Washington and persuaded them for "humanitarian" reasons to withhold publication of the story. Both said they acted on their own initiative and not at White House bidding. On Wednesday evening Dean Burch issued a statement from the Republican National Committee saying there was "a report sweeping Washington that the White House is desperately trying to suppress a major news story affecting the national security." A few hours later United Press International broke the story.

Word had been relayed to Johnson in New York, where he was preparing to address the Alfred E. Smith Memorial Dinner at the Waldorf-Astoria. Stunned, the President could not believe the report, but finally, reluctantly, he agreed there was no other course but to demand Jenkins' resignation. George Reedy, the President's press secretary, soon announced the resignation and said Jenkins had been hospitalized, suffering from "nervous exhaustion." Later in a statement on Jenkins, the President said he had ordered the F.B.I. to make "an immediate and comprehensive inquiry and report promptly to me and the American people."

Goldwater was in Denver when the story broke. A tense air of expectancy gripped his aides. This was the kind of break they had been waiting for; the Jenkins case seemed to be the missing piece in the picture puzzle of immorality in high places in Washington that Goldwater had been hopefully assembling. His aides foresaw a terrific impact on the campaign. But, typically unpredictable, Goldwater refused to comment. Stopped in the lobby of the Brown Palace Hotel on his way to a speech, he said, not quite candidly, that he had heard of the Jenkins case "five minutes ago and I have no comment." In his speech—he was hoarse from a cold—he again touched on the morality issue, saying that Americans wanted to see in their Government clear and constant evidence of the highest morality. Example, he said, "begins at the top and a government that is to hurl stones at corruption must be without sin." The speech had been mimeographed and distributed the previous night in Milwaukee, apparently well before the Goldwater people knew of the Jenkins case.

As the days passed, the Senator technically maintained silence. He would not be quoted directly, and he refused to make an issue solely of the personal problems of Jenkins. He said he would speak up if later developments showed that national security had been involved. The security question arose because of the belief that a person with an arrest record such as Jenkins might be vulnerable to blackmail or coercion by foreign agents. Besides, the Senator felt that the case had been given widespread publicity and nothing he could do would add to it. Indeed, perhaps, he might generate a counterwave of sympathy and support for Jenkins—and eventually Johnson. However, Goldwater made many indirect references to immorality and Johnson's "curious crew" in a way that suggested he was speaking with the Jenkins case in mind.

Other Republicans were less reticent than the nominee. Their questions centered mainly on the fact that although the Washington police forwarded Jenkins' fingerprints to the F.B.I. after his 1959 arrest, the description of the offense and the accused person were so vaguely worded as apparently to have failed to alert the F.B.I. to the importance of the case. Jenkins at the time was administrative aide to Johnson, who was Senate Majority Leader. Republicans wondered, too, why the Secret Service, which had received Jenkins' dossier in 1963 from the F.B.I. for a routine security check had apparently failed to run down the full facts about the 1959 arrest and report them to the President. But these security questions did not seem to reach Johnson himself.

On a lower plane, probably the lowest of the campaign, automobile bumper stickers appeared, reading: "Light Bulb Johnson. No wonder he turned out the lights in the White House."

The President had been more than politically hurt; the anguish was deep because Jenkins had been so close to him. In downtown Dayton, Ohio, he was confronted on a campaign trip by several crudely lettered signs—"What About Walter Jenkins?" and "Corruption Patrol"—and came close to losing his temper. His voice edged with anger, he took note of the signs, saying he was not on hand to indulge in muckraking or mudslinging since these are weapons of desperation and of fearful, frightened men. He added, "You can always tell them by their words, if not their signs." Then he went on to give a fiery political speech that evoked shouts of "L.B.J., L.B.J., L.B.J."

As the days went by Goldwater continued to hold his fire. In Sioux City, Iowa, after being hit by an egg, he talked about the need for going slow in scrapping farm price supports, about Communist China and about civil rights—but not about Jenkins. Finally, on October 19, five days after the disclosure of Jenkins's arrest, Goldwater broke his silence. In a letter to J. Edgar Hoover, the F.B.I. Director, Goldwater asked why Jenkins had not received a "thorough security check and investigation upon moving into a highly sensitive position in the White House." The Senator disclosed in his letter that two F.B.I. agents had called on him "around 6:30 A.M." October 17 in Chicago and had asked if he knew anything about Jenkins's personal habits. He said he had told the agents his knowledge of Jenkins was limited to "the fact that he is a member of my Air Force Reserve squadron on Capitol Hill." Goldwater wrote that it seemed curious that two agents had called on him, that the unusual hour had reflected apparent urgency and that during the interview of a few minutes the agents had not asked his opinion of Jenkins' loyalty to the country.

On Thursday, October 22, the F.B.I. made its report to President Johnson on Jenkins. It said an exhaustive investigation had revealed no information that Jenkins had "compromised the security or interests of the United States in any manner." Although Jenkins did admit having engaged in the indecent acts for which he was arrested, he did not confirm rumors that he had been enticed into the episodes that led to the second arrest. He told the F.B.I. that his mind was "befuddled by fatigue, alcohol, physical illness and lack of food." The Times article listed these other points made in the F.B.I.'s summary of its report:

Jenkins told the F.B.I. that no blackmail attempt or attempt to compromise him had ever been made against him and that "he would lay down his life before he would disclose any information that would damage the best interests of the United States."

When Jenkins was issued a White House pass in 1961, neither President Kennedy nor any member of his staff, nor Mr. Johnson, then the Vice President, "had any knowledge of the 1959 incident nor any reason to suspect its existence."

Johnson still did not know of the incident when he became President in 1963. "When questioned regarding his failure to order an investigation of himself" at that time, "Mr. Jenkins stated that he thought he had been investigated in 1961."

The summary also said that Jenkins had been given an Air Force top-secret clearance in 1956, a Department of Defense top-secret clearance in 1956 and an Atomic Energy Commission "Q" clearance in 1958 for access to restricted information on nuclear weapons, following a full field investigation by the F.B.I. As to why no action was taken after the 1959 arrest, the F.B.I. explained that the report it received from the Washington police merely stated that one "Walter Wilson Jenkins" who was unable to give his occupation had been arrested for investigation as a suspicious person. "No mention of a sex or morals offense appears on this card," the summary of the F.B.I. report said, "nor did it show any indication of Government employment." In 1961, when Jenkins sought a White House pass, the F.B.I. reported the 1959 arrest to the Secret Service. One man there noted the arrest, but he did not consider it as a serious matter or call it to the attention of his superior.

A day after the F.B.I. report was issued, Goldwater launched a full-scale attack. He said, in San Diego, that the White House had shown a careless disregard of security procedures in the case. True, he said, Johnson had now ordered new security checks for all White House staff members, but he said this was also a frank admission of how lax things had been for year after year. As another example, he said, "150 persons in the State Department alone have been given emergency clearance to deal with secret matters without waiting for a full field investigation." He noted that the Eisenhower Administration had resorted to this emergency clearance technique only five times.

Replying at once, the State Department said the emergency clearances Goldwater mentioned had been given in 1961 when the Democrats took over the Administration. They had been followed, it said, by complete investigations and the 150 had received a full security clearance.

In this same period, the Goldwater operation ran into an immorality issue of its own. It concerned a half-hour campaign film titled "Choice," which implied forcefully that Johnson was presiding over a morally deteriorating society. The film was being distributed by a newly organized division of the Citizens for Goldwater-Miller organization, called the Mothers for Moral

America. It was scheduled for release on the National Broadcasting Company national television network in mid-afternoon, when women would be watching. Before the film could be shown, however, the Democrats succeeded in getting a copy of it, and promptly screened it for reporters on Tuesday, October 20. The film included shots of a girl in a topless bathing suit being ogled by young men; a man clad only in a fig leaf; montages of pornographic magazines and book covers; scenes in strip-tease joints and the legends on the marquees of "nudie" theatres. Nan Robertson's dispatch in The Times explained how the film tried to link all this to Johnson:

> The President is neither shown nor mentioned by name, but he is symbolized by a speeding Lincoln Continental that screeches at intervals across the screen, with beer cans being tossed from time to time out of the driver's window.
> Republicans say this is the only staged portion of the film. It contains scenes showing violence, looting and chaos in the streets; twisters gyrating in riotous abandon; Billie Sol Estes, the bankrupt Texas financier; Robert G. Baker, former Senate Democratic secretary, and other instances of what the narrative pinpoints as "moral decay."
> The automobile sequence is an obvious reference to much-publicized accounts last Easter saying that Mr. Johnson was speeding and drinking beer at the wheel of his Continental near the LBJ Ranch.
> A recurring theme is that the nation's morals have gone down hill since the death of President Kennedy. The narrator, Raymond Massey, points out that Mr. Kennedy dreamt of an "honest, decent, law-abiding America."
> "The young, inspiring leader is gone," Mr. Massey says. The clear implication is that corruption now extends from the White House on down.

The Democrats, of course, protested. John Bailey, chairman of the Democratic National Committee, called the film "the sickest political program to be conceived since television became a factor." N.B.C. said it was undecided whether to cut some of the racier portions of the film. On Wednesday, October 21, the day before the film was scheduled to be shown, N.B.C. deleted some sequences with the cooperation of Mothers for Moral America.

But Goldwater was not satisfied; he ordered the film temporarily withdrawn and the N.B.C. program was postponed. For the first time Goldwater watched an unexpurgated version at a private screening in Philadelphia and the entire film was canceled. He said he did not regard the film as pornographic because it was made up mostly of newsreel clips. However, he added: "It is nothing but a racist film. There is nothing but riots. I think the film would incite trouble. . . . If it is shown I will publicly repudiate it. I said I would do nothing to incite riots."

The Democrats in a way were pleased by the whole "Choice" episode. Attacked for months on the morality issue, they now were able to charge that the Republicans had planned a dirty movie and that Goldwater's action seemed to bolster their view.

A welcome light moment in the Goldwater campaign was provided by his remarkable verbal political "appearance" of October 22 before 750 Arizona Republicans at a $100-a-plate dinner in Phoenix. The candidate was in shirtsleeves, at a table in the forward cabin of his plane, a microphone in his hand and the floor cluttered with electronic gadgetry. Over his head a sign proclaimed, "Better brinkmanship than chickenship." Goldwater peered through the window into the darkness below. At 11:07 P.M. a green light flashed on a box on the floor and a man wearing headphones pointed his finger at the Senator. Goldwater blew on the microphone and said:

"Hello, Bob [his brother]. Do you read me? Over."

A pause, then:

"Okay, it's good to talk to you, old man. This is Barry Goldwater talking to you from a 727, about over Prescott now. We're at 39,000 feet. I can clearly see the lights of Phoenix down to the left. I hate to say 'the left' but that's where it is. We're making about 480 miles an hour over the ground. This is the longest 727 flight yet tried in this country—coast to coast and east to west. [This was news to the reporters, who looked at one another and smiled weakly.] This is the first time that I know that we've attempted, or anyone else has attempted, an air to ground hookup like this to speak to a political meeting. And I wish we had thought of it sooner."

After a brief report on how the campaign was going, he signed off with: "By the way, Bob, you don't feel too bad now being a Republican, do you? Thirty years as a Democrat didn't hurt you. And now you can start living it up, boy, you're in a good party. That's all I have, Bob, I'll turn it back to you. Oh, yes, tell Mum I'll be home after the election."

This kind of informality often spread back through the Goldwater plane to the crowded press quarters. Goldwater's relations with the reporters, while occasionally strained and distant, were far friendlier than those between Nixon and the press corps in 1960 (when they were practically nonexistent). The Senator knew many of the newspapermen and broadcasters did not share his political views, but it rarely seemed to bother him. One night, as the Yia Bi Kin was cruising back to Washington from Wichita Falls, Goldwater went back to the press seats carrying a huge silver-ornamented sombrero and a gorgeous serape that a group of Mexican-Americans had given him in Corpus Christi. He said he was raffling them off, but it was obvious, after reporters had pulled numbers out of the hat, that the drawing had been rigged so that Frank Cancellare, a colorful United Press International photographer, would win. Goldwater put the sombrero on Cancellare's head, draped the serape over his shoulder and began taking pictures himself. When he had finished, Goldwater held up his hand for silence. "Amigos," he began, with a grin, "and I mean amigos. . . ."

Moved by the friendly speech, and a few drinks, the reporters began turning out a parody to the tune of "The Battle Hymn of the Republic" and soon the plane was reverberating with:

> Mine eyes have seen Goldwater at a million speaking dates,
> Mine ears have heard him give the lie to liberal candidates,
> And my head has quaked and trembled as he tells us of our fates

If Lyndon should get in.
Barry, Barry says he'll save us
From A.D.A. which would enslave us,
The curious crew that would deprave us.
He'll save us all from sin.

The campaign was now approaching its climax. It had developed much as Goldwater had thought, with one major exception—the defectors from the party had been greater in number and had been slower in returning than he had anticipated. Some, obviously, would not return, but he still hoped that most of them would. With only one week left before Election Day, it began to be clear that the Jenkins case had not had any fundamental impact on the voters. Goldwater's plan to send Ike to Vietnam had had even less effect. The postponement of the Bobby Baker hearings had not aroused the public against Johnson. Some of Goldwater's closest advisers were bewildered—and almost hurt—at their inability to turn favorable events into political breaks.

22

"Come On, Now,
Let's All Go
to the Speakin'"

Lawrence F. O'Brien, Johnson's director of campaign organization, returned from a scouting trip from Ohio to the West Coast on October 7, and gave a glowing report. The party, he said, was in excellent shape everywhere, with its national candidates leading in all the states he had visited except Nebraska, Colorado, Kansas and possibly Arizona. O'Brien warned, however, of three possible dangers: Overconfidence, the possible impact of the widely-circulated "hate literature" that depicted Johnson as dishonest, socialistic and an ally of communism, and an increase in Goldwater activity on the local level in California, Oklahoma, Texas and several other states. Other O'Brien conclusions: The Johnson-Humphrey ticket was running far ahead because the defection of Republicans from Goldwater continued to be sizable everywhere (up to 25 and 30 per cent in California and Michigan); the defection of Democrats from Johnson on the civil rights issue was diminishing and would probably not be of significance in any of the states he surveyed except Oklahoma and Arkansas; the unions were doing an excellent job on registration in the big industrial states. The key issue for the last half of the campaign, O'Brien suggested, was the question: "Whose finger should be on the nuclear button?"

The day before, the President had set out on a frankly political six-day tour. The same old themes of peace and prosperity were sounded as the President moved into the Republican heartland of the Middle West—Illinois, Iowa, Indiana and Ohio. He told the voters they must decide whether to continue the policies and programs that brought unprecedented national prosperity and that kept the peace under Administrations of both parties. "Let me tell you today," he warned, "those policies are in jeopardy."

Roaring, cheering throngs—and friendly police estimates of their size— greeted the President in the Midwest. In Des Moines, 175,000 persons acclaimed him; in Peoria, 75,000; in Springfield, 25,000; in Indianapolis,

40,000; in Gary, 30,000. Johnson loved it. In Des Moines he left his car ten times on the way to the state capitol to speak to the crowds. Several times he called out, "Come on in closer, people, come in closer," and then took a bullhorn to shout, "All the way with L.B.J."

The next day, as he walked into Monument Circle in Indianapolis he tossed his grey Stetson into the crowd, then autographed white plastic souvenir Texas hats and threw them to the people. As he passed a line of pretty drum majorettes he made an exaggerated gesture of sprucing up for them. So elated was the President by his reception in the Republican bastion of the Middle West that he was soon proclaiming publicly, "The Democratic party, come November, is going to have the greatest victory in the history of America."

As the President's plane turned south the Johnson drawl became noticeably thicker. The invincible theme—peace and prosperity—remained, but there was a tactical change. For the President was not campaigning in the South to win over Republicans; Goldwater had them sewed up. He was trying to bring the restive Democrats back to the party of their fathers, Democrats angered by Johnson's strong support of the Civil Rights Act of 1964.

The President did not try to duck the civil rights issue, but to place it in the perspective of the South's broad economic needs. In Louisville, in Memphis, in New Orleans, the message was the same: The Civil Rights Act was the law of the land "and I'm going to enforce it." He said nothing about the wrongs inflicted on Negroes or the rights denied them. Neither by word or tone did he arouse resentment nor offend the sensibilities of the Southerners by suggesting that they were somehow morally set apart from the rest of the nation.

In New Orleans on October 10, Johnson laid the civil rights issue squarely on the line. His words were not widely reported; they were part of a rambling extemporaneous addition to his prepared text, and most of the reporters had left the fund-raising dinner to write for the next day's papers. What the President said was something only a Southerner could say to a Southern audience—but few before him had. Disguising his own views thinly by quoting an anonymous old Southern Senator on his home state, Johnson said:

"I would like to go back there and make 'em one more Democratic speech. I just feel like I've got one more in me. Poor old state, they haven't heard a Democratic speech in thirty years. All they ever hear at election time"— the President's finger reached out and his voice thundered over the crowd— "is Negro, Negro, Negro!"

It was an amazing statement for a Presidential candidate, a Democrat and, most of all, a Southerner, to make in the South. Southern politicians had been using the race issue for decades to win elections, ignoring the South's other critical problems, both in campaign oratory and in office. The kind of Democratic speech these politicians should have been making, Johnson said, was "about the economy and what a great future we could have in the South if we just meet our economic problems, if we could just take a look at the resources of the South and develop them." And this was the kind of speech the President took it upon himself to make in the South now. He reminded the crowds that, of all sections of the country, the South had been aided most by Federal programs over the last thirty years and had the most to gain by future aid.

In Louisville, he said there was still far too much poverty in Kentucky and "we are not about to go back to 10 per cent terbacker." The Federal Government was helping to bring in new industry, and "I am going to serve the 38 per cent of Kentucky families" earning less than $3,000 a year. In Nashville, he said that T.V.A. "has shown what the Government and the people, working together, shoulder to shoulder, can do to conquer hostile nature and create a blessed home for the human spirit." In New Orleans, he said, "I may turn out the lights in the White House chandeliers but I am determined no one will turn out the lights of R.E.A. in the farmhouses of Louisiana."

"I want to wipe poverty off the face of the South—and off the conscience of the nation," the President declared again and again. But if this vision is to be made reality, he went on, then we must put behind us the problems of the past and resolve our differences. For economic progress would come only hand in hand with a new era of courage and common sense in racial relations, he said.

E. W. Kenworthy commented in The Times:

Only a Southerner could talk that way to Southerners and make them listen. It was not only a matter of understanding or of approach. It was also a matter of style. To the Easterner, President Kennedy had style. In the South, President Johnson has it. It is not the florid, purple-patches style of Senator Tom Connally, nor the gallus-snapping once affected by Governor Gene Talmadge in Georgia's red clay hills. It is part corn pone, as when, traveling in his car on the way to a meeting he grabs an electronic megaphone and calls out: "I like to see the sunshine, I like to see these smiling faces. Come on, now, let's all go to the speakin'." Or it's straight from the "poor hills of Texas": "I am not going to sell T.V.A. In the first place, it doesn't belong to me. It belongs to the people of the Upper South. It really belongs to the people of America. It is part of the blood and bone of Tennessee. It is part of the greatness of America and it is not for sale. Some day—and you mark my prediction, I don't take pride in being a prophet—the time will come in your lifetime when these men of little faith and great fear who are marching around under another banner not of their forefathers, the blush of shame will come to their cheeks and they will hang their heads when they are told by their children that they supported a party that wanted to sell the T.V.A."

Johnson literally wanted to carry all the states, but there was one he especially coveted: Goldwater's home state of Arizona. From the beginning of the campaign he had closely watched the polls for Arizona, which now gave him a narrow lead. Since he planned to visit the West before returning to Washington, why not stop off in Phoenix? The open day was a Sunday, October 11, so the visit should not be blatantly political, but he could go to church—and politics could be served. And on Sunday in Phoenix, thousands lined the route as his motorcade wound through the streets to the First Presbyterian Church. He stopped the procession seven times on the way to the church and ten times on the way back to the airport. He spoke to the crowd over the electronic bullhorn, his text for the Sunday being love thy neighbor. Once he directed traffic when it jammed. It was a hugely successful stopover, so much so Goldwater protested a desecration of the Sabbath.

In the West, the flexible Johnson discarded his Southern mannerisms, became a Westerner and talked like one. But while shifting geographic gears, he never forgot the nuclear trigger issue as he swung through California, Nevada, Montana, Wyoming, Colorado and Idaho. In Butte, Montana, he declared: "We here in the West know how the West was won. It wasn't won by the man on the horse who thought he could settle every argument with a quick draw and a shot from the hip. We here in the West aren't about to turn in our sterling-silver American heritage for a plastic credit card that reads, 'Shoot now, pay later.'"

Back in Washington, the Johnson campaign staff was gleefully in the process of catching the Republicans in a clumsy piece of political espionage. On Tuesday, October 13, the Democratic National Committee passed to a selected group of newsmen an affidavit signed by one Louis Flax, a night-shift teletype operator for the committee's national communications system. The story that Flax told in his sworn statement—the Republicans harrumphed about it but never really denied it—went like this:

On September 28, an anonymous telephone call to Flax had assured him he could make some badly-needed money by keeping friends of the caller "up to date on any prospective campaign plans." When Flax refused, his caller asked if the Democrats knew of "certain things" in his background. Flax, who had served time in Maryland on a bad-check charge, called the number he was given the next day—it turned out to be the Republican National Committee—and eventually agreed, according to his story, to sell Democratic information to John A. Grenier, the committee's executive director.

But Flax almost immediately became a double agent. He told Wayne Phillips, the Democratic committee's news director, what he had done—and about his prison record, too. Phillips told him to keep up his role as a Republican spy, but with appropriately doctored Democratic information. Under these orders, Flax brought an envelope of papers (they contained copies of messages to and from Democratic headquarters) to Grenier on October 2; after looking them over, the politician brought in a man with a limp and told Flax to remember him. Moments later under an awning outside the building, the man with the limp shook hands with Flax and passed him $1,000 in $10, $20 and $50 bills.

Flax said he took the money back to Phillips, who had him deposit it in a nearby bank. According to the Flax affidavit, there were more deliveries, all of material screened by the Democrats. When Phillips decided to tell the story, he also tried to spring a trap by dangling a juicy tidbit—the rest of Johnson's campaign schedule—in front of the Republicans. The Democratic publicist was so confident he invited an inconspicuous group of reporters and photographers to watch the payoff.

But the newsmen found Flax alone on the sidewalk. He had, he said, delivered a large manila envelope to Grenier's office, only to be told, "When you get something hot, we'll come up with some more money." No sidewalk payoff, no pictures, a good deal less than the smashing climax that the reporters had been promised. When the same reporters went up to Grenier's office, they saw a large manila envelope on his desk. But the Republican official, after having read a copy of the double spy's affidavit, said, "I don't know anyone named Flax." Goldwater was reportedly not disturbed by the incident; he thought any guilt would attach to the man who was paid, not to the party that paid him.

For many voters, it was a pure—and welcome—piece of comic opera. But the laughter was short-lived, for only a day after the light-hearted espionage revelation, the Walter Jenkins case broke.

And then, through what leaders of both parties later regarded as an incredible stroke of pure luck for Johnson, great international events pushed the scandal of Walter Jenkins out of the news spotlight. First, Moscow astonished the world on October 15 with the announcement that Khrushchev had been displaced as head of the Soviet Communist party by Leonid I. Brezhnev and as head of government by Aleksei N. Kosygin. On the same day Britain replaced the Conservative Government by a thin margin and Harold Wilson took over as Labor Prime Minister. The next day Peking announced that Red China had exploded its first atomic bomb. It now seemed clear that the campaign's decisive last days would be focused not on the integrity issue, where Goldwater found Johnson weak, but on the foreign policy issue, where the Democrats and the surveys found Goldwater weak. The effort to convince the voters that Goldwater might embark on risky foreign adventures had, by the same stroke of luck that stilled the Jenkins case, been tremendously advanced.

James Reston commented in The Times:

The world has done the American people a favor this week. It has startled us out of our preoccupation with secondary issues in the Presidential election, and clarified the primary issue of the campaign. Who is best qualified to sit in the White House and deal with a world in which Communist China is setting off nuclear explosions, the Soviet Union is moving to reunite Communist parties and Britain has established a weak Labor Government? This is the foremost question.

No matter how the experts interpret the momentous events in the Communist world, or how honest men differ about racial and economic policy in the United States, the lesson of the news out of Peking, Moscow and London is fairly obvious.

It is that this country must have a Government strong enough to maintain economic growth and prosperity, experienced and wise enough to create the largest possible degree of unity within the nation and the free world, and bold enough to review our policies with the allies, with Communist Russia and particularly with Communist China, in the light of the changing facts.

Whatever else may be said for the Senator, it certainly cannot be claimed that he has been a powerful unifying force in the field of foreign policy. He has not unified his party, let alone the country, behind his military or diplomatic programs. There is not a single government in the Western alliance, or a single opposition party in any of the allied countries—not even one—that supports his views.

This was true last week before the Chinese explosion, before the Soviet upheaval and before the British election; and it is even more true today in a highly delicate situation, which depends primarily on a unified America and a unified alliance.

The world has not been kind to the Senator. For, in a few strokes of lightning, it has illuminated the facts, and the facts have always been his downfall.

Goldwater could only respond with what he had said so many times before: He was not trigger happy; he, like all American political leaders, would never start a war, certainly not this way; the question was not who had his finger on the nuclear trigger, but who had his thumb on the country. In Youngstown, Ohio, he discounted the Chinese blast. "I am not overly impressed with this, because I have been convinced for a long time that almost anybody can make an atomic device if you get a little piece of fissionable material," he said. "I don't think you can make them in your kitchens yet, and you can't get do-it-yourself kits, but the fact that China has exploded a device doesn't mean by any means that tomorrow she will become a nuclear threat." He said that a warhead had no military value "unless you can get it from here to there." Without help, he said, it would take China at least twenty-five years to develop a suitable missile.

The President lost no time in exploiting the disturbing news from abroad. For a nationwide television audience he sought to be the calm voice of wisdom and experience, reassuring and cautionary. He said that despite China's atomic bomb and the ouster of Khrushchev, the key to peace was to be found in the strength and good sense of the United States.

Although the President avoided any reference to domestic policies in his speech, the Republicans demanded equal time for Goldwater on the reasonable theory that it had been a political address. All three national networks declined, were upheld by the Federal Communications Commission and eventually the courts. N.B.C. gave Burch fifteen minutes, which he used to repeat a statement charging the President had made a patently political broadcast. The Republican National chairman appealed to all who believed in fair play to send money to put Goldwater on the air to rebut the President. The contributions poured in—more than 30,000 letters and 3,000 telegrams, the Republicans said—and on Wednesday, October 21, three days after Johnson's address, Goldwater replied over one network, the American Broadcasting Company. His theme: "The foreign policy of the present Administration—based on a belief that there are good and bad Communists—has been an utter failure."

Then, in a speech at Pikesville, Maryland, this issue was carried very nearly to its extreme. "I charge that this Administration has a soft deal for

Communism," Goldwater declared. The problems in Cuba, Berlin and Vietnam are the product of this soft deal, he contended. At one point he said he would be willing to substitute another word for soft. Voices in the audience cried, "Treason!"

"That's it," replied Goldwater. Yet the American people seemed neither shocked nor impressed.

Johnson kept up the pressure, denouncing what he called the "smearlash" and keeping the nuclear trigger issue alive. In Akron, he implied that Goldwater was committed to a foreign policy of bluster and bluff and belligerence and said, "The world's hopes for peace cannot be left with those who have no faith in the possibility of lasting agreements and who readily predict war."

A fortnight before the election, The Times sent reporters into key sections of the country to find out the mood of the voters. This is what they reported:

In the Middle Atlantic states:

President Johnson should sweep the four-state Middle Atlantic region by an extraordinary majority of popular votes, according to all heretofor trustworthy political indicators.

It is the consensus of election observers in a survey by The New York Times that the Democratic candidate may win the ninety-two electoral votes of New York, New Jersey, Pennsylvania and Delaware as decisively as President Eisenhower did in 1956.

In the South:

The South, long considered Senator Barry Goldwater's chief source of strength, appears likely to give him less than half its support in the Presidential election.

A decline in popular sentiment for the Republican candidate that began more than three weeks ago, has become apparent even in such Goldwater strongholds as Alabama, Mississippi and Louisiana.

The Arizona Senator is still expected to carry these states and possibly one or two of the eight others in the former Confederacy. But his once promising prospects for winning a majority of the region's 128 electoral votes now seem dim.

In the Border states:

The close division of Democratic and Republican strength that is a political tradition in the Border states seems likely to be submerged this year in a Democratic landslide. It will not be the first time.

This is Presidential "winner's country." From Maryland west to Oklahoma voters in this loosely connected chain of states between the North and the South have compiled a record in Presidential preferences of remarkable near-unanimity for a section that lays no claim to regional homogeniety. . . .

Even the Republican National Committee lists two of the five Border states— Missouri and West Virginia—as "leaning Democratic." The Democrats and most other observers give all five to Johnson.

In the Middle West:

Senator Barry Goldwater's efforts to tuck away the electoral votes of the conservative, traditionally Republican states of the Great Plains are stumbling. . . .

Polls find and informal soundings reinforce the conclusion that for the first time since 1936 the Democratic Presidential candidates could sweep the fifty-three electoral votes of the Plains states in the north-south tier from North Dakota to Texas.

In the Mountain states:

Senator Barry Goldwater is losing where he was strongest—in the rock and sage desert of the mountain West.

Even in his native state and political stronghold of Arizona, the Republican Presidential nominee is thought to be running behind President Johnson.

The Goldwater lag in such states as Utah and Idaho, or Wyoming and Montana, is all the more puzzling because in the spring and summer he was King of the Mountains.

And in the Far West:

President Johnson's political bankers have already confidently deposited to his credit the sixty-two electoral votes of the five states touching the Pacific Ocean.

There was general agreement this week among party leaders, campaign technicians and qualified observers that Mr. Johnson continued to run ahead in Alaska, California, Hawaii, Oregon and Washington.

Except for some Goldwater managers who placed unbounded faith in "the troops in the field," the consensus was that the President's lead was too great to be overcome by the Republican nominee's renewed emphasis on the morality issue.

A week before the election, John Bailey predicted Johnson would carry all but three states; he conceded Alabama and Mississippi to Goldwater and said there was another state "that we could lose." He would not name it but he meant Louisiana. Nevertheless, the Democrats could not forget how Truman upset Dewey in 1948. "I'm still running scared," Bailey said. "I have been in this business too long to take anything for granted. The Republicans did one year, and they wound up with a Democratic President."

23

"I Have Spent My Life Getting Ready for This Moment"

One week before Election Day, the Democrats talked of the biggest land-slide victory since 1936 and the Republicans suggested without much conviction the biggest upset since 1948. One thing seemed clear, the Presidential race was not as exciting as some of the state contests. Observers hesitated to use the word boring to describe the campaign, but they were thinking it. There seemed to be no dramatic issue; neither side had made a serious blunder, but neither side had electrified the nation either. If Johnson appeared to be far ahead, as almost everyone agreed, it was as much because of disapproval of Goldwater as because of approval of Johnson.

At the beginning of the last week Tom Wicker summed up the outlook:

> The Democrats believe President Johnson will win more than 40 states, perhaps as many as 48, if they can assure a big voter turnout—something near the 71 to 72 million that political analysts and the Census Bureau believe is possible.
> The Republicans, on the other hand, are looking for a huge "silent vote," not reflected in published polls and in just enough states to put Senator Barry Goldwater over the 270 electoral votes needed to win.
> As a result, both party organizations are putting major emphasis in the last phases of the campaign on get-out-the-vote drives in their areas of greatest strength.

Thus the last week of the campaign opened with uncertainty and disorder, uncertainty because all of those who were sure of Johnson's victory remembered 1948, disorder because the candidates went their separate ways, scarcely paying attention or answering one another, carrying out their own strategies, regardless of observers who would have liked to impose logic or tidiness on the campaign. Both candidates knew the old political tradition that no one's vote was changed in the last-minute appeals, but Johnson plunged ahead as if every speech, every handshake could mean the difference between victory or defeat, while Goldwater seemed to be going through the motions.

The activities of the candidates were like the tip of an iceberg; everyone saw them, they made headlines in newspapers and were quoted on network television shows. But beneath that surface of the campaign, precinct workers everywhere were rallying the uncommitted and trying to convince the remaining undecideds. There were local rallies, tea, coffee and cocktail parties, telephone campaigns, door-to-door canvassing and tons of mail. And both parties stepped up their last minute television appeals. In New York, you couldn't turn on a television or radio set without seeing or hearing Keating appealing for votes. In Ohio, a television appeal by Ronald Reagan that made a big hit nationally was broadcast over twenty stations in one weekend. The Reagan show, in which the actor gave a pessimistic view of the country's fiscal future and attacked centralized government and the drift to Socialism, ended with these stirring words: "Should Moses have told the children of Israel to live in slavery under the pharoahs? Should Christ have refused the cross? Should the patriots at Concord Bridge have thrown down their guns and refused to fire the shots heard round the world?" It turned out to be the campaign's biggest television hit; it attracted more than $1,000,000 in contributions to the Republicans in the last week. In the last five days alone, the Republicans collected over $4,000,000 in contributions from all sources, much of this in small gifts.

On Monday, Goldwater came into New York for his final appearance in the state with forty-three electoral votes, a state that everybody conceded he would lose by at least a million votes. He had made two perfunctory upstate visits before, but this was his only trip to New York City. Goldwater's appearance was so well-organized that he would have been cheered if he had read the telephone book, and the next morning The Times carried this report:

Senator Barry Goldwater received a deafening 28-minute ovation at Madison Square Garden last night and then went on to predict he would win the Presidency next week in "the major political upset of the century."

More than 18,000 persons jammed the arena, and 5,000 others who were unable to get in listened as loudspeakers brought the program out to 49th Street west of Eighth Avenue.

The Republican Presidential nominee was interrupted with applause and cheers at almost every phrase of a speech that took him 35 minutes. . . .

He set the crowd to roaring when he declared: "If you ever hear me quoted as promising to make you free by forcibly busing your children from your chosen neighborhood school to some other one just to meet an arbitrary racial quota—look again because somebody is kidding you!"

On the same day, campaigning in the South, Johnson continued to hammer away at the theme of responsibility and prudence in the control of nuclear weapons and civil rights. In Florida and Georgia, Negro registration had risen and large numbers of Negroes lined his motorcade routes. At Hemming Park in Jacksonville, Johnson looked out over the heads of some Goldwater supporters and at a large group of Negroes and commented, "We are all equal on Election Day." The Times reported his day's campaigning as follows:

COLUMBIA, S.C., Oct. 26—President Johnson, making a determined attempt to reverse Republican trends in the South, said today that Senator Barry Goldwater of Arizona had advanced "the most radical proposals that have ever been made to the American people."

"Under the wild charges and the impulsive statements of the opposition," Mr. Johnson said, "is hidden a deadly intention that would initiate policies which I think would radically change the American way of life. . . . "

Mr. Johnson recalled to audiences that he was the only President born and reared in the South since Woodrow Wilson, and said:

"I know the burdens the South has borne. I know the ordeals that have tried the South through all these years."

The next day, Tuesday, October 27, Goldwater was in Ohio, speaking out against transporting children to schools outside their neighborhoods to correct racial imbalance, but he also urged his audience to live by the golden rule and to substitute love for hate in their hearts. He said: "No person, whether government official or private citizen, should violate the rights of some in order to further the rights of others. Isn't that the very thing happening across this land of ours today?" The Times reported his day this way:

CLEVELAND, Oct. 27—Senator Barry Goldwater carried his campaign into Ohio tonight with an outspoken attack on the Civil Rights Act of 1964.

Republican strategists number Ohio among the states that the Republican Presidential candidate must carry to win the election. Polls and other soundings, however, indicate that he is running behind President Johnson.

Mr. Goldwater's prospects for taking the state's 26 electoral votes seem to hinge in considerable measure on whether there is a sizable white backlash for him by ordinarily Democratic voters disturbed over Negro militancy.

Cleveland, a Democratic stronghold, has had racial friction. It also has sizable ethnic and worker groups, sometimes said to be particularly resentful about Negro pressure for equality.

In two states that seemed safe for the Democrats, Pennsylvania and Massachusetts, Johnson, meanwhile, pegged his speeches to the theme that Goldwater had opposed almost all Federal programs designed to make the nation's big cities more livable. The President's private polls showed him that almost all the big cities were safely in his column, but he knew, too, that the record or near-record mandate he sought would have to be built with extra votes from everywhere. The Times report of his day said:

EVANSVILLE, Ind., Oct. 27—President Johnson said tonight that while Senator Barry Goldwater of Arizona wanted to talk about "Bobby Baker, Walter Jenkins and Billie Sol Estes," the Democrats wanted to talk about social programs the Republican candidate opposes.

"And we're wrapping them around his neck," the President said.

Speaking to about 13,000 persons in the Pittsburgh Civic Arena, Mr. Johnson mentioned for the first time to a live political audience the case of Mr. Jenkins, who resigned as a special Presidential assistant after disclosure that he had been arrested twice on moral charges.

His reference to the Jenkins case was elliptical, but unmistakable. Sometimes in government "unfortunate things" happen and men disappoint you, he said, adding that in a government of 3,000,000 men some of them make mistakes. The only thing to do, he went on, was to take their jobs away from them, ask for their resignations and order impartial investigations.

In Wednesday morning's Times, James Reston stood back and observed that in the midst of the boring clatter of the campaign "it is hard to believe but it's still true, that the American political system works better than most." He went on to say:

> The main trouble with the American election system is that it exhausts the principals and diverts them from the cool appraisal of serious and complicated problems. No doubt it could be improved. The British found, after centuries of imperial responsibility, that they had to reduce their election campaigns to three weeks, and while this is impossible here, some moves toward a shorter election ought at least to be studied.
> Taken as a whole, however, the system is not as silly as it sounds. Sometimes it takes time to expose the ignorance of candidates. But it does finally come to an end, thank God, and it usually leaves the President free to be as effective a magistrate as he can.
> The people, as Mr. Jefferson observed long ago, are still "the safest depository of power." Churchill put it even better: Democracy, he remarked, is the worst system of Government in the world—"except all those other systems."

On Wednesday, Goldwater made speeches in Wisconsin, Illinois and Iowa and managed to introduce a new and controversial contention into the campaign. The Times account said:

> CEDAR RAPIDS, Iowa, Oct. 28—Senator Barry Goldwater questioned today how the churches could be "concentrating on morality" when "clerical spokesmen" have become "loud advocates" of President Johnson. . . .
> In the speech, Goldwater said:
> "We ask about the churches. And how can they be concentrating on morality when we find the clerical spokesmen who now become loud advocates of Lyndon Johnson, whose desire for power, in my opinion, represents much that is in opposition to the thinking of every church I know?"

The President spent Wednesday in New Mexico and California:

> SAN DIEGO, Calif., Oct. 28—President Johnson, who has maintained a lead in the public-opinion polls, concentrated his campaign today on appeals for a large voter turnout next Tuesday.
> He told an audience at Albuquerque, N.M., this morning that he thought he would beat the Republican candidate, Senator Barry Goldwater of Arizona, but he added:
> "Anybody who counts those votes before they are in the ballot box is gambling with his life and with the future of this nation. The risk is too great."
> Mr. Johnson continued to stress that the key issue in the election was "survival" in a nuclear age and to try to profit from the charge that Senator Goldwater is impulsive.

Stressing the need for restraint and responsibility in dealing with a Communist world armed with nuclear weapons, Mr. Johnson told a Los Angeles audience that "some people have more guts than brains."

He did not mention Mr. Goldwater, but there was little doubt about whom he was discussing.

In Los Angeles Johnson made news as the President, but with political overtones. In fact, The Times considered his views on the possibility of a rise in the price of steel and its consequent effect on the economy the most important story of the day, the lead on the front page:

LOS ANGELES, Oct. 28—President Johnson believes that any increases in steel prices at this time would be extremely difficult to justify.

Contracts between the United Steelworkers of America and the steel companies expire next June, and wage negotiations can begin Jan. 1.

These wage talks could have an important effect on prices, and the President is keeping close touch with all preliminary moves now in progress toward contract changes.

There have been recent reports that a steel price increase is in prospect. Steel executives have been arguing that profits are inadequate and that a price rise is needed.

The President's views on certain economic questions became known today from a qualified source as Mr. Johnson and his party campaigned in California.

Mr. Johnson believes that the economy as a whole can sustain its present momentum at least until mid-1965. His economic advisers, however, have indicated to him that some further action may be necessary by that time to stimulate the economy.

The next day, Thursday, Goldwater made a 245-mile whistle stop train tour of Pennsylvania, where he said he had a "fighting chance" to win despite the polls. As was expected, Republican Senator Scott found it convenient to be campaigning in other parts of the state. But Governor Scranton introduced Goldwater at the last rally of the day in Pittsburgh, saying he did not believe in "walking out on a party" or failing to support its nominee. This was the way The Times reported Goldwater's main speech:

PITTSBURGH, Oct. 29—Senator Barry Goldwater charged tonight that Secretary of State Dean Rusk "has coddled the liars, the wiretappers, the brutal abusers of government power who tried to railroad [Otto F.] Otepka."

Mr. Otepka, the State Department's chief security evaluator, fell into disfavor with his superiors last year for giving information to the Senate Internal Security subcommittee without authorization. Department officials attempted to intercept his telephone conversations in an effort to find out if he was privately in touch with the subcommittee. Mr. Otepka has kept his title but has been assigned to less important duties.

Mr. Goldwater, in a speech here tonight, charged that the Otepka case was "a shocking example of lax security in our State Department."

Johnson chose that day to reply to Goldwater's attack on the clergy and also to repeat his call for sophistication and prudence in the diplomacy of the cold war. The Times story said:

PHILADELPHIA, Oct. 29—President Johnson defended clergymen tonight against attacks by Senator Barry Goldwater, who has charged that some of them are improperly partisan.

Mr. Johnson, speaking at a $100-a-plate Democratic fund-raising dinner here, interpolated in a speech a statement that "men in the pulpit have a place in political leadership of our people and they have a place in our public affairs."

He added that "we should be grateful for their concern for the well-being of this land."

Mr. Goldwater complained yesterday that church leaders "don't have much time to worry about morals if they're worrying about partisan politics" and said that some churchmen were "loud advocates" of President Johnson. Tonight Mr. Johnson told 14,000 persons at Convention Hall, 5,000 of whom had paid for the fund-raising dinner, that "I do not condemn church or clergymen for being concerned that America meet her moral responsibility to peace" and for "doing what a rich nation can and should do to wipe poverty from our land."

He said, "I not only do not condemn them, I thank God for their courage."

On Thursday, too, a group of important clergymen of the three major faiths issued a statement on morality in the campaign, signed by forty clergymen and released to the press by Dr. John C. Bennett, president of Union Theological Seminary. The Times account said:

An "emergency committee" of prominent Protestant, Roman Catholic and Jewish churchmen issued a strong protest yesterday against the use of the Jenkins case in the Presidential election campaign.

They said that the case and a few other "episodes involving personal morality" had been allowed to "obscure fateful moral issues related to public life," such as civil rights, poverty and the danger of nuclear war. . . .

Several of the clergymen who signed it, however, acknowledged yesterday that the campaign of Senator Barry Goldwater of Arizona, the Republican Presidential candidate, had been the major impetus for the protest.

On Friday morning, *The New York Daily News*, the nation's largest newspaper, which had been decidedly pro-Goldwater in its editorials, declined to take a stand for either Presidential candidate. *The News* summarized its views this way, "The Goldwater campaign has been so clumsily conducted up to now, and the Senator has made so many unfortunate remarks in public, that one wonders how capable a President he would be." With regard to President Johnson, *The News* said, "On the other hand, we wonder whether the country could stand four more years of Lyndon B. Johnson in the White House. And when we think of Senator H. H. Humphrey as being within a heartbeat of succeeding President Johnson, we—like Senator Goldwater—shudder and shake."

The Times on the same day gave a final accounting of how the nation's press was lined up editorially for the candidates:

A larger number of the nation's daily newspapers are supporting President Johnson in the election Tuesday than are supporting Senator Goldwater, the Republican candidate.

It is the first time a Democratic candidate has had a majority since *Editor & Publisher,* the weekly trade magazine, began polling the nation's press in 1932.

The magazine's final tabulation showed Mr. Johnson supported by 440 newspapers, or 42.4 per cent of the 1,036 that answered a questionnaire.

The Republican candidate was supported by 34.7 per cent—359—while 237 said they had taken an "independent" position.

James Reston had a few sour reflections on the campaign:

WASHINGTON, Oct. 29—Anything that stains the reputation of America, or weakens the confidence of the people or the world in her institutions, injures mankind. And this election campaign has done just that.

No matter who wins on Tuesday, the nation has lost something. For the campaign has disillusioned and divided the people, revived their ancient feelings that politics is a dirty business, raised doubts about the integrity of the press, and even cast a shadow on the White House.

This could not possibly have happened at a worse time. In the last year a President of the United States has been murdered in the streets, and his accused assassin in turn murdered in the hands of the police.

A great party, which emancipated Negroes 100 years ago, has nominated for the Presidency a man backed by every racist gang in the country and lent its name to an attack upon the whole trend of foreign, economic and social policy of the last generation.

We shall deceive ourselves if we think all will be redeemed by an overwhelming defeat of Barry Goldwater. This is essential if we are not to be even more divided among ourselves and isolated from our allies, but it will not be enough.

For it is not Goldwater the man who is the central issue of the election, but Goldwater ideology and the Goldwater apparatus, now deeply entrenched in the Republican National Committee and in control of the party machinery in many of the states.

In fact, it is still more than a mere possibility that Goldwater could be overwhelmed in the voting on Tuesday and that many of his followers could be elected to carry on his obstructionist policies in the House and Senate.

This is especially true in the Mountain States and the Middle West, where right wing Republican candidates still have a good chance of unseating liberal incumbent Senators such as McGee of Wyoming, Moss of Utah, Cannon of Nevada, Hartke of Indiana and Burdick of North Dakota.

Paradoxically, the prospect of a Johnson landslide, which would help these men, hurts the chances of liberal Republicans like Keating and Lindsay of New York, Scott of Pennsylvania, Percy of Illinois and Romney of Michigan, whose defeat would leave the Republican party all the more in the hands of the most conservative elements.

Even if Goldwater is repudiated, not only in the Presidential but in the Congressional elections, much will have to be done to restore confidence in the political parties, in the judgment and integrity of the political process, and in the methods and purposes of the Administration.

It is not only Goldwater but President Johnson who has been hurt in this election, and it is he who will have to represent and guide the nation long after Goldwater has retired to his ranch house in Arizona.

A clear distinction has to be made between the immorality of policies that would leave the Negro's yearning for equality to the states, weaken the social legislation of a generation, and impose aggressive policies that would not be tolerated by either the allies or the Communists—this on the one hand—and the immorality or unethical practices of influential Government servants on the other.

This country is not likely to establish the principle that a President is responsible for the misdeeds of all his friends or associates, but it is likely to expect him to be more candid than President Johnson has been about his television ventures and about Baker and Jenkins.

It would be difficult to underestimate the number of people who are going to vote for the President next week with a profound sense of uneasiness, not because he has removed their doubts or convinced or exalted them, but simply because he is the only alternative to Goldwater.

In fact the disillusion and even disgust of the people with the political practices of this campaign hurt him more than he deserves, simply because in appearance and style and by reputation he is the arch symbol of the professional politician.

He has the same problem overseas. Not so long ago we were talking in this country a great deal about our national purposes, and half the world, seeking guidance for its own political process of the future, was watching intently. Under Kennedy, it seemed, the world began to change its impression of America as an inexperienced and violent giant, but the violence has returned in the last year, doubt has been spread once more about our judgment and our institutions, and this has hurt us and the free world much more than we have dared to admit.

On Friday, with Goldwater still on the West Coast, The Times reported:

LOS ANGELES, Oct. 30—Senator Barry Goldwater stumped the West today, concentrating his attack heavily on the Administration's foreign policy.

He charged that the United States might be in the beginning of World War III in South Vietnam. And he cited a lengthy catalogue of alleged Administration foreign policy failures to back up his assertion that President Johnson, running a "circus" campaign for "personal power," had "turned his back on the pressing problems of foreign policy."

Johnson spoke in Milwaukee and Detroit before going to Chicago for a torchlight parade and a speech at the Chicago Stadium:

CHICAGO, Oct. 30—President Johnson solicited the votes of both big city Democrats and the nation's Republicans today.

He shook hands and talked his way through four major cities in an attempt to offset white backlash among ethnic groups. And in the Republican stronghold of Rockford, Ill., he pictured himself as the kind of candidate who was more faithful to traditional Republican principles than was Senator Barry Goldwater.

In a campaign technique that was highly unusual for a Democrat, he even praised the "humane leadership" of the late Herbert Hoover.

On Saturday, Johnson flew into New York for the formal closing speech of the campaign in Madison Square Garden. The hall was less crowded than it had been for Goldwater five days before and there was less frenetic applause. But the only question in New York State was how much higher than a million Johnson's plurality would be. The Times reported Johnson's remarks as follows:

President Johnson offered the vision of "a society of success without squalor" and "rewarding leisure" for all in a speech last night at the New York windup of his election campaign in Madison Square Garden. . . .

He ripped into the opposition led by Senator Barry Goldwater, the Republican Presidential nominee, branding them "radicals" who would tear down institutions, not conservatives. He charged his foes with helping create "the atmosphere of hate and fear and suspicion in which individual liberty faces its maximum danger."

"Extremism in the pursuit of the Presidency is an unpardonable vice," Mr. Johnson declared in his prepared speech. "Moderation in the affairs of the nation is the highest virtue."

Goldwater was back in the South. In Columbia, South Carolina, he was greeted by a roaring, shouting, cheering outpouring of support and affection, the most enthusiastic demonstration of his entire campaign. The speech he delivered was almost identical with one he had made several days earlier in Cleveland, a slashing attack on the Civil Rights Act. But, in these closing days of the campaign, Goldwater seemed to be slowing down. His pace appeared deliberately leisurely; he did not act as a candidate fighting for every vote down to the wire. But for public consumption, he, like all candidates, maintained an optimistic posture. This attitude was reflected in the next day's Times report from Phoenix:

PHOENIX, Ariz., Oct. 31—Despite the overwhelming evidence of the polls and other soundings to the contrary, Senator Barry Goldwater thinks he will win the election Tuesday. A source in the best position to know the Republican Presidential candidate's views says that Mr. Goldwater is willing to concede only five states and the District of Columbia to President Johnson.

The states are Massachusetts, Rhode Island, Connecticut, Alaska and Hawaii. With the District, they account for only 36 of the 270 electoral votes needed for victory. . . .

Although Mr. Goldwater does not believe that he will carry all of the 45 other states, the source said, he believes he will do very well in them. The Republican nominee's view is that he is moving up throughout the nation in much the same way that brought him what had seemed an unlikely victory in the Republican Presidential primary in California in June. The impetus, he was said to feel, will enable him to win.

On Sunday, Russell Baker, who had been traveling with Johnson for a week, summarized the President's campaign tactics as follows:

WASHINGTON, Nov. 1—The strange thing about Lyndon B. Johnson's Presidential campaign has been its early-19th-century styling.

It exploits all the latest 20th-century gadgetry, but its spirit derives from Andrew Jackson, who dispelled the early grandeur of the Presidency and opened the White House to the folks.

"Come on down to the speakin' " is the call that comes from the Presidential bullhorn in the custom-built, bubbletop, armorplated limousine. And what the folks hear when they do is not a new-fangled, ghost-tailored image-builder, but an honest-to-goodness 19th-century speakin' that is liable to go on until they are limp, glassy-eyed and begging for mercy.

In Pittsburgh the other night, the crowd laughed when the President told them he was "not going to take over an hour or so" to speak—but an hour later he was still talking.

There has been nothing quite like it in recent memory. For President Kennedy, 20 minutes was a long speech. Dwight D. Eisenhower was a 30-minute speech reader and Harry S. Truman favored the short, punchy style. But loquacity alone is not the essential difference.

The trend in this century has been to isolate and glorify the Presidency, to call it a "splendid misery," to maintain it aloof and mysterious to the masses. Mr. Johnson's campaign has changed this.

All week long, from Boston to Los Angeles, from Wichita to Milwaukee, he has put the Presidency on display at street corners, urging the crowds to come and touch it and trying to make his audiences not merely understand but also feel what it is like to be President.

In his effort to establish a personal communion with every individual within earshot, he uses the old-shoe technique. His crowds are "you folks," and a constant refrain is, "I want you folks to know . . ."

A consummate showman, he takes them into the White House council rooms and reconstructs the thermonuclear confrontation between President Kennedy and Nikita Khrushchev in 1962 in a vernacular narrative that makes one's hair stand on end.

"As he and the leader of the Soviet Union came eyeball to eyeball, and their thumb started getting closer to that nuclear button, the knife was in each other's ribs, almost literally speaking, and neither of them were flinching or quivering."

The crowds are invariably silent at this point, mesmerized by the imagery and by the President's big thumb creeping theatrically up toward an invisible nuclear button. And then he asks them:

"Which man's thumb you want to be close to that button, what man you want to reach over and pick up that receiver on that hot line when they say, 'Moscow is calling'?"

The next moment he is talking to them like a rich uncle who hasn't become too successful to ask the family's help.

"I want you to do something for me," he tells a crowd at San Bernardino, Calif. "If you don't do it, I'm not going to get mad at you. I'm going to forget all about it."

What he wants is for San Bernardino to give the Democratic ticket the biggest majority in its history.

"I'm going to be down on the banks of the Pedernales in a little village in Texas, and I am going to be waiting," he tells them. "I'm going to be wondering how well you do your job."

Those who have come to prefer the aloof Presidency of the mid-20th-century complain that the style is "corny," much as the admirers of the Adams family complained about Jackson's having the street crowds into the White House for cheese.

Mr. Johnson resents such criticism, but when he is at his best on the stump he cannot resist the compulsion to talk to his audiences in the easy common style with Texas vernacular. When the crowd is responsive, he tries to establish even closer contact with them by giving them small items of family gossip.

"I met Luci coming out of the elevator on my way to Boston, and I said, 'Well, where have you been, young lady?' " goes a typical recital in Albuquerque. "She said, 'I have covered the Dakotas, I have made speeches there and in Nebraska, and it is pretty difficult country but I think we are going to carry it, and I will be so happy because I haven't had a weekend of my own since last May.' "

Or, to 13,000 persons in Pittsburgh:

"I have to meet Lady Bird in Evansville, Indiana, for another speech, and then she and I are going to kind of have a little anniversary, kind of a little 30-year honeymoon over in Albuquerque tonight. You know that poor girl has been traveling since daylight this morning."

In Los Angeles, before a large lunch-hour crowd at City Hall, he dismisses the campaign of his opponent, Senator Barry Goldwater, by citing reasons for the electorate to be happy, then asks, "Why do we want to go around being grouchy?"

And, in a long personal anecdote, he sums up his own view of the Republican opposition by declaring:

"Any jackass can kick a barn down. It takes a carpenter to build one."

Mr. Johnson carries an amplifier in his limousine, and at intersections where the crowds are big he orders his motorcade stopped, lets the hordes press against him, reaching for his hand, then climbs on the car trunk and tells them "the nation needs" whichever local Democrat happens to be riding with him.

It is the fashion to say that the crowds don't "love" him. If true, it is not because he has not given them the chance. No President in modern times has offered himself so completely to the crowds' caresses nor talked so intimately to them.

His compulsion to "press the flesh," as he puts it, is the despair of the Secret Service. When crowds are responsive, he will burst forth, as he did at one stop this week, in a paean to happiness—"What a wonderful land it would be if all of our people were as happy tonight as you are."

It may be that he is not really Andy Jackson in a superjet, but after his campaign it will be a long time before the political scientists can again refer to the Presidency as a lonely misery and keep straight faces.

On that same Sunday, John D. Pomfret, who had been covering Goldwater's campaign in its final phase, summarized the mood in the Republican camp:

PHOENIX, Ariz., Nov. 1—The perspiring young man stood below the speaker's platform, exhorting his candidate through an electronic megaphone.

"Take off the 16-ounce gloves and put on the brass knuckles," he pleaded.

But Senator Barry Goldwater never really did.

The incident occurred last week at Madison Square Garden, in New York City. But what happened there was not an isolated instance. It has been an important element in the campaign.

Time after time, the Republican Presidential candidate has begun his speech after a surging, roaring, pulsating ovation. He has stood with the cheers and the spotlights beating down on him, sometimes waving, sometimes smiling and sometimes looking as though he were embarrassed by the whole business and wished he were alone out in his beloved Arizona desert.

The fact is that Mr. Goldwater's style does not come close to matching the fervor of his audiences. If it did, he would be a different kind of candidate, and this a different kind of campaign.

The Senator rested at his home near here today and made a television tape with members of his family for broadcast Monday night. He will make one final sortie into crucial California tomorrow, going to San Francisco for a rally. Then he will wind up the campaign at Fredonia, Ariz., his "lucky" town, which he visited on the final day of his two successful senatorial races. On Tuesday Mr. Goldwater will vote here and await the verdict of the people.

The dominant mood today among his closest staff members appeared to be that he would win, but that it would be a squeaker. Like Mr. Goldwater, who has already indicated that he believes he will be the victor, they believe that the Senator's appeal to the public has begun to catch hold in the last 10 days and that he is moving up on President Johnson rapidly.

This is a distinctly minority viewpoint. Most political analysts think that Mr. Goldwater is so far behind that he will never overtake the President.

Whatever the outcome, Mr. Goldwater will be glad that the battle is over. He has not left the impression that he is a man who is enjoying himself.

Last week, for example, he confided to a crowd at Dover, Del., that it might be nice if "we could change this crazy system in this country whereby we have to campaign for months and months and months."

"How nice it would be," he added a bit wistfully, "if we could run a campaign like they do in England and get it over with, but I guess we are not going to be able to do it."

Sensing that the crowd might not appreciate these confidences, which are shared by many candidates but are not usually expressed in public, Mr. Goldwater quickly added that he would "kind of hate to see the thing change," because he did not have enough time to see all the people he wanted to.

The Senator seemed to catch fire a bit this week, but it was a flickering fire. He roused his audience in Oshkosh, Wis., for example, with a slashing, off-the-cuff speech in which he waved a copy of the Communist newspaper, The Worker, with a headline that said, "Smash Goldwaterism," and said that the Democrats had not repudiated the Communist party's support.

But the next day, whistle-stopping through Pennsylvania, Mr. Goldwater's performance seemed to some as uninspired as the gray, drizzling skies under which he traveled.

The fact appears to be that Mr. Goldwater is no political Dempsey. At times, when an enthusiastic reception such as some Mr. Goldwater has received might have prompted another candidate to fling away a prepared text and go for his opponent's jugular, Mr. Goldwater's tone has remained almost conversational.

There have been some tough lines in his speeches, but he usually delivers them mildly. Furthermore, despite some of the harsh things he has been saying about President Johnson and particularly about Senator Hubert H. Humphrey of Minnesota, the Democratic Vice Presidential nominee, he genuinely appears to want to be their friend.

Thus, last Thursday in Greensburg, Pa., thanking a group of teen-age Democrats for not heckling him, he said:

"I have had some of the most hair-pulling debates I ever want to have with Hubert Humphrey, but I don't think two people in this country are closer together as friends. And with Lyndon Johnson I have argued, fought and debated, but we can still call each other friends. It is only when we allow disagreement to overrun and overrule good judgment that we forget our basic goodness and decency in this country."

Mr. Humphrey has been saying that Mr. Goldwater is nice, too, but he always adds this kicker:

"I would like to have him as my neighbor, but not as my President."

On Monday morning, November 2, the day before the election, The Times added up the opinions of politicians and came up with the following view of the outcome of the race:

WASHINGTON, Nov. 1—On the eve of the 1964 Presidential election, political professionals and observers believe President Johnson is certain to carry 27 states with a total of 369 electoral votes—99 more than the 270 needed to assure his victory.

Sixteen additional states, having 109 electoral votes, are believed to be "leaning" narrowly toward Mr. Johnson. If the Democratic candidate should carry all of them, he would achieve a landslide, winning 43 of the 50 states and 478 out of a possible 538 electoral votes.

In sharp contrast, political experts believe the Republican nominee, Senator Barry Goldwater, is certain to carry only the two states that have been conceded to him from the beginning—Alabama and Mississippi, with a combined total of 17 electoral votes.

In one other state, Louisiana, with 10 votes, Mr. Goldwater is believed to have a narrow edge in the last days before the voting.

By the most objective judgments, five states with 33 electoral votes are considered genuinely in doubt as the campaign closes. They are Mr. Goldwater's home state of Arizona, Florida, South Carolina, Vermont and Wyoming.

The same Monday, the professional pollsters came out with their final forecasts, indicating that Johnson would win by a popular majority as high as 20,000,000 votes. The Times report said:

Significantly, all the professionally conducted voter opinion surveys, national and in states, are uniform in indicating a landslide for the Democratic ticket of Mr. Johnson and Senator Hubert H. Humphrey . . .

The final report of Dr. George C. Gallup's nationwide poll forecast a Johnson sweep by 64 per cent of the popular vote to 36 per cent for Mr. Goldwater.

Samuel Lubell, whose report does not include percentage figures, predicted a "Johnson landslide."

The national poll of Louis Harris foresaw 64 per cent for Mr. Johnson, 36 per cent for Mr. Goldwater.

On that last day of the campaign, everyone was still predicting a massive turnout the next day, something above 70,000,000 voters, possibly 71,000,000 to 75,000,000, and the candidates made their final appearances of the campaign. Charles Mohr reported the Johnson windup:

AUSTIN, Tex., Nov. 2—President Johnson came back to his home state today to await the results of the election. He told his hill country neighbors that it seemed "I have spent my life getting ready for this moment."

The President traveled from Washington to Houston for three speeches this afternoon and then came to Austin to speak from the steps of the state capitol. Austin gave him a hero's welcome. The crowds were so thick on broad Congress Avenue approaching the Capitol that his car could barely move, and the President happily hung from the open automobile to shake hands with "the folks."

But to say that Mr. Johnson campaigned was less than accurate. The campaign was over, and Mr. Johnson spoke primarily of his hopes and plans if the nation's voters tomorrow give him a full term of his own.

In a final television appearance tonight, Mr. Johnson told Republicans that the health of the two-party system would be restored by "an overwhelming repudiation of the small minority which has seized your party and intends to keep it."

He said that "only a massive defeat" could drive conservative Goldwater followers "from their places of power."

Goldwater flew to Fredonia, Arizona, his "lucky" town, in northern Arizona near the Utah border, the town where he had wound up his two successful campaigns for the Senate. John Pomfret reported the closing minutes of his campaign:

About 1,800 people—Indians, cowboys, farmers and townspeople from six surrounding communities—stood in the chill, flag-snapping wind to hear Mr.

Goldwater wind up his campaign. It was the first time a Presidential candidate had been there.

"I can't think of a better way to end the campaign than at sunset in this beautiful place," Mr. Goldwater said. "I am proud and happy to be back amongst people who I am sure understand every word that I have been saying throughout this campaign across the length and breadth of America, because these are the words you have grown by, the words that you have lived by.

"I've been speaking about man's obligation to himself and to his family, to do things himself, to accomplish things himself and only take help when everything else has failed."

The last moments of the Goldwater campaign were characteristically personal and anticlimactic. The Senator finished his formal remarks and then directed himself to the Indians in the audience. He pronounced a greeting in Navajo and thanked the Hopis for the doll they had given him. "And, if there are any Paiutes out there," he said, peering into the Western sunset, "hello." It was his final word to the American electorate.

And then it was over, the long, hard months of speeches, midnight flights, missed meals, sleepless nights, charges and countercharges.

24

Election Day

Ten months to the day after he had stood in the sun on the patio of his ranch house and formally enlisted in the campaign, Goldwater was back in Arizona. An early riser, he was up at 5 A.M. on Election Day to turn on his radio and get weather reports from fellow hams around the country. They all predicted a good day. After breakfast, the Senator, his wife and their two sons got into the family's blue Lincoln Continental and drove to their local polling place, the Phoenix Country Day School, arriving there at 9:41 A.M. Goldwater declined an offer to put him at the head of the long line, and the family waited for an hour and nineteen minutes until their turn came to enter the voting booth.

While the line moved slowly forward, the Goldwaters signed autographs and chatted with school children. Although he did shake many hands, the Senator scrupulously avoided politics in his conversations as he edged across the line within which electioneering was prohibited. Mrs. Goldwater waved gaily to friends and chatted with neighbors, and kept writing (just the word "Peggy") on slips of paper thrust toward her. Her husband, standing behind her in line, playfully drew tic tac toe marks on her bare neck. She smiled and rubbed them off.

When he reached the voting booth in the school's combination auditorium and cafeteria, he became Voter 465, Cudia Precinct, Maricopa County, Arizona. He spent nearly a minute and a half inside the booth, and afterward reporters asked him if he had split his ticket. "I always split it," he replied, an unpredictable irregular to the end. (When the day was over, his home precinct had cast 896 votes for Goldwater, 254 for Johnson and one for Eric Hass, the Socialist Labor party candidate for President.)

Back home about noon, the Senator took an hour and a half walk over the desert toward the Squaw Peak range, lunched on a hamburger, and spent the afternoon gardening and puttering around the house. Then, as the television returns began to come in, the Goldwaters gathered in the library with a dozen members of the family and some close friends to watch and listen. There were four television sets to watch, the one in the library, another near the pool, another in the kitchen and one in the master bedroom. The atmosphere surrounding all of them was one of stoic gloom, mixed with a few tears.

Two and a half miles away in the Camelback Inn in Phoenix, some hundred newsmen and several hundred Goldwater adherents had been told the Senator would come there for a concession speech if he lost but remain unavailable at home with his family if he won. The Secret Service was standing by to guard him if he won.

Goldwater's running mate, Miller, and his wife, Stephanie, were staying with Mr. and Mrs. Raymond J. Lee, their oldest friends in Lockport, who had traveled with them throughout the campaign. Miller no longer lived in Lockport, where he was born and had spent most of his life, but he kept as a voting residence a summer cottage in nearby Olcott on Lake Ontario. On Tuesday, the Millers drove to the firehouse in Olcott and voted. It took him twenty-five seconds. Unlike Goldwater, the New Yorker went straight down the Republican line, he said, not even skipping Senator Kenneth B. Keating, the Republican who had refused to endorse the national ticket. His explanation, "I'm a team player." Miller played nine holes of golf in the late morning (he shot a forty-three), lunched leisurely and napped for two hours before he began watching television in the Lee's recreation room—with a television camera watching him. Nearby was a phone connecting him with the Goldwater home in Phoenix.

Lyndon Johnson was home, too, in Texas. This is the way Charles Mohr described the voting of the President:

President Johnson voted for himself at Johnson City today by drawing a line through the name of Senator Barry Goldwater.

With customary energy, the President then held an impromptu news conference, gave a guided tour of his boyhood home and told stories, Texas-style.

When someone asked him if he had been consulting his political advisers, he looked at Mrs. Johnson and said, "No, the only political adviser I have talked to is my wife."

Mr. Johnson arose at 6:30 this morning and drove himself and his wife in a white Lincoln from his LBJ ranch the twelve miles into Johnson City (population 611). He entered his polling place in a demonstration kitchen at the Pedernales Electric Co-op seven minutes after the polls opened at 8 o'clock.

Under Texas law, a voter does not mark the candidate of his choice but scratches out all other candidates for the same office.

In Johnson City, the privacy of a curtained voting booth is dispensed with. There are tables scattered around the room where voters can huddle over their ballots in secrecy.

Mr. and Mrs. Johnson did not bother. Sitting across from election officials and in view of reporters and photographers, Mr. Johnson marked his ballot in one minute and ten seconds by drawing vertical lines through the columns of Republican and Constitution party candidates for national and state office.

Mrs. Johnson, who wore a simple red dress, took longer because she industriously drew horizontal lines through each opposition candidate's name.

The President's Johnson City neighbors who had watched him grow up and play in their streets now watched him vote in the open room. When he asked a neighbor if she had voted, she replied, "I'll bet I've been voting longer than you have." Outside, Johnson jokingly remarked to the Blanco

County Democratic Chairman, Mrs. Bill Stribling, "I'm leaving it up to you now—if Blanco County goes Republican, it'll be your fault."

Mrs. Stribling leaned over confidentially and said: "I've done everything I can. I even carried Mama down to vote and she's eighty-six!" (When the vote was counted in Precinct Four of Blanco County, where Johnson had voted, it was 205 for Johnson, 41 for Goldwater.)

The President invited reporters to walk two blocks with him to the little white frame house where he had lived from the time he was seven until he was graduated from Johnson City High School. He sat on the porch swing with his wife and reminisced, noting that the only election he had ever lost, the Senate race in 1941, he had closed on the porch. Then he recalled how he and his wife as a young couple had wanted to buy 600 acres of nearby land at six dollars an acre. His father, he went on, got up from the front of the fireplace, stalked into the kitchen and said to his wife, "Rebekah, I never thought I'd raise a boy that didn't have more sense than to pay six dollars an acre for land."

As the President talked, the piped-in music system he had installed played "Everything's Coming Up Roses."

When Mrs. Johnson was asked if she had been courted on the front porch swing, she said, "Not us, not here."

The President's eyes twinkled and he said, "I've done some courting on swings, though."

Mrs. Johnson smiled demurely. "Yes, I was preceded," she said.

After an hour in Johnson City, the President and his wife returned to the LBJ Ranch for a day of relaxation, characteristically punctuated by an afternoon on the telephone for the President. He watched the early television returns but after less than an hour, he and his wife and Federal Judge Homer Thornberry and his wife flew to the nearby ranch of A. W. Moursand, an old friend and the Johnson family financial trustee. There the growing party watched more election results for another hour before flying to Austin for the climactic events of the evening.

Predictably, Hubert Humphrey was the candidate least able to cast off the campaign and relax. The only one of the four to make political appearances on the final Sunday, he moved from California into Utah on Monday for a last swing, and it was well after midnight on Tuesday morning before he flew into Minneapolis for a few hours sleep before voting. Not until 1:30 in the afternoon, after a forty-mile drive through a heavy rain, did the Humphreys reach Waverly, where they have a four-bedroom home on a small lake in predominantly farm country. There, in the white wooden town hall of Marysville Township, he and his wife, Muriel, marked their paper ballots, folded them in quarters and dropped them into the box. When reporters asked how he had voted, the Democratic Vice Presidential candidate was only slightly evasive. "It's a big secret," he replied, "but you can tell the President he can rely on me." After chatting with two dozen voters, Humphrey drove back to Minneapolis to hear the results in a suite at the Sheraton Ritz.

These four men poised at the corners of a parallelogram formed by Johnson City, Phoenix, Lockport and Minneapolis, did not have long to wait. From the states where the polls had closed early, the evidence began to pour in, clear and conclusive from the beginning.

From Connecticut, a Democratic state watched closely for Eastern voting trends, the word came early: Johnson was winning by a landslide; he was running better than two to one ahead of Goldwater. From Indiana, a state that had not gone Democratic since the Roosevelt landslide of 1936, the returns showed Johnson with an early but insurmountable lead. In the border state of Kentucky, which last went Democratic in 1952 and then by 700 votes, it was not even close: The President was sweeping to victory.

The early returns also made it clear, however, that Goldwater was making a major challenge in the South, the only time in his party's history except when Hoover defeated Smith in 1928, that a Republican Presidential candidate had been able to penetrate the Democratic political domination over the states of the Old Confederacy. Goldwater captured Alabama by default— Johnson's own party had not put him on the ballot—and Mississippi, where the Democrats had waged only a token fight for the national ticket. More important, the Republican took South Carolina, a state in doubt up to the end, and he threatened to carry Georgia.

But these were only small flickers of good fortune in a steadily blackening night for Goldwater. Early in the evening, it became evident that Johnson had carried Ohio, a state considered essential to the Goldwater strategy; he appeared likely to win Illinois, similarly vital to the Republicans.

West with the sunset, the tide of Democratic victory moved steadily. At 8:30 P.M., for its first election night edition, The New York Times credited Johnson with ten states and 114 electoral votes, Goldwater with three states and twenty-five votes. At 11:15, for its second edition, The Times reported that Johnson had carried twenty-nine states with 363 electoral votes—a clear-cut victory. By the same time, Goldwater had only edged up to a total of four states with thirty-seven votes, adding Georgia to his earlier conquests in the South. For The Times' third edition, under the banner headline "JOHNSON SWAMPS GOLDWATER," Tom Wicker had the 1964 Presidential story all wrapped up:

Lyndon Baines Johnson of Texas compiled one of the greatest landslide victories in American history yesterday to win a four-year term on his own as the 36th President of the United States.

Senator Hubert H. Humphrey of Minnesota, Mr. Johnson's running mate on the Democratic ticket, was carried into office as Vice President.

Mr. Johnson's triumph, giving him the "loud and clear" mandate he had wanted, brought 44 states and the District of Columbia, with 486 electoral votes, into the Democratic column.

Senator Barry Goldwater, the Republican candidate who sought to offer the people "a choice, not an echo" with a strongly conservative campaign, won only five states in the Deep South and held a narrow lead in his home state of Arizona. Carrying it would give him a total of 52 electoral votes.

After flying to Austin at about 9 P.M., Johnson munched sandwiches in a suite at the Driskill Hotel with his daughters. Then he attended a reception at the Executive Mansion of Governor John B. Connally Jr. He also made a point of stopping off at the campaign headquarters of Senator Ralph W. Yarborough, a leader of the liberal Texas Democratic wing with whom the President had often been at political odds; Yarborough was also winning handsomely in the Texas sweep.

Later in the long election night Johnson himself formally acknowledged his victory. Well after 1 A.M., Texas time, he stood with his wife and two daughters before thousands of cheering partisans in Austin's Municipal Auditorium, which moments before had echoed to a swelling, spontaneous chorus of "The Eyes of Texas Are Upon You." His overwhelming election, the President told the Austin crowd and late-staying television viewers, was "a mandate for unity, for a government that serves no special interest—no business government, no labor government, no farm government, no one faction, no one group—but a government that provides equal opportunity for all and special privileges for none."

Of the size of his imposing majority, Johnson would only say, "I doubt that there has ever been so many people seeing so many things alike on decision day." But he appealed to his supporters and their opponents "to forget our differences because there are many more things in America that unite us than divide us and our nation."

Goldwater had agreed to make an election night statement if it became necessary for him to concede, but he changed his mind. At 8 P.M., Arizona time, about an hour after the television networks had elected Johnson, the Senator stopped watching, ate dinner and retired to his bedroom to work on his mail. It was not until several hours later that a press aide told reporters Goldwater would have nothing further to say until the following morning because "he wants to analyze the vote." But Goldwater had gone to bed at 11 o'clock, long after his defeat had become clear to all, without conceding the election. The next morning Goldwater sent Johnson a sharp but nominally congratulatory telegram, the conservative's first admission that he had lost:

Congratulations on your victory. I will help you in any way I can toward achieving a growing and better America and a secure and dignified peace. The role of the Republican party will remain in that temper but it also remains the party of opposition when opposition is called for. There is much to be done in Vietnam, Cuba and the problem of law and order in this country, and a productive economy. Communism remains our No. 1 obstacle to peace and I know that all Americans will join with you in honest solutions to these problems.

Goldwater's reluctance to speak had held back any statement by Miller who, early in the evening, had tacitly conceded defeat when he told re-

reporters he and Goldwater would have made a better showing if all Republican leaders had united behind the national ticket. Humphrey was also trapped by the protocol of deferring to the Presidential candidate. He waited so long in his Minneapolis hotel suite for Johnson to claim victory that when he arrived in a local auditorium for his own speech of triumph, several thousand of the weary Minnesota celebrants had already gone home to bed.

Although it had taken the candidates a long time to acknowledge formally what happened on election night, it had taken the voters of America the shortest time in history to find out the same results. The three television networks and the two newspaper wire services had joined forces to finance and organize a single collection system for election returns. Replacing a group of competitive lesser efforts, the new effort spotted 100,000 workers in precincts all over the nation, producing faster counting, faster transmission and earlier news for the papers and radio and television stations.

Equally important, the decisive 1964 election news came early because the election was so one-sided. Four years before, the margin of the vote in key states like Illinois, Minnesota and California had been so small that no one could be sure until well into the night—and even for days—which way these blocs of electoral votes would go. In 1964, only seven states could be called close—Arizona, Florida, Idaho, Kansas, Nebraska, Utah and Virginia—and their total electoral vote was fifty-one out of 538. In almost every other case, the Johnson majorities were large enough so that their certainty became clear early in the evening.

A third source of speed in spotting the Johnson victory went partially unrecognized because it was not a night on which anyone needed any special equipment to hear the thundering approach of the landslide—although all the news media had prepared complicated projection systems. The competition between the National Broadcasting Company, the Columbia Broadcasting System and the American Broadcasting Company was fierce. All three networks had installed systems of electronic computers that could take partial returns and project a final result from them for any given state. On a relatively easy workout, the projection systems, using computer techniques, proved accurate in predicting the final outcome on the basis of seemingly fragmentary evidence.

Jack Gould, The Times' television critic, assessed their coverage:

The Columbia Broadcasting System turned in a superb journalistic feat last night, running away with the major honors in reporting President Johnson's election victory.

In clarity of presentation, the network led all the way, and in speed it was up in front for at least an hour and a half. In a medium where time is of the essence, the performance of C.B.S. was of landslide proportions. The difference between C.B.S. and the National Broadcasting Company and the American Broadcasting Company lay in the C.B.S. sampling process called Vote Profile Analysis. By quickly reporting the results in key districts that represented a microcosm of a state, the C.B.S. staff called the outcome in state after state before its rivals. . . .

The figures that the new collection system ultimately assembled made some new American election records and fell just short of others. Johnson's 61 per cent of all the popular votes cast exceeded the previous record of 60.8 per cent recorded by Franklin D. Roosevelt in 1936 and the 60.4 per cent of Harding in 1920. But Johnson's share of the two party vote, 61.4 per cent, fell short of the vote of three other Presidents, Coolidge with 65.2 per cent in 1924, Harding with 63.9 per cent in 1920 and Roosevelt with 62.5 per cent in 1936. The difference between these two kinds of measurement was caused by the relatively large third party votes in 1920, 1924 and 1936.

Johnson's popular vote was 43,126,218, 20 per cent higher than the Eisenhower total of 35,000,000 in 1956 that had been regarded as basically unrealistic by politicians for the past eight years. Goldwater's vote was 27,174,898, giving Johnson a plurality of 15,951,320, and converting the 1936 Roosevelt plurality of 11,000,000 from a record to an interesting bit of American political history. The total vote in 1964 was 70,621,479, far short of the 71,000,000 to 75,000,000 that had been forecast. 320,363 went to third party candidates or unpledged electors. The number of Americans eligible to vote had been estimated at 113,931,000.

How accurate were the polls in predicting a Johnson victory of these proportions? From the point of view of the average layman, interested in who's going to win and by roughly how much, the polls scored a resounding triumph. Both the Gallup and the Harris polls in their closing estimates gave Johnson 64 per cent of the vote; he got 61. Louis Harris pointed out in his final report that trying to pinpoint so huge a lead was really a waste of time from a political point of view. Concededly, a 3 per cent error—more than the pollsters' normal margin of error—in an election of the 1964 variety confused no one. But in another year, an error of that size could mean the difference between predicting a candidate's share of the popular vote at 48.5 per cent or 51.5 per cent, a potentially critical difference. Such problems the pollsters shrug off with the explanation that their national vote percentages cannot pick the winner in very close elections anyway, because of the vagaries of the electoral vote system.

The value of the polls, which after all did predict a landslide for Johnson, was more in surveying public opinion. Polls, in attempting to measure reaction to both issues and events, provided information for voters, the press, politicians and, more important, the candidates themselves. The growing use of polls by almost all candidates who can afford them to determine effective issues and the reaction of voters poses an old problem in new guise: Will the candidate say what he thinks or what he thinks the voter wants to hear? Politicians have usually tempered their views to their audiences (Barry Goldwater being a notable exception in many of his speeches); polls now give them a "scientific" basis for doing so.

Pollsters, who sell their reports to either the public or to politicians, argue that they should not be judged merely by the figures, which, they say, are interesting, but not as important as what they reveal about the dynamics of the political process. In this, they always get into arguments with newspapermen, who say that pollsters who publish election predictions stand or fall on the accuracy of those figures. According to the view of pollsters, though, the most valuable information from continuous polling is insight into public opinion. Lou Harris, for example, says without polls, it would not have been possible to document the fact that peace was the dominant issue of the 1964 campaign, that the white backlash faded in the latter stages of the campaign, that the welfare state was out as a major issue, that Goldwater was considered more of a radical than a conservative and that Johnson's reputation as a wheeler-dealer also enhanced confidence in his ability to get things done.

Goldwater was not the only Republican member of Congress who found himself going to bed early and quietly on election night. For in the wake of the Johnson sweep, the Democrats had improved an already impressive position in the Senate and made the greatest gains in two decades in the House. Unlike the one-sided Presidential race, the Congressional picture was still cloudy on election night. But the following day in The Times, its chief Congressional correspondent, John D. Morris, wrote, "President Johnson is assured of the biggest Democratic majority in the House of Representatives since the high point of the Roosevelt New Deal in 1936."

In the Senate, the Democrats increased their majority by two seats; there would be sixty-eight Democrats and thirty-two Republicans in the new chamber. In the House of Representatives, the Democrats gained forty seats, despite Republican inroads in the South; the new House would have 295 Democrats and 140 Republicans. It was true that Republican candidates had made an historic breakthrough in the South, carrying five House seats in Alabama and one each in Georgia and Mississippi. But elsewhere in the country, it was not enough for a Republican Congressional candidate to run well ahead of Goldwater; unless he ran far ahead, he was lost. On Wednesday morning the political battlefield was littered with sorry examples.

In New York, Senator Kenneth B. Keating had refused to support Goldwater, running an independent campaign against Robert F. Kennedy. Goldwater lost the state by a record-shattering 2,600,000 votes. Keating ran 860,000 votes ahead of his party's national ticket, but still lost by 400,000.

The Ohio Senate election was much closer, but the final result was the same. Representative Robert Taft Jr., lost to Senator Stephen M. Young. The figures told the story: Goldwater lost Ohio by 1,000,000 votes; Taft succeeded in making up all but 17,000 of that deficit, but he still fell short.

In California, however, a Republican Senate candidate was able to overcome the dead weight of the Goldwater candidacy. There George Murphy won by a little more than 200,000 votes over Pierre Salinger while Goldwater was losing the state by 1,300,000. But in Pennsylvania, the vote was so close that it wasn't known for weeks that Scott had eked out a narrow victory over Miss Blatt.

In the House, the Republicans lost seats they already held: Two in Indiana, five in Iowa, three in Michigan, four in New Jersey, seven in New York, four each in Ohio and Washington and by ones and twos elsewhere. In New York there was one remarkable exception. Representative John V. Lindsay, the attractive young Republican from the Seventeenth "silk stocking" District of New York City, who had not supported Goldwater, swept to an easy victory, despite the Democratic tide. But in Westchester County, Richard L. Ottinger, a Democratic newcomer, gave his party its first victory in that suburban, traditionally Republican area by defeating incumbent Robert Barry, after a campaign devoted to what he called curing the "Barry-Barry" disease.

Republican candidates for Governor more than held their own in the face of the low Goldwater vote. Of the twenty-five states choosing Governors, the Republicans captured three new state houses—in Massachusetts, Wisconsin and Washington—and held on to five others they had. Democratic candidates for Governor ousted Republicans in Arizona and Utah and retained control in fifteen other states. This represented a net gain of one governorship for the Republicans, but they were still outnumbered, thirty-three to seventeen, in the nation as a whole. A major Republican disappointment was the defeat in Illinois of Charles H. Percy. He ran nearly 335,000 votes ahead of Goldwater, but this was not enough to defeat Governor Otto Kerner, the Democrat, who won by 180,000 votes. And in Goldwater's home state, Richard Kleindienst, one of his aides, lost the gubernatorial election to Sam Goddard by 30,000 votes.

In Michigan, Republican Governor George Romney, who had opposed Goldwater at the Convention and never supported him afterward, defeated his Democratic opponent, Neil Staebler, by 380,000 votes, despite Johnson's triumph in the state by more than a million votes. Romney thus put himself in the forefront for leadership of his party and for consideration as a Presidential possibility in 1968.

Around the country, the Democratic sweep carried the party to control of numerous state legislatures which normally contain the bread and butter jobs for local politicians. In New York, the Democrats won control of both houses of the legislature for the first time since 1935; in Maine, a Democratic legislature was elected for the first time in fifty-six years; the Democrats carried the lower house in Pennsylvania; in Michigan, despite Romney's victory, the Democrats carried both houses; in Montana, Nevada and Washington, the Democrats also won control of both houses.

In the relative tranquility of Thursday morning's Times, Tom Wicker wrote, "The Republican party, divided by Barry Goldwater and smashed by Lyndon Johnson, surveyed yesterday the wreckage of one of the worst election defeats in American history."

25

"Poor Strategy,
Poor Content,
Poor Delivery"

Senator Barry Goldwater lost the 1964 election in the vain hope that a huge conservative vote awaited his call.

Even during the campaign, Sentor Goldwater appeared to many observers to be throwing away his chances of winning.

He did it, in the main, by permitting and even aiding in his own isolation from the Republican party. It was a minority party when the campaign started, and its deliberate fragmentation, which President Johnson skillfully abetted, ended all hope of any majority-producing coalition.

That simple explanation appeared on the front page of The Times on November 8. For Goldwater, the loser, it was inescapably a humiliating defeat, a vote of "no confidence" that all the rhetoric of the irreconcilable conservatives could not explain away. More than a man had lost, and more than a political party. Into the contest with Goldwater had gone a set of ideas about how the American government should be run and about the nation's role in the world. Some of these ideas had been inchoate, half-formed; others were implied rather than explicit; still others were so direct as to be startling. What did Goldwater's loss mean to these ideas and their future? On the morning after Election Day, James Reston summed up this way:

Barry Goldwater not only lost the Presidential election yesterday but the conservative cause as well. He has wrecked his party for a long time to come and is not even likely to control the wreckage.

It is not only that he ran behind President Johnson by a larger popular majority than any other loser in the history of Presidential elections, but he ran so far behind the very progressives he scorned in his own party that he now faces a G.O.P. revolt against his leadership and associates in the Republican national and state organizations.

The only theory he proved is that part of the Deep South, particularly of the rural South, favors his policies of leaving the Negro revolution to the judgment of the states. His gamble that the North would put its prejudices against the Negro ahead of its conscience was disproved. His belief that the American

273

people would turn against the principles of social security at home and collective security abroad was rejected. Even the Middle Western Bible Belt, on which he centered his moral yearnings, turned against him.

The American people followed the historic voting pattern of the nation in yesterday's 45th Presidential election. In a time of comparative peace and prosperity, they voted once more for continuity rather than for radical change. They voted, as usual, for the incumbent President rather than for his opponent. Whatever their doubts, they went along with the welfare state at home and coexistence with the Communists overseas, rather than reverse the trend of the last generation.

Accordingly, Lyndon Baines Johnson of Texas, like Theodore Roosevelt, Calvin Coolidge and Harry S. Truman—the three other Americans who went to the White House in this century from the Vice Presidency—was elected by the people in his own right, and he was elected overwhelmingly.

The voters answered the major questions of the election quite clearly:

Would the United States reject the policy of trying to reach an honorable accommodation with the Communist world, despite all their disappointments since the last world war, and accept instead a more aggressive policy toward the Communist world? They said "No."

Would they go along with Barry Goldwater, the Republican nominee, in his efforts to reverse the trend toward centralized government direction of economic policy within the nation? Again, they seem to have said "No."

Would they intervene to oppose the efforts of the Supreme Court of the United States and the Congress to gain a more equal place for the Negro in American life? And their answer was "No."

The last question had been the one that concerned political analysts the most during the campaign. Most of the other issues could be measured with some degree of accuracy by public opinion sampling—and were. But the pollsters were not convinced that they could gauge the white backlash. The trouble was that voters who willingly gave their views on Social Security and nuclear weapons could not always be trusted on their answers to civil rights questions. A Northerner who opposed a law that would let a Negro buy the house next door would not always admit it. So, right down to Election Day, some poll takers and many others feared that there might be a larger, subterranean Goldwater vote in city neighborhoods of shifting racial complexion and in the suburbs, a movement that would rise to the surface only on Election Day and might confuse if not confound their predictions.

But it became clear early on the night of November 3 that this was not going to happen. Statistical sampling systems, like the Vote Profile Analysis (developed by C.B.S., I.B.M. and Louis Harris) which was used by The New York Times, demonstrated as the returns flowed in that the white backlash had very largely failed to materialize. In general, city and suburban areas that might have been sensitive to the civil rights issue gave Johnson just as strong, if not stronger, support than they had given Kennedy in 1960. Anthony Lewis of The Times wrote:

The white backlash had shown up during last spring's Presidential primaries, especially among heavy industrial workers, many of them Catholics of East European origin. Gov. George C. Wallace of Alabama carried such areas in Gary, Ind., and Baltimore.

Yesterday, Mr. Goldwater showed some gains over Mr. Nixon among Polish and other East European ethnic groups in Baltimore and the Indiana steel areas, and also in Ohio, Pennsylvania and Illinois.

He cut the Democratic margin by as much as 8 per cent in these districts— but there were just not enough of these precincts to matter very much.

Moreover, the signs of backlash among the Polish and East European ethnic groups were scattered. In New York, New Jersey and Connecticut, the trend among these groups was just the opposite. In New York, the Democratic margin in three substantially Polish precincts rose from 75 to 82 per cent. And it was up in Michigan and Wisconsin.

What this seemed to show was that the unpopularity of Mr. Goldwater had transcended all the usual ethnic and regional and economic categories of voters.

In no section of the country was the Republican trend away from the Republican Presidential candidate more pronounced than in the Northeast. In the New England states, once an impregnable G.O.P. preserve, one of every two Republicans deserted his party to vote for Johnson. Vermont, which had never supported a Democrat for President since becoming a state, gave more than 60 per cent of its votes to Johnson. In Maine, the only other state that had eluded Roosevelt in 1936, the Democratic vote of 68.8 per cent was among the highest in the country. And New Hampshire, where the 1964 campaign had opened and where Goldwater and Rockefeller had campaigned intensively, went for Johnson 63.6 per cent.

Attempts to measure the vote by religion produced some interesting contrasts with 1960, when, in the Southern and Border states, Kennedy lost some Protestant Democratic votes because of his Roman Catholic faith, while picking up some compensatory votes from Catholic Republicans in the urban centers of the Northeast and elsewhere. In 1964, apparently, Johnson regained the Protestant ground without losing the Catholic. In Kentucky, for example, typical Protestant districts that had voted 57 per cent for Nixon went 61 per cent for Johnson. At the same time, heavily Catholic precincts in Kentucky increased their Democratic margins from 65 per cent in 1960 to 75 per cent.

The South was the only exception to the proposition that Johnson had improved on Kennedy's showing with all segments of the population. But the South demonstrated that it was changing in more than one direction. On election night, John Herbers of The Times reported that President Johnson had carried a majority of Southern states by turning the normal voting patterns inside out. The rural Deep South, solidly Democratic in the past, had voted for Goldwater but the states on the border of the region, which had gone Republican in recent Presidential elections, returned to the Democrats.

After detailing the Republican conquests in the South—five states, forty-seven electoral votes, seven new Congressmen—Herbers concluded:

Despite Senator Goldwater's strong showing in the Deep South, the results clearly demonstrated that a Presidential candidate can no longer carry the South on the civil rights issue alone.

In virtually every state, the voting followed this pattern:

The urban and suburban areas that had been building Republican strength in recent years voted Democratic, partly on the basis of a rising Negro vote.

The rural "Black Belt," which previously had shunned the two-party system and voted Democratic, gave its votes to Senator Goldwater, almost purely on the race issue.

If Goldwater did not profit measurably from any white backlash in the North, he certainly suffered under the most severe black backlash of any Presidential candidate of this century. Negro precincts in New York and Maryland went 94 per cent Democratic, in Pennsylvania 96 per cent and in Ohio an almost unbelievable 99 per cent. These were not states that Johnson needed a good deal of help to carry, but the demonstrable appearance of such massive bloc voters was a pointed lesson to leaders of both parties. It taught Republicans that they could never win an election in those states with a candidate who, like Goldwater, aroused distrust and outright hostility in the Negro community.

In the South, the achievements of the Negro vote were the most impressive. Election night analysis indicated that votes cast by Negroes had prevented three states—Virginia, Tennessee and Florida—from casting their electoral votes for Goldwater. All these states had gone Republican in the three previous Presidential elections, but all went for Johnson. Two weeks after the election, the Southern Regional Council reported that Negro voters had also wielded the balance of power for Johnson in Arkansas and, probably, in North Carolina. The only Southern states in which the President had received a clear majority of the white vote taken by itself was his home state of Texas.

Who then voted for Goldwater? What kind of American had determinedly fought his way upstream against the onrushing consensus of almost every racial, religious, ethnic and economic group in the country? Ben A. Franklin of The Times asked the question and offered the best available answers:

An acknowledged broad statistical sketch of Goldwater voters, drawn with broad "average voter" strokes, discloses several main types under a general heading of "hard-core Republican." Not all of Mr. Goldwater's supporters were Republicans, but a large majority were. And not all his supporters fit into the categories.

. . . the average Goldwater voter was white. In the cities and towns, he was a young man on the rise professionally and financially.

On the farms, he was distinctly Southern. Among the aged, he was financially independent, reasonably secure without the help of Social Security. And among low income persons, he was a rarity.

The upper-income majorities the Senator won were somewhat smaller than those normally accorded a Republican Presidential candidate. Goldwater's support was pretty substantially Protestant. He received a majority of the Catholic vote in only one state—Mississippi—and of the Jewish vote in one other—his home state of Arizona. Among ethnic groups, the Senator got his highest percentages from voters of German and Scandinavian extraction, but he did not do as well with these groups, or with Polish and Italian voters, as Nixon had. Among women who had voted Republican in three successive elections, Goldwater was a failure. The Senator got only 38 per cent of the women's vote, the Gallup Poll reported later, compared to 51 for Nixon and 58 and 61 for Eisenhower. The women, in fact, were just a shade more enthusiastic about Johnson than the men, 62 per cent in the Democratic column compared to 60 for the male vote.

These statistics inevitably raised the broadest question of all: What had the two candidates done, or failed to do, in the campaign that had induced all kinds of people—except the rich and the unreconstructed Southerners—to support Johnson in such large numbers? Four years before, neither Kennedy nor Nixon had been able to command more than 50 per cent of the vote, and the difference between their national totals was measured in tenths of 1 per cent.

The reappraisal of the Goldwater campaign undertaken by its closest observers after it was over produced a summary something like this: Goldwater and his views stood apart from the majority of the American people from the beginning; rather than moving over to join the people, he invited them to move to join him; very few of them were prepared to take such a trip.

In retrospect, Goldwater had enjoyed the luxury of a clear majority only once in 1964: At the Cow Palace in San Francisco. But his majority had been within the ranks of his own party, a conceded minority itself. The ease with which it had been mustered, against the clumsiest opposition, made it look like much more of a consensus than it was. Goldwater, after all, had won exactly one contested primary, and that by a scant 51 per cent in one state, California. As a demonstration of national popularity, his nomination had really been something of a fraud. It had demonstrated two things: (1) That there were many states in which Republican leaders—if not voters—were initially favorable to Goldwater, and (2) that skilled, dedicated Goldwater strategists had been able to sign up Republicans who were likely to become convention delegates and then see that they were chosen for this service.

Presidential nominations are not infrequently captured by men who could not win a national popularity contest among members of their own party. Such nominees almost immediately move to reassure disaffected party elements. The one thing Goldwater really never did, from beginning to end, was to reassure anyone. In the first weeks of his active campaign for the nomination, he had set the divisive pattern: He proposed making the Social Security system voluntary, he aligned himself against the civil rights movement, he said he would consider breaking diplomatic relations with the Soviet Union to force such concessions as "free elections" in Eastern Europe and he suggested in his first major speech that the poor were in many ways to blame for their own poverty. The election demonstrated in the boldest terms, that these views were not calculated to attract Republican voters, much less the millions of Democrats and independents that a Republican candidate needs to win a national election.

If Goldwater had made a fundamental error by espousing—and in most cases sticking to—such radical positions, what had Johnson done in the campaign to capitalize on this weakness? In a post-election summary, Fendall W. Yerxa of The Times described the evolution of the Democratic approach this way:

> In shaping his campaign strategy, the President found in Senator Goldwater an antagonist who made his problem easy.
> Mr. Goldwater made it clear that his campaign would be based on dissent. Mr. Johnson, from the moment he had succeeded to the Presidency, had called for national unity.
> Mr. Goldwater could be counted on for hard negative criticism of the Administration. Mr. Johnson espoused positivism, holding out a vision of prosperous progress at home and peace abroad.
> Mr. Goldwater could be counted on to mount a personal campaign. Mr. Johnson had commanded Congress "to always debate principles, never debate personalities."
> Mr. Goldwater took an uncompromising stance that made it difficult to unify his party. Mr. Johnson invited Republicans to join with the Democrats.
> Mr. Goldwater indicated his aloofness from the voter, disdaining mingling with the crowds. "Meeting the people" became the most distinctive characteristic of the President's campaign.
> In short, the Goldwater campaign appeared to the Johnson strategists to be vulnerable in almost every sector.

One of the criticisms of the Goldwater campaign from his fellow Republicans, ironically enough, was that his managers did not spend enough. For the first time in memory, a major political party wound up a Presidential campaign with a surplus, provoking even some Republicans to comment ruefully that "the Democrats have a President, but we have money in the bank." Reports filed in Congress showed that various Republican groups had gathered $18,800,000 and spent $17,500,000 as of December 31, 1964; in the same period, the Democrats received $12,400,000 and spent $12,700,000. These reports, required by law, were obviously incomplete. As one official in Washington said, "When they wrote that law, the loopholes were built in, just like Swiss cheese." The best estimate of the total spending for the 1964 campaign, national, state and local, was about $200,000,000, with at least $40,000,000 going for national television time.

Not all this spending was for the Presidential campaign; large sums were also spent in the Congressional races. It was reported that $2,000,000 was spent in the Bobby Kennedy Senatorial race; Keating spent almost as much in losing. Even for seats in the House of Representatives, large sums were expended, $75,000 being a not uncommon figure. One successful candidate, Richard L. Ottinger, a Democrat in a strongly Republican district of Westchester and Putnam Counties in New York, spent almost $200,000, all strictly within the law. Publicity about expenditures of this magnitude raised questions about the law which was supposed to regulate campaign spending and, more important, about whether only rich men could afford to run for office.

Another aspect of the campaign that occupied post-election analysts was whether it really had been such a bitter struggle after all. In midsummer, both parties were freely predicting that it would be the dirtiest campaign in American political history. Looking back, it did not seem to measure up to this dubious distinction. Phrases such as "soft on communism" and words like "fascist" and "traitor" certainly are dirty words, but they had been used before. Charges of immorality in government circles were not new either, and even some Republicans displayed genuine restraint on the Jenkins case. The one new element that did seem to frighten people was the open proliferation of right-wing organizations and their well-financed support of Goldwater. After the election, which was clearly a repudiation of these forces, the question still remained: Would they disappear or would they renew their efforts, using as an argument that Goldwater, after all, did receive 27,000,000 votes?

Goldwater had a try himself at answering. On the morning after the election he rose early, composed his telegram of concession to Johnson, conferred with members of his staff and then drove, under brilliant Arizona sun, to the Camelback Inn. About a hundred well-wishers applauded and cheered as he approached the Peace Pipe Room, which, according to a poem on the wall, has "room for everything but gloom." Somewhat tired, Goldwater was still remarkably composed, considering the circumstances. The room was crowded with reporters and members of his staff, the men grim, some of the women crying.

He was applauded frequently as he made a brief statement and answered questions, making these points: That in 1968 he thought the Republicans would choose another man to run for President; that he intended to devote his time to strengthening the Republican party and that he did not think his defeat had hurt the conservative cause. (No one reminded him that before the campaign started he had said that if he could pull 45 per cent of the popular vote, the conservative movement would not be hurt, and that he had received only 38.5 per cent of the vote.)

He was asked about the future of conservatism:

QUESTION: Have the Republican voters not shared in repudiating this philosophy you say the party must cling to?

ANSWER: Well, unfortunately I think you're right—that my defeat to some degree, although, I would not say a major degree, was occasioned by Republicans in this country who did not vote for the—or work, I should say—for the top of the ticket. Now this is in direct contrast to times when the conservatives did not win at the convention, when we would go out and work our hearts out for the more liberal or moderate members of the Republican party.

But I don't—this is not a repudiation. This was announced. They announced as soon as the convention was over, and I think they're entitled to do what they want, but I don't think we can build a Republican party on their concepts, which in my opinion have no difference with the Democratic concepts.

Another issue that Goldwater addressed himself to was the role of the press. Was it true, as some of his supporters said, that he lost the election because the press distorted his views? At the Republican convention in San

Francisco, the outspoken hostility to newspaper and television reporters made some of them apprehensive. Then in the succeeding months, both Goldwater and Miller spoke in critical generalities about "columnists and commentators," and some of their followers organized campaigns of writing letters to editors, complaining, as it sometimes seemed, that the news reporters were quoting Goldwater accurately. At one meeting, a Goldwater supporter shouted to the press, "Don't quote what he says, say what he means."

At his farewell press conference, Goldwater elaborated a little his views on the press coverage of his campaign. He denounced newspaper, radio and television columnists who had criticized him, but he had a kind word for the working reporters who had covered his campaign, saying they had been fair. In criticizing the columnists, he said: "I have never in my life seen such inflammatory language as has been used by some men who know better, who should write better, who should have enough decency, common ordinary manners about them to know that no man in this country, for example, is ever going to start a war, that no man in this country is ever going to deny anybody what they have coming to them. I think these people should, frankly, hang their heads in shame because I think they have made the fourth estate a rather sad, sorry mess."

Goldwater's own analysis was only the first of many post-mortems and even he continued to produce further second thoughts. In an interview in *U.S. News & World Report,* Goldwater said he was beaten on July 15, when Rockefeller, Romney and Scranton—although he absolved Scranton for backing the ticket later—refused to unite behind him. "I think it made it virtually impossible for us to do anything to retain the Republicans that they, seemingly, influenced by the bomb scare and the Social Security scare," he said. Many Republicans agreed that Goldwater had indeed been beaten in San Francisco, but said it was because he had turned his back on any attempts to bring the moderates back into the fold. One Republican strategist, who had attended the Sunday campaign strategy sessions, had a simpler answer: "Poor strategy, poor content, poor delivery." A post-election survey for the Republicans disclosed what everyone knew by this time, that the major liability of the Republican campaign of 1964 was Barry Goldwater.

"The weaknesses of Goldwater virtually overshadowed all positive motivations for support of Johnson," the survey reported. It listed these other factors in Johnson's victory: "The advantages accruing to Johnson as the incumbent in a time of peace and prosperity; Johnson's record in office; Johnson's personal appeal; the legacy of John F. Kennedy; and Democratic party identification."

"The Republican Party
Has Been Hurt..."

Bitter, frustrated and shocked, the Republicans, surveyed the damage the Johnson flood had caused. It was as if the Pedernales had overflowed and swept the party down to the Gulf of Mexico. Apart from disaster in the national elections, more than 500 Republicans had gone down to defeat in lesser elections in the fifty states. The soul-searching—and backbiting—began. Within forty-eight hours after the election, Earl Mazo reported in The Times the developing party crisis:

Moderate Republican leaders and even a few conservatives, stung by the magnitude and backwash of President Johnson's victory, began a struggle yesterday to wrest control of the national party organization from supporters of Barry Goldwater.

Many Republicans agreed privately that Senator Goldwater's apparent intention of retaining the leadership of the national organization portended a harsh internal conflict that is not likely to be resolved for months.

The target of the G.O.P. moderates soon became clear: Dean Burch, chairman of the Republican National Committee. Goldwater himself was now out of public office, not even a member of the Senate after January 4. But Burch remained and it was Burch who symbolized Goldwater, who symbolized defeat, who symbolized all that was ideologically repulsive to the liberals and moderates and the professional politicians of the party seeking a "new look."

Returning to Washington, Goldwater was greeted by about fifty supporters on a windswept strip at Dulles International Airport. Looking composed and feeling "like a million dollars," he said Burch had done a very, very commendable job and should continue as chairman. He added it would be wrong to go off half-cocked with recommendations and suggestions now regarding the party's future. Then Goldwater and his closest associates, including Burch and Miller, decided to think it all over by going to Montego Bay, Jamaica, to fish, golf, swim, sun themselves on the beach, and work on ways to save Burch's job.

Back home, there were pleas to keep Burch, with Goldwater supporters contending that, in spite of the crushing defeat, the Republican party had at least been returned to the custody of conservatives, its rightful inheritors, and it should never be allowed to revert to a "me-too" shadow of the Democratic party. There were private talks among others on the best way to ease Burch out, to create the new image the party desperately needed, and to destroy the racist, right-wing mold into which it had fallen. The anti-Burch callers were emphatic: The party must be a home for all Republicans from conservative to liberal.

The bickering continued publicly in these days following November 3:

Richard M. Nixon—"I know as a loser what it means. So I urge my fellow Republicans to take into account that Goldwater deserves a cooling-off period before the great battle for leadership of the party begins. . . . The blood is still too hot and we're too close to the disaster. . . . There is a strong conservative wing of the Republican party. It deserves a major voice in party councils, and the liberal wing deserves a party voice, but neither can dominate or dictate—the center must lead. . . . [Rockefeller] had his pound of flesh and I do not think that he can exert leadership out of New York. . . . [He] pledged, as did Senator Goldwater, that he would support the winner. After he lost he proceeded to drag his feet. . . . He was a spoilsport . . . a party divider."

Nelson A. Rockefeller—"This kind of peevish post-election utterance has unfortunately become typical of Mr. Nixon. It is neither factual nor constructive. The nomination of the Goldwater-Miller ticket divided the Republican party so severely that despite the efforts of Republican state organizations like New York, the nation rejected the national ticket by unprecedented pluralities. . . . My difference and those of other moderate Republicans with Senator Goldwater were not personal but were matters of principle. . . ."

George Romney—"Obviously there is great need in this situation to broaden and unify the party. [But] you don't broaden the party by kicking a lot of people out."

Dwight D. Eisenhower—"The Republican party has been hurt, but not irretrievably. We need now to consult among ourselves as to methods for correcting the false image of Republicanism which, far too long, has confused so many of our citizens and led them to think of it as a political doctrine designed primarily for the rich and privileged. . . . This I believe is the proper time to remind ourselves and the country that we are the party of Lincoln. We remain true to his concepts of human liberty, dignity and equality. . . ."

William W. Scranton—"[I intend] to join with other like-minded Republicans to make it clear that the party of Lincoln is a great national party, eager to return to its heritage and welcome all Americans to our ranks. . . . Apparently many Americans during the recent campaign gained the impression the Republican party was opposed or indifferent to so-called ethnic or minority groups."

Henry Cabot Lodge—"We Republicans must rebuild our party. . . . We need a program that will accomplish the goals toward which the country is trying to move, and not demagoguery, and on that basis the voters were not offered a choice this time. . . . There is a small minority trying to move us back to the nineteenth century system of having one party represent one point of view and the other something opposite. . . . A true conservative is ready to accept new developments and to innovate them."

On the beach in Jamaica, Goldwater and his colleagues came to a decision: They would fight to the end to hold the Republican leadership. At a news conference on the sun-baked veranda of the Half Moon Hotel's golf club, Goldwater said Burch had been elected for a four-year term and had, in effect, a contract. "I would expect the Republican party to live up to it," he added. Looking rugged and relaxed (and patriotic) in red slacks, white polo shirt, blue tennis shoes and a floppy wool hat, he also put forth a suggestion that caught even his colleagues by surprise. He said the country needed a real realignment of the political parties into two new groups. "The time has come to choose up two new teams and get going," he declared, suggesting that they be called the Liberals and the Conservatives.

Some Goldwater friends and supporters tried out a little "reverse-think" by asserting that 27,000,000 votes was really a vote of support for conservatism. But that was before polls estimated that the hard core votes for Goldwater amounted to about 5,000,000. Most of the others, these surveys estimated, voted for Goldwater, although they had doubts about him, out of loyalty to the Republican party. Another 2,000,000 were said to have come from the South because of Goldwater's vote against the 1964 Civil Rights Act.

But the anti-Goldwater forces rejected all his arguments. Among those leading the early fight was Governor Robert E. Smylie of Idaho, who called a meeting of the Republican Governors Association he headed. "In the face of the greatest disaster in the modern history of Presidential elections, surviving leaders of our party have to regroup and revitalize the party machinery," he said. "We have to do this regionally and nationally—and soon—if we are to fight again and win." At their June meeting, the Republican governors had fallen on their gubernatorial faces before an onrushing Goldwater bandwagon. Now it was December and they were more determined. They met in Denver and issued a statement calling for a complete remodeling of the party's national organization and for a major role by governors in rebuilding and leading the party from then on. Earl Mazo reported:

The governors went beyond the question of removing Dean Burch as national chairman. They proposed that the national committee itself be totally revamped to include governors, members of Congress, young Republicans and others representing "all the basic strength of the party."

Regarding Mr. Burch, the statement, which did not specifically mention him, was interpreted by the overwhelming majority of governors as meaning he should be removed as chairman. . . .

The declaration was adopted over the strong objections of Gov. Paul Fannin of Arizona who flew to Denver last night and argued for more than three hours against any criticism, implied or otherwise, of Mr. Goldwater's leadership or any effort designed to oust Mr. Burch.

Early this morning he grudgingly consented to the statement, insisting the "leadership" paragraph did not apply to Mr. Burch anyway. . . .

But Governor Rockefeller of New York insisted that the paragraph was a call for Mr. Burch's removal and said, "If it isn't, you can shoot me."

The critical paragraph read as follows: "The first step in marshaling Republican party strength for the future must be the uniting of Republicans themselves. Any policy of exclusion must be changed and cannot be tolerated. We strongly recommend to the national committee that, in determining its leadership at the forthcoming meeting in January, it adopt leadership which clearly represents a broad view of Republicanism and practices a policy of inclusion, rather than exclusion."

However, Burch didn't view the resolution the way most of the governors did. He endorsed the statement as a request for new policymaking machinery but added that he would fight for his job. He said he had discussed the governors' actions with Goldwater, who concurred in the aims and goals. At the same time, Burch announced the resignation—obviously a reluctant one—of John Grenier, a top Goldwater strategist, as executive director of the national committee.

Seeking a way out to end the blossoming dissension, Goldwater requested a meeting with Eisenhower and Nixon. With Burch waiting outside the door, the three met privately in Eisenhower's suite at the Waldorf Towers in New York. They agreed, in essence, that if Burch could not achieve a broad base of support within the party before the national committee meeting in Chicago on January 22, he should step aside as chairman. Eisenhower also advanced his idea for a two-man leadership of the party—the chairman to deal with organization and a leader of equal status to serve as spokesman on policy and issues. The General suggested that the leadership crisis could be solved with the selection of a strong, generally acceptable figure like Ray C. Bliss of Ohio as national chairman. He also thought a well-known, highly respected Republican like Walter H. Judd of Minnesota should be chosen as party spokesman.

Eisenhower's use of the name Ray Bliss gave new support to a movement that had already been started to give him Burch's job. On December 28, Joseph Loftus in The Times reported from Washington:

Republican leaders who want Dean Burch removed as national chairman are coalescing behind Ray C. Bliss, the Ohio party chairman, as a replacement.

Several national committee members acknowledged this today. They also said they were sure Mr. Bliss would accept, implying that they had received his consent to go ahead with a quiet campaign in his behalf.

Two days before, Goldwater had written to all the members of the national committee saying, "I feel the removal of Dean Burch now . . . would be a repudiation of a great segment of our party and a repudiation of me." Burch himself sent a hopeful letter, outlining three things to which he was dedicated: "the unity, the strength and the achievements of the Republican party, across the board and throughout the nation." But Burch was fighting a losing battle.

During the first week of 1965, Bliss and Donald R. Ross, a Nebraska national committeeman, called on Goldwater in his Washington apartment. In effect, they urged him to bring peace to the party by proposing that Bliss become the new chairman. Whatever his decision, Goldwater was informed, Bliss would be nominated anyway.

Goldwater, however, was still holding out for Burch, as were some of the hard-core conservatives in his political entourage. But other important Goldwater supporters, particularly Bill Miller and George M. Humphrey, argued in favor of Bliss, the neutral and non-ideological professional politician from Ohio, as the only man upon whom all factions could unite. On Thursday night of that week, a dozen Republican leaders, including Goldwater, met for a briefing on a confidential post-election poll that reported, among other things, that fewer than 25 per cent of the Republican voters now wanted Goldwater to continue at the party's helm.

There was no further argument. A tentative decision was reached at a meeting between Goldwater, Miller and Burch on Friday that Goldwater would publicly urge the national committee to accept Burch's resignation and elect Bliss. The change would be effective April 1, with the delay becoming a face-saving device.

On Saturday, Goldwater left Washington and flew to his home at Phoenix. By then, the plan was fully accepted. As part of it, Bliss announced on January 11 that he would not accept the chairmanship unless Goldwater asked him to do so. The next day, on the same patio of his Phoenix home where he had declared his Presidential candidacy a year before, Goldwater hauled down his flag of leadership and announced that Burch would resign April 1 and Bliss had agreed to succeed him. Goldwater, Miller, Burch and Bliss all smiled and shook hands, and then read statements of unity.

The Times' News of the Week in Review summed up the Goldwater decision as follows:

Mr. Goldwater's decision represented a choice between two brands of conservatism—on the one hand, the hard-core rightists who had assumed command of the party after his nomination; on the other, the old-line party members who backed his candidacy out of loyalty to the party's nominee.

By accepting Mr. Bliss, he sided with the old-liners in what he said was the interest of party unity, and thereby rejected the rightists' contention that abandonment of Mr. Burch would be a betrayal of that cause.

The expected happened at the national committee meeting on January 22. The fifty-seven-year-old Bliss, a party organization man with no particular ties to either the liberal or conservative wing, a technician in politics since he accepted his first precinct job in 1932, was elected as the new $30,000-a-year national committee chairman. Burch turned in his resignation with regret and said he would go back to practicing law in Tucson.

Addressing the national committee, Goldwater accepted full responsibility for his defeat in the race and absolved Burch of any blame. He was far from humble, jabbing at times at President Johnson, but he said: "I'm sorry I couldn't produce better results. I'm sorry that so many good men . . . went down with me."

It took weeks of doing, but the Republican party machinery was patched up. Some observers felt that the party had been split irrevocably, that the conservative ideologues, having tasted power, would not be content to sit back and support a moderate; others pointed out that political parties have a habit of springing back from defeat. Whatever the guesses about the future of the party, there was also speculation about the future of Barry Goldwater. Two days after the national committee met, The Times carried this story by Earl Mazo:

Republican leaders in Arizona and elsewhere are almost certain that Barry Goldwater will run for Senator from Arizona again at the first opportunity.

Another Ending,
Another Beginning

On the morning of January 20, 1965, Lyndon B. Johnson awoke at 6:45 and, still in bed, consulted with two aides, Bill Moyers and Jack Valenti, about last-minute changes in his inaugural address. He worked with them for almost an hour, making minor revisions. Then he showered, shaved and put on a dark blue suit. He joined Mrs. Johnson for breakfast, eating light, a piece of Crenshaw melon and some tea. He read his secret daily intelligence briefing and skimmed through the morning papers a little more rapidly than usual. In The Times that morning, Tom Wicker had written about the day:

WASHINGTON, Jan. 19—Another man might have been standing up at noon tomorrow to take the oath as President of the United States. But circumstance won't have it so, and it is Lyndon Baines Johnson of Texas who will lead the nation for the next four years. Jan. 20, 1965, was a date to which John Kennedy looked forward. He was aware of Jefferson's dictum that "great innovations should not be forced on slender majorities," and he was inhibited by the narrowness of his own election victory, and the tenuous grip on Congress it gave him.

So he looked forward to the second term he was confident he could win, particularly as it began to appear more likely that Barry Goldwater of Arizona would be his opponent. It was to be the term of the great achievements that political deadlock and foreign crises had prevented in his first.

But an assassin's bullet changed everything and now the next four years and the great hopes are Lyndon Johnson's.

How do they differ, these two men who will share in history the credit or the blame for a great nation's leadership in what may prove to be one of the crucial decades of an era? Aside from the obvious divergences of appearance and voice and manner, what has been changed fundamentally by Mr. Johnson's accession to the role fate took from John Kennedy?

Not the program Mr. Johnson saw through to completion last year, nor the one he has proposed in his own right this year. Not their fundamental aims; in fact, Mr. Johnson regards his own election as having been a national endorsement of domestic and foreign policies that he inherited from Mr. Kennedy and that to some extent Mr. Kennedy inherited from his own predecessors.

The real change is in the approaches of the two men to the great office that passed from one to the other on Nov. 22, 1963. One way to describe the difference may be as follows:

Mr. Kennedy made demands; Mr. Johnson makes promises. Mr. Kennedy preached sacrifice; Mr. Johnson proffers affluence. Mr. Kennedy said, "You must." Mr. Johnson says, "You can."

"The principal power that the President has," Harry S. Truman said, "is to bring people in and try to persuade them to do what they ought to do without persuasion. That's what I spend most of my time doing. That's what the powers of the President amount to."

The question, then, is political: How to persuade men "to do what they ought to do without persuasion."

One question the student of the Kennedy years must grapple with is how he achieved such great personal popularity without at the same time building up overwhelming support for his domestic proposals. Aside from the obvious fact of his thin Congressional majorities, there may be at least two explanations.

One is that Mr. Kennedy's appeal for sacrifice and struggle, his frequent references to "difficult years" that might get worse before they got better, his habit of questioning myths and assumptions, his repugnance for political posturing and easy answers, his youth and fire, had a divided effect.

To idealistic young people, to skeptical intellectuals, to Americans weary of the materialism and mass culture of their society, he struck all the right notes. They listened to his eloquence, were fascinated by his style, approved of his distinction and his wit.

To the most powerful interests of the country, however—even to business leaders who shared the national fascination with the glamour of the first family— the same qualities were unsetting. Mr. Kennedy seemed to threaten stability, or at least the status quo. He disturbed them with a new economics, spent tax money too freely, and attacked cherished notions and prerogatives.

The second explanation is that Mr. Kennedy, more than most, was also handicapped by the dual nature of his office. The panoply and attention that surrounds any President—for instance, his ability to command an instant audience on television—tends to elevate him beyond human stature into something like a national symbol. When that symbol is challenged or insulted at home or abroad— as, for instance, when Dwight D. Eisenhower was vilified by Nikita Khrushchev during the U-2 crisis—the nation rallies instantly to his support.

Mr. Kennedy's remarkable personal appeal, his photogenic self and family, and their knack for making interesting headlines, placed him perhaps even more than Mr. Eisenhower had been at the center of the national consciousness. All eyes were fixed on him for three years.

But when any President steps out of his role as a national symbol and unifier, and speaks out as a partisan leader in favor of or against particular solutions to domestic problems, he seems to many Americans to have abandoned his right character and to have demeaned his office. He becomes a politician.

Thus, if Mr. Kennedy was higher than most Presidents in public esteem as the national leader and symbol, he had all the further to fall when he became a partisan and an advocate of a particular program. In the latter role, driving down steel prices, arguing the cause of the Negro in a Boston accent, defending budget deficits, he antagonized and divided even some of those who admired the figure he cut.

"In the wider national interest," he said at Yale, "we need not partisan wrangling but common concentration on common problems." But his became a time of intense partisan wrangling, not least because of his conviction that "the great enemy of the truth is . . . the myth."

Circumstances that he quickly seized, together with his own approach, gave Mr. Johnson a chance to create a different atmosphere. He never has achieved—perhaps never will—Mr. Kennedy's personal popularity. But he has been able to diminish sharply the gap between his role as national leader and his work as partisan leader.

For instance, chance took him into office at a time of domestic crisis in race relations. As a Southerner himself, Mr. Johnson could hardly have hoped to win election at such a time; when he took power by accident, however, he was in a sound position to press forward on the civil rights program but to offer conciliation and friendship to the South in a Southerner's voice and idiom. He was able to substitute national leadership for partisan or sectional leadership in a way no non-Southerner could have done.

Again, it was Mr. Johnson's fate—or fortune—to be pitted in 1964 against the divisive and, to many Americans, foreboding Presidential candidacy of Barry Goldwater. Mr. Johnson seized upon the race as opportunity. For the first time since the New Deal, a Democratic President could campaign on a liberal Democratic platform and still be the "safe" candidate, the one who least threatened stability and continuity.

The radical nature of Mr. Goldwater's candidacy gave Mr. Johnson an almost unlimited chance to picture himself as a national leader advancing a national program that could command wide support in both parties and in all sections. The immediate result was the greatest election majority in American history, achieved through enormous Republican defections to the Johnson-Humphrey ticket.

A more far-reaching result may be that Mr. Johnson has been enabled to maintain the position of national leader in his actual conduct of his office. Aided by his election victory and by the shattering of the Republican party, as well as by his huge majorities in Congress, he has seldom resorted—so far—to purely partisan leadership or tactics.

Thus, it is Lyndon Johnson who has been given the opportunity to take the lead in that "common concentration on common problems" that eluded John Kennedy.

The opportunity did not arise entirely through happenstance. Mr. Johnson's natural inclinations neatly complemented the circumstances in which he found himself. All his life a politician of the massive middle, who could point to a liberal record and a conservative record, Mr. Johnson's primary instinct was to reach out in all directions, for every hand.

He has attacked almost no person or group except the right wing—and certainly has disturbed few myths. He woos as ardently as Mr. Kennedy debated. His vision is of Americans marching shoulder to shoulder toward the future, not of inevitable conflict and a struggle that will get worse before it gets better. In advancing the cause of any group or interest, he seeks to stop short of an open threat to any other.

He propounds no grand concepts; the Great Society seems to be one that will simply seek its solutions in the Johnsonian manner, and the "war on poverty" is only a clever label for stepped-up economic and education programs.

But conceptions can be imprisoning. On the evidence of his speech to the National Press Club during his campaign, Mr. Kennedy came to the White House with a strongly developed conception of what a President should be and how he should act. Sometimes it seemed that the conception, rather than the circumstance in which he found himself, was guiding his actions.

Mr. Johnson, on the other hand, has made the Presidency fit not only circumstances but also his own experience and inclinations. That approach may not always work, either, and the really hard challenges are yet to come. But it was Lyndon Johnson, not John Kennedy, who brought railroad management and labor together at last, who closed dozens of surplus military bases and won both Congress and business by convincing them that he was serious about economy, who reversed the long slide of the foreign aid program toward oblivion, and who put a new vitality into the Congressional-Executive relationship.

His leadership may not seem so bold or demanding or inspiring as Mr. Kennedy's but it has persuaded some men to do what they ought to do without persuasion and thus it serves the good wishes of the nation, at least on Inauguration Day.

At 8:55, wearing no hat or coat despite the cold weather (but with thermal underwear under his suit), Johnson left the White House for the first ceremony in a long, eventful day. Accompanied by Mrs. Johnson, who was dressed in an American Beauty red wool coat with a wide Puritan collar and a wide-brimmed roller hat, and their two daughters, he attended a special inter-denominational prayer service at the National City Christian Church. It was so crowded that many of the 1,200 persons who attended had to stand along the walls. The Reverend Floyd S. Smith, the associate pastor, read one of the President's favorite passages from the Scriptures, one that he frequently quotes, an admonition from the prophet Isaiah, "Come let us reason together."

An hour later, the President was back in the White House. He changed his dark blue suit for a dark Oxford grey one—gone by his own orders were the morning coats and top hats of previous inaugurations. He and Mrs. Johnson spent some time with the twenty-two relatives and friends from Texas who had been invited to stay in the White House for the inauguration—sisters, brothers, cousins, aunts, nieces and nephews, and in-laws. The mood, according to a White House spokesman, was of "great, great joy."

In The New York Times Magazine the preceding Sunday, James Reston tried to define the man who was preparing to take the Presidential oath:

Lyndon Baines Johnson is to the politics of America what his State of Texas is to the other states. He is a gargantuan figure; he is a whopper. Measuring him for history is like measuring an active volcano with an inch-tape. He barbecues people who try and eats them for breakfast.

When you interview him, he ends up with your life story. He does not want to be analyzed or classified; he wants to be loved. Anything you say he said, he can usually neutralize with something else he said on the other side. If you say he's liberal, he can prove he's conservative, or vice versa. If you suggest he's from the South, he will insist he's from the West, or the other way around. If you don't tell the precise truth about him, which is almost inevitable, he thinks you are dishonest, and if you do, he feels you are disloyal.

This, however, is the caricature of Mr. Johnson and, like all caricatures, it magnifies one feature and minimizes all the rest. It is amusing, but it is unfair. The big slouching Texas Ranger on the ranch, the master politician on the telephone, the restless, sleepless "arm-twister," trading favors for votes in the smoky back room—all so dear to the cartoonists—are all true, but misleading.

He is more than that—far more. It is too early to say that he is a leader of men in the classic sense of being "quick to know and to do the things that the hour and his nation need," particularly in the foreign field. He has not yet proved that he can get and keep and inspire the best men in the nation to serve him, or even that he has mastered the art of using his staff and his time effectively. But he is a shrewd and knowledgeable man, an elemental force of nature who commands respect and even a certain amount of fear.

"When you come into the presence of a leader of men," Woodrow Wilson observed, "you know you have come into the presence of fire—that it is best not incautiously to touch that man—that there is something that makes it dangerous to cross him."

Johnson conveys this feeling and it is both his strength and weakness. His technique works but it hurts. He can make men do what he wants them to do but he does not make them like it or him in the process. There is a kind of intimidating shamelessness about him that makes men feel that if they don't go along there may be the most frightful and embarrassing row. But he is a highly intelligent man who is not to be dismissed as just another brilliant political operator. . . .

Since his spectacular victory in November he has seemed more calm, as if he had tamed his inner demons at last. He is not a deeply religious man, and his attitude toward life was little changed by his heart attack in 1955, but it would be surprising if he were not now affected by the startling change in his fortunes.

At 45, he was convinced that he was as well prepared for the Presidency as any man in his party. At 52, he was denied the nomination because of what he regarded, with some bitterness, as prejudice against his Southern background. At 55, all was changed by the assassination of President Kennedy, precisely when Mr. Johnson had finally concluded he would never reach the White House.

This is the central paradox of his story. The things he planned and manipulated in pursuit of the Presidency failed, and the thing he did not plan—he took the Vice Presidency for the sake of the party and against the opposition of his wife—carried him in the end to the top.

He does not talk about the election now; he doesn't even analyze the results, as he analyzed the polls before the vote. He merely talks unity, and who is to say at this moment that he is wrong? "The art of free society," wrote Alfred North Whitehead, "consists first in the maintenance of the symbolic code, and secondly, in the fearlessness of revision. . . . Those societies which cannot combine reverence to their symbols with freedom of revision must ultimately decay."

This is Johnson's theme and method. He does not study these things; they are in his bones. Kennedy's purpose was to make men think; Johnson's is to make men act. Both were reformers but went about it in different ways. Kennedy demanded reforms by challenging the conformists; Johnson got Kennedy's reforms by seeming to be a conformist himself.

At 11:15, Johnson and his wife walked out of the north portico of the White House accompanied by Senator B. Everett Jordan of North Carolina, who was the chairman of the Joint Congressional Inaugural Committee. They climbed into an armored Lincoln Continental limousine with bullet-proof glass top— the same car in which (without the top) Kennedy had been shot—and drove up Pennsylvania Avenue, where the stands for the parade were just beginning to fill. At the Capitol, he was ushered into a ground-floor room to wait for the moment to make his entrance onto the inaugural stand.

Under a bright sunny sky, the inaugural platform at the east front of the Capitol was filled with members of the government and other notables. At about 11:30, Mrs. Johnson and Mrs. Humphrey came down the great stairs and took their places. Next came Humphrey, bare-headed, accompanied by John McCormack, Speaker of the House of Representatives. Humphrey walked over to Mrs. Johnson and kissed her on the cheek and then took his place. At 11:40, Johnson appeared, still without an overcoat and hat despite the cold. He walked briskly down the steps and joined Mrs. Johnson.

A few minutes before noon, Humphrey raised his right hand, placed his left hand on a Bible belonging to his wife's family and repeated the oath of office intoned by McCormack. For the first time since November 22, 1963, the nation had a Vice President. Humphrey shook Johnson's hand and then kissed his wife.

At 12:03, Johnson stepped forward and faced the Chief Justice of the United States, Earl Warren, in his black judicial gown. Between them stood Mrs. Johnson, holding a Bible that had been given to her and her husband thirteen years before by his mother, inscribed "To Lyndon and Lady Bird, love, Mother." It had been used when Johnson took the oath of office as Vice President four years before, but this was the first time in the history of Presidential inaugurations that a wife had held the Bible for her husband.

For a moment at the start of the oath, both Johnson and Warren forgot to raise their right hands. But then they remembered and Johnson repeated after Warren the words that made him the President, "I, Lyndon Baines Johnson, do solemnly swear that I will faithfully execute the office of the President of the United States and will to the best of my ability preserve, protect and defend the Constitution of the United States." And then he added, "So help me God." It was 12:04 in the afternoon. Mrs. Johnson, who had not moved her eyes from her husband, smiled, but tears filled her eyes. She put her hand on his arm and they looked at each other for a few seconds, as if they were having a private conversation.

Johnson moved to the microphones and began his inauguration speech, about 1,500 words, one of the shortest on record, at a slow pace, with few gestures. He spoke in broad terms, for twenty-two minutes, defining the nation's aspirations as "man's dominion over tyranny and misery."

James Reston commented in The Times:

WASHINGTON, Jan. 20—President Johnson's Inauguration was a dramatization of the American Dream. It was all there, "bigger and better" than ever before: The poor boy, the country boy at the pinnacle of the world; the lovely wife holding the Bible for the oath; the eternal American combination of religion and politics; and above all, the optimism of America transmitted by a man-made satellite in the sky to a distracted and pessimistic world.

The ceremony was one long paradox: A sermon and a circus; a prayer and a parade; the Bible and the ballyhoo. Change is our problem, said the 36th President of the United States; reason and faith our shield; unity our only hope—this thrown out with painfully slow evangelical overtones to an unreasoning, skeptical and disunited world.

The echoes of past Presidential inaugurals were unmistakable today. "The problems are new," said Teddy Roosevelt in his Inaugural Address, "the tasks before us differ from the tasks set before our fathers who founded and preserved this republic."

"Ours is a time of change," said President Johnson, "rapid, and fantastic

Top:
Staebler proved unable to drape
Goldwater around Romney's neck.
(United Press International photo)

Bottom:
"You can't get anywhere
attacking Grandpa."
(The New York Times photo)

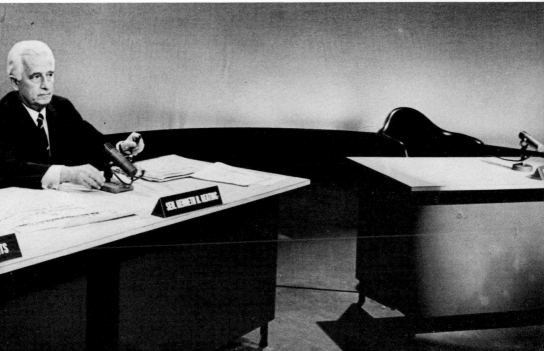

Top:
"His name is Barry Goldwater," the voice went on,
"so if he's elected, they might start
testing all over again."
(Doyle, Dane and Bernbach, Inc., photo)

Bottom:
"You have probably been reading and hearing about
some of the unorthodox things I have been doing."
(United Press International photo)

Stunned, the President could not believe the report,
but finally, reluctantly, he agreed there
was no other course but to demand Jenkins's resignation.
(Between Mr. and Mrs. Johnson is
the hand of Robert F. Kennedy.)
(Associated Press photo)

Left:
And then, through what leaders of both parties
later regarded as an incredible stroke of pure luck...
Peking announced that Red China had exploded
its first atomic bomb.
(United Press International photo)

Right:
1972?
(photo by George Tames, The New York Times)

Negro precincts in New York and Maryland
went 94 per cent Democratic, in Pennsylvania 96 per cent
and in Ohio an almost unbelievable
99 per cent....
(photo by Jay Leviton)

Right:
"You take an oath,
step into an office,
and must then help guide
a great democracy."
(photo by Yoichi Okamoto)

Opposite top left:
The room was crowded
with reporters and
members of his staff,
the men grim,
some of the women
sobbing quietly.
(The New York Times photo)

Opposite top right:
November 4, 1964.
Meanwhile,
back at the ranch...
(Associated Press photo)

Opposite bottom:
January 20, 1965,
12:04 P.M.
(Associated Press photo)

Following page:
*(photo by George Tames,
The New York Times)*

change, baring the secrets of nature, multiplying the nations, placing in uncertain hands new weapons for mastery and destruction, shaking old values and uprooting old ways."

"These dark days," said Franklin D. Roosevelt in his first depression Inaugural Address, "will be worth all they cost us if they teach us that our true destiny is not to be ministered unto but to minister to ourselves and to our fellow men."

John F. Kennedy said it better in his famous statement, "Ask not what your country can do for you—ask what you can do for your country."

And Lyndon Johnson reiterated the same theme today.

"Each of us," he said, "must find a way to advance the purpose of the nation, and thus find new purpose for ourselves. Without this, we will simply become a nation of strangers."

The parallels could be extended a dozen times in the inaugural addresses from Washington to Johnson—and even to the words of that tragic Johnson who followed Lincoln into the White House—but the question about today's Inaugural Address was clear enough.

Is it reasonable to apply reason to an unreasoning world? Will a divided and disbelieving world listen to the counsels of unity and faith?

Lyndon Johnson was his mother's son today—an unbeliever who believes in believing. In the poignant moment of commitment, he went back to the eternal things: justice, liberty, and unity. He was William Jennings Bryan on the Chautauqua circuit. He was Franklin Roosevelt telling us that we believed what he wanted us to believe and what we probably should believe.

"We are one nation and one people," he said. "Our fate as a nation and our future as a people rests not upon one citizen but upon all citizens. This is the majesty and the meaning of this moment."

Nobody who watched him up close could doubt his sincerity. He was tanned and strongly masculine. He spoke every word as if it were his last. He was asserting that the faith of the old frontier could be relevant and even triumphant on the new frontier of science and regional and international contention.

And he went beyond this: He asserted that in a land of great wealth, families must not live in hopeless poverty, that in such a land, rich in harvest, children must not go hungry; that in a country of healing miracles, neighbors must not suffer and die untended; that in a nation of learning, young people must see the glories of knowledge.

"The American covenant," he said, "called on us to help show the way for the liberation of man. And that is our goal today. . . . Justice requires us to remember—when any citizen denies his fellow, saying, 'His color is not mine,' or 'His beliefs are strange and different'—in that moment he betrays America, though his forebears created this nation."

What he was saying was said many years ago by other men in other times. "And I saw a new heaven and a new earth, for the first heaven and the first earth were passed away," it says in Revelations. "Is our world gone?" President Johnson asked. "We say farewell. Is a new world coming? We welcome it—and we will bend it to the hopes of man."

Obviously, a weary and disillusioned world does not believe that America will bend this radically changing world to the "hopes of man" or that Lyndon Johnson or anybody else can liberate the human race or produce "justice and unity" upon earth.

But the inauguration of an American President is one of the few remaining ceremonies of man's hopes and dreams. It is a time for talking as Lyndon Johnson did today about "the uncreased desert and the unclimbed ridge, the star not reached and the harvest sleeping in the unplowed ground."

He was talking in the old American idiom today. "Have the elder races halted?"

Walt Whitman asked. "Do they droop and end their lesson, wearied over there beyond the seas? We take up the task eternal, and the burden and the lesson, pioneers! O pioneers!"

All the hoopla—the high school bands, the Tournament of Roses atmosphere, the blue-kneed twirlers, the red-faced pols, the cheerful guests, rendering unto Lyndon the things that are Lyndon's, and the preachers rendering unto God the things that are God's—merely adds to the main point of an American inaugural, namely, that America is still young enough to hope and dream and believe.

The rest of the world, having lived longer and suffered more, may think it is all a little naïve, but they probably accept Lyndon Johnson's promise: "I will lead and I will do the best I can."

Thus the election of 1964 reached its end. Lyndon Johnson had climbed the road to the White House and there he was, as he said in his State of the Union message, with no special gift of prophesy or foresight. "You take an oath, step into an office, and must then help guide a great democracy," he said. The hardest job of the President was not to do what is right, he said, but to know what is right. And then he told how he found the answers to what was right in the land where he was born:

It was once barren land. The angular hills were covered with scrub cedar and few live oaks. Little would grow in the harsh caliche soil. And each spring the Pedernales River would flood the valley.

But men came and worked and endured and built.

Today that country is abundant with fruit, cattle, goats and sheep. There are pleasant homes and lakes, and the floods are gone.

Why did men come to that once forbidding land?

Well, they were restless, of course, and had to be moving on. But there was more than that. There was a dream—a dream of a place where a free man could build for himself, and raise his children to a better life—a dream of a continent to be conquered, a world to be won, a nation to be made.

Remembering this, I knew the answer.

A President does not shape a new and personal vision of America.

He collects it from the scattered hopes of the American past.

It existed when the first settlers saw the coast of a new world, and when the first pioneers moved westward.

It has guided us every step of the way.

It sustains every President. But it is also your inheritance and it belongs equally to the people we serve.

It must be interpreted anew by each generation for its own needs; as I have tried, in part, to do today.

It shall lead us as we enter this third century of the search for "a more perfect Union."

THE VOTE FOR PRESIDENT—1964

State	Total Vote	Johnson	(per cent)	Goldwater	(per cent)
Alabama	689,817	(1) ——	——	479,085	69.5
Alaska	67,259	44,329	65.9	22,930	34.1
Arizona	480,783	237,765	49.5	242,536	50.4
Arkansas	560,426	314,197	56.1	243,264	43.4
California	7,050,985	4,171,877	59.2	2,879,108	40.8
Colorado	772,749	476,024	61.6	296,725	38.4
Connecticut	1,218,578	826,269	67.8	390,996	32.1
Delaware	201,334	122,704	60.9	78,093	38.8
District of Columbia	198,597	169,796	85.5	28,801	14.5
Florida	1,854,481	948,540	51.1	905,941	48.9
Georgia	1,139,157	522,557	45.9	616,600	54.1
Hawaii	207,271	163,249	78.8	44,022	21.2
Idaho	292,477	148,920	50.9	143,557	49.1
Illinois	4,702,779	2,796,833	59.5	1,905,946	40.5
Indiana	2,091,606	1,170,848	56.0	911,118	43.6
Iowa	1,184,539	733,030	61.9	449,148	37.9
Kansas	857,901	464,028	54.1	386,579	45.1
Kentucky	1,046,132	669,659	64.0	372,977	35.7
Louisiana	896,293	387,068	43.2	509,225	56.8
Maine	380,965	262,264	68.8	118,701	31.2
Maryland	1,116,407	730,912	65.5	385,495	34.5
Massachusetts	2,344,798	1,786,422	76.2	549,727	23.4
Michigan	3,203,102	2,136,615	66.7	1,060,152	33.1
Minnesota	1,554,462	991,117	63.8	559,624	36.0
Mississippi	409,038	52,591	12.9	356,447	87.1
Missouri	1,817,879	1,164,344	64.0	653,535	36.0
Montana	278,628	164,246	58.9	113,032	40.6
Nebraska	584,154	307,307	52.6	276,947	47.4
Nevada	135,433	79,339	58.6	56,094	41.4
New Hampshire	286,094	182,065	63.6	104,029	36.4
New Jersey	2,846,770	1,867,671	65.6	963,943	33.9
New Mexico	327,647	194,017	59.2	131,838	40.2
New York	1,424,983	(1) 4,913,156	68.6	2,243,559	31.3
North Carolina	258,389	800,139	56.2	624,844	43.8
North Dakota	3,969,196	149,784	58.0	108,207	41.9
Ohio	932,499	2,498,331	62.9	1,470,865	37.1
Oklahoma	(2) 7,166,015	519,834	55.7	412,665	44.3
Oregon	783,796	501,017	63.9	282,779	36.1
Pennsylvania	4,818,668	3,130,228	65.0	1,672,892	34.7
Rhode Island	390,078	315,463	80.9	74,615	19.1
South Carolina	524,748	215,700	41.1	309,048	58.9
South Dakota	293,118	163,010,	55.6	130,108	44.4
Tennessee	1,144,046	635,047	55.5	508,965	44.5
Texas	2,626,811	1,663,185	63.3	958,566	36.5
Utah	400,310	219,628	54.9	180,682	45.1
Vermont	163,069	108,127	66.3	54,942	33.7
Virginia	1,042,267	558,038	53.5	481,334	46.2
Washington	1,258,374	779,699	62.0	470,366	37.4
West Virginia	792,040	538,087	67.9	253,953	32.1
Wisconsin	1,691,815	1,050,424	62.1	638,495	37.7
Wyoming	142,716	80,718	56.5	61,998	43.5
TOTALS	(3) 70,621,479	43,126,218	61.0	27,174,898	38.5

(1) Alabama—No Democratic electors pledged to Johnson were on the ballot. Unpledged Democratic electors vote was 210,732.

(2) New York—Johnson total includes 342,432 Liberal party votes.

(3) Total includes 320, 363 for unpledged electors and candidates.

THE VOTE FOR SENATOR—1964

State	Democrat		Republican	
Arizona	Roy Elson	227,712	Paul Fannin	241,089
California	Pierre Salinger	3,411,912	George Murphy	3,626,555
Connecticut	Thomas Dodd	781,008	John Lodge	426,939
Delaware	Elbert N. Carvel	96,854	John J. Williams	103,767
Florida	Spessard Holland	997,585	Claude R. Kirk Jr.	562,212
Hawaii	Thomas P. Gill	96,789	Hiram Fong	110,747
Indiana	Vance Hartke	1,128,505	D. Russell Bontrager	941,519
Maine	Edmund S. Muskie	253,511	Clifford G. McIntire	12,040
Maryland	Joseph D. Tydings	678,649	J. Glenn Beall	402,393
Massachusetts	Edward M. Kennedy	1,716,907	Howard Whitmore Jr.	587,663
Michigan	Philip Hart	1,996,912	Mrs. Elly M. Peterson	1,096,272
Minnesota	Eugene J. McCarthy	931,353	Wheelock Whitney	605,933
Mississippi	John C. Stennis	343,364	No candidate)	
Missouri	Stuart Symington	1,186,666	Jean Paul Bradshaw	596,377
Montana	Mike Mansfield	180,643	Alex Blewett	99,367
Nebraska	Raymond W. Arndt	217,605	Roman L. Hruska	345,772
Nevada	Howard W. Cannon	67,336	Paul Laxalt	67,288
New Jersey	H. A. Williams Jr.	1,677,515	Bernard M. Shanley	1,011,280
New Mexico	Joseph M. Montoya	178,209	Edwin L. Mechem	147,562
New York	Robert F. Kennedy	3,539,103	Kenneth B. Keating	3,104,056
North Dakota	Quentin N. Burdick	149,264	Thomas S. Kleppe	109,681
Ohio	Stephen M. Young	1,923,608	Robert A. Taft Jr.	1,906,781
Oklahoma	Fred R. Harris	466,782	Bud Wilkinson	445,392
Pennsylvania	Genevieve Blatt	2,359,052	Hugh D. Scott	2,429,495
Rhode Island	John O. Pastore	319,607	Ronald R. Lagueux	66,715
Tennessee	Albert Gore	570,542	Dan H. Kuykendall	493,475
	Ross Bass	568,905	Howard Baker Jr.	517,330
Texas	R. W. Yarborough	1,463,958	George Bush	1,134,337
Utah	Frank E. Moss	227,822	Ernest L. Wilkinson	169,562
Vermont	Frederick J. Fayette	76,457	Winston L. Prouty	87,879
Virginia	Harry F. Byrd	592,270	Richard A. May	176,624
Washington	Henry M. Jackson	875,950	Lloyd J. Andrews	337,138
West Virginia	Robert C. Byrd	515,015	Cooper P. Benedict	246,072
Wisconsin	William W. Proxmire	892,013	Wilbur N. Renk	780,116
Wyoming	Gale W. McGee	76,485	John S. Wold	65,185

THE VOTE FOR GOVERNOR—1964

State	Democrat		Republican	
Arizona	Sam Goddard	252,098	Richard Kleindienst	221,404
Arkansas	Orville E. Faubus	337,489	Winthrop Rockefeller	254,561
Delaware	Charles L. Terry	102,797	David P. Buckson	97,574
Florida	Haydon Burns	933,554	Charles R. Holley	686,297
Illinois	Otto J. Kerner	2,418,394	Charles H. Percy	2,239,095
Indiana	Roger O. Branigan	1,164,763	Richard O. Ristine	901,362
Iowa	Harold E. Hughes	794,610	Evan Hultman	365,131
Kansas	Harry G. Wiles	400,264	William H. Avery	432,667
Massachusetts	Francis X. Bellotti	1,153,416	John A. Volpe	1,176,462
Michigan	Neil Staebler	1,381,442	George Romney	1,764,355
Missouri	Warren E. Hearnes	1,110,651	Ethan A. H. Shepley	678,949
Montana	Roland Renne	136,862	Tim M. Babcock	144,133
Nebraska	Frank B. Morrison	347,026	Dwight W. Burney	231,029
New Hampshire	John W. King	190,863	John Pillsbury	94,824
New Mexico	Jack M. Campbell	191,497	Merle H. Tucker	126,540
North Carolina	Dan K. Moore	790,343	Robert L. Gavin	606,165
North Dakota	William L. Guy	146,414	Donald M. Halcrow	116,247
Rhode Island	Edward P. Gallogly	152,165	John H. Chafee	239,501
South Dakota	John F. Lindley	140,419	Nils A. Boe	150,151
Texas	John B. Connally	1,824,119	Jack Chrichton	645,774
Utah	Calvin L. Rampton	226,956	Mitchell Melich	171,300
Vermont	Philip H. Hoff	106,611	Ralph A. Foote	57,576
Washington	Albert D. Rossellini	548,692	Daniel J. Evans	697,256
West Virginia	Hulett C. Smith	433,023	Cecil H. Underwood	355,559
Wisconsin	John W. Reynolds	837,901	Warren P. Knowles	856,779

Index

Acheson, Dean, 139
Alcorn, Meade, 94
Anderson, Robert B., 156
Apple, R. W., Jr., 225
Arizona Republic, The, 172
Ashbrook, John M., 77
Atlantic City, New Jersey, Democratic National Convention (1964) in, 104–111

Babcock, T. M., 95
Bagdikian, Ben H., 128
Bailey, John M., 152, 213, 239, 249
Baker, Howard, 221
Baker, Robert G. (Bobby), 8, 138, 179, 233, 241
  Lyndon B. Johnson and, 9, 52–54, 134, 143, 156, 241
  Cabell, Phillips on, 52–53
  Republican use of, 171, 187, 198, 239
  John J. Williams and, 155
Baker, Russell, 55
  on Democratic National Convention (1964), 108
  on Barry M. Goldwater, 203
  on Lyndon B. Johnson, 108, 155, 258–259
  on Republican National Convention (1964), 55
Baroody, William J., 90
Barry, Robert, 272
Bennett, John C., 255
Bimson, Walter, 84
Blatt, Genevieve, 224, 228, 272
Bliss, Ray, 146, 147, 284, 285
Bontrager, D. R., 224
Bownes, Hugh, 117
Bree, Rita, 78
Brennan, Walter, 164
Brewster, Daniel B., 158
Brezhnev, Leonid I., 246
Brooke, Edward W., 198
Brown, Edward G., 12, 109, 226
Brown, George R., 134
Brown, T. W., 33
Buckley, William, 76, 80
Bundy, McGeorge, 113, 116, 135, 136
Burch, Dean, 59, 76, 126
  on Billie Sol Estes, 233
  Barry M. Goldwater and, 89, 286
  moderate Republicans and, 281, 283–285
  as Republican National Committee Chairman, 144, 147, 168, 247
Burns, Arthur, 163
Burns, James MacGregor, 21
Busby, Horace, 138, 139
Byrd, Harry F., 7, 48, 132, 196
Byrnes, John W., 33

Caidin, Martin, 129
California, 32
  Presidential primary (1964) in, 32, 34, 38–43

California, Republican National Convention (1964) in, 55–71
Cancellare, Frank, 240
Capehart, Homer, 97
Carpenter, Elizabeth, 138, 217
Carpenter, Les, 138
Carter, Clifton F., 139, 152, 153
Case, Clifford P., 230
Castro, Fidel, 154
Cater, Douglass, 139
Celler, Emanuel, 167
Choice Not an Echo, A (Schlafly), 215
Clay, Henry, 137
Cleveland, Grover, 134, 156
Clifford, Clark M., 139, 235
Clifton, Chester V., 139
Cohen, Ben, 128
Congressman From Mississippi (Smith), 103
Connally, John B., 109, 139
Connell, William J., 114
Conscience of a Conservative, The (Goldwater), 143
Cook, Fred J., 215
Coolidge, Calvin, 110, 142, 154, 270
Corbin, Paul, 116–117
Corcoran, Thomas G., 128, 131
Cordiner, Ralph J., 142, 147
Cotton, Norris, 20, 22

Darnton, Byron, 129
Davidson, Roy E., 50
Davies, Lawrence E., 36
  on California Senatorial campaign (1964), 227
  on Oregon's Presidential primary (1964), 36
Democratic party, 46
  National Convention (1964), 104–111
  Presidential campaign (1964), 151
    advantages in, 154–155
    Democratic National Committee in, 152–153, 154, 245
    election day, 268
    elections, 265–272
    funds for, 154–155, 156
    issues in, 46–47, 162–168, 208–219, 235–239, 243–248, 251–255, 257–258
    Negro vote and, 158
    opinion polls, 173–174, 205–206, 248–249, 261–262, 270
    popular vote, 270
    press support, 172, 206, 255–256
    strategy in, 151–160, 175–184, 200, 243, 258–260
    tours, 209–219, 242–245, 251, 257–258
    Vice Presidential candidate selected, 112–122
    Voter Identification Program and, 153
Der Spiegel, 168
Dewey, Thomas E., 20, 92, 97, 205
Dillon, Douglas, 163, 211

Dirksen, Everett McKinley, 56–57, 62, 65–66, 75, 182
Dodd, Thomas J., 100, 114
Dutton, Frederick G., 118

Editor & Publisher, 174, 255–256
Egan, Leo, on Barry M. Goldwater, 72
Eisenhower, Dwight David, 147, 148, 156, 162, 197, 207, 248, 270, 284
 and All-Republican Conference, 75
 Lyndon B. Johnson and, 3, 8
 and National Citizens Committee of prominent Republicans, 75
 Presidential primary (1964) and, 40–41
 on qualifications for Presidential candidate, 40
 on Republican defeat (1964), 282
 at Republican National Convention (1964), 56, 60, 63–65, 71
 U-2 crisis and, 288
 Tom Wicker on, 41
Eisenhower, Earl D., 221
Eisenhower, John, 56
Eisenhower, Milton, 56, 60
Engle, Clair, 226
Erhard, Ludwig, 113, 127
Erskine, Bernard, Mrs., 83
Ervin, Sam, 218
Estes, Billie Sol, 143, 233, 239

Fact, 206
Fannin, Paul, 95, 283–284
Farley, James A., 186
Farmelo, Neil R., 102
Faubus, O., 149
Feldman, Myer C., 135
Felknor, Bruce L., 226
Fenton, John, 17
 on Barry M. Goldwater, 26
Fernald, Judy, 77
Field, Mervin D., 39
Flax, Louis, 245–246
Folsom, Marion B., 156
Fong, Hiram, 65
Ford, Gerald, 95
Ford, Henry, II, 156
Fortas, Abe, 139, 235
Fraase, Elmer, 194
Frankel, Max, 195
 on foreign policy, 52, 195
Franklin, Ben A., 203
 on Goldwater voters, 276
Friedman, Milton, 76, 163
Fulbright, J. W., 178

Gabrielson, Guy George, 94
Gallup, George C., 262, 270, 277
Gaulle, Charles de, 8, 9
Gold, V., 200, 201
Goldberg, Arthur J., 115
Goldberg, David, 27–28, 35
Goldman, Eric, 139
Goldwater, Baron, 83
Goldwater, Baron, Mrs., 83
Barry Goldwater: Extremist on the Right (Cook), 215

Goldwater, Barry M., 258, 260–261, 262, 263, 270, 281–289
 advisors to, 88–91
 birth of, 83
 as chairman of Senatorial Campaign Committee, 74, 76
 as candidate for Republican Presidential nomination (1964), 12–17, 33, 43–44
 in California primary, 32, 34, 38–43
 in New Hampshire primary, 19, 20, 22–31
 in Oregon primary, 34–37
 at Republican National Convention, 55–71
 on conservatism, 72–73, 74–75, 279
 conservative Republican development and, 72–81
 Democratic National Convention (1964) and, 105, 106, 108, 111
 early political career of, 86
 education of, 83
 family background of, 82–83
 as ham radio operator, 85
 hobbies of, 86
 and John F. Kennedy, 14
 on man, 73
 as merchandiser, 83–84
 as mechanic, 86
 and William E. Miller, 92–96, 102
 as pilot, 85–86
 at Republican National Convention (1960), 72
 Republican Presidential campaign (1964), 141
  antipoverty program and, 171
  Congressional campaign (1964) and, 222–224
  crowds and, 184
  Democratic strategy and, 156–159, 209
  election day, 264–265
  farm policy and, 194, 198
  foreign policy and, 8, 165–166, 195, 202, 204, 247–248, 257
  funds for, 142, 251
  Gettysburg meeting and, 147–148
  government and, 196
  issues of, 143–144, 148–149, 162–171, 194–199, 201–203, 207, 230–239
  military draft and, 162–163
  moderate Republicans and, 170, 176, 177, 179, 207, 229
  morality and, 166, 170–171, 198, 253
  Negro riots and, 145–146
  neighborhood schools and, 252
  nuclear issue and, 168–169, 197
  polls and, 172–174, 205–206, 208, 261–262
  post election analysis of, 273–280
  press and, 172, 205–207, 255–256
  Republican National Committee and, 146
  Republican National Finance Committee and, 142
  strategy in, 141–150
  Supreme Court and, 167
  tactics of, 147, 200, 231
  taxes and, 164, 197
  television and, 167, 197
  test ban treaty and, 8

Goldwater, Barry M., tours, 164–174, 194–204, 217, 219, 230–233, 236–240, 251–254, 257
    unity conference and, 148–149
    Vietnam crisis and, 147
    as Senator, 87–88
    as Senatorial Campaign Committee chairman, 87
    Social Security and, 24
    United Nations and, 23–24
    wealth of, 126
Goldwater, Barry M., Jr., 84, 219
Goldwater, Barry M., Mrs., 16, 84–85, 161, 219, 264
Goldwater, Michel, 82–83, 84, 219
Goldwater, Michel, Mrs., 82, 83
Goldwater, Morris, 83
Goldwater, Robert, 83, 165
Good Housekeeping, 84
Goodwin, Richard, 177
Gould, Jack, 269–270
Greer, Walter, 129

Hailey, Foster, 129
Haley, J. Evetts, 214
Hall, Leonard W., 65, 94, 146, 147
Halleck, Charles A., 66, 75, 92, 93
Harding, Warren G., 270
Harlow, Bryce, 148
Harriman, Averell, 60
Harris, Louis, 35, 234, 262, 270–271, 274
Hass, Eric, 264
Hatfield, Mark O., 62, 183
Hayden, Carl, 85
Heckling Hare (airplane), 129
Heller, Walter, 50
Herbers, John, on Southern voting patterns, 275
Herman, Dick, 81
Hess, Karl, 59, 90–91, 148, 170
Hill, Gladwin, on California's Presidential primary (1964), 38
Hill, Lister, 90
Hinman, George L., 21, 32, 145
Holmes, Oliver Wendell, 137
Holt, Richard Arlen, 84
Holt, Richard Arlen, Mrs., 84
Hood, Wayne, 81, 147
Hoover, Herbert, Sr., 154, 202
Hoover, J. Edgar, 237
How to Win Elections (Shadegg), 91
Hughes, Sarah, 2
Humphrey, Douglas, 122
Humphrey, George M., 56, 60, 156, 285
Humphrey, Hubert Horatio, 4, 125, 151, 156, 178, 202, 261
    birth of, 122
    Democratic National Convention (1964) and, 105–110
    education of, 122
    election campaign (1964), 185–188, 190–194
    election day and, 266–267
    oath of office, 291–292
    political career of, 122–124
    selected as Democratic Vice Presidential candidate, 112–115, 118–119, 124

Humphrey, Hubert Horatio, West Virginia primary (1960) and, 20
Humphrey, Hubert Horatio, Mrs., 122, 266–267, 291
Humphrey, Nancy, 122
Humphrey, Robert, 122
Hymoff, Edward, 129

Ickes, Harold, 128

Jackson, Andrew, 106, 134
Jackson, Robert A., 100
Jaffa, Harry, 59, 91
Janson, Donald, 215
Javits, Jacob K., 67, 75, 143
Jenkins, Walter W., 8, 189, 235, 237–238, 246, 252–253
    Lyndon B. Johnson and, 135, 137, 138, 152
Johnson, Andrew, 133
Johnson, Hiram, 20
Johnson, Luci Baines, 126, 128, 218
Johnson, Lynda Bird, 111, 218, 126, 128
Johnson, Lyndon Baines, 1, 127, 131, 275, 281
    on assassination of John F. Kennedy, 1–2
    Robert G. (Bobby) Baker and, 9, 52–54, 134, 143, 156, 241
    Berlin crisis (1961) and, 133
    birth of, 127
    as candidate for Democratic Presidential nomination (1960), 130, 132–133
    in Congress, 128–129
    Cuban missile crisis and, 133
    at Democratic National Convention (1964), 104–111
    education of, 127
    health of, 134–135
    inaugural day, 287, 291–292
    John F. Kennedy's legislative program and, 5
    Kennedy-Johnson civil rights bill (1964), 46–47, 49
    "My Political Philosophy," excerpts from, 132
    oath of office (1963), 1, 2
    oath of office (1964), 292
    as President, 5
        address to joint session of Congress (1963), 5
        advisors to, 135–139
        antipoverty program, 217
        Civil Rights Act (1964), 217
        Congress and, 48–50
        Federal aid for nurses' training and, 155
        Federal workers' pay raise bill (1964), 50
        food for peace program, 155
        food stamp program (1964), 50
        foreign aid bill and, 50
        foreign securities tax (1964) and, 50
        Panama and, 52, 134
        rail labor dispute (1964) and, 50–51
        Russia and, 51
        South Vietnam and, 46–47, 51–52
        State of the Union message (1964), 7
        tax reduction bill (1964), 48
        "Texas Mafia" and, 135–139
        war on poverty bill, 49

Johnson, Lyndon Baines, wheat-cotton voluntary price supports (1964), 50
  wilderness preservation bill (1964), 50, 155
  Presidential campaign (1964), 151
    advantages in, 154–155
    Democratic National Committee in, 152–153, 154, 245
    election day, 268
    election victory of, 268, 269–270
    elections, 265–272
    foreign policy and, 165, 202
    funds for, 154–155, 156
    issues in, 46–47, 162–168, 235–239, 243–248, 251–255, 257–258
    Walter W. Jenkins and, 235, 237, 238, 239
    military draft and, 163
    Negro riots and, 146
    Negro vote and, 158
    "non-political" activities of, 45–46
    opinion polls, 173–174, 205–206, 248–249, 261–262, 270–271
    popular vote, 270
    press support in, 47–48, 172, 206, 255–256
    public relations, 47–48
    strategy in, 151–160, 175–184, 200, 243, 258–260
    Supreme Court and, 167
    tax cuts and, 217
    television spots and, 168
    tours, 209–219, 242–245, 251, 257–258
    Vice Presidential candidate selected in, 112–122
    Vietnam crisis and, 147
    Voter Identification Program and, 153
  and Sam Rayburn, 130
  on Franklin Delano Roosevelt, 130
  as Vice President, 4, 130, 133
  wealth of, 125–126
  in World War II, 128–129
Johnson, Lyndon Baines, Mrs., 2, 8, 47, 127–128, 176, 290–292
  business enterprises, 126, 138, 139, 180
  campaign tour of, 217–218
  election day and, 265–266
Johnson, R. P., 84
Johnson, Sam Ealy, 127
Jordan, B. Everett, 233, 291
Judd, Walter H., 65, 284

Kansas City Star, The, 156
Kaiser, Edgar F., 156
Kampelman, Max, 114, 115
Keating, Kenneth, 75, 143, 170, 199, 224–226, 271, 278
  at Republican National Convention (1964), 67, 70–71
Kefauver, Estes, 20
Keisling, William, 58
Kellems, Vivian, 156
Kennedy, Edward, 198, 213, 221, 227
Kennedy, John F., 126, 131, 133, 238, 239, 280, 287, 288, 289, 290, 291
  "antibusiness" reputation, 156–157
  assassination of, 1, 211, 214
  civil rights and, 3
  Cuban missile crisis and, 3, 165, 189

Kennedy, John F., election campaign (1960), 81, 159, 172, 176, 196, 197, 205, 212, 220, 275
  on elections (1960), 126
  Barry Goldwater and, 14
  "Irish Mafia," 135
  Lyndon B. Johnson on, 1–2
  nuclear test ban treaty and, 3
  Presidential primaries (1960) and, 20, 21
  quoted, 293
Kennedy, John F., Mrs., 1, 2, 110, 119, 121
Kennedy, Robert F., 2, 9, 110, 130, 163, 170, 199, 271
  as contender for Vice Presidential nomination (1964), 113, 115–121
  Senatorial campaign (1964), 221, 222, 224–227, 278
Kenworthy, E. W., 191, 224
Kerner, Otto J., 222, 229, 272
Kerr, Clark, 114
Khrushchev, Nikita, 195, 288
King, John W., 117
King, Martin Luther, Jr., 5, 6, 107, 146
Kirk, Russell, 76
Kirkpatrick, Evron, 114
Kitchel, Denison, 30, 59, 76, 88–89, 146–147, 164, 169
Kleberg, Richard M., 127
Kleindienst, Richard, 80, 81, 95, 272
Kosygin, Aleksei N., 246
Knowland, William F., 32, 43, 66
Krock, Arthur, 58, 109, 178
  on California's Presidential primary (1964), 42, 43
  on Barry Goldwater, 42, 43, 71, 72
Kuchel, Thomas H., 32

Lackey, E. Dent, 98
Landon, Alfred M., 20, 172
Lee, Raymond J., 99, 102, 265
Lee, Raymond J., Mrs., 265
Lee, William, 99
Lewis, Anthony, 104, 107
  on Atlantic City, 104
  on white backlash, 274–275
Life, 206
Lincoln, Abraham, 133, 214
Lindsay, John V., 272
Literary Digest, The, 153
Lodge, George Cabot, 29, 52, 80
Lodge, Henry Cabot, 187, 203
  as candidate for Republican Presidential nomination (1964), 17, 18, 33–38
    in New Hampshire primary, 27–28, 29, 31
  on Republican defeat (1964), 282
  at Republican National Convention (1964), 56, 58, 65, 71
Lodge, John Davis, 221
Loftus, Joseph, 228
  on California's Presidential primary (1964), 38
  on Republican National Convention (1964), 56
Lubell, Samuel, 206, 262
Luce, Clare Booth, 66, 206
Luna, Charles, 50

MacArthur, Douglas, 129
McCabe, Edward, 59, 60, 90, 147, 148
    Charles Mohr on, 89
McCarthy, Eugene, 5, 113, 115, 118–119, 121
McCarthy, Joseph R., 90, 174
McCloskey, Matthew, 198
McCone, John, 166
McCormack, John, 292
McCulloch, William M., 93
McFarland, Ernest, 85, 87, 129
McKay, David O., 213
McNamara, R. S., 113, 115, 119, 202, 211
Manchester Union Leader, The, 22–23
Martin, Joseph W., Jr., 90, 93
Massey, Raymond, 239
Mateos, Adolfo Lopez, 210
Mazo, Earl, 172
    on future of Goldwater, 286
    on remodeling of Republican party, 283–284
    on Republican party crisis, 281
Meany, George, 6, 115
Middendorf, William, 76
Miller, Elizabeth Ann, 99, 219
Miller, Mary Karen, 99, 219
Miller, William E., 69, 75, 161, 178, 180–181,
    206, 211, 281, 285
    and Bell Aircraft Corporation strike, 100–
    101
    birth of, 99
    in Congress, 96–99, 102–103
    education of, 99
    election campaign (1964), 185–190, 192–193
    election day, 265
    and Barry M. Goldwater, 92–96, 102, 144,
    147
    on national unity, 11
    as Republican Congressional Campaign
    Committee chairman, 93
    as Republican National Chairman (1964),
    93–94, 97
    as Republican Vice Presidential nominee
    (1964), 92, 94–96
    and Nelson Rockefeller, 92, 93, 94
    as United States Commissioner, 99
Miller, William E., Jr., 99
Miller, William E., Mrs., 99
Mission, The (Caidin and Hymoff), 129
Mohr, Charles, 147, 148, 161, 200, 232
    on California's Presidential primary (1964),
    42, 43
    on Barry M. Goldwater, 87, 88, 161
        advisors, 90, 91
        ambivalence on the United Nations, 23–
        24
    in New Hampshire primary (1964), 19, 30
    on Wayne J. Hood, 90
    on Lyndon B. Johnson's campaign windup,
    262–263
    on Edward A. McCabe, 89
    on New Hampshire primary (1964), 19, 23–
    24, 30
Montana, Monte, 164
Moore, Dan K., 218
Moore, Roger Allan, 76
Morris, John D., 223, 271
Morton, Thruston B., 58, 64, 93, 144
Moursand, A. W., 139, 266

Moyers, Bill D., 135, 136, 139, 278
Mundt, Karl E., 197
Murphy, George, 221, 222, 226–227, 271
Muskie, E. S., 114
Musmanno, Michael A., 228
"My Political Philosophy" (Johnson), excerpt
    from, 132

National Review, The, 76
Nellor, E., 59
New Hampshire, Presidential primary (1964),
    in, 19–31
New York Daily News, 226, 255
New York Herald-Tribune, 40, 206
Niagara Falls Gazette, The, 101
Niemeyer, Gerhardt, 76
Nixon, Richard M., 12, 18, 77, 80, 202, 203,
    240, 275, 284
    California gubernatorial race and, 78, 226
    as candidate for Republican Presidential
        nomination (1964), 33–36, 41
    in New Hampshire primary, 28
    at Republican National Convention (1964),
        56, 65, 69, 71
    party unity and, 147, 148
    as Presidential candidate (1960), 72, 73, 74,
        172, 196, 197, 201, 212, 220
    on Republican defeat (1964), 282
    as Vice President, 93
None Dare Call It Treason (Stormer), 215
Nutter, Warren, 163

O'Brien, Lawrence, 120, 135, 242
O'Connor, Moira, 200
O'Donnell, Kenneth, P., 1, 117, 120, 135, 214
O'Donnell, Peter, Jr., 76, 79, 80
Oregon, Presidential primary (1964) in, 34–37
Oswald, Lee Harvey, 211
Otepka, Otto F., 254
Ottinger, Richard L., 272, 278

Passman, Otto, 7
Pastore, John, 108, 114
Pearson, Lester B., 182
Percy, Charles H., 222, 229, 272
Peter, Walter, 127
Peterson, Elly M., 224
Peterson, Esther, 46
Pfeiffer, William L., 101
Phillips, Cabell, 52–53
Phillips, Wayne, 245–246
Pillon, John R., 95
Pinaire, Hoyte, 84
Pomfret, John D., 190, 260
    on Republican campaign (1964), 260–261,
    262–263
Porter, Paul, 175
Powell, Wesley, 28
Pulliam, Eugene C., 172
Pyle, Howard, 86, 87

Quayle, Oliver, 234

Rauh, Joseph L., Jr., 107, 114
Raymond, Jack, 211

Rayburn, Sam, 130
Reagan, Ronald, 39, 164, 251
Reardon, Timothy J., 135
Reedy, George E., 134, 138, 139, 181, 236
Reese, Carroll E., 94
Republican party, 11
  Congressional campaigns (1964), 221–229
  conservative development in, 72–81
  damage to, 281–286
  Gubernatorial campaigns (1964), 228–229
  moratorium on political campaigning, 11
  Presidential campaign (1964), 32
    in California primary, 32, 34, 38–43
    candidates for Presidential nomination, 11–18
    funds for, 142, 251
    Gettysburg meeting and, 147–148
    issues of, 143–144, 148–149, 162–171, 194–199, 201–203, 207, 230–239
    in New Hampshire primary, 19–31
    in Oregon primary, 34–37
    polls and, 172–174, 205–206, 208, 261–262
    post election analysis of, 273–280
    press and, 172, 205–207, 255–256
    strategy in, 141–150, 200, 231
    tours, 164–174, 194–204, 217, 219, 230–233, 236–240, 251–254, 257
    unity conference, 148–149
  Senatorial Campaign Commitee, 87
  twenty-seventh National Convention (1960), 72
  twenty-eighth National Convention (1964), 55–71
Reston, James, 214, 219, 246–247, 253, 256–257
  on Democratic National Convention (1964), 106
  on Barry M. Goldwater, 37, 57, 61–62, 149–150, 162, 165–166, 171, 273–274
  on Lyndon B. Johnson, 6, 9–10, 46, 50–51, 109–110, 131, 177–178, 214, 290–291, 292–293
  on moderate Republicans, 80
  on New Hampshire primary (1964), 28, 29
  on Republican National Convention (1964), 57, 61–62, 64–65, 67–69
  on Nelson Rockefeller, 13
Reuther, W. P., 115, 176
Reynolds, Don B., 138
Reynolds, J. W., 158
Richardson, Elliot L., 198
Roberts, Wesley, 94
Robertson, Nan, 239
Rockefeller, Margaretta Fitler Murphy, 199
Rockefeller, Mary Todhunter Clark, 22
Rockefeller, Nelson, 11, 75, 77, 78, 80, 94, 142, 145, 148–149, 199
  as candidate for Republican Presidential nomination (1964), 11, 12, 13, 17, 18, 33
  in California's primary, 32, 38–43
  divorce issue and, 22–23, 41
  in New Hampshire primary, 19–23, 25–31
  in Oregon primary, 34–37
  at Republican National Convention, 56, 58, 64, 65, 67, 71
  and William E. Miller, 92, 93, 94
  on Republican defeat (1964), 282

Rockefeller, Nelson, Jr., 41
Rockefeller, Winthrop, 221
Roll Call, 95
Romero, Cesar, 164
Romney, George, 13, 18, 34, 142, 149, 176, 199, 203, 222, 229
  on Republican defeat (1964), 282
  at Republican National Convention (1964), 56, 64, 65, 69
Roosevelt, F. D., 8, 108, 128, 129, 130, 159, 172, 193, 270, 293
Roosevelt, Theodore, 110, 154, 292
Rose, Alex, 115
Rosenberg, Marvin, 114
Rosenzweig, Harry, 86
Ross, Donald R., 285
Ross, Thomas, 84
Ross, Thomas, Mrs., 84
Rossant, M. J., 156, 163
Rowe, James H., Jr., 120, 139
Rusk, Dean, 113, 121, 165, 211
Russell, Richard B., 6, 129, 132

Salinger, Pierre, 135, 221, 222, 226–227, 271
Saltonstall, Leverett, 33, 198
Sandburg, Carl, 47
San Francisco, California, 55
  Republican National Convention (1964) in, 55–77
Saturday Evening Post, The, 174
Sayre, Francis B., Jr., 181, 232
Schlafly, Phyllis, 215
Schlesinger, Arthur, Jr., 135
Schumach, Murry, 204
Schweitzer, Albert, 213
Scott, Hugh, 56, 75, 94, 143, 179, 228
Scott, Randolph, 164
Scranton, William W., 12, 18, 28, 29, 80, 94, 95, 96, 203, 254
  on Republican defeat (1964), 282
  as candidate for Republican Presidential nomination (1964), 33, 34, 36, 41
  at Republican National Convention, 55–60, 62–65, 67, 71
Scranton, William W., Mrs., 67
Shadegg, Stephen, 35, 81, 91
Shanahan, Eileen, 126
Sitton, Claude, 145
Smith, Flloyd S., 290
Smith, Frank E., 103
Smith, Howard W., 7, 98
Smith, Margaret Chase, 17
  as candidate for Republican Presidential nomination (1964), 17, 27, 33, 34, 36
  at Republican National Convention, 65
Smylie, Robert E., 283
Sorensen, Theodore, 135
Staebler, Neil, 222, 229
Stassen, Harold E., 20, 27
  as candidate for Republican Presidential nomination (1964), 33
Stenger, John H., 102
Stevenson, Adlai, 20, 75, 114, 119, 121, 151, 163, 193, 220, 221
Stevenson, Coke, 129
Stormer, John A., 215

Stribling, Bill, Mrs., 266
Summerfield, Arthur E., 94

Taft, Charles P., 226
Taft, Robert A., Jr., 33, 221, 228, 271
Taft, William Howard, 212, 228
Taylor, George W., 51
Taylor, Maxwell D., 52
Taylor, Zachary, 127
Texan Looks at Lyndon, A (Haley), 214–215
Thornberry, Homer, 266
Thurmond, Strom, 106, 170
Tilton, Martha, 164
Tower, John G., 66, 76
Travell, Janet, Dr., 14, 85
Truman, Harry S., 3, 60, 106, 108, 110, 114, 133, 154, 159, 193
   on Presidential powers, 288
Tuck, Richard, 201
Turner, Wallace, 189

U.S. News & World Report, 279

Valenti, Jack J., 135, 136–137, 139, 278
Vinson, Fred, 128
Volpe, John A., 198

Wagner, R. F., 114
Wallace, C., 106
Wallace, George C., 145, 158, 274

Wallace, Henry A., 122–123
Walsh, William E., 35
Waring, Lloyd K., 17
Warner, William S., 147
Warren Commission on the Assassination of
   President Kennedy, excerpts from Lyndon
   B. Johnson's report to, 1–2
Warren, Earl, 6, 292
Weaver, Warren, Jr., 2, 187, 222
   on Lyndon B. Johnson, 4
   1964 nomination possibilities of, 4–5
Welsh, Matthew E., 158
Whistlestop, 200–201
White, F. Clifton, 76–81, 89, 147
White, William S., 139
Whitener, Basil, 218
Whitmore, Howard, Jr., 198
Wicker, Tom, 8, 109, 136, 139, 174, 205, 231, 249
   on All-Republican Conference, 75
   on Eisenhower, 41
   on Barry M. Goldwater, 73–74, 87
   on inaugural day, 278–291
   on Lyndon B. Johnson, 8, 264
      first month in office, 6–7, 46
   on Republican defeat (1964), 272
Williams, G. Mennen, 84, 229

Yerxa, Fendall W., 184, 278
Young, Stephen M., 228, 271